Human Rights and the Environment

Conflicts and Norms in a Globalizing World

Edited by Lyuba Zarsky

Earthscan Publications Ltd
London • Sterling, VA

First published in the UK and USA in 2002 by Earthscan Publications Ltd
for and on behalf of the United Nations Environment Programme

ISBN: 1 85383 815 2 paperback
1 85383 814 4 hardback

Typesetting by PCS Mapping & DTP, Gateshead
Printed and bound in the UK by Creative Print and Design Wales, Ebbw Vale
Cover design by Susanne Harris

For a full list of publications please contact:

Earthscan Publications Ltd
120 Pentonville Road, London, N1 9JN, UK
Tel: +44 (0)20 7278 0433
Fax: +44 (0)20 7278 1142
Email: earthinfo@earthscan.co.uk
Web: **www.earthscan.co.uk**

22883 Quicksilver Drive, Sterling, VA 20166-2012, USA

Earthscan is an editorially independent subsidiary of Kogan Page Ltd and publishes in
association with WWF-UK and the International Institute for Environment and
Development

A catalogue record for this book is available from the British Library

Library of Congress Cataloging-in-Publication Data

Human rights and the environment : conflicts and norms in a globalizing world /
edited by Lyuba Zarsky.
        p. cm.
    Includes bibliographical references and index.
    ISBN 1-85383-815-2 (paperback) — ISBN 1-85383-814-4 (hardback)
    1. Economic development—Environmental aspects—Case studies.
  2. Environmental responsibility—Case studies. 3. Human rights—Case studies.
  I. Zarsky, Lyuba

    HD75.6 .H86 2002
    333.7—dc21

                                                                        2002006464

Contents

PART I: INTEGRATING HUMAN RIGHTS AND ENVIRONMENTAL ETHICS

PART II: CONFLICTS OVER MINERAL AND OIL DEVELOPMENT

PART III: CONFLICTS OVER DEVELOPMENT STRATEGIES

PART IV: CONFLICTS OVER LAND RIGHTS

PART V: CONCLUSION

List of Figures and Tables

FIGURES

TABLES

About the Authors

Douglas Fifi Korsah-Brown is co-founder of Friends of the Earth Ghana, where he works on issues such as trade and environment, climate change and ozone layer protection. Between 1983 and 1985, he studied journalism at the Ghana Institute of Journalism and proceeded to the University of Ghana, where he obtained a BA Honors in sociology. After setting up Friends of the Earth in 1986, he attended the Ghana School of Law, where he obtained his Qualifying Certificate and was subsequently called to the Bar in April 1996.

Pascal O Girot is Associate Professor of Geography at the University of Costa Rica, where he runs the Program in Geographical Research. He received a BS in geography and international development from Clark University and, in 1984, an MS in geography from the University of Wisconsin-Madison. He is an active member of the World Conservation Union's (IUCN) Commission on Environmental, Economic and Social Policy (CEESP) and a consultant for IUCN's Regional Office for Mesoamerica, in its Forest Conservation and Protected Areas Program. He is editor of *Boundaries in the Americas* (Routledge, 1993) and author of numerous papers in English, French and Spanish on Central America's territorial politics and boundaries, including: 'Transborder Cooperation in Central America', *Borders and Border Regions: New Roles in a Changing Global Context* (Berlin, 1996).

Philip Hirsch is Associate Professor of Geography at the University of Sydney and Director of the Australian Mekong Resource Centre. He is actively involved in field-based research in the Mekong Region, mainly in Lao PDR, Thailand and Vietnam. Dr Hirsch has written extensively on development and environment in Southeast Asia. His publications include: *The Politics of Environment in Southeast Asia*, with Carol Warren (Routledge, 1998); *Reclaiming Resources: Politics of Resources and Environment in Southeast Asia* (Routledge, 1997); *Seeing Forests for Trees: Environment and Environmentalism in Thailand* (Silkworm Books, 1997); and 'Competition, Conflict and Cooperation in the Mekong River Basin: Toward a New Framework for Security', *Development Dilemmas in the Mekong Subregion* (Monash Asia Institute, 1996).

Fergus MacKay is a human rights lawyer, specializing in the rights of indigenous peoples. He received his JD from California Western School of Law in 1991. Formerly legal adviser to the World Council of Indigenous Peoples, he is presently Regional Coordinator for the Guyanas in the Forest Peoples Programme of the World Rainforest Movement. Based in the Guyanas, he works with a coalition of indigenous, human rights and environmental organizations from Guyana, Suriname and French Guiana. His publications include: 'International Law, Intergovernmental Organisations and the Rights of Indigenous Peoples' (Global Law Association, 2000); and 'Mining, Land Rights and Indigenous Peoples in the Upper Mazaruni', with L Anselmo (Amerindian Peoples Association of Guyana, Upper Mazaruni Amerindian District Council, Forest Peoples Programme) (Global Law Association, 2000).

John Mugabe is Executive Director of the African Centre for Technology Studies (ACTS). He is a member of Kenya's National Council for Science and Technology (NCST), the Board of Directors of the African Conservation Centre (ACC), Kenya, and the Board of Trustees of Sustainable Agriculture Centre for Research and Development in Africa. He also serves on the International Steering Committee of the Leadership for Environment and Development (LEAD) International Inc, New York, and is on the roster of experts for the Scientific and Technical Advisory Panel (STAP) of the GEF.

His publications include: *Access to Genetic Resources: Strategies for Sharing Benefits*, with C Barber (ACTS Press and Initiatives Publishers, Ltd, 1997); and *Managing Biodiversity: National Systems of Conservation and Innovation in Africa* (ACTS Press, 1997).

Godber Tumushabe is an independent environmental law and policy analyst engaged in research on a broad range of environmental and human rights issues in eastern and southern Africa. He is currently Executive Director of Advocates Coalition for Development and Environment (ACODE), a Ugandan-based independent public policy research and analysis think-tank, and has formally worked as a Senior Research Fellow at the African Centre for Technology Studies (ACTS) in Nairobi, Kenya. He has written extensively on environmental law and human rights issues and co-edited, with Professor Okoth-Ogendo, *Governing the Environment: Political Change and Natural Resources Management in Eastern and Southern Africa* (ACTS, 1999).

Erika Rosenthal directs Earthjustice's Russian project and has worked with Ecojuris, Russia's national environmental law group, since 1994. She has prepared supporting briefs for several of Ecojuris' cases, designed more than a dozen international legal training seminars, and written numerous articles on citizen participation in environmental decision-making and enforcement with a focus on the former Soviet countries and Latin America.

Agus Sari is Executive Director of the Pelangi Organization in Indonesia and a lecturer on the politics of climate change at the University of California, Berkeley. From 1994 to 1999 he was the Senior Research Associate at Pelangi. His publications include 'On Equity and Developing Country Participation' in *On the Flexible Instruments Under the Kyoto Protocol* (Kluwer Academic Publishers, 1999).

Naomi Roht-Arriaza is Professor of Law at Hastings College of the Law, University of California. She teaches international human rights, international and domestic environmental law, and is on the Executive Council of the American Society of International Law. She received her JD from the University of California, Boalt Hall and a Masters in Public Policy from UC Berkeley. Roht-Arriaza is associate editor of the *Yearbook of International Environmental Law* and author of numerous publications on the subjects of human rights, environment, trade, indigenous populations and international law, including: 'Shifting the Point of Regulation: The International Organization for Standardization and Global Lawmaking on Trade and the Environment' (*Ecology Law Quarterly*, 1995); 'Environmental Management Systems and Environmental Protection: Can ISO 14001 Be Useful Within the Context of APEC?' (*Journal of Environment and Development*, 1997); and 'Institutions of International Justice' (*Journal of International Affairs*, 1999).

Robert Thornton is a professor in the Department of Anthropology, University of Witwatersrand, Johannesburg, South Africa. After receiving a PhD from the University of Chicago in 1978, Professor Thornton accepted a teaching position at the University of Cape Town in South Africa, where he was promoted from Lecturer, to Senior Lecturer to Associate Professor. In 1989 he went to the Institute for Advanced Study in Princeton, New Jersey for one year. The following year, he became Raoull Wallenberg Associate Professor of Human Rights in the History Department, Rutgers University, and a Fellow at the Rutgers Center for Historical Analysis, in New Jersey.

His publications include: 'A "vague and baggy monster"? Finding Culture Between the Cracks in the Disciplines', in *Openings: Studies in South African Culture*, edited by S Nuttall and C-A Michaels (Oxford University Press, 2000); and 'Culture-based Management Solves the Street Hawker Problem at Village Walk, Sandton [Johannesburg, South Africa]', *Planning: Architectural and Planning Review for Southern Africa* 159:6–9, 1998.

Changhua Wu is Senior Associate and Director of China Studies and directs the World Resources Institute's (WRI)' work in China. Her areas of work include strategic planning, project design and management, research and outreach, environment and health, energy and climate change, urban transportation, institutions and governance, and biodiversity and watershed management in China. She has an ML in journalism from the Chinese Academy of Social Sciences and an MPP in environmental policy from the University of Maryland. As a World Press Institute Fellow in 1993, she travelled, with nine other international journalists throughout much of the US, interviewed Federal and State congressional leaders and legislators, government officials and Presidential advisers, policy researchers and scientists, US media and NGO representatives, prisons and hospices, and gained a broad and objective view of the US.

Wu is co-founder, President and Board Member of the Professional Association for China's Environment (PACE). An enlarging network of people working on environmental issues in China, PACE is playing an increasingly important role in networking those people with common interest, exchanging and sharing information and ideas, and providing advice for Chinese decision-makers to chart a sustainable future for China. She is editor of *Sinosphere*, an English quarterly on China's environmental policy issues, and executive editor of *Chinese Environmental Perspectives*, a Chinese environmental policy journal.

Lyuba Zarsky is cofounder and Director of the Globalization and Governance Program at the Nautilus Institute for Security and Sustainable Development in Berkeley, California. She has designed and directed a number of collaborative research and advocacy projects, most recently: the California Global Corporate Accountability Project, which explored the global environmental and social dilemmas of California-based high tech and oil multinational corporations; and the International Sustainable and Ethical Investment Rules Project. An economist by training, she has acted as consultant for the Asian Development Bank, the Organisation for Economic Co-operation and Development (OECD) Environment Directorate and the UNDP Northeast Asia office. In the early 1990s, she created and managed a national programme on sustainable development at the Australian Commission for the Future.

Zarsky has written widely on the ethics and sustainability in the governance of international trade and investment, especially in the Asia–Pacific region. Her recent publications include: 'Beyond Good Deeds: Strengthening Corporate Social Responsibility With Public Policy' (*Forum Magazine*, forthcoming 2002); 'APEC: The "Sustainable Development" Agenda', in R Steinberg (ed) *The Greening of Trade Law* (Rowman and Littlefield, 2002); and 'Havens, Halos and Spaghetti: Untangling the Relationship Between FDI and the Environment' (OECD, 2000).

Preface

This book grew out of an initiative by the Earth Council, a Costa Rica-based non-governmental organization (NGO), to explore the creation of an international environmental ombudsperson. Founded by Maurice Strong, the Earth Council was launched after the United Nations Conference on Environment and Development (UNCED, also known as the Earth Summit) held in Rio de Janeiro in 1992.

The Earth Council had a vision of an ombudsperson function which would help to define new international norms by mediating in conflicts involving environment, human rights and development. The Council sought the help of experts to develop the conceptual foundation for the ombudsperson's function, especially to present design options for its scope and modality.

In October 1996, the Nautilus Institute for Security and Sustainable Development was engaged to lead the project, From Concept to Design: Creating an International Environmental Ombudsman. We quickly determined that the first task was to improve our understanding of what was happening 'on the ground'. We commissioned 12 case studies of local or regional conflicts centred on human rights and environment issues. Each conflict involved at least one international actor or set of issues linked to globalization. To consider whether the ombudsperson could function effectively as a global institution, or should be located within a specific locale or region, the case studies spanned Latin America, Europe, Asia and Africa.

The case studies were undertaken by researchers based in NGOs, universities and think-tanks from around the world – from Suriname to Ghana, from Indonesia to the Russian Far East. All the researchers are exceptionally astute and creative analysts, as well as highly committed social advocates and problem-solvers.

The case studies were completed and submitted to the Earth Council at the end of 1998, along with a summary report outlining design options and recommendations. While the Earth Council weighed alternatives and negotiated with potential partners, the case studies were not made public. With the establishment of the International Ombudsman Centre for Environment and Development (OmCED) in 2000, the Earth Council released the project papers for publication. We are pleased to present them here.

All the case studies have been updated and incorporate those changes, some dramatic, which have occurred since 1998. In one example, an entire country experienced a political and social explosion, overturning a 35-year-old government. Most of the conflicts were a long time in the making – and will be a long time gone. They provide insights not only about effective mediation but also about how deeply and profoundly human rights and environmental protection are entangled in the process of globalization. The case studies also highlight the creative ways in which communities from around the world are mobilizing to hold governments and corporations accountable to higher ethical standards. This book is dedicated to these communities.

Lyuba Zarsky
Director, Globalization and Governance Program
The Nautilus Institute for Security and Sustainable Development

Acknowledgements

Special thanks are due to Tani Adams, Coordinator of the From Concept to Design project for her persistence and brilliance in bringing the research project to fruition; and to Maximo Kalaw, the late Executive Director of the Earth Council, for his patience and commitment in seeing it to completion. Thanks to Leif Brottem of the Nautilus Institute for able assistance in editing and preparing the manuscripts for publication, and to Megan Keever for securing a publisher. Thanks to Michelle Leighton for helping to frame the project's thinking on the emergence of international jurisprudence on human rights and the environment. For helpful comments and pointers to new literature, many thanks to Eva Herzer, Peter Hayes, Jason Hunter, Barbara Johnson, Jacob Scherr, Dinah Shelton and Edith Brown Weiss. Thanks to Kira Schmidt for editorial assistance and to Natalie Bridgeman and Jason Hunter for research assistance. A special thanks to Naomi Roht-Arriaza for co-directing the project with a delightful mixture of wit and whip. Finally, thanks to the Ford Foundation, New York Office, for supporting the staff time needed to bring the case studies to publication.

Lyuba Zarsky

Acronyms and Abbreviations

ACHR	1969 American Convention on Human Rights
ADB	Asian Development Bank
ADR	alternative dispute resolution
AFTA	ASEAN Free Trade Area
AGC	Ashanti Goldfields Company Limited
AMDAL	Analisis Mengenai Dampak Lingkungan (environmental impact assessment)
ANC	African National Congress
ANCON	Asociación Nacional para la Conservación
ASEAN	Association of Southeast Asian Nations
BIDA	Batam Industrial Development Authority
BILIK	Bina Lingkungan Hidup Batam (Batam Industrial Environmental Improvement Council)
BOOT	build-own-operate-transfer
BP	British Petroleum Corporation
BPKP	Bolisat Phatthana Khet Phudoi (Mountainous Regions Development Corporation)
CBD	Convention on Biological Diversity
CBO	community-based organization
CEC	North American Commission for Environmental Cooperation
CERD	Convention on the Elimination of All Forms of Racial Discrimination
COP	Conference of the Parties
COPD	chronic obstructive pulmonary disease
CRLR	Commission on Restitution of Land Rights (South Africa)
CSD	Commission on Sustainable Development (United Nations)
CSR	corporate social responsibility
CTE	Committee on Trade and Environment
DEAT	Department of Environmental Affairs and Tourism (South Africa)
DHMT	District Health Management Team
DLA	Department of Land Affairs (South Africa)
DSR	debt-service ratio
EBRD	European Bank for Reconstruction and Development
ECA	export credit agency
EDC	Export Development Corporation (Canada)
EGAT	Electricity Generating Authority of Thailand
EIA	environmental impact assessment

EP	European Parliament
EPA	Environmental Protection Agency
EPL	Ejercito Popular de Liberación
FARC	Fuerzas Armadas Revolucionarias de Colombia
FDI	foreign direct investment
FHWA	Federal Highway Administration (US Department of Transportation)
FPP	Forest Peoples Programme
GATT	General Agreement on Tariffs and Trade
GDP	gross domestic product
GDRP	gross domestic regional product
GEF	Global Environment Facility
GMS	Greater Mekong Subregion
GoL	government of Laos
GRASSALCO	Grasshopper Aluminum Company
GRI	Global Reporting Initiative
GSR	Golden Star Resources
HRC	Human Rights Committee (United Nations)
IACHR	Inter-American Commission on Human Rights
IADB	Inter-American Development Bank
IAG	International Advisory Group
IAIP	International Alliance of Indigenous-Tribal Peoples of the Tropical Forests
IBRD	International Bank for Reconstruction and Development (World Bank)
ICA	Colombian Agriculture Institute
ICCPR	International Covenant on Civil and Political Rights
ICEAC	International Court of Environmental Arbitration and Conciliation
ICESCR	International Covenant on Economic, Social and Cultural Rights
ICJ	International Court of Justice
ICSID	International Center for the Settlement of Investment Disputes
IDA	International Development Agency
IFC	International Finance Corporation
IFI	international financial institution
IGAD	Intergovernmental Authority on Development
ILO	International Labour Organization
IMF	International Monetary Fund
INCORA	Colombian Institute for Colonization and Agrarian Reform
IOI	International Ombudsman Institute
ISO	International Standardization Organization
IT	information technology
IUCN	World Conservation Union (*formerly* International Union for Conservation of Nature and Natural Resources)
IWGIA	International Work Group for Indigenous Affairs

JD	Juris Doctor
JEXIM	Japanese Export-Import Bank
KDA	Karamoja Development Agency (Uganda)
KNP	Kruger National Park
Lao PDR	Lao People's Democratic Republic
LARRRI	Land Rights and Resources Research Institute (Tanzania)
LRA	Lords Resistance Army (Uganda)
MDB	multilateral development bank
MDTs	multidisciplinary teams (ILO)
MIGA	Multilateral Investment Guarantee Agency (World Bank)
MIT	Massachusetts Institute of Technology
MNC	multinational corporation
MOPT	Ministry of Public Works (Colombia)
MRC	Mekong River Commission
NAFTA	North American Free Trade Agreement
NALC	North American Labor Commission
NBCA	Nakai-Nam Theun Biodiversity Conservation Area
NEPA	National Environmental Protection Agency (China)
NGO	non-governmental organization
NP	National Party
NPC	National People's Congress
NPPR	National Pollution Prevention Roundtable
NRA	National Resistance Army (Uganda)
NRM	National Resistance Movement (Uganda)
NT2	Nam Theun II
NTEC	Nam Theun Electricity Corporation
OAS	Organization of American States
OAU	Organization of African Unity
OECD	Organisation for Economic Co-operation and Development
OmCED	International Ombudsman Centre for Environment and Development
OPIC	Overseas Private Investment Corporation (US)
OREWA	Organización Regional Emberá Waunana (Indigenous Organization in Colombia)
PAC	Pan Africanist Congress
PCBs	polychlorinated biphenyls
PDG	Project Development Group
PDIP	Partai Demokrasi Indonesia Perjuangan (Indonesian Democratic Party for Struggle
PNDC	Provisional National Defence Council
POE	Panel of Experts
PPA	power purchase agreement
PSA	production sharing agreement
PTA	Preferential Trade Area
PWC	PriceWaterhouseCoopers
RCAP	Royal Commission on Aboriginal Peoples
RMB	remimbi (Chinese national currency)

SADC	Southern African Development Conference
SDC	Semarang Diamond Chemical
SEIC	Sakhalin Energy Investment Company Ltd
SEPA	State Environmental Protection Administration
SLORC	State Law and Order Restoration Council (Burma)
SMEC	Snowy Mountains Engineering Corporation
SPLA	Sudanese Peoples Liberation Army
SPLM	Sudanese Peoples Liberation Movement
STEA	Science, Technology and Environment Agency (Lao PDR)
TGL	Teberebie Goldfields Ltd
TLC	Transitional Local Council (South Africa)
TNC	transnational corporation
TRANSMEC	Transfield with SMEC
TSP	total suspended particulates
UN	United Nations
UNCED	United Nations Conference on Environment and Development
UNCITRAL	United Nations Commission on International Trade Law
UNCTAD	United Nations Conference on Trade and Development
UNDP	United Nations Development Programme
UNESCO	United Nations Economic, Social and Cultural Organization
UNGA	United Nations General Assembly
UNHCR	United Nations High Commissioner for Refugees
UPD	Unit for Promotion of Democracy (OAS)
USDA	United States Department of Agriculture
USSR	Union of Soviet Socialist Republics
WALHI	Wahana Lingkungan Hidup Indonesia (Indonesian Forum for the Environment)
WCD	World Commission on Dams
WCED	World Commission on Environment and Development
WCS	World Conservation Society
WGIP	Working Group on Indigenous Populations (United Nations)
WTO	World Trade Organization
WWF	*formerly known as* World Wide Fund For Nature (World Wildlife Fund *in Canada and USA*)

Introduction: Conflicts, Ethics and Globalization

Lyuba Zarsky

The intersection between human rights and the environment is a chaotic and contested terrain. For many international human rights lawyers, it can best be mapped by clarifying new 'rights to the environment', such as rights to clean air and water, and a minimum standard of health. Whether such rights can ultimately be justiciable is a matter of debate.

For environmental philosophers, the terrain is less about expanding than contracting human rights, that is, clarifying and honouring ecosystem limits to individual human rights. The goal is to define not rights but responsibilities to care for the environment. Sometimes, these responsibilities are encapsulated in the 'rights of future generations' to inherit a living, life-sustaining planet.

For many public interest advocates, the human rights–environment terrain is about social justice. The allocation of environmental resources, like political and economic resources, is typically skewed towards the rich and powerful. This is as true within a nation as it is at the global level. The poor and marginal suffer the brunt of environmental pollution and natural resource degradation. Indeed, they often suffer outright expropriation of land, forests, fisheries and other natural resources. Moreover, because the rights of the poor to have a political voice receive the least protection, they are often least able to press for just compensation – or to just say 'no' to unwanted development.

From all three vantage points – the emergence of new, international norms, the embrace of environmental responsibilities and the deepening of social justice – the human rights–environment interface became, in the 1990s, an arena of growing ethical concern. In North America and Europe, an 'environmental justice' movement took root, as studies revealed that poor communities and communities of colour disproportionately bear the brunt of industrial pollution and waste. At the global level, 'equity' emerged as the conceptual fulcrum for social justice advocates in defining how to allocate both the burden of global environmental protection and access to 'environmental space'.

But, it was the explosion of the process of economic globalization that catapulted the human rights–environment interface onto the radar screen of a wide circle of analysts and advocates. Globalization means that developing country governments have new opportunities to attract foreign investment. In countries around the world, manufacturing enclaves have been established, displacing local communities and undermining local ecosystems. Multinational energy and mining corporations sent probes to new frontiers, often teaming up in joint ventures with governments whose human rights record was, at best, problematic. With rising levels of production and consumption, new demands for regional transport, energy infrastructure and waste management have emerged, generating both local and transboundary tensions.

The rapid expansion of global investment, production and consumption, in short, has collided in many places and in many ways with local communities. The collisions take place in both developed and developing countries. However, most developing countries have weak institutions to uphold the rule of law, and poor or non-existent judicial systems in which to raise grievances and seek redress and compensation. Lacking the protection of either national or global norms and institutions, poor and marginal communities in developing countries are left either to suffer or to fight – or both.

This book explores conflicts sparked by processes of globalization that involve human rights and the environment. It presents nine case studies of conflicts spanning Latin America, Africa and Asia around three broad axes: energy and mineral development; the development process as a whole; and land rights.

Part I outlines ethical toolkits and norms for the integration of human rights and the environment into the global economy. Fergus MacKay (Chapter 1) considers the rights of indigenous peoples under international law. While a number of international treaties protect specific and individual rights, there is as yet no overarching framework that protects the collective rights of indigenous peoples, especially the right to participate in the drafting of international environmental and other treaties.

Lyuba Zarsky (Chapter 2) explores the emergence of an incipient, voluntary ethical framework governing the global operations of multinational corporations. This framework, which defines the voluntary 'corporate social responsibility' (CSR) model, incorporates norms concerning human rights, labour rights and environmental protection. Zarsky argues, however, that government action is needed to move towards ethical corporate accountability and suggests two potentially fruitful arenas for policy innovation: mandatory social disclosure and international 'sustainable and ethical' investment rules.

Part II presents three case studies of conflicts involving mineral and energy development. More than any other sector, energy and mineral development has sparked conflict with international environmental and human rights groups, as well as local and indigenous communities in dozens of countries around the world.

Mineral development has collided often with indigenous communities in Australia, North America, South America and other 'new world' countries. Pushed back to the least desirable and most marginal lands in the 19th century, indigenous communities found themselves sitting astride valuable mineral resources in the 20th century. Mineral development has, in some cases, brought welcome royalties. In others, it has brought involuntary displacement and expropriation, as well as large-scale pollution.

Fergus MacKay (Chapter 3) examines the conflict between a multinational mining company and the indigenous, maroon community of Nieuw Koffiekamp in the South American nation of Suriname. In the aftermath of a still smouldering civil war, the Surinamese government is actively pursuing foreign investment in mining. Claims, however, are located in home regions of indigenous peoples, including maroon communities, for whom the natural environment provides not only livelihood but also spiritual sustenance and cultural identity. With their government-granted mineral rights in hand, the mining company has tried repeatedly to resettle the residents of Nieuw Koffiekamp, who refuse both relocation and compensation. In the face of mutual intransigence, the conflict continues and an essential question remains unanswered: Does the community have the right to say no?

The process of mineral extraction can be degrading to and demanding of the local environment. Water resources are especially vulnerable. Ground or river waters are often diverted for mining operations, especially washing, and then used as a repository for mining wastes. Douglas Korsah-Brown (Chapter 4) examines two case studies of local villages in Ghana whose water supply was diverted and polluted by mining company operations. In both cases, the villages fought back and won, despite the weakness of Ghanaian environmental law. However, the poor villages have been hard pressed to make the big companies honour the promises they made. The best hope for enforcement not only for these particular cases but for the entire class of conflicts is for Ghana to strengthen both its environmental institutions and its non-governmental organizations (NGOs).

Vera Mischenko and Erika Rosenthal (Chapter 5) examine conflicts over offshore oil leases off Sakhalin Island in the Russian Far East. Rich in fisheries and endangered marine resources, these North Pacific waters provide a livelihood for local and indigenous communities. In a landmark 'David vs. Goliath' case, Russian environmentalists won a lawsuit forcing transnational US and Japanese energy companies to comply with Russian law in assessing and mitigating environmental impacts of offshore drilling. The case is far from settled, however, because the energy companies are fighting back.

Part III presents four case studies where the fundamental issue of contention is the content and direction of the development strategy. The overarching question is: Who gets to participate in designing a development strategy? Agus Sari (Chapter 6) examines the rapid transformation of the island of Batam in Indonesia from a community of 6,000 fisherfolk, traders and pirates to a major industrial city with an urban population of 200,000. Foreign investment and export-led growth have greatly changed not only the social but also the physical environment of the island, and degradation is widespread, not least because waste management infrastructure is lacking. Urban and fishing communities have protested, with some success. Sari examines 'who wins, who loses' and considers the crucial role of inclusive, participatory local institutions in resolving environment–development conflicts.

A development strategy proposed for Laos centres on harnessing the Mekong River through the building of hydroelectric dams and exporting electricity to neighbouring Thailand. Philip Hirsch (Chapter 7) examines the proposed Nam

Theun II dam, a large-scale project which entails the displacement of thousands of people in indigenous and subsistence communities. Largely due to the involvement of the World Bank, processes have been established to 'consult' local Laotian communities. Hirsch examines the dilemmas raised by the application of global norms to help justify a project whose host country has poorly established institutional and cultural means of dealing with such norms. 'Consultation' and 'participation' can have little depth where free and open political speech is neither protected by law nor practised by tradition.

Globalization is both made possible by and stimulates the expansion of transport systems. In the Western Hemisphere, Pan-American road systems run continuously – except for a 130 kilometre gap – from Alaska to the tip of South America. Pascal Girot (Chapter 8) examines the complex politics of the battle over the Darien Gap, which harbours one of the most culturally and biologically diverse ecosystems of the Neotropical region. Straddling the border between Panama and Colombia, the Gap is also a geopolitical battleground. At stake is both human and environmental security in the region.

The scale and pace of the development process in China has no parallel in human history. Whether China can maintain growth without seriously compromising the environment or public health is far from clear. Changhua Wu and Simon Wang (Chapter 9) examine the nexus of development, environment and human rights in China through a case study of foreign dumping of hazardous wastes. The Chinese government has defined the human rights–environment interface in response to foreign waste dumping, thus conflating human rights with national sovereignty. However, the case study shows that the lack of capacity to manage foreign wastes extends also to domestic wastes, raising serious questions about protection of public health in the development process.

Part IV of the book turns to conflicts over land rights, with two case studies in Africa. Robert Thornton (Chapter 10) examines claims to lands in and around the Kruger National Park in South Africa. Acting on offers by the post-apartheid government to restore land taken on the basis of race, a host of overlapping and competing claims have been made. The land itself, however, has high ecological value in terms of watershed management, biodiversity protection and international ecotourism. Institutions to resolve the conflict are still evolving.

Eastern and central Africa have experienced some of the most persistent conflicts in the world over the last several decades. John Mugabe and Godber Tumushabe (Chapter 11) examine the role of natural resource degradation in conflicts in the Sudan, Uganda and Rwanda. They argue that environmental stress is at the root of these conflicts, a fact that explains why efforts to resolve them, which have focused narrowly on the political underpinnings of the conflicts, have largely failed. A regional approach to mediation which focused on the shrinking subsistence base would potentially have a much better chance of resolving conflicts.

Part V concludes the book with a look at institutional mechanisms for mediation and conflict resolution. Naomi Roht-Arriaza (Chapter 12) maps existing institutions and considers institutional innovations at the global, regional or local level, which could help to 'amplify the voice of the powerless'. Such innovations could be especially useful given the lack of clear and/or enforceable global norms. Rather than adjudication, innovative institutions for mediation would utilize a 'soft law' approach which would reference a wide set of evolving norms and would aim to be inclusive and participatory.

The conflicts described in this book span three continents and a myriad of issues. Three central themes, however, thread through all the case studies. The first is that the root of the conflicts is political exclusion. The lack of effective institutions in which all stakeholders can be heard, including those 'representing' environmental responsibility and future generations, exacerbates conflict and undermines environmental sustainability. While there are serious and deeply felt conflicts of interest, the lack of institutional mechanisms for all parties to be heard, for scientific information to be brought forward and for trade-offs to be deliberated, makes true 'conflict resolution' difficult, if not impossible.

The second theme, exemplified so well in the Suriname case, is the right of local communities to fundamentally shape the development process. Do local communities, including indigenous communities, have the right to refuse a development project or process which makes them cultural, economic or political losers? By what right can development be imposed on unwilling communities? Is social justice served by ensuring that losers are compensated?

The third theme is about what drives normative change. The case studies explore the relationship beween legal norms and state capacities to uphold them, on the one hand, and 'soft law' and incentives for conflicting parties themselves to discover and uphold norms, on the other hand. Most case studies highlight the potential role that mediation-based institutional innovations could play both in resolving a conflict and in clarifying new norms. However, the mediation process itself must be robust, that is, all information must be brought to light and all parties must sit at the table and speak for themselves. Most important, the conflicting parties must themselves be committed to seeking and honouring a mediated resolution. This is a tall order. In the end, it will take a combination of both legal and institutional innovations, including mediation, to clarify and enforce new ethics in the global economy which promote human rights and environmental sustainability. This book seeks to make a contribution to that process.

Part I

Integrating Human Rights and Environmental Ethics

Chapter 1

The Rights of Indigenous Peoples in International Law

Fergus MacKay

INTRODUCTION

The rights of indigenous peoples have assumed a prominent place in intergovernmental human rights discourse in the past 30 years. During this time, there has been a steady evolution in normative development towards a greater recognition of indigenous rights that can only be described as remarkable. Some scholars argue that these rights, in whole or part, have already achieved the status of customary international law and are therefore legally binding. Even a cursory look at the treatment of indigenous peoples by states, however, demonstrates that there is a long way to go before indigenous peoples are secure in the enjoyment of these guarantees. This is especially the case when indigenous rights conflict with state development plans and multinational operations, which in many cases are supported by powerful local elites capable of manipulating political, legal and judicial systems.

There is also a growing awareness among development theorists and conservation planners of the need to recognize indigenous rights to lands and resources, as well as indigenous legal systems and traditional knowledge.[1] Recognition of these rights, it is argued, is in many cases a precondition for the ecologically sustainable use, management and preservation of tropical rainforests and other ecosystems.[2] Nonetheless, although the situation is improving, conflicts between indigenous peoples and conservationists, biodiversity prospectors and others occur regularly. Indeed, state, NGO or intergovernmental conservation initiatives that fail to incorporate indigenous rights, however laudable, are generally perceived by indigenous peoples to be no different from other activities that affect their control over their ancestral domain.

This chapter provides an overview of indigenous rights in international law. It begins with an outline of selected conceptual issues related to indigenous rights, such as collective rights and definitional criteria, and goes on to examine indigenous rights as defined by United Nations and regional human rights instruments including the Organization of American States (OAS). It then explores emerging standards as developed in draft United Nations and OAS instruments, and concludes with an examination of international instruments on environment and development.

CONCEPTUAL ISSUES

On one level, indigenous rights are straightforward: they are rights that attach to indigenous persons and peoples by virtue of being human and indigenous. However, in certain cases, applying these rights to actual situations may present, at least in the abstract, a number of conceptual and other problems. For instance, there is no official or generally accepted international definition of the term 'indigenous'. Nor is there an international definition of what constitutes a people (as in indigenous peoples), nor an accepted definition of 'minority'. Indeed, in most cases, indigenous peoples can be classified as both a minority and an indigenous people at the same time, yet, as we will see below, two distinct (at times overlapping) bodies of law have evolved to account for indigenous and minority rights.[3] Moreover, indigenous rights as developed by intergovernmental organizations are far more extensive, stronger and detailed than minority rights.

Furthermore, emerging human rights standards relating to indigenous peoples are in large part rights that apply to collectivities, focusing on the indigenous people as a whole rather than the indigenous individual. This accords with indigenous aspirations and cosmovisions, but is rejected by certain governments and theorists, who state (erroneously) that international law does not and should not recognize collective rights.[4] Many of these objections are directly related to fears of recognizing the self-determining status (and international subjectivity) of indigenous peoples and attendant issues of resource sovereignty and political power.

The distinction between rights of general application ('established') and 'emerging' indigenous rights is somewhat artificial as the majority of the so-called emerging standards either build on existing human rights or are contextualized restatements or elaborations thereof. Nonetheless, indigenous rights, both established and emerging, exist as a body of law distinct from the rights that apply to persons belonging to minorities or rights of universal application. The primary distinction may at first appear semantic, but has far reaching consequences (see the discussion on the right to self-determination below) – the use of indigenous *peoples* as opposed to indigenous people, groups or populations. Indigenous rights are collective rather than individual rights. Minority rights, on the other hand, are individual rights to be exercised in 'community with other members of their group'. While some measure of collective rights are implicit in this language, it is the individual, rather than the minority as a group, that holds the right.

Collective rights have been described as 'an inherent and essential element of indigenous rights' (WGIP, 1988, para 68). While human rights law, with few exceptions (self-determination, the right to development, the prohibition of genocide, for instance), has traditionally been concerned with the rights of individuals, international consensus is developing that other human rights can also adhere to collectivities. Sanders (1991, p369) defines collectivities as: 'Groups that have goals that transcend the ending of discrimination against their members … for their members are joined together not simply by external discrimination but by an internal cohesiveness. Collectivities seek to protect and develop their own particular cultural characteristics'. As evidenced by numerous statements from indigenous peoples, cultural integrity and survival are paramount concerns. The importance of collective rights in this context is that they redefine the legal terms of indigenous cultural survival and future development insofar as they represent the 'legitimation and affirmation of the value of protecting indigenous peoples' ways of life and cultures per se' (Williams, 1990, p687).

The collective rights of indigenous peoples are therefore about taking the imperative of decolonization to its logical conclusion and recognizing the inherent equality and dignity of all peoples to maintain their distinct socio-cultural-political organization, free from unwanted, external interference. This is the essence of the right to self-determination, denied to indigenous peoples by centuries of colonial and racist discourse and practice translated into and ensconced in international law. In this context, collective rights include the recognition of and respect for indigenous political and cultural institutions and legal systems. According to Gray (1997, pp18–19), indigenous legal systems 'constitute an important, but frequently ignored, area of indigenous rights. This is because indigenous legal systems are embedded in the daily practices and knowledge of a people, consisting of the duties and obligations that are necessary for social life to continue'. Also included are ownership and control of territory and the right to give or withhold consent to activities related to that territory and its attendant resources.

The concept of territory, as used here, encompasses the multiple and various forms of indigenous interaction – spiritual, physical, social, economic, cultural, etc – with their lands and resources. Accordingly:

> *Property law must acknowledge Native difference beyond the limited notion of a usufructory right and permit the freeing up of the multiple processes by which aboriginal identities are constructed out of individual and communal encounters with nature and land. To do so requires a significant shift away from the fiction that the [state] owns underlying title … and the notion that aboriginal interests in land rest on the continuing goodwill of the [state]* (Macklem, 1993, p26).

Opponents to collective rights assert that individual rights will be eroded and threatened by the exercise of collective rights. While there is some degree of inherent tension between the rights and interests of individuals and collectivities, these tensions are by no means restricted to indigenous peoples. In all societies and legal systems, to varying degrees, the interests and rights of the collective (for example, society, the nation, the state) and individuals are measured against each other. The power of eminent domain, for instance, is often wielded by states in the name of the general interest even though individuals may perceive that their rights or interests are compromised in the process. State claims to ownership of sub-surface or other natural resources are also normally made in the name of the common good, and in many cases exploitation thereof comes at the expense of individuals and groups within the larger population. The objective of this discussion should not be to dismiss or reject collective rights, but rather to determine the mechanisms by which rights that may conflict can be accommodated and reconciled. Neither indigenous peoples, as self-governing entities, nor states are exempt from respecting international human rights standards applicable to individuals (WGIP, 1993a, article 33).

The preceding points may be classified as theoretical conceptual issues, whereas the issue of the legal concept of indigenous peoples, or in other words, a legal definition for the term 'indigenous', presents a number of applied problems in addition to the theoretical.[5]

Various definitions of indigenous peoples have been developed by intergovernmental organizations. A definition for tribal peoples has also been developed, sometimes synonymous with indigenous, more recently as a distinct category, although equal in terms of the rights that attach to such a designation. Indigenous peoples have consistently opposed such definitions on the grounds that the right to define, both individually and collectively, who is an indigenous person or people is part and parcel of the right to self-determination and would include the power to deny rights that attach to that status. They point to the fact that history bears graphic witness to abuse of this power by states. Perhaps in response to this, definitions developed by intergovernmental organizations all include self-definition as a 'fundamental criterion' (ILO 169, article 1; IACHR 1997a, article 1; Cobo, 1986, 50). The UN Draft Declaration goes further, leaving out any definition and including in Article 8 a right to individual and collective self-definition.

Clearly, an unrestricted right to self-definition raises multiple concerns and fears, some legitimate, others not, for many states. Asian and African governments especially continue to insist on a definition that includes historical continuity with a given pre-invasion/settlement territory and population so as to restrict the scope of indigenous rights to the so-called 'settler states' of the Americas, Australasia and the Pacific (Gray, 1995).

The UN Working Group on Indigenous Populations (WGIP) conducted an in-depth study on the question of a definition, deciding, in accordance with statements made by indigenous representatives, that a definition was neither necessary nor desirable and concluding 'that the concept of "indigenous" is not capable of a precise, inclusive definition which can be applied in the same manner to all regions of the world' (Daes, 1996, p5). The Chairperson-Rapporteur stated that this conclusion was not intended 'to minimize the concerns expressed by some governments, but to demonstrate that their concerns cannot effectively be met through an exercise in definition. The result of undertaking such an exercise would be a definition which lacked any scientific or logical credibility...' (Daes, 1996, p21).

The Chairperson did, however, note a number of factors that have been 'considered relevant to the understanding of the concept of "indigenous"' by international organizations and legal experts (Daes, 1996, p22). These factors include:

(a) Priority in time, with respect to the occupation and use of a specific territory; (b) The voluntary perpetuation of cultural distinctiveness, which may include the aspects of language, social organization, religion and spiritual values, modes of production, laws and institutions; (c) Self-identification, as well as recognition by other groups, or by State authorities, as a distinct collectivity; and (d) An experience of subjugation, marginalization, dispossession, exclusion or discrimination, whether or not these conditions persist (Ibid).

She concluded by stating that:

the foregoing factors do not, and cannot, constitute an inclusive or comprehensive definition. Rather, they represent factors which may be present, to a greater or lesser degree, in different regions and in different national and local contexts. As such, they may provide some general guidance to reasonable decision-making in practice (Ibid).

Some definitions focus primarily on cultural distinctiveness and internal and external perceptions of cultural difference without reference to priority in time or historical continuity. The World Bank's Operational Directive 4.20 on Indigenous Peoples (1991), for instance, states that: 'the term "indigenous peoples", "indigenous ethnic minorities", "tribal groups", and "scheduled tribes" describe social groups with a social and cultural identity distinct from the dominant society that makes them vulnerable to being disadvantaged in the development process.' Article 1(2) of the Proposed OAS Declaration does not include any definition for indigenous peoples, but, borrowing from ILO 169, does define other groups to whom the Declaration applies. It states that the 'Declaration applies to indigenous peoples as well as other [tribal] peoples whose social, cultural and economic conditions distinguish them from other sections of national community, and whose status is regulated wholly or partially by their own customs or traditions or by special laws or regulations.' Accordingly, Afro-American peoples, such as Suriname and Jamaica maroons, would enjoy the same rights as Amerindian peoples under this instrument.

EXISTING HUMAN RIGHTS STANDARDS

The United Nations system

The International Covenant on Civil and Political Rights (ICCPR), the Convention on the Rights of the Child and the Convention on the Elimination of All Forms of Racial Discrimination (CERD) all contain provisions relevant to indigenous rights. Other instruments, such as the International Covenant on Economic, Social and Cultural Rights (ICESCR), are also relevant, but will not be addressed in detail here.

Common article 1 of the ICCPR and ICESCR states in part that:

(1) All peoples have the right to self-determination, by virtue of that right they freely determine their political status and freely pursue their economic, social and cultural development (2) All peoples may, for their own ends, freely dispose of their natural wealth and resources... In no case may a people be deprived of its own means of subsistence.

The United Nations Human Rights Committee (HRC) applies this right to indigenous peoples when examining state-party reports under article 40 of the ICCPR. In its Concluding observations on Canada's fourth periodic report, for instance, the HRC stated that:

With reference to the conclusion by the [Royal Commission on Aboriginal Peoples] that without a greater share of lands and resources institutions of aboriginal self-government will fail, the Committee emphasizes that the right to self-determination requires, inter alia, that all peoples must be able to freely dispose of their natural wealth and resources and that they may not be deprived of their own means of subsistence (article 1(2)). The Committee recommends that decisive and urgent action be taken towards the full implementation of the RCAP recommendations on land and resource allocation. The Committee also recommends that the practice of extinguishing inherent aboriginal rights be abandoned as incompatible with article 1 of the Covenant.[6]

The right to self-determination as enumerated in common article 1 has also been applied to indigenous peoples by the Working Group on Indigenous Populations (WGIP) and the UN Sub-Commission on the Prevention of Discrimination and the Protection of Minorities. The Inter-American Commission on Human Rights has recognized some measure of this right – autonomy and self-government – in its Proposed Declaration. Self-determination in all its manifestations, political, territorial, economic, cultural, etc, is the key demand and central right of indigenous peoples.

Article 27 of the ICCPR applies to minorities and recognizes, *inter alia*, an individual right to enjoy one's culture in community with other members of the cultural collective. The HRC has interpreted this article to include the 'rights of persons, in community with others, to engage in economic and social activities which are part of the culture of the community to which they belong' (HRC, 1990, 1). In reaching this conclusion, the HRC recognized that indigenous peoples' subsistence and other traditional economic activities are an integral part of their culture, and interference with those activities can be detrimental to cultural integrity and survival (among others, HRC, 1990; 1988). By implication, the land, resource base and the environment thereof also require protection if subsistence activities are to be safeguarded. The HRC further elaborated on article 27 in its General Comment No 23, stating that:

With regard to the exercise of the cultural rights protected under Article 27, the committee observes that culture manifests itself in many forms, including a particular way of life associated with the use of land resources, specifically in the case of indigenous peoples. That right may include such traditional activities as fishing or hunting and the right to live in reserves protected by law. The enjoyment of those rights may require positive legal measures of protection and measures to ensure the effective participation of members of minority communities in decisions which affect them. The Committee concludes that article 27 relates to rights whose protection imposes specific obligations on States parties. The protection of these rights is directed to ensure the survival and continued development of the cultural, religious and social identity of the minorities concerned, thus enriching the fabric of society as a whole… (HRC, 1994, p3).

The HRC has also found violations of indigenous rights under other articles of the ICCPR – the right to family and the right to privacy – although this was largely due to the fact that France had registered a reservation to article 27.[7] This case involved the construction of a hotel complex on an ancestral burial ground of indigenous Polynesians in Tahiti. The petitioners had argued that the hotel would interfere with and deny their ability to maintain their relationship with and duties to their ancestors. Finding that a violation had occurred the HRC stated that:

cultural traditions should be taken into account when defining the term 'family' in a specific situation. It transpires from the authors' claims that they consider their relationship to their ancestors to be an essential element of their identity and to play an important role in their family life… The Committee considers that the authors' failure to establish a direct kinship link cannot be held against them … where the burial grounds in question pre-date the arrival of European settlers and are recognized as including the forebears of the present Polynesian inhabitants of Tahiti.[8]

Employing language consistent with article 27 of the ICCPR, article 30 of the Convention on the Rights of the Child should be interpreted in conformity with the views of the HRC above and with the decisions of the Inter-American Commission on Human Rights discussed below. This requires a recognition of the right to participate in the cultural life of the collective, especially as it relates to subsistence practices, relationship to land and territory, and their educational and religious significance to the indigenous child. States-parties have affirmative obligations to facilitate the enjoyment of these rights by, *inter alia*, recognizing, respecting and enforcing rights to land, territory and resources, and all aspects of productive organization. Article 30 and ICCPR article 27 embody one manifestation of the general norm of international law relating to the right to cultural integrity (Anaya, 1991, 15).

Under CERD, states-parties are obligated to, *inter alia*, respect and observe the right 'to own property alone as well as in association with others'(article 5(d)(v)). In a 1997 General Recommendation, CERD elaborated on state obligations and indigenous rights under the Convention (CERD, 1997). The Committee called on states-parties to 'ensure that members of indigenous peoples have equal rights in respect of effective participation in public life, and that no decisions directly relating to their rights and interests are taken without their informed consent' (ibid, p1). Additionally, states-parties should:

> *recognize and protect the rights of indigenous peoples to own, develop, control*
> *and use their communal lands, territories and resources and, where they have*
> *been deprived of their lands and territories traditionally owned or otherwise*
> *inhabited or used without their free and informed consent, to take steps to*
> *return these lands and territories* (ibid).

This General Comment is surprisingly strong and undoubtedly influenced by the UN Draft Declaration.[9] The reference to 'informed consent' is particularly important as is the inclusion of 'control' in the scope of indigenous rights to lands and resources. Moreover, interpretations of CERD should carry additional weight given that the prohibition of systematic racial discrimination has acquired the status of *jus cogens* under international law and, therefore, will void any law or practice found to be in violation of the norm (Brownlie, 1990, 513).

This section on UN instruments concludes with International Labour Organization (ILO) Convention No 169. ILO 169 and its predecessor, Convention No 107, are presently the only binding international treaties that exclusively focus on the rights of indigenous peoples. The stated aim of ILO 107 was, and remains for its states-parties, the integration and assimilation of indigenous peoples.[10] Due to this lack of respect for indigenous culture and identity, ILO 107 became an 'embarrassment' to the ILO (Berman, 1988, pp48–9) and, in 1986, a decision was made to revise it according to the principle that indigenous peoples should 'enjoy as much control as possible over their own economic, social and cultural development'(ILO 1988, p117). After a two-year revision process, ILO 169 was adopted in 1989 by the International Labour Conference.[11]

ILO 169, while not declaring a right to environment, is the first international instrument to relate environmental concerns explicitly to indigenous peoples. Article 4(1), for instance, requires states to take 'special measures' to protect the environment of indigenous peoples. These special measures include environmental impact studies of proposed development activities (article 7(3)), the recognition of subsistence rights (article 23), protection of natural resources (article 15(1)), and measures to protect and preserve the territories of indigenous peoples (article 7(4)).

Article 7(1) contains one of the most important principles of the Convention. It provides that:

> *The people concerned shall have the right to decide their own priorities for the*
> *process of development as it affects their lives, beliefs, institutions and spiritual*
> *well-being and the lands they occupy or otherwise use, and to exercise control,*
> *to the extent possible, over their own economic, social and cultural development.*

This article is one of the general principles of the Convention and provides a framework within which the other articles are to be interpreted. It recognizes that indigenous peoples have the right to some measure of self-government with regard to their social and political institutions, and in determining the direction and nature of their economic, social and cultural development. Other general principles of the Convention require participation, consultation, good faith negotiation and the recognition of indigenous land and resource rights. Of particular importance is article 13(1), which requires that 'governments shall respect the special importance for the cultures and spiritual values of the peoples concerned of their relationship with the lands or territories, or both as applicable, which they occupy or otherwise use, and in particular the collective aspects of this relationship'.

While ILO 169 is being promoted by indigenous peoples all over the world, it has nonetheless been severely criticized by many, especially in the period immediately following its approval in 1989. Criticism focused on, among other things, the lack of indigenous participation in the drafting process, the absence of self-determination language and consent standard, particularly in connection with the exploitation of indigenous resources, and the many qualifications included in the various articles that substantially weaken the protections defined therein, the majority of which are procedural rather than substantive guarantees. The Convention's deficiencies are especially apparent in comparison with the UN and OAS Declarations discussed below. Indeed, the argument can be made that ILO 169 is in many ways out-dated ten years after its approval and the results of its implementation and enforcement so far are mixed.

Inter-American system

In 1972, the Inter-American Commission on Human Rights (IACHR) issued a resolution entitled *Special Protection for Indigenous Populations, Action to Combat Racism and Racial Discrimination* (IACHR, 1972, pp90–1). This resolution stated, *inter alia*: 'That for historical reasons and because of moral and humanitarian principles, special protection for indigenous populations constitutes a sacred commitment of the states' (ibid). The need for special protection for indigenous peoples was recently reaffirmed by the IACHR in its 1997 *Ecuador Report*. Specifically, the IACHR stated that:

> *Within international law generally, and Inter-American law specifically, special protections for indigenous peoples may be required for them to exercise their rights fully and equally with the rest of the population. Additionally, special protections for indigenous peoples may be required to ensure their physical and cultural survival – a right protected in a range of international instruments and conventions* (IACHR, 1997b, p115).

Although dated, the IACHR's *Report on the Situation of Human Rights of a Segment of the Nicaraguan Population of Miskito Origin* is illustrative of state obligations under the American Convention. It found that:

> *special legal protection is recognized for the use of [indigenous peoples'] language, the observance of their religion, and in general, all those aspects related to the preservation of their cultural identity. To this should be added*

> *the aspects linked to productive organization, which includes, among other*
> *things, the issue of ancestral and communal lands* (IACHR, 1984, p81).

For the attendant rights to be respected, the IACHR stated that participatory mechanisms must be developed within the institutional framework of the state that open political space for indigenous peoples to assert their aspirations, needs and rights.

In 1985, the IACHR examined the rights of the Yanomami people in the context of the construction of the Trans-Amazonia highway in Brazil, invasion of their territory by small-scale gold miners and devastating illnesses brought in by the miners (IACHR, 1985). The IACHR found, due to Brazil's failure to take 'timely measures' to protect the Yanomami, that violations of, *inter alia*, the right to life and the right to the preservation of health and well-being under the American Declaration had occurred (ibid, p33). In reaching this conclusion, the IACHR reiterated the widely held conclusion that the right to life has broad application beyond intentional or arbitrary deprivation of life; it also requires that governments take affirmative steps to protect life by ensuring environmental integrity and promoting policies that guarantee the basic survival of persons subject to state jurisdiction.

In its *Third Report on the Situation of Human Rights in The Republic of Guatemala*, the IACHR found Guatemala responsible for acts and omissions detrimental to indigenous 'ethnic identity and against development of their traditions, their language, their economies, and their culture' (IACHR, 1986, p114). It characterized these as 'human rights also essential to the right to life of peoples' (ibid). Note that this is stated as a right of peoples, as opposed to individuals, and therefore a collective right. Persistent and pervasive violations of these rights are generically referred to as ethnocide or cultural genocide, which is prohibited by international law.

In its *Ecuador Report*, IACHR directly relates the right to life to environmental security stating that, 'The realisation of the right to life, and to physical security and integrity is necessarily related to and in some ways dependent upon one's physical environment. Accordingly, where environmental contamination and degradation pose a persistent threat to human life and health, the foregoing rights are implicated' (IACHR, 1997b, p88). This report also recognized that state policy and practice concerning resource exploitation and land use cannot take place in a vacuum that ignores its human rights obligations. In doing so, the Commission stated that it:

> *recognizes that the right to development implies that each state has the freedom*
> *to exploit its natural resources, including through the granting of concessions*
> *and acceptance of international investment. However, the Commission*
> *considers that the absence of regulation, inappropriate regulation, or a lack of*
> *supervision in the application of extant norms may create serious problems*
> *with respect to the environment which could translate into violations of human*
> *rights protected by the American Convention'* (IACHR, 1997b, p89).

Building on principles adopted at the United Nations Conference on Environment and Development (UNCED) and various articles of the American Convention, the IACHR highlighted the right to participate in decisions affecting the environment (ibid, pp92–5). An integral part of this right is access to information in an understandable form. Emphasizing procedural guarantees and state obligations to adopt positive measures to guarantee the right to life, the IACHR stated that:

> *In the context of the situation under study, protection of the right to life and physical integrity may best be advanced through measures to support and enhance the ability of individuals to safeguard and vindicate those rights. The quest to guarantee against environmental conditions which threaten human health requires that individuals have access to: information, participation in relevant decision-making processes, and judicial recourse* (ibid, p93).

With regard to land rights, the IACHR stated:

> *For many indigenous cultures, continued utilization of traditional collective systems for the control and use of territory are essential to their survival, as well as to their individual and collective well-being. Control over the land refers to both its capacity for providing the resources which sustain life, and to 'the geographical space necessary for the cultural and social reproduction of the group'* (IACHR, 1997b, p115).

Although it fails to fully address the serious and pervasive nature of human rights violations connected with the oil industry in Ecuador, the *Ecuador Report* is a significant elaboration of state obligations with regard to the human rights–environment nexus that deserves detailed analysis. The OAS Proposed Declaration has also addressed and contextualized to indigenous peoples many of the issues noted above.

Most recently, the IACHR found that Niacaragua had violated the right to property and to judicial protection (articles 21 and 25, respectively, of the American Convention on Human Rights (ACHR)), by failing to identify, title and demarcate lands traditionally occupied and used by an indigenous people and by granting logging concessions on those lands without the participation of the affected communities.[12] This case is presently pending before the Inter-American Court of Human Rights for an examination of the merits.

EVOLVING HUMAN RIGHTS STANDARDS RELATING TO INDIGENOUS PEOPLES

The internationalization of the indigenous rights movement can be traced back to the formation of the International Indian Treaty Council and the World Council of Indigenous Peoples in North America in the mid-1970s. Afterwards, this movement expanded to encompass indigenous peoples and organizations from all regions of the world. The 1977 NGO Conference on Discrimination Against

Indigenous Peoples of the Americas, followed by a conference on indigenous land rights in 1981, firmly placed indigenous issues on the international agenda (Gray, 1997). Within the United Nations, indigenous issues arose in the context of an expert study on racial discrimination. This study, submitted in 1969, concluded that the issue of discrimination against indigenous peoples had not been adequately dealt with and required further attention. Consequently, a study on the *Problem of Discrimination Against Indigenous Populations* was authorized. Also known as the Cobo Report, this multi-volume report, completed in 1983, recommended that a declaration on the rights of indigenous peoples be elaborated, with a view to ultimately developing a binding international convention.

Against this background, the Commission on Human Rights recommended the establishment of a Working Group on Indigenous Populations (WGIP) within the United Nations system. Established in 1982, the Working Group's most notable achievement to date has been the completion of a draft declaration on the rights of indigenous peoples.[13] This instrument, drafted with substantial indigenous participation, is by far the most comprehensive and responsive attempt to recognize indigenous rights drafted to date. It is presently being examined by an inter-sessional Working Group of the Commission on Human Rights. This Working Group, composed entirely of political-level delegates, rather than human rights experts like the WGIP and Sub-Commission, has the authority to amend, change or modify the text and substance of the instrument and may well do so in the coming years. After it is approved by the Commission, the Draft Declaration will pass via the Economic and Social Council to the UN General Assembly for adoption.

The OAS Proposed Declaration, started in 1989 and approved by the IACHR in 1997, was in part inspired by developments within the United Nations and the adoption of ILO 169 in 1989. It was drafted in relative secrecy by the IACHR's technical staff with minimal indigenous participation and lacks the consistency, depth and detail of the UN Draft Declaration. Its use by the IACHR in interpreting state obligations under other Inter-American instruments may be its greatest significance. The OAS Declaration is currently under review by a working group of the OAS Committee on Juridical and Political Affairs; the first session was held in November 1999.

Both the UN Draft and OAS Proposed Declarations, although to varying degrees, build on existing standards, including ILO 169, and attempt to redefine prevailing political, economic and cultural relations between indigenous peoples and states (Daes, 1993a, p4; Daes, 1993b, pp8–9; Barsh, 1994, p39). They do so by recognizing rights in three main areas: 1) self-determination, autonomy and self-government; 2) lands, territories and resources; and 3) political participation rights. These rights are all in some way related to fundamental guarantees of non-discrimination and cultural integrity, which are also elaborated on by the instruments in question. The primary distinction between the two instruments is that the UN Declaration is framed by the right to self-determination, whereas the OAS Declaration, in common with ILO 169, fails to recognize this right without qualification. Although the results of exercising the rights defined in each instrument may in many cases be similar, this distinction is nonetheless profound and fundamental.

Full and unqualified recognition of indigenous peoples' right to self-determination has been and is the most prominent demand of the indigenous rights movement (Barsh, 1994; Anaya, 1996; Sambo, 1993). This right is viewed as the mechanism by which indigenous peoples can enjoy all other human rights and ensure their cultural integrity and survival, and can broadly be defined as the right to freely determine the nature and extent of their relationship with the state and other peoples and to control their internal affairs. The Cobo report, for instance, stated that: 'Self-determination, in its many forms, is thus a basic pre-condition if indigenous peoples are to be able to enjoy their fundamental rights and determine their future, while at the same time preserving, developing, and passing on their specific ethnic identity to future generations' (para 269).

Responding to this, the UN Draft Declaration states in article 3 that, 'indigenous peoples have the right to self-determination. By virtue of that right they freely determine their political status and freely determine their economic, social and cultural development'. This language is consistent with common article 1 of the ICCPR and ICESCR, which include the right to be secure in the means of subsistence, rights to the requisite resource base and the right to development in accordance with indigenous priorities, cultural characteristics and needs.[14] It also includes recognition of and respect for indigenous governing institutions and legal systems, which are also explicitly provided for in both the UN and OAS instruments.[15]

The OAS Proposed Declaration, as does ILO 169 (article 1(3)), explicitly states that the use of the term peoples 'shall not be construed as having any implications with respect to the rights which may be attached to that term under international law'. In effect, this sidesteps the contentious issue of the application of the right to self-determination as defined by the International Covenants and the UN Draft Declaration, while still recognizing indigenous peoples as collective rights-bearing entities. It does not say that indigenous peoples do not have the right to self-determination nor does it say they do; it is silent on the issue. At the same time, the OAS instrument does recognize rights that amount to a possible expression of the right to self-determination – autonomy and self-government within existing states. Article XV(1) provides that:

> *States acknowledge that indigenous peoples have the right to freely determine their political status and freely pursue their economic, social and cultural development, and that accordingly they have the right to autonomy and self-government with regard to their internal and local affairs, including culture, religion, education, information, media, health, housing, employment, social welfare, economic activities, land and resources management, the environment and entry by non-members; and to the ways and means for financing these autonomous functions.*

The first part of this article is, with the deletion of the word 'self-determination', identical to that of common article 1 of the Covenants and article 3 of the UN Draft Declaration. However, it specifically – 'and that accordingly' – designates autonomy and self-government as the mode by which indigenous peoples shall exercise their right to determine their political status and pursue their economic, social and cultural development. Article 31 of the UN Draft Declaration contains similar language to that quoted article XV(1), but is framed by the explicit recognition of the right to self-determination in article 3 and provides that autonomy and self-government is the preferred, but not exclusive, means of exercising that right. Daes explains that self-determination in this context requires that indigenous peoples exercise their right to self-determination through the state's political and legal systems unless these systems are 'so exclusive and non-democratic that [they] can no longer be said to be representing the whole people' (Daes, 1993a, p5). States have a corresponding duty to adopt legal, administrative and constitutional reforms that recognize the rights of indigenous peoples to, among others, autonomy, self-government, territory, cultural integrity and participation based on consent. Secession is only possible as an exceptional measure should the state fail to accommodate these rights and be so abusive and unrepresentative 'that the situation is tantamount to classic colonialism...' (ibid).

An indigenous right to self-determination has been contentious as certain states claim that recognition of this right will lead to secession and territorial dismemberment. For their part, indigenous peoples, with few exceptions, have stated that they have no desire to secede from states. They argue that the failure to recognize their right to self-determination constitutes discrimination insofar as 'all peoples have the right to self-determination' and perpetuates their domination by other peoples. Some states counter that indigenous peoples are not peoples in law and that self-determination is restricted to decolonization from geographically distinct colonial powers. However, in her Explanatory Note on the UN Draft Declaration, Daes asserts that, 'indigenous groups are unquestionably "peoples" in every political, social, cultural and ethnological meaning of this term' and that 'it is neither logical nor scientific to treat them as the same "peoples" as their neighbours, who obviously have different languages, histories and cultures' (Daes, 1993a, p2). She continues that, 'The United Nations should not pretend, for the sake of a convenient legal fiction, that those differences do not exist' (ibid).

Territorial rights are integral to indigenous peoples' right to self-determination and cultural survival. Consequently, recent normative developments relating to indigenous lands, territories and resources are expansive, requiring legal recognition, restitution and compensation, protection of the total environment thereof, and various measures of participation in extra-territorial activities that may affect subsistence rights and environmental and cultural integrity. Article 26 of the UN Draft Declaration, for instance, provides that:

> *Indigenous peoples have the right to own, develop, control and use the lands and territories, including the total environment of the lands, air, waters, coastal sea, sea-ice, flora and fauna and other resources which they have traditionally owned or otherwise occupied or used. This includes the right to the full recognition of their laws and customs, land-tenure systems and institutions for the development and management of resources, and the right to effective*

measures by states to prevent any interference with, alienation or encroachment upon these rights.

The OAS Proposed Declaration, while not as broad and detailed as the UN Draft Declaration, also provides a substantial measure of protection. Both recognize and require protection of indigenous peoples' unique relationship with their lands, territories and resources traditionally occupied and used.

The UN and OAS instruments recognize a right to restitution of indigenous lands, territories or resources which have been 'confiscated, occupied, used or damaged', without indigenous consent (OAS, article XVIII(7); UN, article 27). If restitution is not possible, then compensation is to be provided. They also include a right to environmental protection (articles XIII and 28, respectively). The OAS Proposed Declaration includes many of the elements identified by the IACHR in its *Ecuador Report* and elsewhere – relationship to the right to life, measures to ensure effective participation and the right to information and remedies. Due to the importance attached to indigenous cultural, spiritual and economic relationships to land and resources, relocation is treated as a serious human rights issue. Strict standards of scrutiny are employed and free and informed consent is required.[16] Additionally, relocation may only be considered in extreme and extraordinary cases. The implicit statement contained in these standards is that forcible relocation is prohibited as a gross violation of human rights.

In conformity with rights to self-determination, autonomy and self-government, standards relating to indigenous participation are expansive and strong (UN, articles 4, 19 and 20; OAS, article XV(2)). This is due to the recognition that indigenous peoples will undoubtedly be affected by the larger policies and actions of the state despite their status as autonomous, self-governing entities. Free and informed consent is required by the UN Draft Declaration before states may enact and implement legislative, administrative or other measures that may affect indigenous rights or interests (article 20). In connection with this, indigenous peoples have the right to determine their representatives in accordance with their own procedures.

Informed participation in decision-making processes concerning resource exploitation, especially sub-surface resources, is required. Article XVIII(5) of the Proposed OAS Declaration requires that states 'must establish or maintain procedures for the participation of the peoples concerned in determining whether the interests of these peoples would be adversely affected and to what extent, before undertaking or authorizing' operations on indigenous lands.[17] It also requires that the affected peoples or communities share in any benefits and that compensation be rendered for damages sustained. The UN Draft Declaration goes further, requiring that states obtain the 'free and informed consent' of indigenous peoples prior to authorizing exploitation of indigenous lands and territories. The consent standard is fundamental to ensuring the right of indigenous peoples to cultural integrity and it is a major failing of the ILO and OAS instruments that it is not included therein. If indigenous peoples are unable to control their territories, they will also be unable to determine and control their social and cultural well-being and development as the two are inseparably related.

The effect of these provisions is to establish procedural obstacles to proposed resource exploitation on indigenous lands, rather than recognizing substantive rights to indigenous subsoil resources. This has allowed intergovernmental organizations to minimize politically sensitive debates over resource sovereignty, while providing indigenous peoples with some leverage to protect their interests. Veto power or participation rights concerning resource exploitation are coupled with provisions safeguarding subsistence and other resources, territorial rights, broad political participation rights, environmental protection measures and autonomy and self-government, including authority over development decisions and resource management. The effect is, as one commentator has noted, that state sovereignty over natural resources is burdened and restricted by the rights and interests of indigenous peoples (Schrijver, 1997, p391).

As illustrated by the preceding discussion, indigenous rights are receiving detailed and progressive treatment by intergovernmental human rights bodies. These standards are also having an impact on interpretations of indigenous rights under general human rights instruments. It is important to bear in mind, however, that indigenous peoples have severely criticized ILO 169 (Venne, 1989), and have stated that they consider both the OAS Proposed and UN Draft Declarations to be statements of minimum rights. Consequently, as progressive as many of the standards discussed above may be within the larger context of state-dominated international law, for many indigenous peoples they do not adequately reflect the full extent of their rights and concerns. This has important implications as conflicts may hinge more on what indigenous communities believe their rights to be than on how their rights are defined by either national or international law.

INTERNATIONAL INSTRUMENTS ON ENVIRONMENT AND DEVELOPMENT

As described above, the IACHR, the ILO and various United Nations organs have all taken a number of important steps towards the recognition and protection of indigenous rights. They have also recognized the nexus between human rights and environmental and resource security. How do international environmental organizations and instruments account for indigenous rights? Have they matched the attention accorded by human rights bodies? In this context, I believe that it is important to bear in mind, as stated by Croll and Parkin (1992, p9) (paraphrasing the Brundtland Report), that 'many problems of resource depletion and environmental stress arise from disparities in economic and political power so that sustainable development is conceived not so much to be about resources of the physical environment as about issues of control, power, participation and self-determination'. Therefore, indigenous rights, established or emerging, particularly the right to self-determination with all its attributes, must be considered as inseparable from larger discussions centred on sustainable development and environmental security.

The instruments adopted by the 1992 United Nations Conference on Environment and Development (UNCED) include a number of references to indigenous peoples. These instruments also established bodies mandated to monitor state compliance with, or progress in achieving, their terms and objectives. As we shall see, the UNCED instruments deal with some of the same issues that are covered under the human rights instruments. Indeed, in some ways, the two are mutually reinforcing. However, the UNCED instruments fall far below the level of recognition of indigenous rights set by the human rights standards.

Both Agenda 21 and the Rio Declaration promote indigenous participation, but do not go much further. Chapter 26 of Agenda 21, devoted entirely to indigenous peoples, contains two principal elements: 1) objectives to be pursued 'in full partnership with indigenous people and their communities'; and 2) activities to be undertaken with regard to indigenous peoples. Chapter 26 recognizes that some of its goals are also addressed in both ILO 169 and the UN Draft Declaration (26.2). Chapter 26 is focused on strengthening and facilitating indigenous peoples' participation in their own development and in external development activities that may affect them, and on recognizing indigenous peoples' traditional knowledge of ecological management and sustainable development. This is to be accomplished by a variety of means including greater political participation; greater self-control over indigenous lands and resources 'in accordance with national legislation'; recognition of traditional subsistence practices; and the strengthening of national legislation (26.3).

A binding international environmental treaty of great relevance to indigenous peoples is the Convention on Biological Diversity (CBD). The Treaty was drafted without indigenous participation and, consequently, is substantially deficient with regard to indigenous rights and concerns related to natural resources and biological (and cultural) diversity[18] (IAITPTF, 1997, p42). It attempts to address indigenous intellectual property rights in article 8(j) by requiring that states-parties 'Subject to [their] national legislation, respect, preserve and maintain knowledge, innovations and practices of indigenous and local communities … relevant for the conservation and sustainable use of biological diversity…' With regard to potentially substantial benefits derived from indigenous intellectual and cultural property, it only requires that states-parties 'encourage the equitable sharing of [those] benefits…' (Secretariat of the Convention on Biological Diversity, 2001, p8). Article 8(j) is disappointing to say the least and substandard in comparison with the UN and OAS Declarations' provisions concerning indigenous intellectual property rights (see UN, articles 12 and 29 and OAS article XX).

Article 10(c) of the CBD may have more potential, especially as land and resource rights could be included within its ambit. It provides that States shall 'protect and encourage customary use of biological resources in accordance with traditional cultural practices that are compatible with conservation or sustainable use requirements'. Although the precise scope and meaning of this article has yet to be articulated, it would most likely include indigenous agriculture, agro-forestry, hunting, fishing, gathering and the use of medicinal plants and other subsistence activities. By implication, it should also be read to include a certain measure of protection for the ecosystem and environment in which those resources are found. These conclusions are supported by the analysis of the Secretariat of the CBD in its background paper on Traditional Knowledge and Biological Diversity, which interpreted 10(c) to require respect for indigenous tenure over terrestrial and marine estates, control over and use of natural resources and respect for indigenous self-determination and self-government.[19]

Both the CBD's Conference of the Parties (COP) and the Commission on Sustainable Development (CSD) for Agenda 21, have yet to adequately accommodate the participation and rights of indigenous peoples in their respective areas of competence (IAIP, 1997). The COP took a partial step towards remedying this at its fourth meeting by establishing an open-ended, ad hoc Working Group on article 8(j) and related articles in 1998.[20] Indigenous participation in the CSD, however, remains minimal. This is in large part due to CSD procedures that limit indigenous participation, a lack of resources to attend CSD meetings in New York and unfamiliarity with the CSD among indigenous peoples (IAIP, 1997).

In short, while indigenous peoples are making in-roads, environmental fora have fallen far short of recognizing indigenous rights. It is likely that this will change only if indigenous peoples are able to directly and effectively participate in the drafting, negotiation and implementation of international environmental and development instruments. The need for effective indigenous participation is especially important in the context of the environment, biological diversity and sustainable development as indigenous peoples' territories encompass vast areas of the Earth's remaining biological diversity and threatened ecosystems. Moreover, indigenous knowledge of and management strategies for their territories and resources are essential to the design and implementation of global conservation initiatives. Indigenous knowledge is also highly coveted and frequently expropriated by pharmaceutical and agro-industrial corporations and research institutes with few benefits returning to their communities. It remains to be seen, however, whether the CSD, COP and others will accomplish much, with or without indigenous participation, in the light of government indifference and the tendency of international trade and investment rules to prioritize the rights of multinational corporations over indigenous rights.

CONCLUSION

The premise that indigenous rights are qualitatively and quantitatively distinct from minority rights has been widely accepted and incorporated into intergovernmental policy and action. The primary distinction involves the recognition of the collective rights of indigenous peoples as a means to remedy historical and contemporary forms of colonial domination and discrimination. The right to self-determination is the framework within which indigenous rights and aspirations take form. Subsumed within this framework are rights to give and withhold consent to activities, on whatever level, that may affect indigenous rights and interests; the right to the full ownership and control of territory and resources, which includes protection of the various modalities of indigenous interaction therewith; recognition of indigenous legal systems and institutions of governance; and, in general, respect for indigenous cultural integrity and future development. This distinction is fundamental, for, as expressed by a representative of the International Indian Treaty Council, 'The ultimate goal of their colonizers would be achieved by referring to indigenous peoples as minorities', thereby, denying their equal rights and dignity as distinct peoples and further entrenching and legitimizing their colonization (Deschenes, in Thornberry 1991, p331).

The issue of indigenous territorial rights arises frequently in conflicts involving human rights and the environment, particularly in the context of resource exploitation. Indigenous rights to control their ancestral domains have repeatedly been implicated in mining, logging, dam building, biodiversity prospecting or protected area or other conservation initiatives. To be consonant with human rights norms, these activities, and underlying claims of state ownership of resources, must be viewed, at a minimum, as substantially burdened and restricted by the rights of indigenous peoples.

The consequences of such restrictions will vary depending on the nature of the activity and the rights affected and may result in some form of negotiated compromise between the various parties. The negative environmental effects of resource exploitation are also a major human rights concern as many indigenous peoples remain physically and culturally dependent on their environment. That indigenous peoples have focused mostly on human rights avenues to deal with resource exploitation and environmental degradation is not surprising given the failure of international environmental instruments and institutions to adequately account for their rights. Human rights and environmental standards and policies need to be reconciled. Central to such a reconciliation is the removal of restrictions on indigenous participation in environmental (and other) fora.

NOTES

1   See, for instance, Lynch, 1992; WWF, 1996; IUCN, 1997.
2   Lynch (1992, p1) states that 'Acknowledging the value and legitimacy of community-based tenurial systems should be a crucial and complementary component of any viable effort to conserve and develop tropical forest resources in an equitable and sustainable manner'.
3   See, generally, UN, 2000.
4   The Governments of France, Japan and especially the United States have consistently stated that international law does not, nor should it, recognize collective rights.
5   For a detailed discussion of the international legal concept of indigenous peoples, see, Kingsbury, 1995.
6   *UN Human Rights Committee*, Concluding Observations of the Human Rights Committee: Canada. 07/04/99. UN Doc. CCPR/C/79/Add.105 *(Concluding Observations/Comments) (1999)*, para. 8.
7   Hopu v France. Communication No. 549/1993: France. 29/12/97. *CCPR/C/60/D/549/1993/Rev.1, 29 December 1997*.
8   Ibid, para 10.3.
9   Compare with UN Draft Declaration, articles 30, 25 and 26.

10   ILO 107 remains in force for those states that have ratified it, but have not ratified ILO 169.
11   As of August 2000, the following states have ratified ILO 169: Mexico, Norway, Costa Rica, Colombia, Denmark, Guatemala, Ecuador, Peru, Bolivia, Honduras, The Netherlands, Paraguay, Fiji and Argentina.
12   Case 11.577 (Nicaragua), *Annual Report of the Inter-American Commission of Human Rights*, OEA/Ser.L/VII.98. Doc.7 rev.at 46 (1998).
13   The authoritative text of the UN Draft Declaration is annexed to WGIP, 1993b.
14   Both the UN and OAS instruments provide explicitly for subsistence rights and the right to development. See UN, articles 21 and 23 and OAS articles VII(3) and XXI.
15   OAS, article XVII; UN, articles 4, 33 and 34.
16   The Proposed OAS Declaration (article XVIII (6)), the UN draft Declaration (article 10) and ILO 169 (article 16(1)(2)) incorporate this general prohibition of forcible relocation.
17   ILO 169, article 15(2), in contrast to the Proposed OAS Declaration merely requires that indigenous peoples be consulted.
18   The IAIPTF states that: 'There are substantial deficiencies in the text of the Convention: it does not understand the difference between biodiversity as a scientific or commercial concept and as a principle that encompasses all aspects of indigenous cultural life and production' (IAIP, 1997, p42, authors translation of original in Spanish).
19   *Traditional Knowledge and Biological Diversity*, UNEP/CBD/TKBD/1/2, 18 October 1997.
20   COP 4, Decision IV/9 'Implementation of Article 8(j) and related provisions', Bratislava, May 1998 (Secretariat of the Convention on Biological Diversity, 2001, pp489–93).

REFERENCES

Anaya, S J (1991) 'Indigenous Rights Norms in Contemporary International Law', *Arizona Journal of International & Comparative Law* 8:1
Anaya, S J (1996) *Indigenous Peoples in International Law*. New York/Oxford: Oxford University Press
Barnes, R H, et al (1995) 'The Indigenous Movement in Asia', in R H Barnes, A Gray and B Kingsbury (eds) *Indigenous Peoples of Asia*, Monograph no 48. Ann Arbor, MI: Association for Asian Studies
Barsh, R L (1994) 'Indigenous Peoples in the 1990s: From Object to Subject of International Law?', *Harvard Human Rights Journal* 7:33–45
Berman, H R (1988) 'The ILO and Indigenous Peoples: Revision of ILO Convention No 107 at the 75th Session of the International Labour Conference', *International Commission of Jurists Review* 41:48
Brownlie, I (1990) *Principles of Public International Law* (4th edition). Oxford: Oxford University Press
CERD (1997) *General Recommendation XXIII (51) Concerning Indigenous Peoples Adopted at the Committee's 1235th meeting, on 18 August 1997*. UN Doc. CERD/C/51/Misc.13/Rev.4
Cobo, J (1987) *Study on the Problem of Discrimination Against Indigenous Populations, Conclusions, Proposals, and Recommendations*. UN Doc. E/CN.4/Sub.2/1986/7/ Adds. 1-3. UN SALES NO. E.86.XIV.3

Croll, E and Parkin, D (1992) 'Anthropology, the Environment and Development', in E Croll and D Parkin (eds) *Bush Base: Forest Farm: Culture Environment and Development*. London: Routledge

Daes, E-I (1993a) *Explanatory Note Concerning the Draft Declaration on the Rights of Indigenous Peoples, Chairperson of the Working Group on Indigenous Populations*. UN Doc.E/CN.4/Sub.2/1993/26/Add.1

Daes, E-I (1993b) 'Some Considerations on the Right of Indigenous Peoples to Self-Determination', *Transnational Law & Contemporary Problems* 3:1

Daes, E-I (1996) *Working Paper by the Chairperson-Rapporteur, Mrs Erica-Irene A. Daes. On the Concept of 'Indigenous People'*. UN Doc. E/CN.4/Sub.2/AC.4/1996/2

Gray, A (1997) *Indigenous Rights and Development: Self-Determination in an Amazonian Community*, Oxford: Berghahn Books

HRC (1988) Kitok vs Sweden, *Report of the Human Rights Committee*, 43 UN GAOR Supp (No 40) at 221, UN Doc. A/43/40

HRC (1990) Bernard Ominayak, Chief of the Lubicon Lake Band vs. Canada, *Report of the Human Rights Committee*, 45 UN GAOR Supp (No 43) at 1, UN Doc. A/45/40, vol 2

HRC (1994) *General Comment No. 23 (50) (art. 27)*, adopted by the Human Rights Committee at its 1314th meeting (fiftieth session), 6 April. UN Doc. CCPR/C/21/Rev.1/Add.5

IACHR (1972) *Annual Report*. Washington, DC: Inter-American Commission on Human Rights

IACHR (1985) *Report on the Situation of Human Rights of a Segment of the Nicaraguan Population of Miskito Origin*, OEA/Ser.L/V/II.62, doc.26. Washington, DC: Inter-American Commission on Human Rights

IACHR (1985) OEA/Ser.l/V/II. 67, doc. 9. *Yanomami Case,* Case 7615, IACHR 24, OEA/Ser.L/V/11.66, doc.10 rev.1. Washington, DC: Inter-American Commission on Human Rights

IACHR (1986) *Third Report on the Situation of Human Rights in The Republic of Guatemala*. Washington, DC: Inter-American Commission on Human Rights

IACHR (1997a) *Proposed American Declaration on the Rights of Indigenous Peoples*, approved by the Inter-American Commission on Human Rights on 26 February at its 1333rd session, 95th regular session, OEA/Ser/L/V/II.95 doc 6. Washington, DC: Inter-American Commission on Human Rights

IACHR (1997b) *Report on the Situation of Human Rights in Ecuador*, OEA/Ser.L/V/II.96 doc 10, rev 1. Washington, DC: Inter-American Commission on Human Rights

IAIP (1997) *Participation of Indigenous Peoples in Global Environmental Negotiations*, London/Brussels: International Alliance of Indigenous-Tribal Peoples of the Tropical Forests/European Alliance with Indigenous Peoples

ILO (1988) Partial Revision of the Indigenous and Tribal Populations Convention, 1957 (No 107), *Report VI(1),* International Labour Conference, 75th Session, Geneva.Geneva: International Labour Organization

IUCN Inter-Commission Task Force on Indigenous Peoples (1997) *Indigenous Peoples and Sustainability: Cases and Actions*. Utrecht: International Books

Kingsbury, B (1995) '"Indigenous Peoples" as an International Legal Concept', in R H Barnes, A Gray and B Kingsbury (eds) *Indigenous Peoples of Asia,* Monograph no 48. Ann Arbor, MI: Association for Asian Studies

Lynch, O (1992) *Securing Community-Based Tenurial Rights in the Tropical Forests of Asia: An Overview of Current and Prospective Strategies*. Washington, DC: World Resources Institute

Macklem, P (1993) 'Ethnonationalism, Aboriginal Identities and the Law', in M Levin (ed) *Ethnicity and Aboriginality: Case Studies in Ethnonationalism*. Toronto: University of Toronto Press

Sambo, D (1993) 'Indigenous Peoples and International Standard Setting Processes: Are State Governments Listening?', *Transnational Law and Contemporary Problems* 3:13

Sanders, D (1991) 'Collective Rights', *Human Rights Quarterly* 13:368

Schrijver, N (1997) *Sovereignty Over Natural Resources: Balancing Rights and Duties*. Cambridge: Cambridge University Press

Secretariat of the Convention on Biological Diversity (2001) *Handbook of the Convention on Biological Diversity*. London: Earthscan

Thornberry, P (1991) *International Law and the Rights of Minorities*. Oxford: Clarendon Press

United Nations (1988) *Discrimination Against Indigenous Peoples, Report of the Working Group on Indigenous Populations on its sixth session* (UN Doc. E/CN.4/Sub.2/1988/25

United Nations (2000) *Working Paper on the Relationship and Distinction between the Rights of Persons Belonging to Minorities and Those of Indigenous Peoples*. UN Doc. E/CN.4/Sub.2/2000/10

Venne, S (1989) The New Language of Assimilation: A Brief Analysis of ILO Convention No. 169, 2 *Without Prejudice* 59

WGIP (1993a) *The UN Draft Declaration on the Rights of Indigenous Peoples*. UN Doc. E/CN.4/Sub.2/1993/29, Annex

WGIP (1993b) *Report of the Working Group on Indigenous Populations on its Eleventh Session*. UN Doc. E/CN.4/Sub.2/1993/29

Williams, R A (1990) 'Encounters on the Frontiers of International Human Rights Law: Redefining the Terms of Indigenous Peoples Survival', *Duke Law Journal* 660

World Wildlife Fund (1996) *Indigenous Peoples and Conservation: WWF Statement of Principles*. Gland: WWF

Chapter 2

Global Reach: Human Rights and Environment in the Framework of Corporate Accountability

Lyuba Zarsky

INTRODUCTION

Globalization – the spread of capitalism to ever more areas of social life and parts of the world – is the central story of the current era. From the depths of the Amazon to the farthest reaches of Central Asia, from California's Silicon Valley to Taiwan's Hsinchu Industrial Park, people around the world are ever more deeply interconnected via long and complicated chains of market-based production and consumption, selling and buying.

Multinational corporations (MNCs) are key players in the process of globalization. They are the primary drivers of cross-border investment and the conveyor belts of international trade. Increasingly, multinationals operate through complex, integrated global production networks. Many small and medium sized companies, and even tiny family businesses, are connected to MNCs via supply chains where orders cascade from primary to secondary suppliers and on to tertiary subcontractors.

Although controversial, the role of MNCs in economic development has been well studied. In the accounts of most mainstream economists, MNCs and the capital, technology and know-how they bring are vehicles to generate wealth, fill the purse of government, stimulate local employment and enhance social progress. In other accounts, often by local analysts and activists, MNCs are the cutting edge of a development strategy which destroys local cultures, exploits workers, bankrupts the rural poor and widens the gap between the rich and often politically repressive elite and the rest of society.

Ideological and empirical arguments aside, the reality is that MNC investment is highly sought after by most developing and 'transition' country governments. Throughout Africa, Asia, Latin America and Eastern Europe, local and national economic planners compete hard to attract MNCs, especially from the rich OECD countries of North America, Europe and Japan. The promise of MNC investment is not only a large inflow of capital and jobs but integration with the pulsing heart of the global economy.

The local economic impacts of investment by MNCs are often palpable, although benefits may well be captured by the elite. But what *is* the role of multinationals in promoting – or undermining – environmental protection, human rights, good working conditions, political pluralism, and social and economic justice? Are MNCs part – or even most – of the problem, or a key part of the solution to the global human rights and environmental challenges of the 21st century?

This chapter explores the ethical challenges that MNCs face – or are pressed to confront – as they extend their global reach. First, it examines the role of MNCs as drivers of globalization and describes the ethical dilemmas they face in operating in a world where markets are global but regulation is local. It describes three broad strategies MNCs have adopted in response.

Second, the chapter maps a broad range of ethical concerns raised by a growing 'corporate social responsibility' movement, including labour rights and working conditions, environmental and resource degradation, and human rights. It suggests that an ethical framework is emerging that embraces these three issues and encapsulates social expectations for good corporate behaviour.

Third, it argues that, while it is an important step forwards, the voluntary 'corporate social responsibility' (CSR) model is limited in its capacity to grapple with the ethical demands on MNCs of globalization. It argues that corporate accountability requires government action to complement and strengthen the CSR approach. The chapter concludes by outlining two innovative policy approaches, one based on information disclosure and the other on 'ethical and sustainable' investment rules.

MULTINATIONALS, GLOBAL INVESTMENT AND ETHICS

International investment is the cutting edge of globalization. Capital flows around the world largely determine the geographic and sectoral composition of global production. Investment is the key to economic growth and often a key component in social, political and cultural development.

The two primary forms of investment flows are foreign direct investment (FDI), defined as flows to enterprises in which the investor has at least a 10 per cent equity stake, and portfolio flows, defined as equity shares of anything less than 10 per cent. In most developing countries, FDI is the leading form of foreign investment. The leading players in FDI are multinational corporations.

Spurred by the end of the Cold War, global outflows of FDI grew by a hefty 15 per cent per year in the first half of the 1990s. In the second half, however, FDI outflows exploded, growing by an average 27 per cent each year between 1996 and 1999. By 1999, total global outflows of FDI from home to host countries totalled US$800 billion (see Table 2.1).

Table 2.1 *The Explosion of FDI*

	Global outflows (US$ billions)
1988	58
1990	209
1996	380
1997	475
1998	649
1999	800

Source: UNCTAD *World Investment Report 1999–2000*

The geographic distribution of FDI is highly skewed. The lion's share, over 70 per cent in 1998, flows from one rich 'home' country like the US to another, like the UK or other Western European nation. The US leads the world as both the top investor and the top recipient of FDI, followed by the UK. In 1998, the US accounted for about 20 per cent of global outflows of FDI – and 30 per cent of inflows. Largely as a result of the Asian financial crisis, FDI inflows to the US bulged in the second half of the 1990s, nearly doubling in terms of share of total global outflows (see Table 2.2).

Developing countries, which have the majority of the world's population and the greatest need for investment capital, receive only about a quarter of global FDI flows. Of that, nearly half goes to East Asia, especially to China, which alone accounts for about a quarter of all the FDI inflows to developing countries (Jacobs, 2001, Table 1). Africa, the poorest region of the world, receives only 1 per cent of global FDI inflows (Table 2.2).

While it is a small share of global flows, FDI inflows in developing countries can have large economic, social and environmental impacts on local areas. In the late 1990s, FDI emerged as the primary source of capital to developing countries, far outstripping public sources such as the World Bank and foreign aid. In the smallest and poorest developing countries, foreign investment is often the largest component of domestic industrial investment. One MNC may be the largest single business operation in a region or even the entire country. Foreign mining and oil companies, for example, tend to be large players with high economic and often political profiles.

By sector, the largest share of FDI inflows to developing countries – nearly 48 per cent in 1997 – is in the service sector. Manufacturing is second, with 42 per cent. The primary sector, composed of agriculture, mining, forestry and fishing, receives the smallest share – only 4.5 per cent in 1997 (UNCTAD, 2000). However, despite the smaller portion of FDI they receive, the environmental and social impacts of primary sector industries such as oil, mining and forestry are often highly visible and extensive.

Multinational corporations are the primary transmission belts of FDI. Through their investment strategies, MNCs are propelling the most fundamental and transformative feature of globalization – the internationalization of production. Working through subsidiaries, joint ventures, mergers, direct suppliers, subcontractors and other arrangements, MNCs construct complex

Table 2.2 *Global Distribution of FDI Inflows*

	1995	1998
	(% of total inflows)	
Developed countries	63.4	71.5
US	17.9	30.0
Western Europe	37.0	36.9
Japan	–	0.5
Other	8.5	4.1
Developing countries	32.3	25.8
Africa	1.3	1.2
Latin America and Caribbean	10.0	11.1
East Asia	20.4	12.0
Other	0.6	1.5

Source: UNCTAD *World Investment Report 1999*

global networks linking a wide variety of aspects of company production, management and marketing in countries throughout the world.

There are currently about 63,000 MNCs in the world, with around 690,000 foreign affiliates and a vast number of inter-firm arrangements. MNCs operate in virtually all countries and engage in virtually all types of business. They are, in the words of the United Nations Conference on Trade and Development, a 'formidable force in today's world economy' (UNCTAD, 2000, p1).

The world's 100 largest MNCs are based almost exclusively in industrialized countries. These 100 mega-companies account for over 15 per cent of the total assets of MNCs worldwide and for 4–7 per cent of world gross domestic output (ibid, p84). They are concentrated in five sectors: electronics and electrical equipment, automobiles, petroleum, chemicals and pharmaceuticals.

The US claims four of the world's ten largest MNCs, including the biggest of them all, General Electric (see Table 2.3). Royal Dutch Shell, a British and Dutch multinational, operates in over 140 countries (Schwartz and Gibb, 1999).

REGULATORY GAPS, ETHICAL DILEMMAS

The social and environmental regulation of industry is vastly different in different parts of the world. Even highly similar industrialized countries like Canada, the US and Germany, have different social norms and expectations of industry. In Germany, for example, workers have greater job security and work fewer hours than in the US, and environmental regulations are more stringent.

The gaps are largest, however, between the 30 rich, developed countries of the OECD as a whole and the rest of the world – the 170 or so developing and 'transition' economies of the 'global south'. In general, OECD countries have adopted a democratic form of government, with a strong embrace of civil and political rights and the rule of law. There is a large, generally affluent middle class.

Table 2.3 *World's Top Ten MNCs*

Company	Home country	Sector	Foreign assets (US$ billions, 1998)
General Electric	US	Electronics	141*
ExxonMobil Corporation	US	Petroleum	99
Royal Dutch Shell	Netherlands/UK	Petroleum	69
General Motors	US	Motor vehicles	69
Ford Motor Company	US	Motor vehicles	n/a
Toyota Motor	Japan	Motor vehicles	56
DaimlerChrysler	Germany	Motor vehicles	56
Total Fina SA	France	Petroleum	n/a
IBM	US	Computers	44
BP	UK	Petroleum	39

* Foreign assets, billions of dollars, 1999
Source: UNCTAD *World Investment Report 2001*

Many developing countries, on the other hand, are either fledgling democracies or are ruled by an authoritarian elite. Civil society is often weak or repressed and ordinary people are poor. In the US, per capita income in 2000 was US$25,379. In Mexico, it was US$5070 and in Vietnam, US$390 (US Census Bureau, 1999; World Bank, 2001).

These broad socio-economic differences are mirrored in gaps in social and environmental regulation. Systems of environmental regulation, for example, were not established in most developing countries until the 1990s, 20 years after OECD countries. Moreover, most developing countries modelled regulation on the command-and-control systems of the US or Europe. Lacking top-down enforcement capacities and, often, political will, as well as avenues for civic involvement, environmental regulations are on the books but not enforced. In some cases, enforcement is made nonsensical by the lack of local physical infrastructure. In the Philippines, for example, semiconductor assembly operations may comply with a law requiring that hazardous wastes are not stored on site by having it 'hauled away'. The trucks come, they load up, but where the waste goes, nobody knows (Salazar, 1999).

The lack of national environmental regulation is an issue not just for the poorest and least developed countries of the global south, like most of Africa and South Asia, but also for the most industrialized and affluent. East Asian countries, for example, have been heralded as economic success stories for the last 20 years. According to the Asian Development Bank, resource degradation and environmental pollution in both East and South Asia is so 'pervasive, accelerating, and unabated' that it risks human health and livelihood (Asian Development Bank, 2001, p2).

Protections of basic civil and political rights, guaranteed by the Universal Declaration of Human Rights, are not extended to citizens in many developing countries. Rights to political speech, freedom of assembly, union membership and general political involvement are constrained or denied. In some countries, the penalty for pressing the limits of civil and political rights is imprisonment, torture and even death.

The global reach of investment and production thus poses a dilemma for Western MNCs and their stakeholders. The crux of the dilemma is that markets are global while regulation and ethics are not. In the absence of either global or national norms, MNCs are often left to 'self-regulate', that is, to set their own standards or to simply follow local practice in the different countries in which they operate.

Local practice, however, can involve not only a lackadaisical attitude to industrial pollution or a free-for-all attitude to resource exploitation, but also the violation of internationally accepted human rights. Environmental degradation and concerns about human rights have triggered a host of community–MNC conflicts and a storm of global criticism about poor global 'corporate citizenship'.

Three MNC responses

Faced with the central ethical dilemma of globalization, Western MNCs have adopted one (or more) of three broad strategies. The first, which might be called 'duck and cover', is to follow local standards wherever they operate. The strategy is to embrace the competitive opportunities offered by lower local standards and wages, then duck ethical criticism with the cover of compliance with national law or custom. In practice, the adoption of this strategy makes a company guilty as charged by advocacy groups of both 'sticking their head in the sand' on ethical issues and practising 'double standards'. The pervasive and noxious pollution that characterizes oil company operations in the Amazon, Nigeria and, increasingly, the Caspian region, would not be tolerated in Oklahoma or off the coast of California (see California Corporate Accountability Project, 2002).

Companies who adopt the 'duck and cover' strategy are often 'bottom feeders' in the industry, taking market positions and opportunities left by larger, leading edge companies. In the semiconductor industry, for example, companies are either 'leaders' or 'laggards' in terms of innovations in technology and management (Mazurek, 2000). The 'laggards' tend to follow local standards, whether in California, Thailand, Singapore or southern China. They also tend to offload older, dirtier technology in developing countries.

The second strategy, which might be termed 'no regrets', is for MNCs to adopt company-wide, global standards for production processes, often including environmental, health and safety measures. The logic for global standards is twofold. First, it is more efficient and easier for a company to manage one set than a patchwork of dozens of different national standards. This is especially the case for production processes and procurement policies. With one set of standards, a large multinational chemical company, for example, can generate one standardized approach to training engineers and safety inspectors as well as equipment maintenance and other aspects of day-to-day management in overseas operations.

The second rationale for a global standards policy is that it reduces several kinds of company risk. The most important for many MNCs in the manufacturing sector is the risk of product defect. With integrated production and supply chains, companies need assurance of quality control. Other risks reduced by global standards include: 1) environmental and on-the-job accident and injury, with concomitant down time; and 2) legal liability for accidental death or injury, either in host or home country courts.

The global standards policy became widespread among multinational chemical companies after the 1984 disaster at a Union Carbide pesticide plant in Bhopal, India. More than 3,000 people were killed and tens of thousands permanently injured when a tank leaked five tons of poisonous methyl isocyanate gas in the air. Thousands more have died since then, due to the lingering effects of the poison. To date, Union Carbide has got off easily. The company successfully argued to have the court case tried in India, rather than New York, and the Indian government accepted a compensation settlement of only US$470 million. Nonetheless, the case sent a shockwave through the chemical industry and beyond.[1]

Global, company-wide standards are an improvement over following national standards. In some cases, a company will make a complete or selective commitment to 'best practice', that is, identifying and applying the highest relevant standard or benchmark. The silicon chip giant Intel, for example, applies the higher of Arizona or California water quality and waste management standards to its Costa Rica operations (Roht-Arriaza, 2000).

But the 'no regrets' strategy has limitations. Standards might be the same but a different political, cultural and socio-economic context will affect how adequate they are. Company-wide environmental, health and safety standards, for example, do not take into account the limited administrative capacities of many developing countries for disaster planning or for providing waste management infrastructure. Indeed, in the Bhopal case, the lack of local disaster planning was a key factor in the large number of deaths and injuries from the deadly chemical gas.

In a more repressive political climate, workers cannot organize and are likely to feel constrained in bringing health and safety issues to the attention of managers. Or, as in the case of workers in the high-tech industry in Taiwan, jobs are so valuable and prestigious, relative to the options, that complaints of illness as a result of chemical exposure are stifled (Taiwan Environmental Action Network, 2001). In short, the adoption of global, company-wide standards goes only part of the way to ensure that workers, communities and the environment receive the same quality of care regardless of where the company operates.

The third approach employed by MNCs to deal with the ethical dilemmas of globalization is the 'good guy' strategy. The centrepiece is the adoption by a company of a voluntary code of conduct outlining conduct in areas of ethical concern and pledging company commitment to 'best practice' in environmental and/or social management. Typically, the company itself chooses which environmental and ethical issues are included in (and excluded from) its code of conduct. Some companies stress a commitment to energy efficiency, pollution emissions reductions, high standards of worker safety or philanthropic contribution to local social development.

Corporate ethical targets, however, have been highly influenced by advocacy campaigns. Apparel companies charged with using sweatshop labour, for example, are likely to highlight 'fair labour' issues in supply chain management, while forestry companies highlight environmental sustainability and energy companies showcase an enlightened approach towards dealing with poor communities, security and authoritarian governments.

There is a wide range of MNC 'good guy' behaviour. For some, a code of conduct seems to live primarily as a public relations document, with little attempt to set internal company benchmarks, change management practices or provide real data to the public about performance improvements. Others have embraced a broad commitment to 'corporate social responsibility', which entails changing the company's mission, setting benchmarks, and establishing systems to implement them, including public reporting systems. One of the key features of a CSR approach to corporate governance is an embrace of 'stakeholder consultation'. If adopted fulsomely, stakeholder consultation means that companies are open to considering the implications of their behaviour not just over a narrow set, but also across a broad range of environmental and social issues.

ETHICAL CHALLENGES: LABOUR RIGHTS, ENVIRONMENT AND HUMAN RIGHTS

Around the world, advocates and analysts from a wide range of groups and perspectives – labour, environmental, human rights, religious and development – have highlighted a broad range of ethical concerns about MNC global investment. Their strategies have included consumer boycotts, publicity campaigns, shareholder resolutions, investigations and exposés, pickets and other attempts to 'name and shame' and thus prod corporations to face the ethical challenges of operating globally.

Advocacy campaigns have targeted one or more of three sets of issues: 1) labour conditions, wages and worker rights; 2) environmental and resource degradation; and 3) human rights, mostly civil and political but also including economic, social and cultural rights. A new wave of human rights-and-environment advocacy is concerned with all three sets of issues and the links between them. This set of ethical concerns is emerging as a set of core global ethical principles for a 'corporate accountability' approach to business management and government regulation.

Working conditions and labour rights

The highest profile campaigns about working conditions and labour rights have focused on 'sweatshop labour'. A sweatshop is a workplace where people work long hours for low wages under unsafe and/or unfair working conditions. A sweatshop can be a large factory owned or licensed by a multinational corporation, or a kitchen table where families subcontract to MNCs or their suppliers on a piecework basis. Working conditions in sweatshops may include exposure to toxic materials; inadequate ventilation; use of products banned in OECD countries because of human health impact; inadequate heating/cooling;

overcrowding; fire safety violations; long working hours; no breaks; physical, mental and sexual abuse; and poverty-level wages.

Sweatshops are illegal throughout the OECD, yet many still operate in back-alleys, warehouses and the crowded apartments of recent immigrants. In California's Silicon Valley, for example, an investigation by a local newspaper discovered that 'industrial home assembly', that is, piecework, is rampant in the high-tech industry. These piecework operations evade US and California laws on wages, occupational health and safety, and working conditions. Many of the home assemblers are recently arrived immigrants from Vietnam. Young children have been found to be involved in assembling circuit boards with toxic chemicals close at hand (*San Jose Mercury*, 1999).

American and European labour groups and NGOs have especially targeted the use of sweatshops by brand-name global apparel and shoe retailers, such as Gap, Nike, Levi Strauss, J.C. Penny, Calvin Klein, Brooks Brothers and others. These companies have extensive supplier networks in low wage countries such as Vietnam and China. While many suppliers comply with national laws and offer 'fair' or at least average local wages, others are egregiously exploitative and abusive of workers.

A recent federal class action lawsuit, for example, charged 18 US clothing retailers of subcontracting with companies who used indentured labour, predominantly young women from Asia, to produce clothing on the island of Saipan, in the Northern Mariana Islands, a Commonwealth of the US. In the first ever attempt to hold upstream companies legally liable for the actions of subcontractors, the suit included Gap, Tommy Hilfiger, the Limited, J.C. Penny, Wal-Mart and Sears. The lawsuit alleged that the subcontractors brought the women to the island, where they worked up to 12 hours a day, 7 days a week for about US$3.00 per hour, often without overtime pay, and lived in overcrowded housing in unsanitary conditions. Moreover, the women owed a sizeable, unpayable debt to the subcontractor for bringing them to Saipan and could not leave. In August 1999, four retailers – Nordstrom, Cutter & Buck, J. Crew and Gymboree – settled claims out of court (Meadows, 2000; Global Exchange, undated).

In addition to sweatshops, NGOs and labour groups have charged MNCs with complicity in the use of forced or slave labour. The charge is that corporations turn a blind eye to repressive governments who use forced or slave labour either directly in joint ventures with MNCs, or indirectly, in creating infrastructure needed for MNC investment. A lawsuit against the US energy company Unocal, for example, alleges that villagers were forced by the Burmese military government to clear forests without food or pay for the construction of the Yadana natural gas pipeline (Earthrights International, 2000). Along with the French company Total, Unocal is a joint venture partner with the Burmese military government. The federal district court found that Unocal knew about and benefited from the abuses, but could not be held liable for the actions of its joint venture partner. Upon appeal, however, a California state court agreed in June 2002 to hear the case (Schrage, 2002).

Another key labour rights issue involving MNCs is child labour. The International Labour Organization (ILO) estimates that there are at least 250 million working children between the ages of 5 and 14 in developing countries in Asia, Africa, Latin America and the Caribbean (ILO, 1998). Families who live in abject poverty may have little choice but to send their children to work in factories, where they often face poor working conditions. Because their bodies and brains are still developing and their metabolisms are faster, children are generally more vulnerable than adults to the damaging and often irreparable effects of toxic chemicals.

In the 'global reach' world of MNC production and supply networks, child labour is intimately caught up with sweatshops. Advocacy groups in the US, for example, singled out the giant retail company Wal-Mart, for a 'right-to-know' campaign about the use of sweatshops in general, and children in particular. 'How can you tell if the product you are about to purchase was made by a child, by teenaged girls forced to work until midnight seven days a week, or in a sweatshop by workers paid 9¢ an hour?' challenges the Peoples' Right to Know Campaign, a US coalition of faith-based and labour groups.[2] The answer is – you can't. While broad country sources are made public, the specific factories from which US MNCs purchase their brand name products is not public information.

Worker health and safety is another key ethical concern of labour rights groups. In many developing countries, policies and procedures to protect workers from occupational hazards, including exposure to hazardous and toxic chemicals, are either in the formative stage or are lacking. MNCs who adopt a 'duck and cover' strategy and follow local standards do not extend to their workforce the basic protective procedures and gear available to workers in home countries. Even in companies with global standards and 'best practice', however, workers may face significant health and safety risks. The problem is not only that standards may not be fully enforced in developing country operations but that the standards may not be high enough in the first place.

In the high-tech sector, for example, an alarming number of former and current employees in the US and elsewhere suffer from rare cancers and their children from birth defects. Although it is very difficult to scientifically link exposure to workplace chemicals and health problems, victims have taken legal action to seek compensation. A landmark legal settlement was concluded in January 2001 involving the impacts to workers in a semiconductor manufacturing 'clean room'. IBM settled the case, which involved the child of two former employees born with congenital blindness and a severe breathing disorder, for US$40 million (Huffstutter, 2001). Although IBM claimed no liability, the case set a precedent for over 200 similar cases that are still pending against IBM and National Semiconductor.

With an image as a 'clean' and cutting edge industry, high-tech investment has been heavily pursued by developing countries. The Taiwanese government, for example, made the growth of information technology (IT) the centrepiece of its industrial policy starting in the 1960s. The industry grew rapidly as big US and European companies established downstream operations to assemble and later to manufacture components and electronic products. IBM, Compaq, Dell and Hewlett Packard are all important procurers of Taiwanese IT products – 50 per cent of Hewlett Packard's computers, for example, were manufactured and assembled in Taiwan in 1998 (Taiwan Environmental Action Network, 2001).

The growth of Taiwan's IT industry, however, was not accompanied by 'due diligence' in managing the highly toxic chemicals used in IT manufacture and assembly. The Hsinchu Science-Based Industrial Park, for example, was given jurisdiction over its own environmental management, exempting it from regional environmental standards. However, the Park established neither an adequate waste management infrastructure nor occupational heath and safety policies. The result has been the widespread toxic pollution of the region's ground water, including waters used for both fishing and drinking water supply. In a highly publicized incident, the Shengli Chemical Company, one of the IT industry's major waste haulers, was found to have simply dumped the toxic waste into the Kaoping River – a major water source in a highly populated region (Taiwan Environmental Action Network, 2001).

Gaining protection from chemical exposure and other occupational hazards is made more difficult for developing country workers because they often lack the right to organize and bargain collectively. Although recognized as a 'core labour right' by the ILO, worker rights to organize and/or associate are severely curtailed in many parts of the world. In Malaysia, for example, national laws require a permit to hold a meeting of five or more people. In China, workers who start independent labour unions are likely to end up in prison. In one recently reported case, a man who was imprisoned for trying to start a union during the 1989 Tiananmen protests now battles against forced labour in prison (Pan, 2001).

MNCs do not set or control broad societal policies on rights to organize or other civil and political rights. Governments do. What labour rights groups assert is not that MNCs are responsible but that they do not exercise the power they have on behalf of workers. MNCs can provide opportunities for workers to air grievances with impunity and to organize plant-level organizations. They can also negotiate with developing country host governments for a greater measure of worker freedom within their own operations. In cases where violation of workers rights is egregious, such as Burma, MNCs can use their influence to pressure governments. If governments are recalcitrant, MNCs can divest or refuse to invest.

Environmental pollution and resource degradation

MNCs operate in many countries in which environmental regulations are lacking, inadequate or not enforced. Widespread air, water and soil pollution is a major concern for local communities, environmentalists and, increasingly, as the costs of pollution became more evident, for economic planners. Widespread toxic, chemical and bacterial pollution afflicts not only local communities and ecological media but regional, transboundary and global ecosystems, such as rivers, seas and oceans, air and watersheds, and the global atmosphere and ozone layer (UNEP, 2001; Asian Development Bank, 2001).

In developing countries, the levels of human exposure to toxic and hazardous waste are often amplified because of ignorance and lack of regulation. Chemicals such as DDT and paraquat, which are banned in the US owing to environmental and/or human health impacts, are legal in developing countries. Since people are rarely educated about the potential effects of the chemicals, there is room for abuse. For example, farmers may use unsafe doses or 'cocktails' of pesticides on their crops, unaware of the potential harm to the environment or their health.

Pollution in developing countries stems from many sources, including urbanization, the lack of adequate water and waste management infrastructure, the use of old and dirty industrial technology, growth in transport systems and unsustainable consumption patterns. Overall, pollution is often the result of policy failures in the context of rapid industrialization. Blame cannot be laid at the feet of MNCs, at least not alone. But MNCs are responsible for their own choices and behaviour in the situation. Criticism of less than environmentally responsible behaviour has focused on two key issues.

First, Western MNCs are often the cutting edge of an economic development strategy based on luring foreign investment in order to stimulate local industrialization. They have been willing to accept the lure without ensuring that adequate environmental infrastructure and oversight is in place. In Thailand, for example, incentives provided by the Board of Investments greatly increased the pollution intensity of Thai industry in the 1980s (Panayotou and Sussangkorn, 1991). By 1991, hazardous waste-generating industries accounted for 58 per cent of Thailand's industrial gross domestic product (GDP), double that of a decade before (Reed, 1992). Rather than press local governments to raise environmental standards, there is some evidence that MNCs work in the opposite direction, that is, to encourage local governments to bargain down or at least freeze environmental protection standards.

Second, when regulations are lacking or not enforced, companies have the discretion to set their own environmental standards at the firm or even plant level. Numerous studies have found that the environmental performance of plants operating side-by-side can vary enormously, in both developing and developed countries (Laplante and Rilston, 1995; Dion et al, 1997). Many MNCs claim that they perform better than local firms, especially small and medium sized companies, because they have cleaner technology and better management. Statistical studies, however, have found little support for the claim that foreign ownership or financing positively influences plant-level performance in developing countries (Hettige et al, 1996). The factors that seem to matter most are plant size, community pressure and effective government regulation.

Agri-business MNCs are rapidly transforming the landscape of farming around the world. With expected liberalization of global trade, they will extensively penetrate developing country agriculture, and greatly expand the use of agro-chemicals such as pesticides. Moreover, unless regulatory constraints are put in place, agricultural biotechnology will spread rapidly in developing countries. There is little study, however, of the environmental, health or social impacts of the widespread use of genetically modified seeds, plants and animals.

In addition to pollution, resource degradation is the second broad area in which globalization in general and MNCs in particular affect the environments of developing countries. Indeed MNC global investment in resource and extractive industries has been at the centre of global storms of criticism and controversy.

Mining is an inherently dirty industry. According to the Mineral Policy Center, a US mining watchdog NGO, hard rock mining releases more toxic waste than any other industry in the US. The pollutants released from mining include arsenic, lead, cyanide and mercury. The destructive environmental impacts of mining include 'mountain-top removal', where mountains are literally cut in half to expose coal and other mineral deposits. Tailings, which are the by-product of removing ore, can create a massive disposal problem and in many cases are dumped directly into a nearby river or open-air pit. The legacy of toxic tailings can continue to pollute soil, rivers and groundwater over a century after the original mining process (Mining, Minerals and Sustainable Development Project, 2002).

Gold mining can be particularly problematic. Many gold-producing companies, including the giant MNC Newmont Corporation, use cyanide leaching to extract small amounts of gold from tons of rock. The gold is removed, leaving an extremely hazardous, cyanide-laced sludge for disposal. According to one study, Newmont's operations in Indonesia, Peru, California, Nevada and the Philippines have destroyed fisheries, polluted water and caused widespread health problems (Project Underground, 2000). In developing countries, where economic options are few, the destruction of local resource-based livelihoods can be catastrophic.

The worst single incident occurred in Romania on 30 January 2000, when a massive toxic stew of cyanide and heavy metals from the Baia Mare Gold Mine, operated by the Australian company Esmeralda and a Romanian joint venture partner, flowed into the Tisza and Danube rivers. Caused by the collapse of the tailings dam, the spill created the worst ecological nightmare since the 1986 Chernobyl nuclear disaster. Tisza is now considered a 'dead' river (Hungarian Ministry for Environment, 2000). An international coalition is pressing for an end to cyanide leaching.

Forestry is another extractive industry in which MNC investment has large ecological and social impacts. Forests are the repositories of a large portion of terrestrial biodiversity. They are also important in maintaining watersheds, stabilizing local climate and sequestering carbon. Forest cover is disappearing rapidly in developing countries. In Asia, 70–90 per cent of original wildlife habitat had been lost by 1985 owing to agriculture, infrastructure development, deforestation and land degradation (Asian Development Bank, 2001). While it is not the only or even the primary source of forest loss at a global scale, unsustainable logging practices by both domestic and foreign companies are largely to blame in particular countries, including those of Southeast Asia. Moreover, logging roads and operations often pave the way for farms or settlements that widely impact the forest.

Many forestry companies engage in *clear-cutting* or other unsustainable logging practices. After pulp and paper companies have removed the valuable 'old-growth' timber, the land may be replanted, if at all, with exotic and invasive fast-growing tree species such as eucalyptus. These plantations are raised for quick re-growth to be harvested repeatedly. Replacing old-growth forests with monoculture species has a detrimental impact on plant and animal diversity.

Human rights

MNC operations are located in many countries in which the rule of law is weak or non-existent. In the absence of legal and judicial institutions and protections, MNC operations must rely on personal connections to government leaders or establish their own policies and institutions. In either case, they are vulnerable to corruption and to complicity in human rights abuses of the governments.

An overarching area of ethical concern is the denial of basic civil and political rights. Throughout the world, local communities and NGOs have organized in opposition to the penetration of MNCs in their cultural, economic and political lives. Refusing to protect rights to free speech and assembly, many governments have responded with political repression. In extreme cases, protestors have been shot and/or imprisoned.

Multinational energy companies, including Royal Dutch Shell, Chevron, BP Amoco, Occidental, Unocal, ExxonMobil and others have been highly visible in developing country conflicts involving human rights. Energy projects, such as oil drilling or the construction of a pipeline, are typically organized through leases from or joint ventures with local governments. These governments can be highly repressive, even military dictatorships, or otherwise lack credibility and/or popularity. In some cases, including Indonesia, Colombia and Nigeria, the government is engaged in what amounts to a civil war with ethnic, tribal, political or other groups.

The joint ventures are seen to be – and indeed are – ways that the central government maintains and finances its power and position vis-à-vis its domestic opponents. The alliance makes the on-the-ground MNC operations vulnerable to criticism, opposition and sabotage. In Burma, for example, the political opposition led by Aung San Suu Kyi has made clear that they do not oppose but, indeed, favour foreign investment. What they oppose is the alliance between the MNCs, Total and Unocal, and the military dictatorship that stole a democratic election and has quashed democracy for over 20 years (Fink, 2001).

Moreover, the energy MNCs have become targets in their own right when they have been found to be negligent in their protection of workers, communities and the natural environment. The widespread choking pollution caused by oil exploration and drilling activities in the Ecuadorian Amazon region is a leading example (Kimmerling, 2001).

To protect their operations and personnel, energy MNCs have either engaged their own private security forces, sometimes with connections to paramilitary groups, or relied on government military or police forces. An investigation by a human rights group found that ExxonMobil Oil, for example, spends about US$500,000 per month for military protection for its gas fields in the Aceh region of Indonesia. Although ExxonMobil denies spending that much, it admits to paying the government for logistics support, such as food and housing, for soldiers who guard the gas fields (Kwok, 2001).

In several documented cases, government- and/or company-sponsored security forces have attacked civilians and protestors. In Colombia, an official inquiry alleged that American civilian airmen, under contract to Occidental Petroleum, coordinated and marked targets in an anti-guerrilla air attack in 1998 that mistakenly killed 18 civilians. The airmen used a Skymaster plane which, according to the Colombian pilots involved in the raid, was paid for by Occidental Petroleum (Penhaul, 2001).

In addition to the use of security forces, a key human rights issue involved in MNC-led globalization is the encroachment and expropriation of the lands of indigenous peoples. Many resource-intensive MNC activities, including mining, energy and forestry operations, involve expanding to remote areas inhabited by indigenous groups. The rights of indigenous people as a group to control traditional lands or otherwise to maintain themselves as a culture have not yet been fully defined at the international level (see Chapter 1). In many developing countries, neither the individual nor the group rights of indigenous people are protected. They are treated as marginal, second-class citizens who lack a voice (see Chapter 4).

An integrated ethical framework?

While not exhaustive, the ethical issues outlined above provide a good sampling of the key labour, environment and human rights issues confronting MNCs. Advocacy groups and MNCs themselves increasingly perceive links between the three sets of issues. Worker exposure to hazardous chemicals, for example, is at once a labour rights and an environmental concern. The expropriation of indigenous peoples from ancestral lands to make way for a mining operation has implications for both human rights and environmental protection. An alliance of an energy multinational with a repressive government is likely to generate both human rights violations and environmental pollution, not least because of the inability of community groups to advocate for better performance. Burgeoning coalitions have formed between labour groups and environmentalists, and between human rights and environmental groups.

Within forward-looking 'good guy' corporations, too, there is an increasing tendency for integrated 'corporate responsibility' units to replace or work in parallel with managers responsible for environment, health and safety, government relations or public affairs. Levi Strauss, for example, has created the post of Corporate Responsibility Manager. Within the Global Reporting Initiative integrated 'sustainability reporting' has replaced earlier efforts to develop a reporting template based primarily on environmental indicators.

A number of efforts to develop a coherent set of guidelines have blossomed, generally outlining labour, human rights and environmental standards, including the Global Sullivan Principles and the OECD Guidelines for Multinationals. These various frameworks have varying levels of specificity. At the United Nations, the Global Compact articulates nine principles spanning the three ethical issue areas to guide corporate behaviour (United Nations, 2001). An international coalition is working to standardize social and environmental guidelines for export credit agencies (ECAs) and to develop a binding convention.

In short, an ethical framework is emerging outlining broad social expectations for 'socially responsible' corporate behaviour in a global economy. At the moment, however, the adoption and implementation of this framework remains at the level of company discretion.

FROM SOCIAL RESPONSIBILITY TO CORPORATE ACCOUNTABILITY

Despite the rapid advance of economic globalization and the preponderant role of MNCs in it, a coherent global framework of ethical norms for multinational corporations has not yet been adopted. A substantial body of international law governs human rights standards but, until recently, was held to apply only to governments. The same applies to the ILO's core labour standards, although increasingly they are being used as voluntary guidelines for MNCs. Moreover, there are no direct international enforcement mechanisms to enforce international human or labour rights norms, and enforcement by national governments is patchy. International environmental law likewise has been aimed at defining government responsibility and is still in an early stage, even though it has burgeoned in the last 20 years. In this context, the 'corporate social responsibility' (CSR) model of corporate governance has offered a channel through which companies and their stakeholders can work to voluntarily embrace, define and raise ethical standards. A necessary and important step forward, it is nonetheless limited in what it can achieve without parallel and supportive action by governments.

The 'corporate social responsibility' model

A business management model based on CSR has three discrete components. First, owners and managers reconceptualize and reformulate the company's *mission* to target public purpose as well as private gain. At its most fulsome, a CSR mission commits the company to the pursuit of a 'triple bottom line': financial, social and environmental (Elkington, 1998). Central to the mission is the recognition that not only shareholders but also a wide circle of 'stakeholders', including local communities where companies operate, are affected by company operations.

The second component of CSR is the creation of *internal management systems* to operationalize the 'triple bottom line' mission. Effective systems focus on two central elements of implementation: auditing and benchmarking. The aim of the auditing system is to make sure the company knows what is going on, that is, to track and monitor information about environmental, labour and human rights impacts in all company operations, both domestic and global, as well as subcontractors and suppliers. Benchmarks set substantive targets for improvements in performance; for example, 'reducing on-the-job accidents by 20 per cent each year for three years' or 'increasing energy efficiency by 30 per cent within five years'. For some companies, an initial benchmark might be to bring labour or environmental standards into compliance with international or even national law. For others, benchmarks aim 'beyond compliance'. The fundamental idea of benchmarking is to aim for 'continuous improvement'.

The third component of CSR has to do with external relations, including *stakeholder engagement* and *public disclosure* of the environmental and social performance data tracked by the internal auditing system. The stakeholder concept is that a company is first and foremost a social construct, embedded in a society and accountable to it. Stakeholders include those who are directly affected by company decisions, including not only owners but workers, investors, consumers and local communities. Stakeholders also include a broader range of public interest and advocacy groups, such as environmental, human rights and labour groups, and government. The larger and more global a corporation, the wider is its circle of both direct and public interest stakeholders.

A robust CSR model entails seeking out stakeholder views and regular consultation with stakeholder groups. Some of the most forward-looking companies have created ongoing advisory panels or other mechanisms for regular stakeholder engagement. Most, however, engage with stakeholders on an ad hoc basis.

Public disclosure can take a variety of forms. Most companies who have created codes of conduct publish environmental and social performance information in annual reports and/or on their websites. Claims about better performance, however, are often vague, with little or no real data. Moreover, the information is reported in many different formats, making comparisons difficult.

The Global Reporting Initiative (GRI) is working to overcome this problem – and company resistance to public disclosure – by creating a standardized reporting framework for voluntary disclosure. Initially conceived as a framework for environmental reporting, GRI has expanded to include both social and environmental issues. However, because information is reported at the firm rather than facility level, community NGOs are concerned about how useful the GRI framework will be in monitoring corporate performance.

Limitations of the CSR model

The essence of the CSR model is that it is voluntary, or at least non-regulatory. Rather than lobbying governments and seeking government enforcement, advocacy and community groups can use market pressures to directly prod companies to adopt higher ethical standards. Because reputation effects can be very costly, companies can feel coerced to respond, an approach to norm-setting one analyst has dubbed 'civil regulation' (Zadek, 2001).

The combination of community pressure and voluntary corporate response makes for an innovative approach to regulation. Voluntarism allows companies to respond flexibly to rising social demands. Flexibility allows companies to choose their own targets and timelines, potentially allowing for higher performance at lower cost. At its best, CSR offers the promise that companies will voluntarily both search for and find continuous improvement, especially if social and environmental improvement also boosts financial performance. It suggests a paradigm shift in business management and strategy, a cultural change in values which would eventually become the norm not only in global but in all business.

CSR also holds the promise of creating better and higher performance practices and standards than those driven by government regulation. Regulation can be poorly designed, creating perverse incentives, such as behaviours aimed more at evading the law and protection from lawsuits than at improving performance. US Superfund legislation is a well-known instance. Command-and-control regulation requires a police-patrolling-the-beat approach to enforcement. Even at home, OECD countries cannot afford an inspection system that assures a high level of compliance. Community pressure is likely to be much more effective than threats of legal or administrative sanctions to enforce both compliance with the law and improvements beyond compliance.

There are serious limitations, however, to CSR as the primary mechanism for defining and universalizing environmental and human rights norms in the global economy.

Company discretion over ethical choices

The first limitation stems from the fact that companies themselves select not only how to respond to ethical demands but which demands to respond to. The ability to pick and choose means that private actors, rather than society as a whole, determine social priorities, a premise that is at odds with a democratic society. It also means that crucial environmental and social issues can be neglected or overridden by company financial concerns.

The problem of company ethical discretion can be mitigated to some extent by the adoption of robust stakeholder engagement strategies. But, since most companies select the stakeholders with whom they will engage, the problem is simply transferred from 'which issues'? to 'which stakeholders'? In many cases, companies have specified that they seek to engage only those with 'direct interest', like local community groups. But what about the larger, public interest issues and implications, like climate change or the welfare of children? Advocacy groups are often at odds with each other, let alone with the company. How should the general public be represented?

Moreover, for MNCs with operations in dozens of countries, even a narrow concept of 'direct interest' stakeholders makes the question of 'which stakeholders?' far from trivial. Within a single community, stakeholders can have a wide range of contradictory concerns, especially when some will win and some will lose from a company decision. Thus, two key choice-variables concerning the social good remain at the discretion of the company: 1) who gets access to the company's ear; and 2) how to deal with trade-offs between the concerns of different stakeholders.

Credibility of environmental and social information

The effectiveness of the CSR model pivots on information. Within the company, obtaining and monitoring information about social and environmental performance is what allows the company to benchmark and to know if its self-selected targets are being met. Externally, information about company environmental and social performance is what enables community pressure and market leverage to work. Communities use it to monitor local companies and press bad performers to improve; investors and consumers to reward good performers and shun or engage bad ones. Without credible, publicly disclosed information, there is little to distinguish the CSR model from a public relations effort.

Most companies, however, are reluctant to significantly expand public disclosure of any information, including on social and environmental performance. Reasons include fear of liability and lawsuit, particularly if disclosure reveals breaches of law, and concerns that competitors will have access to proprietary information. There are also concerns that companies could use environmental or social performance data to undercut competitors.

Some companies, including some who are leaders on environmental or social issues, simply have a culture of insulation and instinctively shun any attempts to shine a spotlight on their affairs. Still others consider voluntary disclosure to be an obstacle, rather than a help, towards better ethical performance, since it encourages empty boasting.

The lack-of-information problem afflicts both companies that do not and those that do disclose performance data. When little information is available, community and shareholder activists have little to grab on to in terms of leverage. Indeed, this is precisely why some companies withhold it. However, they thereby become vulnerable to misinformation campaigns. The use of Asian sweatshops in the apparel industry, for example, is well known. Without company-specific information, advocacy groups paint all companies with the same brush.

When companies do make information available, the problem becomes credibility. How can consumers and others know if the information is robust, or if the numbers are simply cooked? A hundred years ago, companies provided financial information in much the same style – without the benefit of legal standards and regulatory oversight. Examples of cooked books abounded. Indeed, the Enron debacle in the US suggests that the problem has not been fully overcome.

Some companies, especially apparel retailers accused of using sweatshop labour, have engaged auditors to provide third party verification of their social and environmental performance claims. In the main, the auditors are big accounting firms like PriceWaterhouseCoopers (PWC), for whom social auditing is a high-growth market. But the credibility of the verifiers is itself problematic. Accounting firms have a conflict of interest in auditing both the financial and the social performance of their clients. Moreover, 'fly in/fly out' auditors may get a poor picture of actual conditions. In autumn 2000, a group of MIT faculty accompanied PWC in audits of labour conditions in Asian companies producing clothes stamped with US university logos. They found that the auditors either did not speak to workers or spoke only with those handpicked by the company. Nonetheless, PWC 'verified' company claims about the lack of forced overtime and other labour violations (O'Rourke, 2000).

Without independent, high-standard, third-party verification, it is difficult to separate out snake-oil – public relations gimmicks – from real performance improvements. Credible information about the impacts of MNC operations in developing countries is especially difficult – and important – to obtain, not least because a free press is often lacking. Companies like Unocal can present smiling faces of Burmese people who are benefiting from the building of the Yadana pipeline – but what about the thousands of Burmese refugees in Thailand who ran for their lives?

System-wide effects of competition: Do good guys finish last?
The CSR model is premised on the belief that large multinationals have significant discretion over most aspects of their business, including labour, human rights and environmental management practices. There is no doubt that they do. But MNCs operate in larger institutional contexts. Like smaller companies, they are subject to the pressures of market competition structured within systems of rules and regulations. Absent global standards, a company that gets too far ahead of the crowd may find it has left its market position behind as well. In a show of commitment to worker and human rights, Levi Strauss, for example, withdrew from China in the 1990s, expecting other large retailers to follow. When they did not, Levi quietly resumed its Chinese operations (Smith, 1999). In the Caspian region, US energy companies complained to the State Department that less scrupulous French companies would reap the benefits of attempts to press local governments on human rights.

The lack of global standards affects not only competition between MNCs but also the host country governments, both national and sub-national, which seek to attract them. In bargaining with an MNC, especially in manufacturing industries where a large quantity of local jobs are at stake, planners and regulators are reluctant to place more stringent environmental or social standards than competitors. Competition for FDI acts like a low-pressure zone on the global economy, inhibiting standards from rising as fast as local preference and conditions would otherwise demand.

Some business leaders, especially in the US, claim that global ethical standards are not needed because MNCs themselves, through newer technology, better management and corporate governance practices, drive up local standards in developing countries. In effect, they suggest that they are driving a global 'race to the top'. Advocacy groups, however, argue that corporate-led globalization is driving a 'race to the bottom'. In a review of the empirical and statistical evidence, this author found that environmental standards are not racing anywhere but are 'stuck in the mud' (Zarsky, 1999). Because of the effects of competition on both companies and governments, the system-wide tendency is for standards to raise slowly, incrementally and in tandem with competitors. The rate of environmental degradation and social inequity is rising much more quickly.

Mandatory social disclosure

Government action is needed not to thwart or replace the CSR model but to complement and strengthen it. A promising arena for government action is in mandating public disclosure of company social and environmental performance information, including for both domestic and global operations. Disclosure would strengthen the monitoring role of communities and the market leverage of ethical investors.

Companies are already required to make certain social disclosures. In the US, for example, the Toxics Release Inventory mandates disclosure of emissions of some 600 industrial chemicals. The US Security and Exchange Commission requires disclosure of any 'material' information, including environmental liabilities. The International Right to Know Campaign is pressing the US

Congress to extend the same reporting requirements to overseas company operations, plus additional disclosures related to human rights.[3]

Mandatory reporting could be implemented at various levels – global, national, even sub-national. Global requirements, however, will be the most difficult to achieve and might be modelled on successful national efforts. Moreover, like requirements to disclose different kinds of financial information to national and sub-national regulators, mandates for social disclosure could vary by jurisdiction. A 'super-state' like California could take the initiative to mandate disclosure of a wider variety of data, such as plant-level emissions. Disclosure would help state environmental and development planners to set their own benchmarks for 'sustainability planning'. Any initiative to mandate social disclosure would need to be designed in a way that took full account of potential liability, as well as company needs to protect proprietary information.

International 'sustainable and ethical' investment rules

Currently, there is no global set of rules for the governance of investment. An attempt to create one, the ill-fated Multilateral Agreement on Investment, foundered in large part because it defined only the rights but not the responsibilities of investors, host and home governments. A global coalition of environmental, human rights and labour groups worked to defeat it. Since then, the trend towards expanding investor rights at the expense of public purpose has gone even further. North American Free Trade Agreement's (NAFTA's) Chapter 11 allows investors to sue governments for 'regulatory takings' when health or environmental regulations have cut into investor profits (IISD, 2001).

A 'sustainable and ethical' investment rules framework, as currently being explored by a group of NGO analysts, would balance investor rights with public purpose (Nautilus Institute, 2002). It would define and extend the 'right to regulate' in investment agreements and give equal weight to international human rights, labour rights and environmental law in the resolution of investment disputes. It would also link investor rights to good corporate governance, including in the management of environmental and social dimensions of business. In a parallel approach, a coalition led by Friends of the Earth is pressing for a binding global convention on corporate accountability (Friends of the Earth, 2002).

Whether or not a formal global treaty is signed, an international investment regime will emerge over the next decade. The shape of that regime, the balance it strikes between private rights and public purpose, will be of momentous importance in determining how globalization will impact both the environment and society in the 21st century. Combined with rules to promote social disclosure, government action to regulate investment can be the crucial lever to promote corporate accountability.

NOTES

1   See www.bhopal.org/.
2   See http://gbgm-umc.org/umw/endchild.html#coalition.
3   See www.irtk.org.

REFERENCES

Asian Development Bank (2001) *Asian Environment Outlook 2001*,
    (www.adb.org/documents/books/aeo/2001). Manila, Philippines: Asian
    Development Bank
California Global Corporate Accountability Project (2002), reports on field
    investigations on environmental and social impacts of global operations of oil and
    high-tech companies, www.nautilus.org/cap/index.html. Berkeley, CA: Nautilus
    Institute for Security and Sustainable Development
Earthrights International (2000) *Total Denial Continues, Earth Rights Abuses Along the
    Yadana and Yetagun Pipelines in Burma*, May (www.earthrights.org). Washington, DC:
    Earthrights International
Elkington, J (1998) *Cannibals With Forks: The Triple Bottom Line of the 21st Century
    Business*. Stony Creek, CT: New Society Publishers
Fink, C (2001) *Living Silence: Burma Under Military Rule*. London: Zed Books
Friends of the Earth International (2002) *Towards Binding Corporate Accountability*,
    www.foei.org/wssd/prepcom.html
Global Exchange (undated) *Made In USA*, online article,
    www.globalexchange.org/economy/corporations/saipan/overview.html
Hettige H, Huq M, Pargal S, and Wheeler, D (1996) 'Determinants of Pollution
    Abatement in Developing Countries: Evidence from South and Southeast Asia',
    World Development 24(6)
Huffstutter, P J (2001) 'IBM Settles Suit Alleging Its Plant Caused Birth Defects', *Los
    Angeles Times*, 24 January
Hungarian Ministry of Environment (2000) *Preliminary Evaluation of the Cyanide
    Pollution in the Rivers Szamos and Tisza*, February,
    www.zpok.hu/cyanide/baiamare/docs/komreports/cyanide.htm
IISD (2001) *Private Rights, Public Problems, A Guide to NAFTA's Controversial Chapter on
    Investor Rights*. Winnipeg, Canada: International Institute for Sustainable
    Development/World Wildlife Fund
ILO (1998) *Statistics on Working Children and Hazardous Child Labour in Brief*, April,
    www.ilo.org/public/english/bureau/stat/child/childhaz.htm. Geneva:
    International Labour Organization
Jacobs, D (2001) 'The Potential and Limitations of Foreign Direct Investment for
    Development', Paper produced for the *Financing for Development Conference*, Oxfam
    America, 15 June
Kimmerling, J (2001) 'International Standards in Ecuador's Amazon Oil Fields: The
    Privatization of Environmental Law', *Columbia Journal of Environmental Law* 26(2)
Kwok, Y (2001) 'Exxon to Resume Aceh Operation', CNN, www.cnn.com, 22 March
Laplante, B and Rilston, P (1995) 'Environmental Inspections and Emissions of the
    Pulp and Paper Industry: The Case of Quebec', *New Issues in Pollution Prevention*.
    Washington, DC: World Bank

Mazurek, J (2000) *The High Tech Sector and the Environment in the New Millennium: Performance, Prescriptions, and Policies*. Berkeley, CA: California Global Corporate Accountability Project

Meadows, S (2000) 'Six Firms Added to Saipan Sweatshop Lawsuit' (Levi Srauss, Calvin Klein, Brooks Brothers, Abercrombie and Fitch, Talbots), Bobbin Group, May, www.findarticles.com/cf_0/m3638/9_41/63058111/p1/article.html

Mining, Minerals and Sustainable Development Project (2002) *Breaking New Ground: Mining, Minerals and Sustainable Development*. London: Earthscan Publications (www.iied.org/mmsd/finalreport/index.html)

Nautilus Institute (2002) International Investment Rules Project, www.nautilus.org/enviro/Investment.html. Berkeley, CA: Nautilus Institute for Security and Sustainable Development

O'Rourke, D (2000) 'Monitoring the Monitors: A Critique of Price Waterhouse Coopers (PWC) Labor Monitoring', 28 September, http://web.mit.edu/dorourke/www. Cambridge, MA: Massachusetts Institute of Technology Environmental Policy Group

Pan, P (2001) 'China's Prison Laborers Pay Price for Market Reforms', Post Foreign Service, 14 June (see also www.laborrights.org). Washington, DC

Panayotou, T and Sussangkorn, C (1991) *The Debt Crisis, Structural Adjustment and the Environment: The Case of Thailand*. Bangkok: Thailand Development Research Institute

Penhaul, K (2001) 'Americans Blamed in Colombia Raid', *San Francisco Chronicle*, 15 June, page A1

Project Underground (2000) *Newmont, Why Are People Around the World so Mad at This Company?* Berkeley, CA: Project Underground

Reed, D (ed) (1992) *Structural Adjustment and the Environment*. Boulder, CO: Westview Press

Roht-Arriaza, N (2000) 'Semi-Conductor Production in Costa Rica: A Preliminary Field Investigation', report to California Global Corporate Accountability Project, www.nautilus.org/cap

Salazar, C (1999) personal communication with author. See also Salazar's case study, Semi-Conductors in the Philippines, Asian Institute of Management, Philippines, http://iisd.ca/susprod/casestudies.htm

San Jose Mercury (1999) 'Why Piecework Won't Go Away,' *San Jose Mercury* 28 June (see www.mercurycenter.com)

Schrage, E (2002) 'A Long Way to Find Justice', *Washington Post*, 14 July, page B2

Schwartz, P and Gibb, B (1999) *When Good Companies Do Bad Things: Responsibility and Risk in an Age of Globalization*. New York: John Wiley & Sons

Smith, G (1999) Remarks to the 'Hard Issues, Innovative Approaches' Round Table of the California Global Corporate Accountability Project, Berkeley, CA

Taiwan Environmental Action Network (2001) 'Environmental and Social Aspects of Taiwanese and US Companies in the Hsinchu Science-based Industrial Park'. Taipei, Taiwan, and Berkeley, CA: California Global Corporate Accountability Project, www.nautilus.org/cap/index.html

UNCTAD (1999) *World Investment Report, Foreign Direct Investment and the Challenge of Development*. New York/Geneva: United Nations Conference on Trade and Development

UNCTAD (2000) *World Investment Report, Cross-Border Mergers and Acquisitions and Develoment*. New York/Geneva: United Nations Conference on Trade and Development

UNEP (2001) *State of the Global Environment*. Nairobi, Kenya: United Nations Environment Programme

United Nations (2001) *The 9 Principles, A Compact for a New Century*, www.unglobalcompact.org/gc/unweb.nsf/content/thenine.htm

US Census Bureau (1999) *Money Income in the United States 1999*, www.census.gov/hhes/www/income99.html

World Bank (2001) 'Country at a Glance Tables', *World Development Report*, www.worldbank.org/data/countrydata/countrydata.html

Zadek, S (2001) *The Civil Corporation: The New Economy of Corporate Citizenship*. London: Earthscan Publications

Zarsky, L (1999) 'Havens, Halos, and Spaghetti: Untangling the Relationship Between FDI and Environment', in *OECD, Foreign Direct Investment and the Environment*. Paris: OECD

Part II

Conflicts Over Mineral and Oil Development

Chapter 3

Mining in Suriname: Multinationals, the State and the Maroon Community of Nieuw Koffiekamp

Fergus MacKay

INTRODUCTION

All over the world, states are liberalizing investment laws and redrafting mining legislation to encourage investment in the mining sector. As a result, once remote and ignored indigenous lands and territories are increasingly on the front line of state- and corporate-directed resource exploitation operations. These operations are environmentally destructive and socially disruptive. The Guyana Shield – the region that includes Guyana, Suriname, French Guiana, Venezuela and parts of Colombia and Brazil – is no exception, and Suriname, the setting for this case study, is a microcosm (Colchester, 1995).

Suriname is a small, former Dutch colony and is considered by historical and demographic factors to be Caribbean rather than Latin American. Until recently, its tropical rainforests were regarded as having good prospects for long-term, sustainable use and preservation (Colchester, 1995, p7). These forests cover at least 80 per cent of the surface area of the country and are biologically rich and high in endemic species. These forests are also the ancestral home of five distinct indigenous peoples composing up to 5 per cent of the population, and six tribal peoples (maroons) totalling between 10 and 15 per cent of the population. In real numbers, this translates as approximately 20,000 indigenous people and 40–60,000 tribal people. In the past few years, they have been joined by some 30,000 Brazilian *garimpeiros*, licensed by the state.

Less than 30 years ago, Suriname was one of the most prosperous states in South America. A brutal military dictatorship, civil war, endemic corruption, declining prices for bauxite and the suspension of Dutch aid money has left the country with serious economic problems. In recent years, the government has parcelled out vast areas of the rainforest interior to multinational mining and logging companies, claiming that this is needed to finance foreign debt and stimulate economic recovery and growth. For instance, in 1993, the government began negotiations with Asian logging companies for concessions totalling between 3 and 5 million hectares – almost two-fifths of the country. Contracts for these concessions were rejected in early 1997 after enormous international condemnation and pressure. More recently, however, a large number of logging concessions have been granted despite government promises to the contrary.

Suriname has long depended on bauxite mining as its principal export earner, but until recently had done little to exploit the substantial gold deposits assumed to occur throughout the interior. This changed in 1992, when the government began inviting investment in the gold mining sector. The first company to arrive was Golden Star Resources, a Canadian company. It has been followed by numerous others, large and small, all seeking to cash in on Suriname's gold fever. Analyses of contracts for both logging and mining operations have revealed, however, that the Surinamese treasury will receive few if any benefits and that the environment and indigenous and tribal peoples will suffer irreparable harm (World Resources Institute, 1995). Indigenous and tribal peoples, whose rights to their territories and resources are not recognized in Surinamese law, have vigorously condemned this multinational invasion. They have demanded that all existing concessions are suspended and that no more are given until their rights are recognized in accordance with international human rights standards and enforceable guarantees are in place in Surinamese law.

This case study examines the dynamics of a dispute between the tribal community of Nieuw Koffiekamp and two Canadian mining companies authorized and supported by the government. It identifies and discusses the various actors and their respective roles and analyses attempts at conflict resolution, which to date have proved unsuccessful. It concludes with an evaluation of the potential role in the conflict of an international NGO mediator or ombudsperson.

THE CONFLICT

Nieuw Koffiekamp is an Aucaner maroon community of between 500 and 800 persons, located approximately 80 kilometres south of the capital of Suriname. Maroons are the descendants of escaped African slaves who fought for and won their freedom from the Dutch colonial administration in the 18th Century. They succeeded in establishing viable communities along the major rivers of the rainforest interior and have maintained a distinct culture based primarily on an amalgamation of African and Amerindian traditions. Maroons consider themselves and are perceived to be culturally distinct from other sectors of Surinamese society and regulate themselves according to their own laws and customs. Consequently, they qualify as tribal peoples according to international definitional criteria and enjoy largely the same rights as indigenous peoples under international law.[1] Aucaners, also known as N'djuka, are one of the six maroon peoples of Suriname. Their freedom from slavery and rights to territorial and political autonomy were recognized by a treaty concluded with the Dutch (1760, renewed in 1837) and by two centuries of colonial administrative practice. Aucaners and other maroons have even been described as a 'state within a state' (Scholtens, 1994, p147). The recognition of their autonomy has eroded in the past 50 years and the government now asserts that maroons have no rights to their territories and, for the most part, refuses to recognize tribal authorities and law (Kambel and MacKay, 1999, pp55–80).

Nieuw Koffiekamp is one of the so-called 'transmigration villages' (over 20 villages with a population of approximately 6000) that were forcibly relocated from their ancestral lands to make way for a hydroelectric dam and reservoir in 1963–1964. The dam was constructed to provide power for a bauxite and alumina refinery. The community of (old) Koffiekamp split into three parts during transmigration, one going to its present location, one forming another community called Marschalkreek and the remainder moving to the capital of Suriname on the coast.

Community members state that transmigration caused serious social, cultural and economic problems. In particular, they point to a breakdown in traditional authority and social cohesion; lack of compensation for their lands; economic hardship; a shift away from subsistence agriculture; and the loss of ancestral burial grounds and other sacred sites. Maroon culture and identity are a complex web of ongoing relationships with ancestral and other spirits, land and kinship structures. Activities that interfere with the processes by which these relationships are constructed and reinforced have a profound impact on their socio-cultural integrity; relocation is an extreme example. Community members frequently refer in very emotional terms to the pain and loss suffered due to transmigration. Elders, men, women and youth alike state that a second relocation will be tantamount to the cultural and social death of their community as relationships with ancestors, the land and kin will be further weakened, if not destroyed.

In 1992, GRASSALCO, the Surinamese parastatal mining company, transferred its rights to the Gross Rosebel gold and diamond concession to Golden Star Resources. Nieuw Koffiekamp is located at the centre of the southern block of this 17,000 hectare concession. The community and other surrounding communities affected by the concession were not consulted or even informed prior to its granting. In 1994, a Mineral Agreement was signed between Golden Star and the Suriname government granting exclusive exploration rights to Golden Star. In 1996, another Canadian company, Cambior Inc. of Montreal, exercised its option to acquire a 50 per cent interest in the project. In September of the same year, Golden Star announced publicly for the first time that the village of Nieuw Koffiekamp would have to be relocated again to make way for an industrial gold mine. That the relocation was planned had been widely known prior to the public announcement, even though the companies refused to discuss the subject, stating that it was not a pertinent issue.

After the Gross Rosebel concession was granted to Golden Star, the area was invaded by small-scale miners, the majority of whom were from Saramacca maroon communities near Nieuw Koffiekamp. Golden Star threatened to pull out of the project if the miners were not removed from the concession. In response, the Minister of Justice and Police threatened to attack the miners

Photograph: Fergus MacKay

Figure 3.1 *Villagers Blocking the Road to Golden Star's Mining Camp, 1997*

from the ground and air if they did not immediately vacate the area. A detachment of police and the paramilitary Police Support Group were permanently stationed at the mining camp and company security was increased. Around this time, community members began to complain that they were surrounded by armed guards and were being denied access to hunting, fishing and agricultural areas as well as areas used for small-scale mining, seriously impacting their economic well-being. Small-scale gold mining, directly and indirectly, provides an important source of income for many people in Nieuw Koffiekamp. This supplements subsistence hunting, fishing and agriculture as well as small-scale gravel mining and limited logging in community timber concessions.

Tensions escalated as company security guards and the police working with them began using live ammunition to intimidate and frighten community members away from areas in which the company was conducting or planned to conduct exploration activities. Moiwana '86, a Surinamese human rights organization, stated at this time that in its opinion at least eight separate violations of the American Convention on Human Rights had occurred and were ongoing due to company action and government inaction (Moiwana '86, 1995). In response to continued harassment, the community blocked the access road to the mining camp. This lasted five weeks until *Granman* Songo Aboikoni (paramount tribal leader) intervened, installing a Commission using the good offices of the OAS Special Mission to Suriname.[2]

The primary objective of this Commission was to resolve the dispute between Golden Star, the government and community-based, small-scale miners. The *Granman* appointed two of his personal advisers to sit on the Commission; Nieuw Koffiekamp appointed three persons; and representatives of the government (Ministry of Natural Resources, the Geology and Mines Service and GRASSALCO) and Golden Star also participated, the latter only briefly and informally. The Commission met 14 times over approximately a year, disbanding after both the government and the companies failed to respond to a draft agreement. This was the first and only sincere attempt at conflict resolution in the Nieuw Koffiekamp conflict.

The Commission's draft agreement outlined the means by which the activities of the community-based miners and the exploration programme of the companies could coexist. It did this primarily by identifying areas set aside for community miners to use in exchange for promises not to enter or interfere with areas in which the company was working. It also attempted to address the more fundamental issue of land ownership and, implicitly, the subject of relocation, by providing that the companies (and the government) would *de facto* recognize and respect, subject to the other terms of the agreement, the rights of the community under article 10 of the 1992 Peace Accord. The Peace Accord (officially called the Lelydorp Accord) concluded a devastating six-year civil war (1986–1992) that pitted maroon and indigenous insurgents against each other and the military dictatorship of the 1980s. The OAS Special Mission was very influential in drafting the Peace Accord and, in certain respects, is responsible for monitoring compliance with it. With the exception of the provisions relating to the decommissioning of weapons and a few others, the Peace Accord has never been implemented by the government.

In short, article 10 stipulates that indigenous and tribal persons should be issued with (individual) title to their land and that economic zones should be identified and demarcated around communities in which subsistence and other activities, including small-scale mining and community-based forestry, could occur. The inclusion of this article in the draft agreement is related to the issue of relocation for two reasons. First, it was decided that recognition of community rights would substantially increase the amount of potential compensation to be paid when negotiations on relocation commenced (personal communication with Special Mission staff). Second, from the community's perspective, recognition of rights under the Peace Accord would strengthen their opposition to relocation as they would be able to cite rights recognized by agreement with the companies and the government, further legitimized by the involvement of the Special Mission. Although for different reasons, the community and the Special Mission concurred on this part of the agreement. This is instructive about the different positions of the community and the Special Mission: the former sought to support its opposition to relocation, while the latter had decided that it was a forgone conclusion and sought to strengthen the community's position in negotiating the terms of compensation.

Both the companies and the government, however, failed to respond to the agreement as a whole, thereby nullifying the manoeuvres of the community and Special Mission. The reasons are unknown, although I can offer some educated speculation. The companies and the government were clearly concerned about the impact of this agreement on their contractual relationship as defined by the

1994 Mineral Agreement, which contains a derogation clause in which the government warrants that there are no pre-existing rights to the concession area. From their perspective, recognition, even *de facto*, of community rights under the 1992 Peace Accord challenged a fundamental provision of the Mineral Agreement, raising a myriad of legal questions with uncertain results. Also, from the government's perspective, and perhaps also to a certain extent the companies' as well, recognizing the rights of one community under the Peace Accord would have opened a can of worms best left alone. If one community's rights were recognized, then it would have to address the rights of all other indigenous and maroon communities, or at least justify why it would not. It was certainly aware that this was not lost on other communities throughout the country, who were waiting for this kind of opportunity to press their own claims. Nor was it lost on the companies who have interests in a number of other concessions in Suriname, most of which would be affected.

After the October 1996 general election, the new government, which was directly related to the military regime of the 1980s, installed a 'Task Force on the Relocation of Nieuw Koffiekamp'. It was staffed by persons associated with the military dictatorship and considered loyal to the government, and its mandate was to conclude a relocation settlement agreement. In doing so, it attempted to bring the community, the companies and government representatives to the negotiating table. A number of meetings were held between October and December in both the village and in the capital, which were attended by senior company management, high government officials and community leaders. Basically, these talks broke down as neither the government nor the companies were willing to consider options other than relocation of the community.

The Task Force continued to meet after December but was boycotted by the community, which stated that they were opposed to relocation and, therefore, were not interested in participating in a body whose sole function was to negotiate a relocation agreement. A few months later, the community appointed a negotiating body called the *Collectief* to represent its position with the government and the companies. The Task Force handed in its report, which has not been made public, in August 1997. The *Collectief*, which has since ceased to function, declared in a 1997 press release that talks were stalled and that no solution was emerging (*De West*, 1997, p1).

The companies submitted their Environmental Impact Assessment and Feasibility Study and the requisite forms for incorporating a Surinamese holding company in June 1997. The companies also submitted their preliminary applications for political risk insurance to the World Bank's Multilateral Investment Guarantee Agency (MIGA) and the Canadian government's Export Development Corporation (EDC). On 30 September 1997, a press release was issued stating that mine construction would begin in December 1997. It noted that the government had appointed yet another Commission to resolve the Nieuw Koffiekamp 'problem', and that a relocation plan had been submitted by the companies to the Minister of Natural Resources (*De Ware Tijd*, 1997, p1).

Since that time the companies have updated their feasibility study to include additional identified reserves. This updated feasibility study was submitted to the government in December 1997. As of August 2000, the government has yet to issue a licence to exploit the deposit, political risk insurance has not been secured and an agreement for the relocation of Nieuw Koffiekamp has not been reached (GSR, 2000, p36). In 1998, the price of gold on world markets plummeted and still remains below the US$350 an ounce level required to commercially operate the mine (Cambior, 2000). A combination of all these factors, although the last is probably the most important, has forestalled mine construction.

The nature of the dispute at Nieuw Koffiekamp on the surface appears quite straightforward – small-scale miners versus a multinational mining company sanctioned and supported by the government. In other words, the dispute is over gold and access thereto. This is also how the companies and the government portray the dispute. However, the situation is far more complex and involves a variety of interested parties. In the words of the OAS Special Mission Report (UPD Report), Nieuw Koffiekamp is:

> *a conflict fuelled by contrasting ideologies rooted in two worlds very far apart from each other: maroon and corporate culture. Land is of primary importance to the maroons. The social, political and economic system of maroon society is deeply rooted in clan ownership of territory, and the threat to what maroons consider traditional tribal territory is regarded with great seriousness. From the perspective of the large scale mining companies, having full title and unlimited access to concessions under development is a condition* sina qua non *for developing a mine* (OAS/UPD, 1997, Introduction).

In short, the dispute is based first and foremost on competing notions of land and its utility and significance, as well as competing notions of rights to and control over land and resources. In Suriname, the state claims ownership of all unencumbered land and all subsurface and surface resources. Based on this claim, it granted rights to Golden Star and Cambior, who now assert these rights against Nieuw Koffiekamp. Maroons state that their rights of ownership and, importantly, control of territory and resources are based on the struggle for freedom concluded in sacred treaties, the 1992 Peace Accord and international human rights law, and would incorporate a full understanding of all aspects of their relationship to that territory and attendant resources and a recognition of their laws pertaining thereto. International law, to a certain extent, has recognized the maroon perspective and is moving towards a more complete recognition.

Furthermore, maroons make no distinction between surface and subsurface resource rights. Their lands and resources are viewed holistically and are intertwined with the social, ancestral and spiritual relationships that govern their daily lives. Expropriation of their lands or the resources pertaining to those lands are indistinguishable and deeply offensive on a number of levels. In particular, maroon identity is inextricably connected to their struggle to free themselves from slavery, which they refer to as 'First-Time'. First-Time ideology pervades all aspects of maroon consciousness and is so powerful that it cannot be discussed openly or directly for fear of serious spiritual and other repercussions (Price, 1983).

First-Time ideology is also integral to maroon understandings of political and territorial autonomy. Consequently, perceived threats to this autonomy are directly related to fears about a return to the First-Time and a new era of slavery. Generally, the government and multinationals are not perceived to be very different from the brutal colonial regime that figures so prominently in First-Time discourse. It makes no difference that the face is black or white. Indeed, maroons perceive Surinamese Creoles, also of African descent, to have been cowardly collaborators with the slave masters and, therefore, inherently untrustworthy to this day. What is important here is that, in addition to challenging fundamental tenets of maroon political and social organization, government-sanctioned corporate mining invokes the struggle of First-Time ancestors, striking at the heart of maroons' deepest and most powerful belief and value systems.

The ideology of the government of Suriname is also a fundamental element of the dispute. Surinamese politics are dominated by the politics and interests of 85 per cent (in reality much less) of the population who occupy a narrow coastal strip composing 10 per cent of the surface area of the country. Indigenous peoples and maroons who occupy the other 90 per cent are seen as backward, anachronistic and obstacles to national development. They occupy the lowest rung of Suriname's multi-ethnic society and are viewed with contempt by other ethnic groups. Government policy towards them is based on assimilation and integration. Illustrative of this attitude is the statement of the Minister of Natural Resources, when asked about indigenous and maroon objections to logging concessions, that, 'they have to decide whether they want development or whether they want to remain backward people living in the bush' (interview with RFO, French television in French Guiana). Development, as used here and generally in Suriname, refers to the interests of the ruling elite, prime economic indices and the balance books of the state treasury, with which the elite maintains an elaborate system of ethnically based patronage through civil service appointments and government contracts. Development in Suriname is primarily about the interests of the few and appeasing the mostly middle class, voting population of the capital.

In 1997, the nature of the dispute between Nieuw Koffiekamp, the government and the companies radically shifted. Relocation of the community for the second time in 33 years versus the operation of a gold mine became the primary points of discussion and contention.[3] In a meeting with the Forest Peoples Programme, an international NGO actively supporting Nieuw Koffiekamp, Cambior stated that while it did not wish to see the community driven off its land, preferring to convince them of the need to move instead, it was not willing to accept the community's right to give or withhold its consent to relocation as enumerated in international indigenous rights standards. The government and Golden Star have taken a less tactful position, stating bluntly that the rights of the companies by Mineral Agreement supersede any rights claimed by the community. Golden Star's lawyer went so far as to describe the community as 'squatters'.

A relocation plan was drafted by the companies setting out compensation for the community. It was submitted to the government but has never been made available to the public. Judging by discussions between company representatives and myself, this plan probably includes: title to land at a new location (whether individual or collective is unknown); royalty payments at a set percentage (around 0.25 per cent); mining permits issued to the community; equipment and training in mining techniques; agricultural equipment and training; and provision of community infrastructure, such as houses, electricity, potable water, a health clinic and a school. It is unclear exactly how this plan would be implemented and by whom. The companies cannot do it alone as land titles and mining permits require government approval. The government, however, faces a dilemma related to recognizing rights under the Peace Accord, raising questions about how land titles would be issued: according to the Peace Accord or under a separate procedure authorized by the Decree on Issuing State Land.

Under the latter only individual titles can be granted unless the government was to recognize the legal personality of indigenous and maroon communities, something it has not been prepared to do in the past. Alternatively, the communities could organize themselves as corporate bodies, usually a foundation, which is something that indigenous leaders have rejected as it fails to recognize their traditional forms of social and political organization. Furthermore, the highest form of land title that can presently be issued on so-called state land in Suriname is a short-term lease of 15–40 years. This provides little or no protection to maroon subsistence and other economic activities insofar as the land is still subject to logging and mining concessions or other activities that may be inconsistent with its full use and enjoyment. These problems are also, although to a lesser extent, associated with the Peace Accord.

The community is justifiably sceptical that the terms of any agreement with the government and the companies will be honoured. The government of Suriname is notorious for not keeping promises, especially as they relate to the interior, and the community still has a bitter taste in its mouth from the many broken promises of the transmigration and Peace Accord eras. While it may be expected that the companies will be more responsible, their decisions are substantially affected by economic considerations that could affect the extent and quality of compliance. From the community's perspective, there is little difference between the companies and the government. Both are viewed as untrustworthy.

ACTORS

Nieuw Koffiekamp

A wide variety of actors have played a role in the Nieuw Koffiekamp situation. The community is the group most clearly affected. Within the community a number of groups can be identified. First, a group of younger people active in small-scale mining has been one of the most outspoken opponents of the mining project. This is in part due to the fact that one of their members was appointed community representative by the Captain (traditional village authority), and in part due to their interests in mining activities. They were also the group that experienced police and company repression on a day-to-day basis. Another group, the Captain and village council, was subjected to a great deal of pressure and manipulation from the companies and the government. Consequently, they were reluctant to take firm positions, preferring to let the younger people take the lead, supporting them and providing direction in the background. They nonetheless lost credibility and were distrusted by many in the village.

Most of the elders are opposed to relocation and the presence of the companies. One said that the companies are visitors in their house. If one must leave, it should be the visitor and not the owner of the house. Another group in the community, mainly those who had found employment with Golden Star, approved of Golden Star's presence as an income generator. Most of these people and others in the community are not opposed to relocation, citing the benefits of new facilities – school, hospital, houses, electricity, clean water – and additional employment and training possibilities when the mine begins production. Finally, the women of Nieuw Koffiekamp were among the most outspoken against the companies. Women are the primary caretakers of the agricultural plots around the village. In fulfilling this task they were subject to harassment by company security and police and often stated that they were afraid to go to their plots with children because of the shooting. Some of the women were injured fleeing from shooting incidents.

The companies

Golden Star is a Canadian company headquartered in the US. It has been described as one of the most aggressive Canadian juniors operating in the Guyana Shield (Minewatch, 1995, p12). Juniors are companies that focus exclusively on exploration. When a commercially viable deposit has been documented, they enter into an agreement with a major, a company that builds and operates mines, to exploit the deposit. Golden Star's primary focus is the 'acquisition, discovery and development of gold and diamond projects'(GSR, 2000, p3). Once commercially viable reserves have been sold or properties abandoned, 'the company must continually acquire new mineral properties to explore for and develop new mineral reserves'(ibid, p8). This constant acquisition of mining concessions, and the manner in which it conducts its operations, has led Golden Star into numerous conflicts with indigenous peoples and environmentalists throughout Suriname, the Guyanas and elsewhere. This is not surprising given that David Fagin, President of GSR, bluntly stated in 1994, that Golden Star had looked specifically at the Guyana Shield because of 'increased pressure from environmentalists and the government in the USA' (Minewatch, 1995, p10).

Conflicts between junior companies, like Golden Star, and local communities occur more frequently than conflicts with majors given the disproportionate number of juniors operating in most areas. Furthermore, the nature of junior operations is generally not conducive to respect for indigenous rights and community relations. These operations tend to be transitory; they do not consider communities to be stakeholders other than as labourers; they are

Photograph: Fergus MacKay

Figure 3.2 *Signpost near Nieuw Koffiekamp, 1997 ('Entry Forbidden. Golden Star/Grassalco Concession Area')*

driven by the need to produce results in order to survive, develop partnerships and finance further exploration and, therefore, focus on the technical aspects of the project rather than its wider impact and implications; and, finally, they are strongly oriented to fluid venture capital markets which play a major role in determining their policy and behaviour. These characteristics also make juniors less susceptible to political pressure, especially as many are fly-by-night operations that are extremely vulnerable to fluctuations in international gold prices. Majors, with some notable exceptions, are more likely to be shamed into at least adopting responsible policies, although many of the larger companies are able to exert substantial pressure on governments, both at home and abroad, so that enforcement of national laws and company policies is often lacking.

Cambior is one of North America's top ten gold producers. It is sensitive to criticism and has adopted internal policies on the environment and on human rights to mitigate criticism of its operations. A large percentage of its revenue, up to 50 per cent by some estimates, is derived from the Omai mine in Guyana, which it operates in partnership with Golden Star (30 per cent) and the government of Guyana (5 per cent). The Omai mine is best known for the collapse of a tailings facility on 19 August 1995, which dumped 3–4 million cubic metres of cyanide- and heavy metal-laced waste into the Omai and Essequibo rivers, prompting the government to declare the area an environmental disaster zone. This event, described as one of South America's worst mining disasters, was characterized by David Fagin as nothing more than 'one of the many risks of doing business' (*Montreal Gazette*, 1995, A1–A2).

Indigenous peoples, maroons and the government

The government views the Gross Rosebel mine as its flagship and proof to international investors that Suriname is a safe place to do business. It sees gold as a major revenue earner and as a replacement for export earnings from bauxite mining. Gold and diamond mining concessions have been granted to vast areas of the rainforest interior, many to multinationals with dubious records on environmental and human rights grounds. Multinational investment has also spurred rampant speculation by private citizens who obtain mining concessions – it costs about US$3 to obtain a large mining concession in Suriname – and then sign deals with companies to explore their concessions for a fee and percentage of potential royalties. Friends and allies of government officials in particular have benefited from this.

Surinamese law offers little protection for the rights of indigenous peoples and maroons. Their rights to their ancestral lands and resources are not recognized nor are their rights to participate in decisions concerning the use of those lands and resources. The official position is that maroons and indigenous peoples are permissive occupiers of state land, with no rights or title thereto (Kambel and MacKay, 1999, p178). The treaties with the maroons are also dismissed by the government as non-binding, 'domestic political contracts' as is the 1992 Peace Accord.

While Cambior has stated its intent to negotiate with the community to convince it to move, the community is being subjected to a great deal of pressure from other parties. Golden Star and Cambior are aware that this is taking place.[4] For instance, a paid consultant to Golden Star has been accused of bribing key leaders of the opposition to the mine and members of the village council and, in 1996, the former military dictator and present leader of the National Democratic Party, Desi Bouterse, publicly threatened to kill the community's representative after he returned from meetings in Washington, DC. Villagers also report that Bouterse's bodyguard threatened that the community would be driven off its land by the army and the police if they did not agree to move. Bouterse was made an official Advisor of State in 1996.

The role of Bouterse, described by the Inter Press Service as 'the government's special Advisor on [the mining] project', is most troubling (IPS, 1997). Military rule was characterized by gross and systematic violations of human rights, and maroons were targeted and suffered greatly during the civil war.[5] Consequently, Bouterse's involvement has played a substantial role in intimidating the community and stifling opposition. Golden Star's consultant mentioned above is a close associate of Bouterse and, according to a company employee, is an intermediary between it and Bouterse, and as a negotiator with local communities.

Many other indigenous and maroon communities are closely watching the situation. Nieuw Koffiekamp is the first of many conflicts that may arise in Suriname over rights and access to land and resources as multinational miners and loggers further expand their operations into indigenous and maroon territories. Presently at least 75 of the estimated 150 indigenous and maroon villages are located either in or very near mining concessions and this number rises substantially when logging concessions are accounted for. As with Nieuw Koffiekamp, all interior communities are routinely ignored when decisions are taken that affect their land and other rights. For these reasons, Nieuw Koffiekamp is perceived as a test case that must be resolved positively if other communities are to fare well in the future. A positive solution in this context means the legal recognition of collective ownership rights to lands and resources and the right to give or withhold consent to activities relating to those lands and resources.

That indigenous peoples and maroons fought against each other in the civil war was: in large part, due to manipulation by the government, particularly Bouterse, who claims to be of indigenous descent when seeking indigenous support, and to abuses perpetrated by maroon insurgents against indigenous communities. In light of the common threat to their ancestral homelands posed by multinational resource exploitation and the refusal of the government to recognize their rights, maroon and indigenous leaders began a process of attempting to minimize and resolve their differences and to speak with a unified voice.

In 1995 and 1996, two *Gran Krutus* (Great Gatherings) were held to develop a common position and strategy. Although the leaders expressed a multitude of concerns ranging from the lack of adequate health and educational facilities in their communities to the need for increases in government payments to village leaders, their paramount concern was land and resource rights, particularly in connection with multinational operations. In the final resolutions adopted by the *Gran Krutus*, they called for a freeze on additional concessions and a suspension of existing activities affecting communities, at least until their rights were fully recognized in the Constitution and laws of Suriname.[6] They specifically referred to the Nieuw Koffiekamp situation and condemned the activities of Golden Star, both there and elsewhere.

Intergovernmental and non-governmental organizations

The OAS Special Mission to Suriname has played an important role in the Nieuw Koffiekamp dispute, both directly and indirectly. In the first instance, the Special Mission was closely involved in the 1992 peace process that concluded with the adoption of the Peace Accord. Second, the Special Mission acted as an umbrella for the Commission of the Granman and took part in the government's Task Force on the Relocation of Nieuw Koffiekamp. Its most important contribution was writing the only detailed report of the dispute available, some of which is quoted above. Although couched in diplomatic language and deficient in certain important respects, the UPD Report has provided a measure of transparency to the dispute.

The Special Mission's mandate for involvement with Nieuw Koffiekamp arose originally as part of an examination of the means for implementing the Peace Accord. The staff of the Special Mission decided that in order to adequately evaluate means of implementation, baseline data was required concerning community land and resource use. The Nieuw Koffiekamp dispute came to national attention around the same time, so the Special Mission decided that it would be a good place to start. It was asked to participate in the *Granman*'s Commission by the *Granman* himself and was mandated by the Unit for Promotion of Democracy (UPD) in Washington to facilitate dialogue, provide support services and to write a report on the meetings.

Cambior has filed a preliminary application with MIGA to obtain political risk guarantees for its investment in the mine. Coverage will be sought jointly with the Canadian government's Export Development Corporation (EDC). The MIGA application process requires a review of the EIA to determine compatibility with International Finance Corporation (IFC) environmental review standards. Both MIGA and IFC are part of the World Bank's private sector arm. IFC standards are weaker than standard World Bank policy guidelines, such as OD 4.20 on Indigenous Peoples (1991) and OD 4.30 on Involuntary Resettlement, which has subjected MIGA's role in providing guarantees for environmentally and socially sensitive projects to a great deal of scrutiny by NGOs. That MIGA provided guarantees for the Omai mine in Guyana and disclaimed any responsibility for the 1995 disaster has only increased this scrutiny. In response to NGO enquiries concerning Nieuw Koffiekamp, MIGA stated that it will employ ODs 4.20 and 4.30 in its environmental review process and has requested that Cambior provide information on these issues. How MIGA will apply these standards remains to be seen.

A number of NGOs have been involved in providing support to Nieuw Koffiekamp. This began with Moiwana '86, the main Surinamese human rights organization. Working closely with the community, Moiwana put Nieuw Koffiekamp on the national agenda and did much to end the shootings through press releases and letters to the Attorney General's office requesting investigations into human rights violations. The Forest Peoples Programme (FPP), an affiliate of the World Rainforest Movement, has been most active on the international level. The FPP has a staff member permanently based in the Guyanas, who has been able to provide support directly to the community as well as information to international support networks. As noted above, it also met with Cambior to discuss the situation. In doing so, every effort was made to ensure that FPP was not construed as a representative of Nieuw Koffiekamp and that discussions were not a substitute for direct negotiations with the community. Cambior requested that FPP act as an intermediary in an attempt to reach an agreement with the community. No decision has been taken on this to date and it is unlikely that it ever will, given Cambior's refusal to consider alternatives to relocation. Cambior may seek another organization to act as a third party.

FPP and other NGOs attended a meeting with MIGA representatives in November 1997 to discuss MIGA involvement with the mine project.[7] At this meeting it was discovered that Cambior had yet to respond to MIGA's request for additional information and had not upgraded its preliminary application to a definitive application for insurance guarantees. Also, MIGA stated that Suriname had yet to officially become a member of MIGA and, therefore, the project is presently ineligible for guarantees – the Surinamese legislature ratified the MIGA treaty in September 1997, indicating that it was in the process of becoming a member. MIGA concurred with the concerns raised by the NGOs, stating that, if verified, they would be compelling reasons for MIGA not to get involved. They added, however, that it would be possible for Cambior to obtain insurance guarantees solely from EDC or in conjunction with a private insurer. EDC has been subjected to enormous criticism from Canadian NGOs for insuring 'bad' projects and for the complete lack of public accountability in its operations and administration. For example, EDC does not have a public disclosure policy and enquiries are treated at best as annoyances that do not require a response. Consequently, while some pressure may be applied on MIGA, EDC offers few opportunities for even raising issues of concern.

This component of the case study has attempted to analyse the Nieuw Koffiekamp situation by examining the nature of the dispute, underlying and associated factors and the actors involved. It has shown that the dispute is complex – in reality, the dispute is far more complicated than can be shown here – and based primarily on conflicting understandings of land and territory and rights thereto. Maroon territorial rights are fundamental to their identity and integrity as distinct cultures. The Surinamese political and legal systems have failed to account for the rights and interests of Nieuw Koffiekamp, and of indigenous peoples and maroons throughout the country, while at the same time promoting and enforcing their own vision of land and resource ownership, use and management. Assimilation and integration and the corresponding disrespect for maroon culture and identity are also dominant themes in state policy. That disputes have arisen with multinational corporations is in large part symptomatic of this failure to recognize maroon rights. The multinationals, however, are by no means blameless and often use domestic laws as a convenient excuse for ignoring and violating indigenous rights. Corporate ideology is more akin to the position of the Surinamese government and the two are allied by common interests against Nieuw Koffiekamp.

Attempts at dispute resolution have failed because the ultimate objectives of the parties are irreconcilable – the community, for the most part, is opposed to relocation, whereas the companies and the government, for their own reasons, are only interested in talking about the terms for relocation. Domestic remedies offer little hope of providing relief and the community is being intimidated by the former military dictator, who is extremely influential in the government and has a deserved reputation for brutality. This case also has enormous significance for other indigenous and maroon communities confronted with resource exploitation operations. It is a test case that may well determine how these communities will be treated in the years to come. The only positive outcome of the dispute from the perspective of Nieuw Koffiekamp and the other communities is a full recognition of their collective land and other rights, especially the right to freely consent to the use of their lands and resources. Environmental considerations, both in general and in relation to community well-being, are also high on the agenda. The companies involved at Nieuw Koffiekamp and others working elsewhere in Suriname have been responsible for some of the worst mining disasters in recent years. This case clearly requires additional international attention and could well serve as a test case for a mediation effort led by an international NGO ombudsperson.

TEST CASE FOR AN INTERNATIONAL NGO OMBUDSPERSON?

This section will examine the potential role of an ombudsperson in the case of Nieuw Koffiekamp and, briefly, in cases involving indigenous peoples in general. Two key elements will be discussed: potential functions for an ombudsperson, such as analysing technical information and acting as a mediator or broker in negotiations; and problems that an ombudsperson will encounter in carrying out these functions.

In assessing the utility of an ombudsperson in the case of Nieuw Koffiekamp, and for cases involving indigenous peoples in general, a number of criteria must be examined. A paramount consideration is: what will the role of the ombudsperson be in relation to existing indigenous structures and how will it relate to supporting NGOs already involved in the situation? An ombudsperson should not supersede or supplant existing indigenous structures and capacity, but rather should determine in collaboration with the affected people(s) how it can best support and address their priorities and concerns. Related to this, some communities may defer to what they perceive to be the superior knowledge and experience of outside interveners. The ombudsperson must be especially sensitive to this and ensure that its views are not imposed. It should also draw on the expertise and knowledge of NGOs and others trusted by and working with the community or communities in question.

In the case of Nieuw Koffiekamp, an ombudsperson could be very useful. The OAS Special Mission attempted to take on this role, at least with regard to a dispute resolution function, however, it operates under a number of constraints that ultimately render it of limited utility. An international NGO ombudsperson could be far enough removed from local politics to avoid these constraints. Some understanding of the interpersonal nature of politics in Suriname would, nevertheless, be indispensable to approaching the Nieuw Koffiekamp situation. Also, both the government and the companies involved are susceptible to international attention and pressure. Consequently, high profile involvement and internationalization of the dispute may play an important role in at least holding them to certain standards of conduct, although lasting solutions will involve the resolution of underlying issues of ownership of land and resources.

In its meeting with Cambior, the Forest Peoples Programme raised the following issues: 1) that Nieuw Koffiekamp must be considered as the legitimate owner of its land and resources; 2) that relocation should not take place without free and informed consent; and 3) that the companies must respect the community's decision-making process – consensus of the village meeting (krutu) – in particular, the lengthy nature of consensus-based decision-making. In connection with this, it was stressed that free and informed consent, by definition, entails turning over detailed information concerning the mining plans, alternatives and options, and time to consult with experts so that the information can be fully understood by the community. These issues are still highly relevant to determining an appropriate approach to the situation.

Cambior has shown that it is willing to share information. An ombudsperson could be especially useful in identifying technical expertise required to analyse and then communicate complex documents such as an EIA, Mineral Agreements and mining plans to the community in an understandable form. Providing information, if necessary, on larger issues related to industry and company performance, and analysing national legal regimes would also be useful. This 'translation' of technical documentation is essential if the community is to play a meaningful role in discussions about its future and, also, the foundation upon which any agreements must be laid. Consent is not valid unless both parties fully understand what they are consenting to. Nieuw Koffiekamp, in common with many other indigenous and tribal peoples, is primarily a non-literate community whose main mode of communication is verbal. Consequently, the manner in which information is presented to the community is extremely important. Information must be presented in a combination of written and verbal materials, which requires the resources to spend adequate amounts of time in the community. The community has specifically requested this type of support in the past.

If requested, the ombudsperson can also provide information to intergovernmental human rights bodies concerning the human rights issues raised by a particular situation. Also, and again if requested, the ombudsperson can assist in identifying legal expertise to file complaints with these bodies and compile supporting documentation of an anthropological, scientific or other nature. The latter is particularly important as, while the technical staff and members of intergovernmental organizations may be well versed in human rights, they may need additional information concerning the nature and extent of environmental degradation, and its impact on health standards, culture and socio-economic well-being. I have stressed that use of these measures should be requested by the communities in question because they will have to suffer the possible consequences that such action may entail.

In the case of MIGA or other World Bank involvement, analysis of EIAs and other documentation may be essential to ensuring that World Bank standards are complied with or that projects are evaluated in the proper context. The ombudsperson can also play a role in lobbying and informing MIGA and other multilateral institutions about the details of particular projects and how these projects could be improved, or whether multilateral involvement would be appropriate at all. The same can also be said for governmental guarantee agencies like EDC in Canada or the Overseas Private Investment Corporation (OPIC) in the US. Influencing these agencies may require access to high placed government officials that have the authority to intervene in their operations, or that may enact policy guidelines that require attention to human rights, social and environmental issues presently accorded little or no attention by these agencies.

Cambior has requested that a third party act as an intermediary in negotiations with the community. This role, provided it is also requested or agreed to by the community, would permit the NGO ombudsperson to act as a mediator or facilitator of discussions. If this approach is adopted, particular attention should be paid to avoid legitimizing the company's plans or operations. This can be addressed in part by agreed terms of reference for the ombudsperson's involvement, which should also make explicit reference to indigenous rights standards. The community has not specifically requested an intermediary, although I believe that it may be interested in this approach. However, a number of problems will be associated with this approach that may limit its chances of success. In particular, the community is, for good reasons based upon experience, very suspicious of outside intervention. It is more than likely that they will not appreciate the level of neutrality that may be required for mediation. They will expect that intervention, particularly from an NGO, is either for them or against them, and if it is not for them, it will rapidly be considered to be against them. This will substantially limit the extent of the community's participation in any discussions and will result in another dead-end. This perception and the result were part of the process involving the Special Mission. The community will also reject intervention that is in any way funded, even in appearance, by the government or the companies.

While the community will be looking for an advocate for its position, the companies will be looking for intervention that can break the impasse with the community. They will be very nervous of an organization that they perceive as radical or opposed to mining. They will be most comfortable with high-profile, mainstream organizations or academics that are seen to be rational, scientific and understanding of the problems of the business community. These same considerations will also be relevant to the government, who will prefer multilateral or intergovernmental organizations, provided involvement is on an informal level, as they will feel that they have more control over the situation. They will be more comfortable with organizations, or friendly government personnel, who are used to diplomatic interactions, are perceived to be sympathetic to the position of governments and will be unlikely to challenge government policy and fundamental assumptions, such as state sovereignty over natural resources. They will be most receptive to Caribbean- and South and North American-based organizations and will categorically reject any Dutch involvement, financial, technical or otherwise.

As noted above, Cambior refuses to accept that the community has the right to consent to relocation. This is problematic, as Cambior is ostensibly only interested in an intermediary that will further the negotiation of a relocation agreement, rather than address alternatives to relocation. Alternatives do exist that would permit the community to remain at its present location and, with a number of design modifications, also permit mining to go ahead. However, this would require that the company does not mine one of the larger deposits that is closest to the community and that it modifies its infrastructure and other plans in order to allow the community access to and enjoyment of its larger territory. It is unlikely that the company would agree to this. Also, the government cannot be ignored as a factor. It is doubtful that it would be supportive of outside intervention, as it would reduce its ability to manipulate and control the situation as well as expose its role in intimidating the community. Furthermore, it may result in a solution that is unacceptable from its position as self-proclaimed sole owner of natural resources.

Given the fundamental nature of the right to give or withhold consent to relocation in the larger scheme of indigenous rights, extreme caution must be exercised in deciding whether to engage as a mediator. Under these circumstances, an ombudsperson should attempt to facilitate dialogue aimed at securing acceptable terms of reference – if this is possible – for negotiations between the parties, which would explore the feasibility of alternatives to relocation. Once acceptable terms of reference have been agreed, the ombudsperson could then explore the possibility of playing a formal role in negotiations that would, as the prime objective, seek to minimize the power imbalances between the parties. This may mean acting as an adviser to the community in negotiations or locating other persons to act in this capacity. However, given the limited prospects for securing an acceptable basis for negotiations, it would be advisable to consider other approaches. One of these could be an 'eminent person' visit and report aimed at shaming the companies and government into seriously addressing the concerns of the community. This approach has been discussed previously and was agreed on by the community. Publicizing the abuses of the government and the companies has had an effect on their behaviour previously and can be expected to do so in the future. For best results, this approach should be used in conjunction with other forms of pressure, perhaps including resort to intergovernmental human rights procedures, which will complement the underlying objectives.

Another problem that may confront an ombudsperson is identifying legitimate community representatives. International indigenous rights standards provide for the recognition of indigenous authorities and representatives, chosen according to their own procedures. The ombudsperson should also observe these principles when interacting with indigenous communities. However, there may be more than one group or NGO claiming to represent a community and each may be supported by factions therein. Traditional authorities and groups within the community or larger society may be manipulated by the government or companies involved and/or may have contradictory positions. At one point with Nieuw Koffiekamp even those who had been working with the community for years were confused as to who was acting as representative. Both the Captain and the *Granman* were not trusted by the majority of the community and were accused of selling out. Others with dubious ties to the village were claiming to speak for it in the media. Local NGOs and others with a history of working with the community will be invaluable in identifying legitimate representatives or at least in separating out the various groups and their motivations. The best policy may be to involve all groups, other than those that are clearly extraneous or creatures of the government or companies.

Having noted the main issues concerning the suitability and potential role of an ombudsperson in the case study at hand, this section will conclude by noting a few points concerning an ombudsperson's function and organizational structure, applicable to both Nieuw Koffiekamp and situations involving indigenous peoples in general. First, the ombudsperson will need to employ or have access to persons knowledgeable about indigenous rights and issues. It is often assumed, erroneously, that indigenous peoples share the same characteristics as rural populations in general and, therefore, should be treated in the same way. Knowledge of and sensitivity to indigenous issues and rights are essential if the situation is to be analysed correctly and mistakes minimized. Consequently, an advisory board on indigenous issues should be established to guide the ombudsperson's activities, and specialized, experienced staff should be employed. Indigenous persons should be included in both categories.

Second, the ombudsperson will need to have the financial and temporal resources and personnel to gain a full understanding and appreciation of the situation. Indigenous peoples are not monolithic. Concerns, needs and rights awareness will vary from country to country, region to region and even community to community. There are commonalities, but it is essential to precisely determine the operative issues. The issue of land rights, for instance, is a common concern and the underlying cause of many disputes. However, the term 'land rights' can mean different things to different people and involves a whole range of other related factors relevant to the control of land and territories. International, national and especially indigenous law must all be evaluated and accounted for. Resource use patterns must also be documented. This is particularly important as indigenous peoples consider even the strongest international standards to be minimum standards that do not fully account for their rights. National laws in almost all cases do not fully conform to these standards. Even if they come close on paper, there are likely to be problems associated with implementation and/or enforcement. In short, the community's understanding of its territory and attendant social and political relationships must be given equal if not greater weight than competing expressions of rights to land. A complicating factor is that some communities may be reluctant to share information of this kind and various persons, both within the community and larger indigenous society, may have differing understandings of this. Nonetheless, failure to include indigenous understanding risks ignoring what may be one of the primary causes of the dispute.

Finally, the approach to be used by an ombudsperson in a given case will be dependent on the nature of the case at hand. Broadly defined, blanket prescriptions about the role of an ombudsperson will ultimately be counter-productive. The mandate must be flexible to account for various contingencies. In certain cases, it may be more appropriate to function as a publicist or to facilitate international support; in others, analysis and provision of information may be desired. It may also be the case that mediation is requested by the parties involved. In other cases, an ombudsperson may find it necessary to participate in or facilitate filing cases with intergovernmental organizations or to support domestic litigation. However, irrespective of the approach used, in all cases, it must be ultimately decided with the full participation and consent of the affected indigenous communities or people(s).

NOTES

1   Proposed OAS Declaration on the Rights of Indigenous Peoples, article 1 and International Labour Organization Convention No 169 Concerning Indigenous and Tribal Peoples in Independent Countries 1989, article 1. See, also, World Bank Operational Directive 4.20 on Indigenous Peoples (1991).

2   For a more detailed account of OAS Special Mission involvement and the Nieuw
     Koffiekamp situation in general, see OAS/UPD (1997).
3   Golden Star and Cambior intend to exploit at least five open pit mines in the Gross
     Rosebel concession, one of which will be less than 500 metres from Nieuw
     Koffiekamp. Cyanide leaching and a tailings facility will be employed, as will regular
     discharges of 'treated' wastes into the Saramacca River. There are at least five large
     maroon communities downstream of the entry point for the wastes.
4   Letter dated 23 May 1997 to Louis Gignac, CEO of Cambior from Forest Peoples
     Programme summarizing points discussed at meeting held in Montreal.
5   A number of houses were burned down in Nieuw Koffiekamp during the civil war and
     the neigbouring village of Gros was destroyed entirely. For more information on
     human rights during the military regime, see: IACHR (1985); IACHR (1983); Price
     (1995); Wako (1988).
6   The resolutions of the First *Gran Krutu* can be found in IWGIA (1996).
7   Discussion of the meeting with MIGA is based on my notes.

REFERENCES

Cambior (2000) *Gross Rosebel: Investor Information,*
     www.cambior.com/english/4_operations/gross.htm
Colchester, M (1995) *Forest Politics in Suriname*. Utrecht: International Books/World
     Rainforest Movement
De Ware Tijd (1997) 'Mine to Come in December', *De Ware Tijd* 30 September
De West (1997) 'Talks between Nieuw Koffiekamp, Task Force and Government at an
     Impasse', *De West*, 20 August
GSR (2000) *Form 10k, Annual Report pursuant to Section 13 or 15(d) of the Securities
     Exchange Act of 1934*, Golden Star Resources, 1 April
IACHR (1983) *Report on the Human Rights Situation in Suriname*, OAS/Ser.L/II.61 doc 6
     rev.1, Inter-American Commission on Human Rights, 5 October
IACHR (1985) *Second Report on the Human Rights Situation in Suriname*,
     OAS/Ser.L/V/II.66 doc 21 rev.1, 2 October, Inter-American Commission on
     Human Rights
IPS (1997) *Community Doesn't Want Mine*, Inter Press Service, 7 May 1983
IWGIA (1996) *Indigenous Affairs* 1, January, February, March, International Work Group
     for Indigenous Affairs
Kambel, E-R & MacKay, F (1999) *The Rights of Indigenous Peoples and Maroons in
     Suriname*, IWGIA Doc. 96. Copenhagen: IWGIA & Forest Peoples Programme
Minewatch/Moody, R (1995) *Swords in the Shield: Canada's Invasion of the Guyanas*, A
     Report for the Amerindian Peoples Association of Guyana
Moiwana '86 Human Rights Organization Suriname (1995) Press Release, 18
     September
Montreal Gazette (1995) 'On Guyanese river, people don't buy account of spill', *Montreal
     Gazette*, 30 August: A1–A2
OAS/UPD (1997) *Natural Resources, Foreign Concessions and Land Rights: A Report on the
     Village of Nieuw Koffiekamp*, Unit for Promotion of Democracy, General
     Secretariat, Organization of American States
Price, R (1983) *First Time. The Historical Vision of an Afro-American People*. Baltimore:
     Johns Hopkins Press
Price, R (1995) 'Executing Ethnicity: The Killings in Suriname', *Cultural Anthropology*
     10:437

Scholtens, B (1994) *Bosnegers en Overheid in Suriname* (Bush Negroes and the Government in Suriname). Paramaribo, Suriname: Minov

Wako, A (1988) *Summary or Arbitrary Executions. Report by the Special Rapporteur, Mr. Amos S. Wako, pursuant to Economic and Social Council Resolution 1987/60*, UN Doc. E/CN.4/1988/22 & Annex

World Resources Institute (1995) *Backs to the Wall in Suriname: Forest Policy in a Country in Crisis.* Washington, DC: World Resources Institute

Chapter 4

Environment, Human Rights and Mining Conflicts in Ghana

Douglas Korsah-Brown

THE LEGAL CONTEXT

This chapter comprises two sections. First, it briefly sketches international environmental law, focusing on environmental human rights, and considers various roles for an ombudsperson function. In addition, the chapter provides both a legal and situational overview of local legislation in Ghana on enforcement of environmental law and the available mechanisms for dispute control and settlement.

Then the chapter considers two complementary case studies – 'Ashanti Goldfields Company versus the People of Akrofuom' and 'Teberebie Goldfields Limited and others versus the People of Wassa Fiase and others'. Both cases centre on underlying conflicts between mining companies, the local people and the manner in which these conflicts were resolved. The chapter concludes by recommending the possible implementation of the ombudsperson function in promoting environmental human rights in Ghana.

ENVIRONMENTAL LAW

Environmental concerns have emerged as critical issues in international law only in recent decades. After adopting traditional approaches to a number of international conventions, the nations of the world woke up to very urgent issues at the Vienna Convention and Montreal Protocol, and adopted significant shifts in the enforcement and compliance of these treaties. The United Nations Security Council declared in January 1992 that, 'non-military sources of instability in the economic, social, humanitarian and ecological fields have become threats to peace and security' (Sands, 1993a). The 1992 United Nations Conference on Environment and Development (UNCED) became the watershed for the linkage of environmental protection and human security.

Before this epoch-making agreement, only three international human rights treaties expressly provided a link between the environment and human rights (ibid). These are the 1966 International Convention on Economic, Social and Cultural Rights (CSCR), the 1969 American Convention on Human Rights (ACHR) and the 1981 African Charter of Human and Peoples' Rights. However, environmental rights were not specifically categorized for specific rules of protection although they established a conceptual framework and approach, which would allow for the introduction of environmental concerns. For example, the African Charter provides in article 24 that, 'all peoples shall have the right to a generally safe and satisfactory environment favourable to their development'.

This general thrust is the position of various statutory provisions currently in Ghana and underlies the socio-economic context of Africa. The 1989 San Salvador Protocol to the ACHR declares in Article 11, that:

1   *Everyone shall have the right to live in a healthy environment and to have access to basic public services.*
2   *The State Parties shall promote the protection, preservation and improvement of the environment.*

The ACHR and its San Salvador Protocol represented a clearer statement of the linkage between the environment and human rights by distinguishing between the extent of the right of the individual and the obligation of the state. Unfortunately, however, the 1989 Convention Concerning Indigenous and Tribal Peoples in Independent Countries never came into force. This Convention integrated environmental obligations and rights relating natural resources to traditional human rights and fundamental freedoms. It proposed the adoption of special measures to safeguard, protect and preserve the environment of indigenous and tribal peoples; and the adoption of measures to safeguard the rights of these peoples to the natural resources pertaining to their lands, including use, management and conservation of these resources.

According to Fatma-Zohra Ksentini (1995), poverty and underdevelopment are the main concepts of the right to development conceived as a human right. The right to environment, perceived in its entire dimension, includes the human aspects of the right to sustainable and sound development. Poverty has adverse effects on the environment and a degraded environment worsens the problems of underdevelopment. Underdevelopment also impairs the realization of the right to development and other fundamental rights of individuals, groups and peoples. In addition, poor populations, the underprivileged, minority groups and indigenous peoples are most affected since they are most vulnerable and need to be protected from ecological risks and environmental degradation (Sun Lin and Kurukulasuriya, 1995).

Within the context of the right to development and a satisfactory environment is also the notion that the inability of the 'agents of development' to inform and involve the community in the decision-making process carries risks to the environment in that the community cannot fully respond, but merely become passive recipients of aid and projects (ibid). Without processes of information and participation, any form of development would merely be institutionalizing undemocratic forces and reinforcing the very economic structures of exploitation and repression that are responsible for poverty and underdevelopment (ibid).

It has been argued that these concepts do not necessarily entail conferring rights enforceable through legal proceedings but rather ascribe value or status to interests and claims of particular entities (Birnie and Boyle, 1992, p194). By so doing, they seek to force law makers and institutions to take account of these interests – to accord them a priority which they might not otherwise enjoy and to make them part of the context for interpreting legal rules.

This debate leads to interpretation of the right to a decent environment as a procedural right (ibid). The approach ensures that individuals' rights of access to information, to participation in decision-making processes and to administrative and judicial remedies are secured. This procedural approach avoids anthropocentricity to the extent that such rights can be exercised on behalf of the environment or its non-human components (ibid).

The argument that poverty is environmentally destructive can be countered, however, by the notion that wealth also significantly contributes to environmental degradation. This is directly related to the concept of over-consumption in the North, which has a dominant influence on the South's under-consumption and hence poverty. Of relevance is the fact that wealth has contributed in the past and continues to create problems of waste, pollution and inefficiency in the use of resources. The international community has not, however, defined in practical terms the threshold below which the level of environmental quality must fall before a breach of the individual human right will have occurred or above which the level of environmental quality must rise to occasion excess of environmental rights (Sands, 1993b).

It must be noted that the notion of the indivisibility and interdependence of all human rights – whether civil, political, economic, social or cultural – is critical to the link between the right to development and environmental rights. The claim to the right to a satisfactory environment cannot be separated from the claim to the right to develop in its individual and collective aspects as well as in its national and international dimensions (Sun Lin and Kurukulasuriya, 1995).

Therefore, recognizing various commitments of the nations of the world expressed in many international agreements geared towards environmental protection, and of the competing demands on the right to development, the right to sustainable development derives logically from the right to develop. This idea encompasses a whole web and tissue of rights and obligations of all persons and living organisms to ensure that the resources they depend on for their existence are utilized in a way that does not jeopardize the very existence of any sections of the community. This community includes the whole range of organisms, which depend on each other for their existence.

Ghanaian law

Courts in Ghana are reluctant to enforce principles in international law, even when Ghana is a signatory and the government has ratified agreements. In one case, the Supreme Court refused to enforce human rights principles to which the country was signatory on the grounds that the provisions were merely enumerated in a solemn preamble or affirmation by the President and this did not constitute enforceable obligations (Akoto, 1961). The situation seems to be shifting slightly now but more political, judicial and legal space is needed to assert these concepts.

Ghana's 1992 constitution makes no direct reference to the environment and thus creates room for ambiguity. It is the opinion of the writer that greater assertiveness on the part of NGOs and other actors could set in motion the dynamism needed for the judiciary's appreciation and protection of the environment.

Article 15 (1) of the constitution reads, 'The dignity of all persons shall be inviolable'. Applying a larger meaning to this provision, its construction could include violation as a result of environmental damage even though this construction promotes an anthropocentric approach to the protection of the environment.

The constitution directly refers to protecting the environment in the Directive Principles of State Policy Chapter Six, Article 36 (9), 'The state shall take appropriate measures needed to protect and safeguard the national environment for posterity; and shall seek co-operation with other states and bodies for purposes of protecting the wider international environment for mankind.' However, debate continues over whether the Directive Principles are enforceable or justiciable. On the one hand, it is argued that the Constitution does not say it is specifically enforceable as it does for the fundamental human rights (in Chapter Five of the constitution). On the other hand, it is also argued that the principles 'shall guide all citizens' and therefore they are justiciable. These are part of the many grey areas of Ghanaian law and there are no locally decided cases. Although there are many decided cases in other jurisdictions, they are merely of persuasive value. The balance of probabilities, however, tilts in favour of enforcing these provisions and therefore provides opportunities for environmental groups to undertake legal advocacy to develop the law for ensuring environmental sustainability.

In fact, this is the only provision on the constitution that minces no words in the protection of the environment. Other provisions making slight hints are Article 36 Section (2) (e) which provides that 'The state shall in particular, take all the necessary steps to establish a sound and healthy economy whose underlying principles shall include the recognition that the most secure democracy is the one that assures the basic necessities of life for its people as a fundamental duty.' Indeed, by implication this includes a construction that allows for a right to a healthy environment.

The chapter on Fundamental Human Rights and Freedoms (Chapter Five, Article 33 Sections 5) states that:

> *The rights, duties, declarations and guarantees relating to fundamental human rights and freedoms specifically mentioned in this chapter shall not be regarded as excluding others not specifically mentioned which are considered to be inherent in a democracy and intended to secure the freedom and dignity of man.*

This omnibus clause, on a more positive note, can allow for an interpretation that includes the right to a healthy environment.

If there is difficulty in finding clear and express links between human rights and the environment, the Ghanaian courts found it even more difficult enforcing environmental obligations. In the case of CFC Construction Company versus Accra City Council, the plaintiffs brought an action against the defendants for damages and an interim injunction to restrain them, their agents or servants from dumping garbage and refuse near CFC property (GLR 496, 1964).

This refuse caused offensive and pestilential smell from vapours in the surrounding area and the stench emanating from the refuse seriously interfered with their comfort and well-being. Even though the court conceded that the plaintiffs' comfort and well-being had been interfered with, it held that it would not impose a restriction on a statutory body, as this would prevent the performance of a statutory function. This position has not changed since then, though it seems the courts may be more predisposed to enforcing the common law rules on nuisance on property of private individuals and companies.

However, the court process is highly discouraging for citizens to go through. Apart from the onerous burden of producing evidence in these instances under the common law, the judicial process in Ghana is archaic and is very time consuming and expensive. Therefore, a specialized body such as the ombudsperson, and more particularly the Commission for Human Rights and Administrative Justice, can provide needed back up to the process of ensuring environmental sustainability through legal means.

It is interesting to note that an erroneous impression has been created since the advent of the 1992 constitution, that NGOs and other citizen groups need to be specifically empowered to enforce environmental obligations in our courts. In fact, this need not be so. Chapter 1, Article 2 (1) states:

> 2. (1) A person who alleges that
> (a) an enactment or anything contained in or done under the authority of that or any other enactment or;
> (b) any act or omission of any person is inconsistent with, or is in contravention of a provision of this constitution, may bring an action in the Supreme Court for a declaration to that effect. 2) The Supreme Court shall, for the purposes of a declaration under clause (1) of this article, make such orders and give such directions as it may consider appropriate for a giving effect, or enabling effect to be given, to the declaration.

Thus, the appropriate question that needs to be asked is 'what provision of this constitution is the said act or omission inconsistent with?' An answer to this may be found in Chapter 4, Article 11, which states that Ghanaian law comprises the constitution, Parliamentary acts, the existing law and the common law.

Thus, a combination of the provisions on enforcing the 1992 constitution and a definition of the laws of Ghana under the same constitution will permit citizen suits to any extent, whether under the existing law, or the common law, or under any enactment made under the constitution.

Mineral development

The Ghanaian Government places a high priority on developing its mineral resources in such a manner to ensure that the maximum possible benefits accrue to the nation from exploitation of minerals. This barely has any environmental undertones and therefore the environment is relegated to the background. To avert any competition in the ownership of minerals, the state has interfered with land ownership rights. While ownership of land is vested in titleholders, it actually refers to anything upon the land. In contrast, any mineral that is found in any given land belongs to the state. The Minerals and Mining Law PNDCL 153 Section (1) states:

> *Every mineral in its natural state in, under or upon any land in Ghana, rivers streams, water-courses throughout the exclusive economic zone and any area covered by territorial waters or continental shelf is the property of the Republic of Ghana and shall be vested in the Provisional National Defence Council (ie government) for and on behalf of the people of Ghana.*

Furthermore, the government will grant any company 'exclusive rights to work, develop and produce the mineral in the area in question'.

There are three main prohibitions:

> *The Company shall not conduct any operations in a sacred area and shall not, without the prior consent in writing of the minister conduct any operations within 50 yards of any building, installation, reservoir or dam, public road, railway or area appropriated for railway, in an area occupied by a market, burial grounds/cemetery or government office, or situated within a town or village or set apart for, used, appropriated or dedicated to a public purpose.*

It is clear from these prohibitions that there are no clear objectives based solely on protecting the environment. The reference to a sacred area is more cultural than environmental even though such traditionally reserved areas had environmental objectives as well. If environmental protection was the purpose of this prohibition, then it would have made more sense to prohibit mining operations in areas such as those harbouring threatened and endemic species, or steep slopes, to mention a few.

In contrast, provisions for protecting the environment are couched in a non-prohibitive way. For example:

> *The company shall conduct all of its operations hereunder with due diligence, efficiency, safety and economy, in accordance with good mining practices and in a proper and workmanlike manner, observing sound technical and engineering principles using appropriate modern and effective equipment, machinery, materials and methods, and pay particular regard to conservation of resources, reclamation of land and environmental protection generally.*

Other provisions call on the company to conduct its operations in a manner consistent with good commercial mining practices so as not to interfere unreasonably with vegetation or the customary rights and privileges of persons to hunt and reserve game, gather firewood for domestic purposes or to collect snails. These provisions are difficult to enforce and the evidence needed to enforce them is not simple but burdensome. Where provisions clearly intend the protection of the environment, other problems arise in terms of definition.

'The company shall adopt all necessary and practical precautionary measures to prevent undue pollution of rivers and other potable water and to ensure that such pollution does not cause harm or destruction to human or animal life or fresh water fish or vegetation.' How can one define the words 'practical precautionary measures' and 'undue pollution'?

The Chief Inspector of Mines is empowered to ensure the safety and health of persons, protection of the environment and prevention of destruction of potable water. Thus it seems that where a community is of the opinion that the health of its citizens will be affected or their source of drinking water is being polluted, they may inform the Chief Inspector of Mines who can take remedial action. However, this is a function that largely has been left to other bodies such as the Environmental Protection Agency and the Local Government Authority in the area. However it is only fairly recently that these institutions have been to a certain extent empowered to address problems of pollution in the communities. In the case of the local authorities, they are yet to have sufficient resources to be able to adequately deal with such environmental problems.

Again, in its operations, the company shall take practical steps 'to prevent damage to adjoining farms and villages and to avoid damage to trees, crops, buildings, structures and other property in the lease area; to the extent, however, that any such damage is necessary or unavoidable, the company shall pay fair and reasonable compensation.' No definite procedure has been laid out except for disagreements between the government and the company, that is the parties to the agreement.

In the determination of what is fair and reasonable, companies have resorted to the employment of valuers from the Lands Commission which makes such assessments. However, the relationship between the company and the citizens of an affected community is not on an equal basis. Most of the affected citizens are poor peasant farmers who depend directly on the land. Since the process of assessment is fraught with delays, they have a very weak bargaining position. Such communities cannot therefore afford to engage the services of competent resource personnel to handle dealings with corporate bodies on their behalf. An ombudsperson function that, among other things, addresses the needs of the community in asserting their right against powerful corporate bodies will help to ensure that environmental rights are protected.

In disputes between government and company, provision is made for settlement under Ghanaian law or through the process of settlement by arbitration under the Arbitration Rules of the United Nations Commission on International Trade Law (the 'UNCITRAL Rule').

There are other opportunities for reviewing environmental problems or conflicts through the EIA procedures (Ghana Environmental Protection Agency, 1995). This is one of the environmental management tools that has potential to contribute towards the sustainable use of environmental resources and avoid conflicts. The purpose of environmental impact assessment is to: (a) support the goals of environmental management and sustainable development; (b) integrate environmental management and economic decisions at the earliest stages of planning an undertaking, programme or investment; (c) predict the consequences of a proposed undertaking from the environmental, social and cultural perspective and to develop plans to mitigate any adverse impacts; and finally (d) provide avenues for the involvement of the public, proponents, private and government agencies in the assessment and review of proposed undertakings.

This is a tool that, all things being equal, could address and prevent environmental problems and conflicts associated with proposed undertakings. The difficulty arises in the fact that the parties are not equal: being inadequately resourced, they are unable to either discuss the issues or negotiate on equal terms.

The process involved in ensuring environmental safety and harmony is very confusing and involves many actors. This, in turn, does not make it open and transparent. Indeed, one of the provisions of the contract between government and company stipulates as follows:

> *The government shall treat all information supplied by the company hereunder as confidential for a period of five years from the date of submission of such information or upon termination of this agreement which ever is sooner and shall not reveal such information to third parties except with written consent of the company which consent shall not be unreasonably withheld* (Minerals Commission).

Indeed, these contradictory processes do not favour environmental protection. Its effect is to discourage the assertion of the rights of communities and where asserted make them very expensive. Communities are therefore left with fewer choices available to redress environmental problems or conflicts over land or water access rights.

Apart from the Chief Inspector of Mines, there are other statutory bodies that are responsible for mining operations in the country. These are the Minerals Commission, which principally grants all licences in the nature of mining, and the Environmental Protection Agency (EPA), which is expected to be the final authority in all environmental problems arising out of any industrial activity. The newly created Water Resources Commission will be responsible for all matters affecting the utilization of water.

The ombudsperson function

The disparity in human and financial resources among stakeholders creates such an uneven balance in the negotiating process that equity cannot be achieved. Rather than the protection of rights, profit becomes the main motive driving the whole process. With an expanded definition of human rights to include the environment, appropriate mechanisms and institutions need to be put in place.

The ombudsperson function varies in its particularity from country to country, but in all places, it is the modern day court of equity. In considering environmental human rights, care must be taken not to take a narrow perspective, since the question of a social and poverty arbitrator is obviously interlinked with that of the environment. In other words, any envisaged function must adopt a holistic approach, as there are clear links between environment, poverty/wealth and development.

Ghana's ombudsperson is the Commissioner for Human Rights and Administrative Justice. Article 218 of the constitution states some of the functions:

- to investigate complaints of violations of fundamental rights and freedoms, injustice, corruption, abuse of power and unfair treatment of any person by a public officer in exercising of his official duties;
- to investigate complaints concerning the functioning of the public services commission, the administrative organs of the state, the Armed Forces, the Police Service and the Prisons Service in so far as the complaints relate to the failure to achieve a balanced structuring of those services or equal access by all to the recruitment of those services or fair administration in relation to those services;
- to investigate complaints concerning practices and actions by persons, private enterprises and other institutions where these complaints allege violations of fundamental rights and freedoms under this constitution;
- to take appropriate action to call for the remedying, correction and reversal of instances specified through such means as fair, proper and effective.

Such means include:

- negotiation and compromise between the parties concerned;
- legal action to secure the termination of the offending action or conduct, or the abandonment or alteration of the offending procedures;
- restraint of the enforcement of such legislation or regulation by challenging its validity if the offending action or conduct is sought to be justified by subordinate legislation or regulation which is unreasonable.

From these constitutional provisions the main question, it would seem, is what definition the courts and legislature would give to human rights.

Unfortunately, the Ghanaian courts have yet to define human rights to include environmental rights. The constitution in Chapter 5 specifically provides for, among other things, economic rights, educational rights, cultural rights and practices, women's rights and children's rights. However, it does not mention specifically environmental rights. The closest it comes to environmental rights is the provision for the Respect for Human Dignity which when combined with cultural rights could imply environmental rights.

Since the law is not static but dynamic, it would require some legal advocacy and some purposive, but not strict, interpretation on the part of the courts to ensure that a wider and larger meaning is given to the concept of human rights.

GHANA CASE STUDIES

Ashanti Goldfields vs. The People of Akrofoum

Ashanti Goldfields Company Limited (AGC) is based in Obuasi in the Ashanti Region of the Republic of Ghana and owns one of the largest goldmines in the world. Ashanti Goldfields operates a lease, which was created in 1994 and expires in 2024, covering an area close to 474 square kilometres within the principal gold belt in Ghana. The main shareholders are Lonrho Plc, Government of Ghana, The Bank of New York and the Ghana Cocoa, Coffee and Peanut Farmers Association.

The village of Akrofuom falls within the concession area of AGC. After battling with AGC for a decent water supply for 30 years, villagers realized that polite discussions were not making any headway (Friends of the Earth, 1996, p4). On 9 February 1996, about 200 angry young men and women, waving rifles and pistols over their heads, descended on the Gyambuou open pit to disrupt mining operations. The workers fled for their lives and a few hours later the rioters returned to their town triumphant, having seized four of the company's vehicles and forced the AGC's arm into serious negotiations.

The River Jimi is now brown from sediment washed down from mining operations at Obuasi some 10 kilometres away. This river's tributary, the Sibiri, is also polluted. Halfway along the road to Obuasi, the river has been dammed by AGC. On the Akrofuom side of the dam, the water is heavily polluted with signboards warning, 'Don't swim, Don't fish, Don't drink'. For the people of Akrofuom, there is no such luxury as treated water. On the other side, the water passes through a treatment plant and is sent back through pipes to Obuasi. The AGC merely agreed to repair the borehole pump, which was installed by the government in the 1970s. However, according to an official of the Adansi West District Assembly, 'The people have now become enlightened and they are thinking differently'. 'Why shouldn't they provide the fuel for the borehole,' fumes the local school inspector and resident of Akrofuom, Mr Oduro Fosu, 'They polluted the river in the first place so they should provide the full alternative.'

According to Ashanti Goldfields policy, AGC will provide new alternative supplies of water, or improve existing facilities in concession areas if sources of drinking water are likely to be adversely affected by its operations. Furthermore, AGC will ensure that the alternative supplies will, at the time of installation, be of a quality comparable with that of the best supplies currently available in the locality. However, contrary to its own policies, AGC demanded from the people of Akrofuom payment for fuelling and regular maintenance for the water supply system.

Therefore, despite the fact that water is now flowing from the taps and peace and stability appears to have returned to the town, there is still underlying resentment and discontent. This is fuelled further by the fact that the borehole water is often discoloured, especially after heavy rain, and tastes salty.

In the negotiations with the people of Akrofuom represented by their District Chief Executive, the highest political officer in the district, the Presiding

Member of the District Assembly (the 'speaker' of the local parliament) and the member of parliament for the area, AGC agreed to undertake immediate repairs to the water system of Adansi-Akrofuom and continue with regular maintenance for a period of two years. They are also to ensure that the water quality in the borehole meets the Ghana Water & Sewerage standards. The District Assembly agreed to continue with maintenance for a further period of not less than two years. Until the community was linked to the national grid, AGC agreed to provide the fuel required to power the borehole and pumping station in order to mechanize the system of water supply.

As part of the general agreement, the District Assembly is to extend the power from the pumping station to supply the streetlights and the Akrofuom Chief's palace and also provide for the salaries of the pump attendant and the watchman. Finally, AGC was to provide additional standpipes to five sections of Akrofuom.

It is essential to note that before the problems culminated in a conflict, the people of Akrofuom took their drinking water from the Sibiri River, which was free. They therefore had strong incentives to keep the water pure, unpolluted, flowing, drinkable and to prevent degradation of the area. Thus, to be asked to contribute to the maintenance of the water system was unacceptable since this meant new obligations to the people of Akrofuom. If the people of Akrofuom initially requested piped water, they would have appreciated the need to pay for maintenance. Furthermore, the pipe-borne water supply system had been in existence since 1969. Since water from the Sibiri River was seen as a better alternative, the people felt no need to have the piped system repaired when it broke down for lack of maintenance.

These conflicting views over water preferences stem from differences in the perception of development. The company presents a very traditional perspective of development, in which economic values are more important than virtually any others. The community, on the other hand, interestingly presents a very contemporary approach to development, in which environmental, cultural and social values are as important as economic values.

The agreement between the parties was a memorandum of understanding among three parties: the Ashanti Goldfields Company, the Akrofuom Community and the local authority in the area, the Adansi West District Assembly. It seems that the community was not represented by legal counsel since the second Akrofuom representative, an elder, merely left a thumbprint on the document with no evidence of a jurat clause, contrary to statute. Other members of this party were the chief and a youth representative.

The Ashanti Goldfields Company has a long history of natural resource exploitation and conflicts in the industry. Since its first concession was granted in 1897, the AGC has been mining and processing gold at Obuasi. Until the late 1980s, when the company started taking steps to rectify the environmental assault that its operations had unleashed, AGC's entire period of operation had been carried out with gross abuse of the human and physical environment at Obuasi.

Sadly, such practices were standard to all mining areas and companies in the country before the Environmental Impact Assessment Procedure was finalized a few years ago. In fact, a 1991 report of the Assembly's environmental sub-committee stated:

> *People are dying in the District and what caused such deaths is not known because no autopsy was done. Others have developed pneumoconiosis, skin rashes, frequent unexplained diarrhoea, eye diseases, and loss of weight that cannot be explained. The District Health Management Team (DHMT) has every reason to make the committee believe that most of the above related diseases are caused by pollution, either of the atmosphere or water.*

The birth of the new democratic dispensation in 1992 permitted communities to assert their rights in areas that hitherto were regarded as taboo. By confronting the management of AGC they were doing what they were prevented from doing decades ago by totalitarian governments.

Teberebie Goldfields Ltd and others vs. The People of Wassa Fiase and others

Teberebie Goldfields Ltd (TGL) operates in the Wassa Fiase Traditional Area of the Western Region of the Republic of Ghana. Its area of operation covers about 42 square kilometres. The main shareholders are the Pioneer group of companies headquartered in Boston, Massachusetts. More than 50 companies have either rights to mine or are prospecting for gold in the region as a whole. Other goldmining companies in the area include the Goldfields Ghana Limited, the Ghanaian Australian Goldfields Limited and Billiton Bogoso Gold Limited.

Wassa Fiase covers part of the concession area (Friends of the Earth, 1997, pp12–13). Teberebie is a small community of about 2,000 people who are mainly farmers. Confrontation arose when farmers whose activities fell within the concession area had to be moved, preferably on terms acceptable to both parties.

Negotiations between the Wassa West District Assembly, the overseeing authority, TGL and the community wrought an agreement spelling out the terms of the resettlement. The mining company was to provide the following in the resettlement area: 168 housing units made up of 128 single space units and 40 double space units; a school complex containing a nursery and a junior secondary; a community centre; a clinic; and a market. The new facilities would include potable water, access roads, toilets and electricity.

The Teberebie Chief signed the agreement on behalf of his people. However, an examination of the document indicated that he could neither read nor write, as he thumbprinted his signature. Doubts arose as to whether he therefore fully understood what he was doing and the implications it would have for his people, together with suspicions that the gold mining company was dealing unfairly with the inhabitants of Teberebie. The document further ignored vital issues concerning the development of Teberebie. It failed to make provisions for the expansion of the community or for the erection of new structures for the rapidly increasing population. It did not address other economic and social issues, which must be dealt with to make life worth living for the people.

The agreement stipulated that the 168 housing units would be ready within 12 months. Nearly seven years after the agreement was signed, however, the company has still not reached that target. Moreover, the housing units have no kitchens or bathrooms. Instead, TGL constructed communal kitchens and bathhouses. People wait in single-file lines for their turn to cook or wash. The concept of privacy has been brutally and involuntarily discarded.

The Chief's wife, too, joins the long queue at the kitchen, waiting to prepare meals for the Chief. When she has cooked the food, she will return to the 'palace' built by TGL for the Chief. It has three bedrooms, but no hall, no kitchen, no toilet, no bathroom. Large cracks have developed in almost all the houses, attributed to the frequent dynamite-blasting common in mining areas. The people fear that a storm will cause their small, cracked oven-like houses to collapse on them.

In addition, TGL has not provided a clinic, although they have managed to build a well-equipped clinic just a few metres away to serve workers of the mining company. Local people do not have access to it. They must travel 8 kilometres to Tarkwa for medical services. Teberebie still lacks other items laid down in the agreement, such as electricity, a market, access roads and a community centre.

The company has constructed two boreholes for the 2,000 residents of Teberebie but only one is functioning. With clean water in short supply, many have resorted to fetching water from streams that are reportedly heavily polluted with deadly chemicals used in the mining process such as arsenic and cyanide. Many inhabitants complain of skin rashes, which they attribute to the contaminated water they drink. Although no tests have been conducted to confirm this, the disease was not prevalent in the area before surface mining began.

The Teberebie community is usually engulfed in dust generated by mining activities, except when it rains. Then the people worry about flooding. There are no drainage systems and the slightest downpour creates large amounts of standing water in the community.

At the same time, the people protest that TGL refuses to employ them but goes as far as Sekondi and Accra to recruit labourers. 'We have able-bodied men and women here, capable of weeding, carrying sand and doing other menial jobs associated with mining,' fumed an old man '…perhaps the company feels the financial benefits they have given the people are enough compensation.' During the past seven years, the people of Teberebie have received 8 million cedis in royalties. In other words, each of the 2,000 current residents has received a total of 4,000 cedis (at current rates, worth less than US$2.00).

With the rapid expansion of mining activities in the area, a new mining company, Goldfields Ghana Ltd, obtained another concession. A public hearing was organized on the environmental impact of the activities of Goldfields Ghana Ltd. The Deputy Minister of Mines and Energy chaired the hearing. Also present was the Deputy Minister of Environment Science and Technology. There were representatives led by the Chiefs of the particularly affected communities, namely, Atuobo and Akontase. The attendance of top-level politicians demonstrates the extent of political interest in the mining operations in the region. The Chair had earlier cautioned the gathering not to regard the hearing as confrontational.

The basis of the complaints of the communities at this hearing was that the criteria used to determine eligibility for resettlement and relocation were very unsatisfactory. Out of about 18,000 people affected, only 3,300 were selected for compensation. Family members living in family houses were not catered for, as only family heads received a meagre sum of ¢1.75 million, which at the time of the hearing in December 1996 had a dollar value of US$1,800.

Additionally, compensation was made without considering the needs of tenants or the number of rooms in the buildings. The only people considered were farmland owners and building owners (landlords). The citizens also complained that, without first providing alternatives, the company demolished existing facilities like schools and community centres. The Deputy Chief Imam (Muslim spiritual head) also protested against the proposed alternative housing designs.

The hearing also revealed some differences among the members of the various communities. A group calling itself 'The Concerned Citizens of Kontase and Atuabo' alleged that at certain stages of the negotiations, the various community committees set up to negotiate with the company no longer represented their views and also lacked negotiation skills necessary to match those of the company's team. They advocated for people with the relevant skills and knowledge to be on their team but this suggestion led to a misunderstanding with the Chiefs and elders. Subsequent presentations clearly indicated general dissatisfaction with the activities of the company, the consequences of which were bound to lead to destitution and civil strife, the obvious outcomes of social dislocation.

The officials of the company also mentioned that, even though they had started part payment of compensation to affected individuals, some of the citizens collected the money only to relocate themselves on different parts of the concession. Other issues not fully dealt with but raised included CO_2 gas emissions and leachate monitoring.

To protest, the Chiefs representing their people wore traditional mourning clothes and undertook a demonstration through the principal streets of Tarkwa, the district capital. Meanwhile there was deadlock in a number of negotiations with the mining companies.

A negotiating committee was then created to attempt to resolve the problems. To date, this negotiating committee has not achieved any results mutually acceptable to the parties. Only trivial changes have been made to the agreements with the communities and tension is high.

Discussion

In both case studies, the communities in question had been abandoned to their fate, especially considering the history of mining in the country. Had they not taken the law into their own hands, they would not have achieved what they wanted and nobody would have fought their battle. In both cases, it seems there was no clear machinery for either resolving or avoiding disputes, or for ensuring a smooth implementation. It would have been valuable and useful to have a clear process for ensuring that all parties receive fair treatment. In both cases, requisite counsel did not represent the communities solely because of the immense expense involved.

It is clear that the negotiations did not take particular consideration of the community's social structure, particularly the structure and size of the family, the role of elders and the mode of ownership. The presumption that the families undertook consultation within their communities was also forcefully rebutted in the events of the public hearing.

In cases such as these, provisions must be made to ensure that communities have access to the resources required to negotiate effectively and in consultation with all relevant actors. Moreover, the real role of the Valuation Officer is not clear. Is he or she neutral or working for the company? The status of the two committees set up to resolve the disputes is also unclear. Since their composition is government heavy, most communities in such a situation would feel coerced into accepting some of the decisions.

In fact, it is clear that the government has conflicting interests. It is interested in the revenue from taxes that the company would provide; yet it is also supposed to promote the development of the communities. It cannot, therefore, be a neutral party to any such negotiation. Moreover, public officers can be influenced and/or bribed. Many communities thus have reservations about the finality of the decisions of such negotiating committees. In so far as there is no transparency and wide consultation, many decisions are held in doubt. Communities have the right to challenge the decisions in court, but as has been observed, the legal option is not a credible one for all communities. Having a meticulous knowledge of the social structure of the communities can ensure that a consultation process is not limited to the Chief and some of his elders but reaches the wider segments of the communities as a whole. This is what a resource person can bring to the process.

An independent, international ombudsperson is therefore of particular interest to the environmental community. This is where the ombudsperson function can be enlarged to encompass all equity issues linked to the environment, that is, poverty and underdevelopment. Such an expanded role will not only ensure a holistic approach to the concept of environmental human rights but will incorporate the new concepts of development into the whole process.

In this regard, a necessary consideration is the state of domestic law, for this will certainly influence the role of such an ombudsperson function. In Ghana, the dilemma is that the government has barely domesticated any of the conventions and treaties it has so far ratified. That makes it burdensome for any NGO, national or international, to attempt any legal advocacy if the impact is to be felt by the communities that are the intended beneficiaries. This is not to say that NGOs must not venture into legal advocacy. However, it is important to keep the short- and long-term objectives in proper context in this case.

In the short term, any process must aim at building the capacity of existing institutions such as the Commission of Human Rights and Administrative Justice. This should enable them to handle issues of environmental human rights and other social issues. Within this same context, NGOs with a legal and environmental orientation would also be capacitated to ensure that communities have access to the requisite human resources needed in dealing with rich and powerful companies. They would be acting as legal aid organizations assisting communities whose livelihoods are threatened.

It is important to note that these issues have traditionally not belonged to the domain of the ombudsperson, and therefore capacity building is essential in order to handle the environmental rights issues as they come up for resolution. This option has the advantage of creating a healthy synergy between the Commission and NGOs in ensuring effective change in the environmental and development process. Furthermore, within the context of emerging institutions at the district level, environmental management committees of the District Assemblies could greatly benefit from such training.

This approach also reflects the procedural nature of environmental human rights at the moment. The quest for environmental impact assessment (EIA), information access and so on will become the basis for any campaign for environmental justice, equity and sustainability. In the long term, Ghanaian NGOs will advocate the codification of treaties ratified by government and fight for the rights of communities through legal advocacy among other methods.

CONCLUSION

The concept of environmental human rights is relatively new in Ghana and manifests itself primarily as a procedural right. The 1992 constitution of Ghana provides some legal space for enviro-legal advocacy, which can be the basis for strengthening these procedural rights in the short term and constructing substantive rights in the long term. To achieve this, it has been suggested that the best approach is to expand and build the capacities of existing institutions such as the Commission of Human Rights and Administrative Justice. The installation of NGOs in the role of 'watchdogs', with both a legal and environmental orientation, would provide facilitators who would work synergistically with governmental institutions at the community level.

NOTE

1   The ten-member committee consisted of: Chairman/schedule officer, Regional Coordinating Director, Regional Officer of Environmental Protection Agency, Regional Officer of Town & Country Planning Department, Regional Officer of Land Valuation Board, Representative of the District Chief Executive, Senior Inspector of Mines in Tarkwa, Representative of Communities (Atuabo, Mandekrom Sofo Mensah), Representative of Stool (Apinto Stool), Representative of Mining Company (Goldfields Fields Ghana Limited) and a member of the Regional Coordinating Council.

REFERENCES

Birnie, P and Boyle, A (1992) *International Law and the Environment.* Oxford: Clarendon Press

CFC Construction Company vs. Accra City Council (1964) GLR 496

Fatma-Zohra, K (1995) 'Human Rights, Environment and Development', in Sun Lin and L Kurukulasuriya (eds) *UNEP's New Way Forward: Environmental Law and Sustainable Development.* Nairobi: United Nations Environment Programme

Friends of the Earth (1996) FOELINE No 4 (April–June). London: Friends of the Earth

Friends of the Earth (1997) FOELINE No 8 (April–June). London: Friends of the Earth

Ghana Environmental Protection Agency (1995) *Environmental Impact Assessment Procedures* 17. General Framework Contract for Prospecting and Mining Companies. Accra: Minerals Commission

Re Akoto and 7 others (1961) GLR 523

Sands, P (1993a) 'Enforcing Environmental Security: The Challenges of Compliance with International Obligations', *Journal of International Affairs* 46(2):367–390

Sands, P (1993b) 'Human Rights Aspects of Environmental Law', *Inter-rights Bulletin* 7(4)

Sun Lin and Kurukulasuriya (eds) (1995) *UNEP's New Way Forward: Environmental Law and Sustainable Development.* Nairobi: United Nations Environment Programme

Conflicts Over Transnational Oil and Gas Development Off Sakhalin Island in the Russian Far East: A David and Goliath Tale

Erika Rosenthal

INTRODUCTION

In the autumn of 2000, Russian environmental groups won a precedent-setting lawsuit convincing the Supreme Court to order the government and transnational companies to comply with environmental law – even where billion dollar oil projects were concerned.

The project that triggered the suit was the Exxon-led Sakhalin-1 oil development. The State Committee on Environmental Protection had denied Exxon's drilling permit citing the company's insistence on dumping toxic drilling wastes at sea, which has been illegal in Russia since oil pollution caused the collapse of the Caspian Sea fishery in the 1970s. Undeterred, Exxon went to the Prime Minister and quietly arranged a waiver of the inconvenient law. The collusion was discovered. Environmentalists sued. The judiciary found its spine and enforced the rule of law. Exxon loudly threatened to withdraw investment from the country.

The following April Vladimir Putin was elected president. Several days before the election he had a well publicized meeting with transnational oil company executives. In May, he abolished the offending environmental agency. Meanwhile, Exxon quietly agreed to re-injection of drilling wastes, the internationally accepted best practice, and received its drilling permit. This set the precedent for Shell, BP and other companies seeking to drill off the coast of the Russian Far East.

Located about 7,000 kilometres east of Moscow and 45 kilometres north of Japan, Russia's Sakhalin Island and the three seas that wash up on its shores

Photograph: Sakhalin Environment Watch

Figure 5.1 *Sakhalin's Unspoiled Coastline*

(Okhotsk, Japan and North Pacific) hold some of the world's most biodiverse and pristine ecosystems, including rich fisheries that supply over half of Russia's annual catch, and dozens of endangered marine mammals and migratory waterfowl. The Sakhalin shelf waters also hold oil and gas reserves that rival those of the North Sea (Working, 2001). Countries and companies from around the globe are jockeying for a share of the energy pie.

The risks to the environment here are exceptional: the region's natural conditions are more hostile than any other locations where these companies have drilled. A unique combination of ice shears strong enough to crush steel and high seismicity threatens major environmental disasters. Oil spill response capacity is weak, and the companies' liability is limited under Russian law in order to promote foreign investment.

The oil companies stand to profit greatly from their operations in the region. US and Japanese credit agencies, as well as international financial institutions (IFIs), have funnelled hundreds of millions of dollars to the projects. These same institutions have conditioned aid money to Russia on structural adjustment to create an investor-friendly climate. Sakhalin production, destined for the nearby Asian market, will be developed under favourable production sharing terms designed to guarantee the companies full return on their investment before the Russian government ever sees its share of the profit.

What the Russian people stand to gain is much less clear. Although they sit atop huge reserves, the people of the Russian Far East are suffering the worst energy crisis since the Second World War, going without heat for weeks on end in winter temperatures that have plunged to minus 40° Celsius. The production sharing agreements under which the transnational corporations are developing the oil are wildly unfavourable for Russia. Taxes have been waived while the companies buy off the Sakhalin government with 'bonus payments' that are the modern-day equivalent of beads and trinkets. Gas production for Sakhalin Island, a condition of the original tenders to provide a steady source of heat and light and help combat air pollution from coal burning, has never materialized.

What Russians stand to lose though is quite clear. Sakhalin has a sustainable, fisheries-based economy that holds great development potential for the future. Oil development threatens the fisheries, the extraordinary biodiversity and indigenous cultures that are dependent upon healthy ecosystems. Moreover, in a country where the rule of law is fragile at best, the oil companies have leveraged their influence to retool laws to their liking and simply ignored many of the rest.

Other oil developments – Shell in Nigeria or Unocal in Burma – present starker corporate abuses. No one has been killed over Sakhalin oil. To date, the only casualties have been democratic principles and the independent environment agency. But perhaps for this reason the Sakhalin oil conflict is more illustrative of the pervasive structural ways in which global corporations manipulate governments and legal systems as part of routine business practice in the globalized economy, to the detriment of local people and the environment.

The Sakhalin conflict is also instructive because non-governmental organizations (NGOs) won round one against the transnational corporations (TNCs), with significant environmental protection results. And even though the companies convinced the government to counter with the dissolution of the environmental agency, civil society is still in the game. NGOs have filed suit against President Putin petitioning the court to invalidate his unconstitutional decree to abolish the agency.

The globalization of the economy that has opened up Sakhalin resources for the oil transnationals has occurred with no parallel globalization of accountability. The challenge of the 21st century is to reign in corporate-led globalization with globalized accountability.

The conflict over Sakhalin shelf development has generated one of the first high-profile environmental campaigns in Russia to demand transparency and public participation in decision-making, enforcement of environmental laws and responsible resource management. It is a conflict between the world's biggest oil companies and their handmaidens, the global financial institutions and Russian civil society over who gets to determine the region's future, and who will benefit from its development.

Bringing TNCs squarely back within the reach of the democratic institutions and the rule of law is the challenge of the 21st century that will determine in large measure the kind of world that future generations will inherit. The Sakhalin experience suggests that multiple approaches are needed, both to strengthen civil society's ability to hold TNCs accountable, and to internationalize environmental protections and access to justice to match the globalized economy.

Developing enforceable global environmental standards and making corporate codes of conduct enforceable are key strategies. Additionally, accountability and environmental protection measures should be required via the financing agencies, particularly the export credit agencies that back TNC projects around the world. And access to justice must be globalized: a first step is to remove legal doctrines that help TNCs to evade liability.

Finally, international support for civil society should be dramatically increased so that it may fulfil its role as a democratic counterbalance to government and industry and make existing participatory mechanisms more effective. In this way, communities and NGOs will be better able to steer conflicts, like those over oil development at Sakhalin, towards more environmentally sustainable outcomes.

The Rich Biodiversity of Sakhalin Island

The seas off Sakhalin Island are home to 25 marine mammal species, including 11 endangered species. The eastern coast of the island, where the first wells were drilled, provide the only summer grounds for two of the world's most critically endangered populations of whales, the western grey and right whales (US-Russian Joint Commission, 1997). Sakhalin's marshes and wetlands provide critical breeding grounds for large numbers of migratory waterfowl and are a stopover point along the migratory route followed by many of the endangered birds of Asia, including cranes, osprey and Steller's sea eagle.

Photograph: Sakhalin Environment Watch

Figure 5.2 *Sakhalin Island's Wetlands Provide Critical Habitat for Many of the Endangered Birds of Asia*

The Okhotsk Sea off the coast of Sakhalin is one of the most productive fisheries in the world, providing over 60 per cent of Russia's total annual catch. The fishing industry dominates the island's economy, employing over 50,000 of the island's 700,000 residents (BISNIS, 1998). In the shelf waters alone there are 70 different species of fish; in the Sea of Okhotsk, more than 300.

Sakhalin Island is also home to the indigenous Nivkhi, Uil'ta and Evenks. The largest group is the Nivkhi, numbering about 4000, many of whom live in traditional villages on the two northern coasts of the island. Many work in fishing and hunting collectives in the island's northern bays.

Oil and gas development threatens fishing grounds and marine mammals, both key sources of food. Pipeline construction is proposed in the area of a reindeer preserve set up for the Uil'ta. Of all Russians, indigenous people have the lowest life expectancy (between 10 and 20 years below the national average), the highest rate of unemployment and the greatest food security challenges (FIAN and IFOE et al, 1997).[1]

BIG OIL: REMAKING THE SAKHALIN LANDSCAPE

> *It's the new prize for world oil, the biggest risk is the risk of not being there.*
> Yergin (1993) commenting on investment prospects for the oil industry in the former Soviet Union.

In the early 1990s, flights to Sakhalin carried hardy tourists. By the late 1990s, flights were packed with executives from the world's largest oil transnationals.

Photograph: Sakhalin Environment Watch

Figure 5.3 *Oil Contamination from Onshore Development*

Russian companies had been unable to develop Sakhalin's offshore reserves because they lacked the technology and capital to address the huge technical challenges. As Russia's economic position worsened in the early 1990s the government, desperate for foreign revenue, tendered the first international offshore oil leases in the country's history.

The Sakhalin-1 and Sakhalin-2 projects, led by Exxon and Royal/Dutch Shell, respectively, are the first to be carried out under Russia's Production Sharing Law, adopted in 1995. BP, ExxonMobil and Chevron-Texaco won later tenders. Ninety per cent of the oil is slated for export to Asia, primarily to import dependent Japan (Andreev, 1996).[2]

The Sakhalin lease blocks V to IX, forming a ring around the island, are open for tenders (Flanagan, 2000). Reserves off the Russian mainland, across the Sea of Okhotsk from Sakhalin, are being assessed in preparation for expected future tenders. Plans for a series of associated onshore and offshore processing facilities, refineries and pipelines to the Russian mainland and sub-sea to Hokkaido Japan are moving forward (Sabirova and Allen, 2000).

Engineering Experiments: Courting Disaster?

> *From an ecological point of view they're preparing for the crime of the century.*
> Russian oil engineer Anatoli Cherni, quoted in Pravda (Ryabchikov, 1997).

The Sakhalin oil and gas development projects are an engineering experiment. The region's natural conditions are more inhospitable than any other locations where these companies have drilled before, including Alaska and the North Sea, with a unique combination of ice shears, tidal waves and high seismicity. The conditions raise serious questions about whether the companies have the technology to build safe platforms and pipelines.

During the winter, ice floes buckle and compress with enough force to crush steel. In 1995, an earthquake registering 7.6 on the Richter scale struck northern Sakhalin killing 2000 residents and causing pipelines to rupture in over 50 places, contaminating rivers with over 100 tons of crude oil.

The oil companies assert that there will be no environmental impacts and conveniently own the only regularly published newspaper on the island to disseminate their views (Polyakova and Lisitzny, 1997). But offshore oil development anywhere is risky, as spectacular blowouts and tanker accidents around the world have sadly shown. The 1960s saw the Santa Barbara blowout; the 1970s the Amoco Cadiz; the 1980s the Exxon Valdez, to name a few examples. Siberia and the Russian Far East are the newest frontiers at which oil exploration is proceeding with few environmental controls, poor monitoring and astoundingly insufficient clean-up capacity and liability provisions.[3]

Sakhalin's coastal and riparian landscapes and marine ecosystems are extremely sensitive to oil spills; in northern climates cold temperatures slow biological processes and ecosystem recovery (Corwin, 1997). A spill could destroy critical bird habitat and salmon estuaries. Vastly increased tanker traffic will both interrupt marine mammal migratory patterns and increase the chance

Photograph: Dan Lawn/Pacific Environment

Figure 5.4 *Drilling Unit for Sakhalin-2: Shell-led Consortium Retrofitted a 20-year-old Drilling Unit that had been Mothballed*

of major accidents. A spill at sea, under ice conditions, would be impossible to clean up.[4]

The Exxon Valdez spill ultimately spread oil over about 26,000 square kilometres of ocean and about 2400 kilometres of shoreline, including critical estuaries. If a similar sized spill hit Sakhalin – the Sakhalin-2 EIA notes probabilities as high as 50 per cent in the autumn – it could blacken the entire shoreline (SEIC, 1997, section 9.7.2.2). The Exxon Valdez spill caused the death of hundreds of thousands of seabirds and marine mammals, and severely disrupted commercial fisheries and coastal communities (Loughlin, 1994). As herring, crab and salmon fisheries were closed, hatcheries lost their income, canneries closed and local residents lost their jobs (Burger, 1997). Today, almost a decade after the spill, few of the injured species have recovered and fisheries remain closed[5] (Steiner, 1997). Thousands of citizens and businesses, especially fishing interests damaged by the spill, are still awaiting full compensation by Exxon, more than ten years later.

It took only 12 years of tanker operations in Prince William Sound to result in the Exxon Valdez. The Russian Far East has harsher climatic conditions, poorer oil spill response infrastructure, less liability and a poorly developed culture of enforcement and compliance.[6]

GLOBAL IMPACTS OF FRONTIER OIL DEVELOPMENT

Both the plight of the planet's oceans and global warming have been much in the news as the Sakhalin projects go forward. Record weather extremes have plagued the world. Storms and droughts raged; floods and wildfires left thousands dead and millions homeless around the world (Hertsgaard, 1998). Vast forest fires burned in the boreal forests of Russia, Alaska and Canada, as lightning struck trees dried to tinder by global warming (Davidson, 2000). UN scientists are predicting brutal droughts, floods and violent storms across the planet over the next century due to global warming.

According to a United Nations report marine and coastal zone degradation is worsening in most quarters of the globe, including the Asia Pacific and the former USSR regions (Stevens, 1997). A 1998 report issued by 1600 scientists from 65 countries at the start of the UN International Year of the Ocean warned that ecosystem destruction and pollution are threatening the world's oceans as never before (Greenwire, 1998).

Oil and gas development puts fishing grounds, marine mammals, salmon streams and reindeer pasture at risk – all of which are fundamental to the survival of indigenous land-based cultures and subsistence economies on the island. Environmental pollution from onshore drilling and pipelines has already reduced the fish, bird and animal populations on the island that Nivkhi rely on for subsistence.

Through the Looking Glass: The Economics of a Shelf Project

The oil, gas and steel industries were practically given free to plunderers. Alexander Solzhenitsyn, Russian Nobel laureate, 'Russia's Resources "Plundered"' (York, 2001)

These are sweetheart deals for the transnational oil companies. The Russian government signed unfavourable production sharing agreements (PSAs) with the transnational oil companies. The battle over PSAs was hard fought in the Russian *Duma* (parliament). *Duma* members complained loudly that these fields were discovered by Russians, but under the PSAs their output and associated revenue go overwhelmingly to the foreign oil companies and consultants for the better part of the next 25 years. While the companies profit, Russia and the global community assume the environmental risk.

Under the PSA taxes[7] are waived and revenue sharing with the Russian and Sakhalin government does not begin until *after* the investors recoup all their costs and a fair return on their investment.[8] According to calculations by one expert, if the Sakhalin Energy Investment Company Ltd (SEIC) invests US$10 billion, at planned production rates it would take more than 20 years[9] to generate the revenues to repay the investment. And since the project's accounting is not transparent, it may take far longer. Even at that point, under the PSA only 32 per cent of net income would go to the Russian side, leaving a 68 per cent share for the company (Fineberg, 1997).[10]

Until then Russia and Sakhalin receive only 'bonus' payments (premiums given to the government each time milestones in licensing and production are reached) and a 6 per cent royalty share (Fineberg, 1997). Revenues collected by Russia are only a fraction of those that would be generated by Western countries

Although the Sakhalin projects will create significant new economic activity in the short term, there is no guarantee that the local people will enjoy its benefits. To mollify unhappy *Duma* members and create local jobs, the PSAs theoretically require 70 per cent of equipment and services used by the projects to be Russian. But calculations by the Russian Energy Ministry showed that in fact Sakhalin-2 has only 18 per cent Russian content (Sabirova and Allen, 2000). The majority of big contracts for geological surveillance, design engineering, dredging and drilling went to US and European firms. A US government press release states that the project is expected to have 'tremendous benefits to the US economy', supporting about 1000 American jobs and using US$270 million in US goods and services (OPIC, 1998).

Finally, the liability provisions of the PSAs are grossly inadequate. The Exxon Valdez spill cost Exxon over US$2 billion in response costs, US$1 billion in natural resource damages claims by the government and approximately US$300 million in compensation to private plaintiffs.[12] The floating oil storage unit for the Sakhalin-2 project can hold about four times as much oil as the Exxon Valdez, yet the liability limit was set at only US$700 million. As Alaska oil spill expert Rick Steiner (1997, p2) notes:

> *Unless oil companies are enticed ... with sufficient liability, they will seek every opportunity to save money up front – that is, on prevention and response preparedness – as a gamble that it won't be needed, and if there is a major spill, they will attempt to rely on their insurers to pay for it.*

Moreover under the Russian law 'On Foreign Investment' (Russian Federation, 1991) the liability of joint stock companies extends only to the amount of their investment, that is, the dollar amount of its founding capital. This shields the parent company Exxon, for example, from any additional liability over the value of Exxon-Neftegas Ltd, the limited liability company that is the official member of the Sakhalin-1 consortium.

The Russian Economy: Who's Running the Show?

> *We have a government that doesn't follow the nation's laws, but instead the dictates of the IMF.* Venyamin Sokolov, Chief of the Russian Chamber of Accounts (Williamson, 1998).

Why risk a pristine ocean supporting extraordinary biodiversity and a productive local fishery economy for profits that overwhelmingly accrue to distant international oil companies? For the Russian government, the rush to develop Sakhalin oil is spurred by a troika of motivating factors: the need to meet IFI conditions of privatization and liberalization of the economy; a short-term need for revenue to meet international loan payments and keep financial markets from crashing; and geographic proximity to the Asian energy market. Nearly half of Russia's hard currency revenues, vital for repayment of international loans, is generated by oil and gas exports.

The globalized economy brought capitalism crashing down on Russia. In retrospect even the US officials who pushed the rush to liberalize – before financial institutions and the rule of law were established – have owned up to the mistake. Privatization brought vast corruption, an ever-widening gap between the few mega-rich and the millions of very poor, and finally the 1998 currency crisis in which many Russians' savings simply evaporated overnight. During the 1990s, the number of Russians living below the poverty line ballooned to over 50 per cent of the population.

IFIs and bilateral aid agencies provide billions of dollars in project financing and wield extraordinary influence over domestic Russian policy. For example, phase one of the Sakhalin-2 project alone was backed by US$348 million in credits from the US Overseas Private Investment Corporation (OPIC), the European Bank for Reconstruction and Development (EBRD) and the Japanese Export-Import Bank (JEXIM). These three institutions, together with the World Bank and the International Monetary Fund (IMF) have also successfully retooled the Russian economy and Russian laws to fit their needs. Privatization allowed transnational corporations to own and export fossil fuel resources; tax breaks and production sharing agreements open up the fossil fuel sector under favourable conditions.

The US government has funnelled billions to Russia since 1992 with the goal of promoting economic liberalization – and assuring US corporations access to a share of the country's wealth. The US Agency for International Development supported privatization of the Russian economy.[13,14] The US has also concerned itself with the details of Russian regulations. In 1998 the Department of Energy sponsored a workshop in Moscow with the objective of generating regulations to invalidate the environmentally protective, zero waste discharge requirements of the Russian Federal Water Code (US-Russian Government Workshop on Offshore Waste Management, 1998). This kind of self-serving influence has been wielded by oil interests before. As early as 1992, the year after the dissolution of the Soviet Union, companies including Sakhalin consortium members Exxon and Marathon Oil donated an average of US$100,000 each to the Russian Petroleum legislation project. These corporate contributors were allowed to place representatives on legislation drafting teams, and to review draft laws presented to the Russian *Duma* – a privilege that the Russian public did not have (Knaus, 1992).

To date, foreign aid and IFI lending programmes have done little if anything to help the vast majority of Russian people. Living conditions have deteriorated. Workers are not paid. Pensioners receive barely US$20 per month; most price controls and subsidies have been lifted. Moreover, the overwhelming political influence wielded by global capital has contributed to a profound loss of hope among ordinary Russians who just a decade ago had great faith in their country's democratic potential.

In addition to undermining host country domestic governance, IFIs also perversely work to counter donor countries' international treaty responsibilities on global warming. For example, in the five years after the signing of the 1992

Convention on Climate Change, the World Bank funded US$9.4 billion in coal, oil and gas projects. It is estimated that these projects will, over the course of their lifetimes, release the equivalent of more than the entire planet's current annual carbon emissions from fossil fuel burning – 9.5 billion tons. Similarly, in its first five years of operations (1991–1996) the EBRD financed fossil fuel projects that will release more than 6.5 billion tons of carbon dioxide into the atmosphere (SEEN, 1997).

IFI funding also abets TNCs' abuse of the Climate Convention. The Convention allows developing countries unrestricted use of fossil fuels to address overriding problems of economic and social development and gives 'flexibility' to 'countries in transition to a market economy' (article 4, paragraph 6, CIESIN, 1998).[15] However, this loophole is exploited by TNCs, Northern governments and IFIs who together are able to gain access to the energy sector of countries like Russia. Rather than working with the Russian oil industry to make existing infrastructure projects more environmentally and economically sound, the IFIs and Western investors focus on gaining control over undeveloped oil and gas fields. These fields are more often than not in remote, pristine regions like the Sakhalin shelf (SEEN, 1997).

RULE OF LAW IN RUSSIA: TAMING GLOBAL CAPITAL?

Democracies are inconvenient for oil men…Dictatorships are more convenient because they prefer to divide the oil wealth privately with the oil men, imposing personal taxes (bribes) that are kept secret and are much less costly for the producers. Helmer (1996)

Legal reforms since Russia's independence in 1991 have produced impressive constitutional, human and environmental rights, at least on paper. A lack of implementing regulation and weak compliance and enforcement have limited their real world impact. And corruption remains rampant: Russia ranked number one in a 1997 survey of Western executives (Stanley, 1997).

An active environmental NGO sector has emerged in Russia, demanding public participation in decision-making and the enforcement of citizens' environmental rights. Indigenous organizations and environmental groups are coming together around issues of resource extraction and biodiversity protection to speak out against the environmental and social impacts of oil development.[16]

The unrealized potential of new constitutional guarantees and environmental laws, as well as international treaty responsibilities, are key to the conflict over whether and how the Sakhalin projects should go forward. For example, the Russian Constitution guarantees the 'right to a favourable environment' and guarantees 'the rights of indigenous peoples in accordance with the universally recognized principles and norms of international law and international treaties' (Constitution of the Russian Federation, 1993, articles 42 and 69). The framework 'Law on the Protection of the Natural Environment' is also far-reaching (Russian Federation, 1992), giving citizens the right to a 'healthy and liveable environment' (section II) and even forbidding projects '… which involve disruption or destruction of highly productive natural ecological systems, … unfavourable changes in climate or the Earth's ozone layer … [and], other irreversible consequences for human health and the environment' (article 57).

The Russian environmental impact assessment (EIA) scheme, known as an environmental *expertiza*, requires an EIA for proposed projects, as well as all licences and permits (including drilling permits), draft laws and authorization of financing decisions. The law also requires environmental review of production sharing agreements (PSAs) and concession contracts (article 12, paragraph 7). The PSA law itself reiterates the *expertiza* requirement.[17] Finally, the Russian Federation Water Code, which prohibits discharge of industrial waste, including drilling wastes, into water bodies (article 96), also comes into play, along with other wildlife protection and industrial safety laws too numerous to detail here.[18]

Russia's obligations under international conventions are also important to the Sakhalin debate. Agenda 21's 'Rio Declaration' reaffirms the need for meaningful public participation in environmental decision-making. Sakhalin Island wetlands are proposed for listing in the RAMSAR convention as wetlands of international importance for endangered birds from across Asia. The 1992 Framework Convention on Climate Change obliges Russia, the third largest greenhouse gas emitter worldwide, to work towards reducing emissions. And finally, Russia has ratified the European Convention for the Protection of National Minorities, which sets out the principles of promoting conditions necessary to preserve and develop the culture, language, religion and tradition of indigenous peoples, and to promote participation in public affairs, among other things (Council of Europe, 1995; Public-Interest-Law-Network, 1998).

David and Goliath

> …*allowing the discharge of waste waters and drilling wastes into places of the greatest concentration of fish in the Russian Federation and the habitat of rare animals and plants, creates a real threat of irreversible environmental harm and economic damage to the country and its people.* Collegium of the Supreme Court of the Russian Federation, 1999 opinion, Ecojuris Institute et al vs. the Russian Government.

The conflict over oil development around Sakhalin Island is typical of the globalized economy, pitting international capital against the local environment, sustainable economies and indigenous people. The momentum and money behind the projects are impressive; the rights at risk are equally compelling. The line of scrimmage is many layers deep, on both sides.

The oil companies and the Russian governing elite have big guns on their side of the table. International funding institutions, including the World Bank, IMF and EBRD, and bilateral agencies like OPIC and JEXIM, support the projects directly and have used their considerable leverage to retool the Russian economy in favour of the oil companies.

On the other side, all Russians, and indeed the global community, have an interest in biodiversity protection and reducing greenhouse gases. The Sea of

Okhotsk supports wildlife of international importance and buoys the fishing economies of large parts of the Russian Far East. Moreover, non-compliance with the mechanisms of global environmental governance, such as the Climate Convention, affect the worldwide community.

As late as 1997 the first two Sakhalin projects, led by Exxon and Shell, respectively, had proceeded apace behind closed doors. Environmental groups were let in on the secret when they discovered that credit agencies including OPIC and EBRD had committed hundreds of millions of dollars to support the Sakhalin-2 project. A condition of the credit, standard for IFIs, is that the recipient must follow all host country laws. But there had been no environmental expertiza as required by Russian law. Russian NGOs wrote to the EBRD board of directors stressing that if the bank financed the project without the required environmental expertiza both the company and the EBRD itself would be committing actionable offences in Russia. Grudgingly the EBRD and the company revisited the environmental review process.

In the US environmental groups worked to get access to the new environmental assessment prepared for the credit institutions. Although OPIC and EBRD are taxpayer funded institutions, their guidelines did not require public disclosure of environmental assessment documents. When it was finally prised from the bank, the document's deficiencies proved legion. The assessment evaluated the first phase test-well drilling project as though it were taking place in a vacuum. There was no analysis of cumulative environmental impacts, either of the total Sakhalin-2 project (including numerous additional drill sites, pipelines, tanker traffic and on-shore storage and processing) or of the multiple oil developments slated for the area (SEIC, 1997, section 9.7.2).

Environmental risks were discounted cavalierly. The impacts of chronic pollution on fisheries and the marine ecology were not analysed (Corwin, 1997). Internationally accepted best practices for drilling waste management (re-injection of the waste back into the geological formation) were ignored and the document indicated that toxic drilling wastes were to be discharged at sea, which is strictly prohibited by Russian law. A complete oil spill response plan had not been prepared[19] even though the document says that the probability of an oil spill reaching the shoreline is as high as 50 per cent in the autumn (SEIC, 1997, section 9.7.2.2, 9.7-21).[20] Although the EIA was challenged on these points and others by an international coalition of NGOs and scientists, it was clear that the EBRD had made its decision well before the EIA was made public, and the project went ahead with no additional review.

By 1999 though, when Exxon applied for permits for production well drilling, issues around Sakhalin oil development and environmental protection had been brought to centre stage by the environmental community. Russian and US groups were monitoring the government review of the company's EIA documents.

In May 1999, Exxon received a negative governmental review of their EIA documents – because proposed at-sea discharge of toxic drilling wastes violated Russian law – and their drilling permit was denied. Exxon went to then-Prime Minister Stepashin and convinced him to issue a decree waiving the company's environmental review requirements and waiving the zero-discharge standards of the Water Code.

The Russian environmental law group Ecojuris was leaked information about the waiver, and filed suit on behalf of dozens of Russian NGOs throughout the Far East. In October 1999 the Supreme Court sided with the environmentalists against the government, invalidating the Stepashin decree and requiring Exxon to follow the law. It was the first time that the Russian judiciary upheld citizens' rights to environmental protection and applied the rule of law to transnational investments.

Exxon squawked loudly at the 'unjustifiable delay' of not being allowed to flaunt the law. Headlines rang out: 'Exxon kills project off Russia ... a move that could further discourage Western investment...' (Solis, 1999). Nonetheless by the following year Exxon had quietly re-written its environment documents, incorporated re-injection of drilling wastes and received the permit.

Some Days You Eat the Bear. Some Days the Bear Eats You

President Putin met with international oil lobbying groups three days before the April 2000 elections. One month later he issued a decree abolishing the State Committee on Environmental Protection. Now the Ministry of Natural Resources, responsible for promoting the commercial exploitation of Russia's resources for short-term hard currency revenues, is in charge of all EIAs.

Environmental groups are back in court. Putin's decree violated constitutional provisions, including the citizens' right to participate in government decision-making (article 32), as well as numerous federal laws stating that these agencies shall be independent and enumerating their powers. Coming full circle, the decree also violated the Law on Environmental Expertiza, which requires that all draft legislation and decrees that could have negative environmental impacts be submitted for the legally mandated environmental review.[21]

With the environmental agency out of the way, the oil companies are taking up the drilling waste issue again in their tireless quest to avoid environmental protection regulations and lower costs. Their current tack has an echo of Soviet bureaucratic logic. Since Russian law prohibits the discharge of pollutants into waters that provide endangered species habitat or are categorized as having the 'highest' fisheries value, the companies are embarking on a campaign to downgrade the fisheries status of the Sea of Okhotsk, at least on paper, so they can pollute with impunity one of the most biologically productive oceans in the world.

TOWARDS CORPORATE ACCOUNTABILITY

Corporate globalization is forcing ... a competition in which workers, communities and entire countries are forced to cut wages, environmental protections, and social programs to attract footloose capital. US Congress Member Bernie Sanders[22] (Mokhiber and Weissman, 2000).

Globalization has helped TNCs to avoid regulation, increase their public subsidies and avoid liability for overseas operations. Bringing these corporations back under the control of accountable democratic institutions is key to protecting the environment and human and labour rights around the world. Whether and how enforceable mechanisms to internationalize human rights and environmental standards are created will determine in large measure the kind of world that future generations will inherit.

How can TNCs be brought back within the reach of the rule of law? The economy has been globalized, but environmental protections and access to justice have not. The Sakhalin experience suggests that multiple strategies are needed to strengthen civil society's ability to hold TNCs accountable, including:

- developing enforceable global environmental standards;
- requiring accountability through financing institutions, particularly the export credit agencies;
- making corporate codes of conduct enforceable;
- globalizing access to justice to prevent corporations from evading liability for overseas activities; and
- scaling-up international support for civil society so that it may better fulfil its role as a democratic counterbalance to government and industry.

Work towards global environmental standards

International movements for corporate responsibility have called for the establishment of global environmental standards, along with effective mechanisms to monitor and enforce them, to reign in TNC worldwide activities. Examples would include global standards for the implementation of 'best environmental practices' (such as re-injection of oil drilling wastes), or minimum environmental impact assessment requirements. Such standards certainly would have been helpful to buttress existing Russian law in the Sakhalin case, and could be even more useful in countries whose domestic standards are weak or non-existent.

But this strategy is not without risks. Building the political will for global standards will be difficult at best. It will be an uphill battle to achieve international consensus on such a treaty without the standards being hopelessly watered down. And TNCs would probably exercise strong influence in the negotiations.

Equally important, without strong enforcement mechanisms and institutions, there is no guarantee that international standards would have had any greater impact than existing Russian law, which the Russian government did its best to alternately ignore or eviscerate to facilitate the oil company investments.

Even in the wealthier Organization for Economic Cooperation and Development (OECD) countries, agreements that purport to require nations to regulate their corporation's operations overseas have proved to be weak and ineffective. Under the OECD's voluntary Guidelines for Multinational

Enterprises, for example, governments agree to promote the guidelines' standards, including disclosure of information, workers' rights and environmental protection, to their domestic TNCs. But observance is voluntary and no remedies are provided. The Guidelines do not even require public disclosure of company violations.

New environmental human rights standards have and are being promulgated to expand rules for application to TNC activities under international law. The 1994 Draft Declaration of Principles on Human Rights and Environment, for example, suggests standards to address the environmental dimension of a range of human rights.[23] Additionally, a draft Human Rights Code for Companies is being developed within the UN system.

With these standards, as with existing instruments, developing new and more effective enforcement mechanisms will be key. The Russian situation is fairly common: national laws on paper are good, but not enforced. As long as host country governments are in a structural bind – crunched by the international financial system and the need for direct foreign investment – they cannot be relied upon for enforcement. Innovate international law enforcement mechanisms will need to be advanced, including standards that would be binding directly on corporations,[24] but this too will be slow to develop.

Currently, the only international institution with effective enforcement procedures, the World Trade Organization (WTO), is, not surprisingly, run by and for the TNCs. Alternative enforcement tools for environmental and human rights agreements such as monitoring mechanisms and individual complaint procedures will help, but fall far short of enforceable remedies that carry economic hammers like the WTO's trade sanctions or liability for corporate wrongs in home country courts.

Time is of the essence. By some estimates, Russian oil reserves will be largely exhausted in 20 years at the present rate of extraction (SEEN, 1997). By then the wildlife, fisheries and cultures of the region may be irreparably harmed.

So, where else can civil society look to develop mechanisms that will increase meaningful public participation in environmental decision-making and help bring the TNCs under the rule of law?

Require accountability via the export credit agencies

The conflict over Sakhalin's future invokes global concerns over the pace and severity of biodiversity loss, global warming and the health of the world's oceans. Yet taxpayer dollars from the US and other countries fund the Sakhalin projects and many others like them around the world, through credit agencies that operate with glaringly little transparency and accountability.

Export credit agencies (ECAs) like OPIC have become the largest source of public international finance as governments increase loans, guarantees and insurance to help their corporations compete for business abroad. These institutions lack even the basic environmental and public participation standards that the World Bank has been pressured to adopt.

The ECAs are key institutions through which requirements for transparency, public participation, environmental assessments and best practice standards should be imposed on TNC projects. For example, OPIC's conditions of credit already require that recipients, like Royal/Dutch Shell's Sakhalin-2 project, must comply with all host country laws. But as the Sakhalin case shows, there is no straightforward enforcement process.

To help achieve this basic result of following host country laws, breaches of credit agreements should be made actionable in the home country. Taxpayers have a right to ensure that their money is not funding TNCs to subvert democratic institutions and despoil the environment in other countries. Moreover, in the same way that an individual who has failed to meet credit conditions, say on repayment of a car loan, will be deemed ineligible for future loans, TNC credit recipients who have knowingly breached loan covenants should not be eligible for future ECA credit.

Additionally, OPIC and other credit agencies such as the Import-Export Bank should implement EIA requirements equal to US domestic law requirements, including public notice and comment periods.

Finally, the ECAs should develop monitoring and auditing mechanisms at least as strong as the World Bank International Inspection Panel. Although the Inspection Panel can only investigate whether the Bank has abided by its own guidelines, nonetheless, adverse findings can eventually halt or modify environmentally or socially destructive projects carried out by governments or TNCs. ECA inspection panels should be accessible to community groups and NGOs so they may petition directly, and would be able to appoint an NGO to represent a community where there is no local representation.

Make corporate codes of conduct enforceable

Voluntary corporate codes of conduct, while giving NGOs a handle to engage the corporations in dialogue over abuses, impose no legal obligations and often allow corporations to paint their overseas operations with a heavy coat of green-wash.

To make the voluntary codes a more effective tool, new mechanisms are needed to publicly shame corporations that violate them, and to make false statements about the labour, human rights and environmental conditions of overseas operations actionable as unfair business practices. In this way the codes would become more useful tools, less susceptible to abuse by disingenuous TNCs and more advantageous for good corporate citizens.

One initiative to watch is taking place at the European Parliament (EP). In 1999 the EP adopted a resolution instructing the European Commission to draw up a model European Code of Conduct for European Enterprises Operating in Developing Countries. The EP Committee on Development and Cooperation holds public hearings giving civil society a new forum in which to confront TNCs over abuses.[25] Here again, the code will not be legally binding, although it will provide a high-profile forum to shame violators. Additionally, the EP has called for enforcement of an existing requirement – that private companies working for the European Union in third countries respect fundamental rights in accordance with the Treaty of Europe, or lose their funding.

Alternatively, it has been proposed that adherence to a code of conduct be made mandatory, effectively imposing US regulations on US transnationals' activities overseas. In the era of 'what's good for Exxon is good for the US', this kind of bold initiative, put forward by Representative Cynthia McKinney, is unlikely to be adopted soon but nevertheless sets out a strategy that would do much to reign in the TNCs.

The Corporate Code of Conduct Act[26] of 2000 would require US-based corporations with more than 20 employees overseas to enact a code of conduct that would establish legally binding minimum requirements for corporate operations overseas. The code, which would also apply to the corporation's subsidiaries and subcontractors, would require adherence to both international environmental standards and US federal environmental laws and regulations.[27] The bill includes reporting requirements and would establish an investigative process that citizens could initiate to determine compliance. Victims of violations, US and foreign citizens alike, could sue US companies in US courts.

Globalize access to justice

TNCs are adept at avoiding jurisdiction and liability. In host and home countries alike, TNCs hide behind the facade of local subsidiaries created to insulate the parent from legal responsibility for overseas operations. In the US and other home countries, an additional legal fiction called 'forum non coveniens' (literally, 'inconvenient forum') allows corporations to further evade liability for overseas operations, even when the parent company was responsible for decision-making affecting the company's worldwide operations, and profits from subsidiaries flows back to the parent company.

What would happen if an oil spill on the scale of the Exxon Valdez happened in Sakhalin? Exxon's Russian subsidiary, Exxon-Neftegas Ltd, has limited liability in Russia, and its operations on the Sakhalin coast are underinsured.[28] And forum non coveniens will make it very difficult if not impossible to sue Exxon Corporation, the US parent company, in US courts – even though it makes decisions for the Sakhalin project, uses its clout to influence Russian law and will reap significant profits. US courts routinely use the legal fiction of the forum non conveniens doctrine to close the US legal system to foreign citizens injured by a US corporation's activities, effectively allowing US corporations to evade legal responsibility for business decisions overseas.

Corporations regularly make calculations weighing environmental safety against the cost of compensating injuries or environmental damage. The threat of liability acts as a deterrent, prodding companies to use better environmental protection and health and safety measures to avoid liability down the road. But if TNCs know they are able to evade liability for overseas activities, the deterrence factor vanishes. The doctrine acts as a straightforward economic incentive for lowering corporate environmental and health and safety standards overseas, and must be abolished.

Although corporations will fight to maintain the status quo – global profits without any corresponding liability from overseas activities – common sense dictates that a globalized economy requires globalized access to justice. Victims of corporate abuses must be able to sue the corporation in its home country. Forum non conveniens must be abolished in those countries where it still exists, including the US.

Increase international support to civil society

Perhaps the clearest lesson from the Sakhalin experience is indeed the most global: a strong civil society that can fight for public participation in decision-making and the rule of law is fundamental to environmental protection. But as the case study shows, it is an uphill battle.

International support, under the auspices of the UN or other institutions, should be dramatically scaled-up to help empower civil society to fulfil its role as a democratic counterbalance to government and industry, and make existing participatory mechanisms more effective.

For example, the International Sustainable Development Ombudsperson office, launched in 2000 by the Earth Council, could expand its role. The more traditional ombudsperson role of receiving complaints from victims and investigating abuses remains key. Nonetheless, the Ombudsperson, along with other regional institutions, should also take a proactive role helping local communities and NGOs to participate early and more effectively in project negotiation and review. As the Sakhalin case study underlines, timely access to information is crucial. The companies and interested government parties proceed in secrecy for as long as they can get away with it, hoping the projects will be perceived as a *fait accompli* before social and environmental impacts are fully studied, much less debated publicly.

The ombudsperson could also advocate for use of 'best practice', and the use of funding mechanisms such as environmental insurance policies and performance bonds that would promote improved TNC environmental and social performance.

Finally, the ombudsperson and other institutions should help civil society to monitor and reform the international financial agencies that back TNC projects. Together they would be stronger advocates for transparent environmental and social impact assessment policies, and sustainable development and renewable energy lending practices. As civil society's influence continues to grow, it becomes ever more likely that credit institutions could be persuaded to mobilize global capital for the development of renewable energy, promote integrated resources planning in loan decisions, and require EIAs that include both supply-side and demand-side (ie conservation) responses to energy needs.[29]

ACKNOWLEDGEMENTS

This paper chronicles the work of a handful of courageous Russian environmentalists, most especially Vera Mischenko of Ecojuris Institute, whose leadership and determination allowed Russian civil society to square off successfully against international oil companies. Many thanks to Ms Mischenko, and also to Gary Cook, for their invaluable contributions to the chapter as well as their assistance translating original Russian language materials.

NOTES

1   The Association of Indigenous Peoples of the North, Siberia and Far East issued a statement in 1996 denouncing uncontrolled resource exploitation which 'deprives us of our basic right – a right to life' (Evai et al, 1996).

2   In 1998 the Japan Export-Import Bank announced US$1.5 billion for energy projects in Russia.

3   Russia's onshore oil spill record is not good. There are an estimated 700 major spills annually. The most dramatic, a 1994 spill from a Canadian and British joint venture in the Komi Republic was almost eight times larger than the Exxon Valdez, and was shrouded in secrecy.

4   According to a study by the US National Research Council, an oil spill at sea under ice conditions presents the most difficulties of all oil spill clean-up and containment operations (National Research Council, 1994).

5   After the Exxon Valdez accident only an estimated 7 per cent of spilled oil was recovered. The US Department of Energy estimates that only 5–15 per cent of oil from a spill can ever be recovered or cleaned up (Holling, 1990).

6   In 1992, Sakhalin agency Nippmorneft estimated that a winter well blowout could release a comparable amount of oil to that from the Exxon Valdez spill (Steiner, 1997).

7   The projects were exempted from local and regional taxes in 1997, and from federal customs duties and value added tax (the only two federal taxes not covered by the PSA) in 1997 (Delay, 1997). Meanwhile, structural adjustment imposed by the IMF as a condition of multi-billion dollar bail-out loans required increasing rates on a range of taxes that affect ordinary Russians most, including value added tax and income tax.

8   In Russia PSAs are not pubic record, therefore it is difficult to know whether or not the copies of PSAs which are spirited out to NGOs are the latest version. For example, a Russian language copy of the Sakhalin-2 PSA, dated 22 June 1994, states slightly different production sharing figures.

9   Sakhalin Energy's project documents claim optimistically to be able to recoup expenses between 2017 and 2019.

10 Compare this with production-sharing contracts in Indonesia, for example. Under Indonesian production sharing the company may deduct operating costs and 20 per cent of capital investments from gross production. The remaining production is then divided 66 per cent–34 per cent in favour of the Indonesian state oil company. See, generally, Rosenfeld et al (1997).

11 And since the companies are not required to open their books to public inspection, they are susceptible to 'gold-plating', when companies artificially increase reported project costs to reduce the profit base on which the government's share is calculated. A study for the state of Alaska, conducted by the author of a Barclay-World Bank study of international petroleum fiscal regimes, warns that the Sakhalin-2 PSA is very susceptible to 'gold-plating' (Fineberg, 1997). A consultant to the Russian federal Duma noted that the economics of the project became considerably less favourable to the Russian government between 1993 when the tender was won and 1996 when the consortium prepared the first phase project feasibility study. For example, the capital investment (which under the PSA is to be reimbursed fully to the company before any profits are shared with the Russian government) increased by 70 per cent. The cost of the platform increased by more than half and the underwater pipeline by a factor of 2.5. And almost US$500 million was added for 'project management' (Melkov, 1998).

12 In October 2000 the US Supreme Court refused to free ExxonMobil from having to pay the US$5 billion punitive damages verdict.

13   The privatization was famously corrupt; state-run firms and even the assets of entire former Soviet ministries were bought up at bargain basement prices by well-connected insiders, often former high level Communist party functionaries.

14   In a 1997 press release, OPIC's then president, Ruth Harken, used the agency's leverage to threaten Russia diplomatically. She noted that US$30 billion in new investments was on the line if required reforms were not adopted. 'These are not new issues,' she said. 'But I am afraid if they are not dealt with soon, many investors will go elsewhere in an increasingly competitive world economy.'

15   The Convention states that '… a certain degree of flexibility shall be allowed by the Conference of the Parties to the Parties included in annex I undergoing the process of transition to a market economy' (article 4, paragraph 6) (CIESIN, 1998).

16   Many others though, co-opted by oil company contracts, or fearful of reprisals from the oblast (provincial) government, have been silenced. Indeed, Sakhalin's governor labelled Russian NGOs opposing oil and gas development as 'enemies of the people', using an old Soviet tactic in an effort to chill NGO activity.

17   The Production Sharing Law itself reaffirms requirements for environmental and cultural protection, including the requirement for environmental *expertiza* (article 4) and the requirement to defend the native environmental and traditional lifestyle of indigenous groups (article 7).

18   The Water Code also specifically prohibits the discharge of processed waste water into water bodies that are spawning or wintering grounds for valuable or specially protected species of fish and into habitats for rare and endangered species (article 144).

19   US NGOs continue to petition EBRD, OPIC and the other credit agencies to require SEIC to improve oil spill response plans.

20   Greenpeace later would team up with local NGO Sakhalin Environment Watch to hang banners from Sakhalin-2's mobile drilling platform demanding protection of the marine ecology. The photos made a splash across Russia.

21   This time around the Supreme Court is running scared, and clearly would rather not decide whether President Putin has to abide by the rule of law. The court has invented all sorts of legal fictions to avoid hearing this politically charged case; more than six months after filing, the case has yet to be heard.

22   See: The Global Sustainable Development Resolution (H.RES.479, at H.R.4596) at http://thomas.loc.gov.

23   A key provision is article 20, which states that: 'All persons have the right to effective remedies and redress in administrative or judicial proceedings for environmental harm or the threat of such harm.'

24   Certain treaties already impose obligations directly on individuals or corporations or require states to outlaw certain conduct in their national laws. For example, international maritime law treaties place direct liability for oil pollution damage on the 'owner of a ship' and prohibit ship owners from limiting liability below a certain amount (article 6, Protocol of 1992 to Amend The International Convention on Civil Liability for Oil Pollution Damage, 1969). Note though that the minimum liability requirements of this treaty have proved to be grossly inadequate to effectively address oil spill damages.

25   The European Parliament's initiative also requested the European Commission to establish an independent body of experts to monitor implementation of the code, identify best practices and receive complaints.

26   See: H.R. 4596, at http://thomas.loc.gov.

27   Initiatives such as the 'Principles for the conduct of company operations within the oil and gas industry' developed by Bread for the World, address the need for codes of conduct to become meaningful and verifiable by listing regulations covering public

participation in planning oil and gas extraction projects, sustainable development, respect for indigenous peoples, environmental standards, among others, and for independent and transparent monitoring and auditing of codes of conduct. (IRENE, 2000).

28 Moreover, in Russia and other countries, damages can be so low that they probably would not serve as a deterrent to future violations.

29 See generally, Krause and Koomey (1992).

REFERENCES

Andreev, A (1996) *Sovietski Sakhalin*, 15 June

BISNIS (1998) Online, the home page for the Department of Commerce's Business Information Service for the Newly Independent States Russia/CIS Division 'Why YOU should do business in Yuzhno-Sakhalinsk!', www.mac.doc.gov/bisnis/cables

Burger, J (1997) *Oil Spills*. New Jersey: Rutgers University Press

Chair of the State Committee on Environmental Protection (1998) 'Order No. 385. Sakhaln-1', 23 June

CIESIN (1998) Environmental Treaties and Resource Indicators (ENTRI) online. University Center, Michigan, Consortium for International Earth Science Information Network/United Nations Framework Convention on Climate Change (1992), http://sedac.ciesin.org/entri/

Constitution of the Russian Federation (1993) Adopted 12 December. Moscow, Juridichiskaya Literatura

Corwin, R (1997) 'Comments on Sakhalin II Technical and Economic Substantiation, Volume 9, Environmental Protection', prepared for Ecojuris Institute and Earthjustice Legal Defense Fund. 12 November 1997 (unpublished)

Council of Europe (1995) Framework Convention for the Protection of National Minorities, Strasbourg, 1.II.1995, http://conventions.coe.int/treaty/en/Treaties/Html/157.htm

Davidson, K (2000) 'Cold Northern Forests Face Burning Threat: Global Warming Blamed for Huge Fires', *The San Francisco Chronicle* 18 December

Delay, J (1997) 'Nemtsov Plans Tax Breaks for Equipment for Sakhalin Projects', *Pipelines News* 57, 7 May

Ecojuris Institute (1997) Letter to European Bank for Reconstruction and Development, 19 May (unpublished)

Evai, A V, et al (1996) 'Discrimination Against Indigenous People of the North in the Russian Federation: A Statement by Social Organizations and Movements of Indigenous People of the North', 4 March, Moscow, www.lib.uconn.edu/ ArticCircle?SEEJ/russia_indig.html

FIAN and IFOE (1997) 'The right to adequate food (Art. 11) and violations of this right in the Russian Federation: Parallel information to the initial report of the Russian Federation concerning the right to adequate food as enshrined in the International Covenant on Economic, Social and Cultural Rights (ICESCR, art.11)', April, www.koeln-onlin.de/infoe/report.htm1. Heidelberg: International Human Rights Organization for the Right to Feed Oneself/ Institute for Ecology and Action Anthropology

Fineberg, R A (1997) 'A Global Perspective on Sakhalin Energy Investment Corporation and the Sakhalin II Project', http://arcticcircle.uconn.edu/SEEJ/Russia/fineberg1.html. Arctic Circle

Flanagan, D (2000) 'PSA Legislation Key to Progress on Sakhalin', *FSU Oil and Gas Monitor* 28 March

Greenwire (1998) 'Oceans: 1,600 Scientists issue "Unprecedented Warning"', *National Journal's Greenwire: The Environmental News Daily* 6 January, www.cloakroom.com

Helmer, J (1996) 'A Tsar for Oil Men', *The Moscow Tribune*, 1 June, p7

Hertsgaard, M (1998) 'Severe Weather Warning', *The New York Times Magazine*, 2 August, p48

Holling, D (1990) *Coastal Alert: Ecosystems, Energy, and Offshore Oil Drilling*. Natural Resources Defense Council and the Central Coast Regional Studies Program. Washington, DC: Island Press

IRENE (2000) 'Controlling Corporate Wrong: The Liability of Multinational Corporations. Legal Possibilities, Initiatives and Strategies for Civil Society', http://elj.warwick.ac.uk/global/issue/2000-1/irene.html

Knaus, H (1992) 'Greasing the Regs', *Multinational Monitor*, www.essential.org/monitor

Krause, F and Koomey, J (1992) 'The Greenhouse Dividend', *The Electricity Journal* 5(7) August/September

Loughlin, T R (ed) (1994) *Marine Mammals and the Exxon Valdez*, San Diego, CA: Academic Press, Inc

Melkov, G M (1998) Consultant to the State Duma Committee on Geopolitics, 'Expert Assessment on the Documentation for Sakhalin II: An Application for Conducting Work in Building Exploratory Drilling Holes at the Licenses Piltun Astokhskii Site', 23 June (unpublished)

Mokhiber, R and Weissman, R (2000) 'Big Ideas on Corporate Accountability and Global Sustainability', 20 June, www.corporatepredators.org

National Research Council (1994) *Environmental Information for Outer Continental Shelf Oil and Gas Decisions in Alaska*. Washington, DC: National Academy of Sciences

OPIC (1997) 'Overseas Private Investment Corporation Signs Agreements Worth More than $335 Million for Five US Projects in Russia', *OPIC Press Release*, 7 February, Overseas Private Investment Corporation, www.opic.gov

OPIC (1998) 'OPIC Makes First Disbursement to the Historic Sakhalin Oil an Gas Project in Russian Far East', *OPIC Press Release* 8-40, 11 June. Overseas Private Investment Corporation, www.opic.gov

PERC (1996) 'PERC Sues OPIC for Failure to Disclose Environmental Information', *Pacific Environment and Resources Center press release*. San Francisco: Pacific Environment and Resources Center, 22 November

PERC et al (1997) Open letter to Karen Sheppard, US Executive Director, European Bank for Reconstruction and Development, Pacific Environment and Resources Center, 31 June (unpublished)

Polyakova, O M and Lisitzny, D V (1997) 'Resolution from the Round Table on the Environmental Aspects of the Sakhalin-2 Project', 4 December. Translated by Pacific Environment and Resources Center (unpublished)

Public-Interest-Law-Network (1998) 'Russia Ratifies European Framework Convention', message from Public-Interest-Law-Network email list, Columbia University, 24 August, www.pili.org/lists/piln/archives/msg00204.html

Rosenfeld, A B, Gordon, D L and Guerin-McManus, M (1997) 'Reinventing the Well: Approaches to Minimizing the Environmental and Social Impact of Oil Development in the Tropics', *Conservation International* 2

Russian Federation (1991) Law 'On Foreign Investments' of the Russian Federation, *Vedomosti* RSFRS, 29, Item No 272

Russian Federation (1992) Law 'On Environmental Protection' of the Russian Federation, 92WNO327A, 3 March 1992, *Rossiyskaya Gazeta*

Ryabchikov, V (1997) 'Sakhalin Energy Prepares a Flood of Oil', *Pravda*, 9 December (translated by Katie Sauter)

Sabirova, E and Allen, M (2000) 'Year End 2000 Update on Sakhalin Oil and Gas Projects', US and Foreign Commercial Service and US Department of State

SEEN and the International Trade Information Service (1997) *The World Bank and the G-7: Changing the Earth's Climate for Business.* Washington, DC: Sustainable Energy and Economy Network of the Institute for Policy Studies, www.igc.org.ifsp/publicat/wb-g7-report/wb-g7-report.en.html

SEIC (1997) 'Technical & Economic Substantiation for Construction of Facilities PA License Area - Phase 1: Astokhskoye feature, Volume 9, Environmental Protection', Sakhalin Energy Investment Company Ltd, September

Solis, D (1999) 'Exxon kills Project off Russia', *The Dallas Morning News* 20 August

Stanley, A (1997) 'Tycoon Purged from Kremlin as Reform Battle Heats Up', *The New York Times*, 6 November, pA8

Steiner, R (1997) 'Comments on Sakhalin II Technical and Economic Substantiation for construction of Facilities Piltun-Astokhskoy License Area, Volume 9, Environmental Protection', prepared for the Pacific Environment and Resources Center and the University of Alaska Marine Advisory Program, 4 November (unpublished)

Stevens, W K (1997) '5 Years After Environmental Summit in Rio, Little Progress', *The New York Times*, 17 June 1997, pC8

US–Russian Government Workshop on Offshore Waste Management (1998) 'Joint Resolution', 28 April 1998, Moscow (unpublished)

US–Russian Joint Commission on Economic and Technological Cooperation (Gore-Chernomyrdin Commission) (1997) 'Joint Statement on Conserving Biological Diversity', 7 February, www.usia.gov/regional/bnc/usrussia/gcc8/biodiv8.htm

Williamson, A (1998) 'Chief Auditor Venyamin Sokolov Says Western Loans Are Hijacked by the Corrupt Yeltsin Government', *Mother Jones*, 16 June

Working, R (2001) 'Oil Holds Promise for Sakhalin', *Anchorage Daily News*, 14 January 2001

Yergin, D (1993) *The Prize: The Epic Quest for Oil, Money & Power.* New York, NY: Touchstone Books

York, Geoffrey, (2001) 'Russia's Resources "Plundered": Solzhenitsyn Shows His Teeth, Attacks Putin on Environmental Record and Corruption', *The Globe and Mail* (Canada), 27 January

Part III

Conflicts Over Development Strategies

Chapter 6

Environmental and Human Rights Impacts of Trade Liberalization: A Case Study in Batam Island, Indonesia

Agus P Sari

BATAM ISLAND: A RIAU ISLAND, A GLOBAL ISLAND

Located about 16 kilometres south-east of Singapore, Batam Island, Indonesia, has unique characteristics as a fully free-trade zone. The ferry trip from the World Trade Center in Singapore to Sekupang in Batam takes slightly more than 30 minutes. Some 30 people with whom I took the ferry in autumn 1999 seemed to cross the two countries' borders regularly – Singaporean, Batamese, or wanderers from other corners of the world. For concrete jungle-dwelling Singaporeans, Batam serves as a provincial hinterland, whereas for the newly urbanized Batamese, Singapore serves as a cosmopolitan downtown.

It is not surprising that, due to its proximity and its economic interdependence, Singapore is the main geographical reference for Batam. Even to those familiar with Indonesia, Batam's whereabouts are not immediately apparent. After all, Batam is only one of more than 17,000 islands that constitute Indonesia, the fourth most populous country in the world with a population of 200 million. Geographically, from east to west and north to south, Indonesia is larger than the continental United States. Two-thirds of Indonesia, however, is ocean. Sumatra, Java, Kalimantan, Sulawesi and Irian Jaya are the five major islands of Indonesia. One of the 27 provinces in Indonesia, Riau is divided into mainland Riau on Sumatra and the Riau Islands. Batam is only one of the many Riau Islands.

A historical perspective

The history of trade in the region goes back to the Kingdom of Sriwijaya, which ruled the entire Malay region in the 10th century. Centred in Palembang, South

Sumatra, Sriwijaya ruled an extensive region from Java and the western part of Borneo in Indonesia to northern Malaysia and Thailand on the Malay Peninsula. The strength of the Sriwijaya Empire derived from its control over the maritime trade routes between Europe, India and the Middle East on one side and Southeast and East Asia on the other. This trading route linked the kingdom to the rest of Southeast Asia, including a major route through the Straits of Malacca, where both Singapore and the Riau Islands lie (Coedés, 1918, 1936). One century later, the Majapahit Empire, centred in Java, emerged as a new dominating power in Southeast Asia. By the 13th century, Sriwijaya was entirely subsumed by Majapahit, whose influence would eventually reach as far as Australia and India (Régnier, 1987).

Beyond the era of the ancient kingdoms, competition to gain control over the strategic trade route extended through the Western colonial era between the Portuguese, British and Dutch. In 1819, British rulers, notably Sir Stamford Raffles, officially founded Singapore – then known as Tumasik – although by no means did they establish the city. In the post-colonial era, Indonesia continued to battle for control over the territory with Malaysia and Singapore, a battle formerly involving the British (who ruled Malaysia and Singapore) and the Dutch (who ruled the Riau Islands in Indonesia). The confrontational approach remained in place until as recently as 20 years ago, parallel to the historic rivalry between the region's hinterland and the dominant regional trading centres. From 1963 to 1965, Indonesia launched a military attack against Malaysia and Singapore (which was in the process of separating itself from Malaysia to become a sovereign country). The abortive military confrontation was followed by less violent economic confrontation for another decade (Quick, 1995).

The Sijori Growth Triangle scheme

Although the rapid physical changes in Batam in the 1990s took many observers by surprise, a rapid pace of development was unplanned. When the Batam Industrial Development Authority (BIDA) was first established in 1971, Batam was designated to become merely a logistical base for oil exploration in Sumatra. Under the auspices of Pertamina, Indonesia's state-owned oil company, BIDA was first chaired by Pertamina's Chief Executive Officer Dr Ibnu Sutowo. At the time, oil was Indonesia's main commodity for earning foreign exchange, and more than half of Indonesia's oil was produced in the province of Riau. While Riau produced most of the crude oil, however, Singapore absorbed most of the value added by producing refined fuels.

The development orientation of Batam, then, was to compete with Singapore and to cut off Indonesia's dependence on Singapore for petroleum exports. The period between 1971 and 1976 was coined as the 'preparation period' of the island's development. When oil exports reached their peak, contributing more than 70 per cent of Indonesia's foreign exchange earnings (BPS, various years), the leadership of the Authority was handed to Dr J B Sumarlin, then State Minister for Utilization of State Apparatus, for a short period between 1976 and 1978. This period was curiously coined the 'consolidation period' (BIDA, 1997).

BIDA's existence has been more prominent since Dr B J Habibie, who became Minister of Research and Technology, took over the chairmanship of the Authority in 1978. Since then, Batam's development has been reoriented. The first move was to declare the entire island as a duty free zone. In this so-called 'infrastructure development and capital investment period' (BIDA, 1997), the economic relationship between Batam and Singapore was no longer competitive. Habibie, in a speech in 1989, described the Singaporean economy as an expanding balloon that would ultimately explode due to its resource constraints. Singapore has major geographic disadvantages being a small, export-dependent, city nation. The increasing scarcity of land leads to increasing land prices, and the increase in per capita income leads to increasing wages. Moreover, with current high levels of per capita income, its citizens increasingly demand environmental quality. As a result, environmental standards have become tighter every year. The combination of land and labour scarcity and tight environmental standards has translated into constraints on economic expansion.

Singapore's weaknesses could be seen as advantages for Batam, one of the closest neighbours in the region. With less expensive land and labour costs, Batam offers a logical backyard for expansion of Singaporean industries. By shifting economic growth to neighbouring regions – to Batam, in this case – Singapore could pre-empt many serious economic problems. The Riau Agreement, an agreement designed to establish the so-called Singapore-Johor-Riau (Sijori) Growth Triangle, was signed on 28 August 1990 and was the realization of this development reorientation.

The Sijori Growth Triangle scheme was to take advantage of the complementarity of these Southeast Asian nations and to enlarge domestic supply and demand by extending the supply channels for factors of production and expanding markets. However, while transborder economic development may lessen the constraints of national boundaries, it tends to constrain the ability of the nations to map their development plans and policies (ASEAN, 1996).

Adhering to the Growth Triangle concept, Batam is perceived as a region that offers lower land and labour prices compared with those of Singapore and Johor in Malaysia. While the Growth Triangle à la Sijori should be a triad between Singapore, Johor and Batam Island in Riau, it is actually a hub-and-spoke relationship with Singapore as the hub and Johor and Riau as two – among many other – spokes (Davies, 1992; Ahmad, 1993; Horn, 1993). Gereffi (1994) characterizes the triangle as a relationship between a rich region, export processing region and a backward region. In the Batam case, rich countries such as Japan, the US and countries in Western Europe make trading deals with companies in Singapore which, in turn, outsource these deals almost entirely to Singapore's neighbouring backward countries.

Economic progress in Batam

Export-led industrialization is deemed to promise rapid economic growth. Today, the Growth Triangle scheme, the manifestation of export-led industrialization, seems to live up to this promise in Batam. As an almost completely open economy, goods and services, as well as capital, flow easily in and out of Batam. The relative size of the external market shows its significant link with the rest of the world. In Batam, the Rp 7 trillion (approximately US$3 billion) export value in 1995 was more than three times greater than the Rp 2 trillion (approximately US$0.8 billion) gross domestic regional product (GDRP) of the island. Combined with the size of imports, reportedly around Rp 25 trillion (approximately US$11 billion) that year, Batam's economy was dominated by external markets. In addition, the relative size of foreign direct investment with respect to total investment, 45 per cent, is much greater than the approximately 10 per cent in Indonesia as a whole. In addition, the freight-on-board export value has grown 145-fold from US$20.9 million in 1986 to more than US$3 billion in 1996, showing an exponential annual average growth rate of 65 per cent. The growth rate is even higher if visitors' spending in Batam is taken into account, yielding a total foreign exchange income of slightly less than US$3.5 billion in 1996. Indeed, Batam has led the rest of Indonesia in pursuing trade liberalization (BIDA, 1997).

To match booming foreign and domestic investments, BIDA has pushed hard for infrastructure development to catch up with modern trade requirements. For example, the Hang Nadim Airport in Batam is currently the second largest airport in Indonesia after Soekarno-Hatta International Airport in Jakarta. Several ferry terminals have been developed to connect the island with neighbouring islands as well as with Singapore. The Asia Port, deemed to be the largest international cargo terminal in Asia, is currently on the drawing board and may be established on the east coast of Batam. Superhighways have been laid to connect these ports with the rest of the island's strategic corners. Although not without its problems, this world-class infrastructure has facilitated the island's export-oriented industrialization.

The high export growth rate has been cited as the main reason for the island's comparably high income growth. With a solid growth of more than 17 per cent per year at least in the last two years, Batam now boasts the highest income per capita in Indonesia. At US$5000, it was four times the average per capita income of the country as a whole in 1996. Table 6.1 summarizes the economic progress experienced by Batam.

Manufacturing has been the leading sector in the region; its share of GDRP in 1995 was about 64 per cent. Within manufacturing, electronics leads other sectors with a lion's share of 90 per cent. The second largest sector in Batam, largely driven by physical infrastructure development, is construction, followed by transportation and communication. It is encouraging to see that the agriculture sector, though still at the bottom of the list, is catching up, as agriculture is important in keeping inflation down. Currently, due largely to the high price of food products, the cost of living in Batam is already two to three times that in Jakarta, with the inflation rate exceeding 10 per cent annually (BIDA, 1997).

Out of the total export value in 1995 in Batam, approximately 85 per cent, US$2.6 billion, were electronic products. The electronics industry started developing in Batam in 1988, when the industry exported only US$1.6 million,

Table 6.1 *Gross Domestic Regional Product (GDRP) in Batam*

Sectors	1995 GDRP growth (%)	1995 Share of total (%)	1994 GDRP growth (%)	1994 Share of total (%)
Manufacturing	22.17	63.56	22.36	60.56
Trade, hotel and restaurant	8.89	15.4	10.04	16.98
Finance	6.76	7.09	7.26	7.66
Construction	14.70	4.82	20.67	4.78
Transportation and communication	13.67	4.14	8.13	4.84
Other services	8.10	1.96	5.81	2.09
Mining and quarrying	9.88	1.50	10.17	1.51
Electricity, gas and water	5.43	0.94	4.06	0.99
Agriculture	1.11	0.55	-9.99	0.59

Source: BIDA 1995, BIDA 1996.

less than 4 per cent of the total export value in that year. In 1991, for the first time the export value of electronic products exceeded those of other products with US$131 million, more than half of the total export value. In general, the export value of electronic products in Batam is growing at the extremely rapid pace of 150 per cent per year since 1988, more than twice the growth rate of exports of all products (BIDA, 1997).

ENVIRONMENTAL AND HUMAN RIGHTS CONFLICTS

Trade and environment

International trade is deemed to enhance economic advantages and in turn to catalyse rapid economic growth. Both Adam Smith and David Ricardo theorized the benefits of production specialization and trade in terms of 'comparative advantage'. For example, a country with an abundant labour supply may be better off specializing in labour-intensive sectors, whereas another country with extensive land area may be better off specializing in land-intensive sectors. Modern trade theory suggests that, while global trade may open up domestic economies, imperfect competition and industrial external economies of scale – resulting from transaction and transportation costs and technological spillovers – may lead to industrial agglomeration in one geographical region (Piore and Sabel, 1984; Krugman, 1991). As a corollary, the introduction of free trade may lead to two different phenomena. First, as official trade protection through tariff and non-tariff barriers is removed, transaction and transportation costs emerge to become determinants of trade advantage. These costs correlate directly with geographical proximity, suggesting that even when trade is fully liberalized, regional advantages will continue to predominate (Storper and Walker, 1989; Saxenian, 1994). Second, as an industrializing economy is increasingly integrated with the rest of the world, export production and consumption of imports tend to be concentrated in urban areas with better access to international trading facilities, credit and high-income urban consumers (Henderson and Kuncoro, 1996). In sum, geography is prominent in modern trade theory.

An open economy has a different set of environmental and human rights impacts on nations, regions and community groups from those of a closed economy. The domestic impacts refer to the impacts of trade on the centre–periphery relationship within a country, whereas international distributional impacts refer to the distribution of benefits and costs among nations.

How does trade liberalization affect the environment? Trade liberalization may have inconclusive impacts on the local environment, including both positive and negative impacts. The positive impacts have been much more debated than the negative impacts. While relocation of industries may take advantage of lower environmental standards or different levels of enforcement of these standards, foreign industries may bring with them more stringent standards, usually imposed by their countries of origin.

There are three mechanisms by which a change in trade and foreign investment policy can affect the level of pollution and the rate of depletion of scarce environmental resources. The first mechanism is the scale effect; if trade and investment liberalization cause an expansion of economic activity, and the nature of that activity remains unchanged, then the total amount of pollution generated must increase (Grossman and Krueger, 1991).

The second mechanism is the so-called composition effect, the effect derived from different comparative advantages: some sectors in different economies will expand, while others will contract (Grossman and Krueger, 1991). Expansion and contraction of sectors in an economy is related to, among other things, differences in environmental standards between an economy and its trading partners. If comparative advantage is derived largely from lower environmental standards, then the composition effect will be damaging to the environment. This effect has been seen notably in labour intensive sectors. As income increases in industrialized countries, the cost of labour follows suit and labour-intensive production is then relocated to labour-abundant countries with lower labour costs (Fröbel *et al*, 1978; Gereffi, 1994). Similarly, energy-intensive processes tend to relocate away from countries where the cost of energy is high (Gitlitz, 1993). For example, between 1990 and 1992, world production of steel – a heavily energy-intensive product – increased by 15 per cent in Asian Pacific countries, while nominal capacity reductions are expected in Western European countries (World Bank, 1994a). A computable general equilibrium modelling exercise using data from Indonesia asserts that if carbon dioxide emission limitations in the industrialized countries increase the world price of energy-intensive products, carbon dioxide emissions from Indonesia would increase by 1 per cent due to the additional comparative advantage gained by Indonesia for producing energy-intensive commodities (Sari, 1996).

The third mechanism is the efficiency effect, resulting from different technologies utilized in the production system. Some technologies may reduce both input requirements of environmental resources and the pollution produced, but others may not have this effect (Grossman and Krueger, 1991). In Batam, for example, some of the companies have strict environmental standards; while many are ISO 9000 certified, a handful are seeking ISO 14000 certification because their headquarters require them to do so. ISO 14000 is an international industrial standard of practice that includes environmental standards.

To a limited extent, environmental impacts are addressed in global trade negotiations. Articles XX(b) and (g) of the General Agreement on Tariffs and Trade (GATT) include an exception to free trade rules and allow the use of trade measures to protect the environment. The World Trade Organization formed the Committee on Trade and Environment (CTE) to address the relationship between GATT and the use of trade measures for environmental purposes, including those within multilateral environmental agreements (GATT, 1994; Jenkins *et al*, 1996). However, Principle 12 of the United Nations Declaration on Environment and Development, signed in 1992 at the Earth Summit in Rio de Janeiro, suggests that trade measures to protect the environment 'should not constitute a means of arbitrary or unjustifiable discrimination or a disguised restriction on international trade' (UNGA, 1992).

While environmental impacts of foreign investment are ambiguous, the severity of social and environmental problems evident in Batam suggests that negative impacts may be more prominent than positive impacts. However, many developing countries are unwilling to accept stringent environmental and human rights standards. To many of them, the inclusion of environmental and human rights clauses in trade or investment agreements is alleged to be disguised protectionism. Moreover, to many countries, expansion of the economy as demonstrated by high growth rates is of higher priority than environmental protection.

The economic imperatives of trade liberalization in Indonesia

'It was an idea whose time has come', proclaimed Ali Alatas, then Indonesian Minister of Foreign Affairs in 1994, in reference to trade liberalization. He stated that, due to the confluence of new trends in both the global economy and in East Asia, there was a resurgence of interest in the establishment of more formal, intergovernmental cooperation on economic issues among the countries of the Asia Pacific region. With this statement, he confirmed that Indonesia accepts economic globalization as inevitable and is willing to take part. Indonesia is now in a position to anticipate the tides of trade liberalization institutionally, politically and economically (Alatas, 1994).

Embracing trade liberalization has domestic economic imperatives. Until the 1980s Indonesia enjoyed 'easy money' from petroleum exports. Buoyed by high world oil prices, petroleum exports increased rapidly in the 1970s and peaked in 1981 with a value of US$20.7 billion, contributing more than 80 per cent of total exports. When oil prices fell, the export value of petroleum products fell dramatically to only US$7.7 billion in 1988, or 40 per cent of total export value (BPS, various years). The overwhelming dependence upon oil and gas products shocked the Indonesian economy and forced a diversification of exports. Indonesia undertook a deliberate transition from resource extraction and the export of raw materials, to an economy based on value-added industrial-based processes and the export of intermediate and final industrial products. Within two decades, real output of the manufacturing sector increased nine-fold. During the 1990s, up until the financial and political crisis of 1997, Indonesia's economy grew at an annual rate of close to 8 per cent. Indonesia's industrial output rapidly increased at a rate of 18 per cent annually as recently as 1997. Manufacturing's share in total GDP grew from 13 per cent in 1970 to 23 per cent in the 1980s, and is expected to exceed 33 per cent in the 1990s and approach 45 per cent in the following decade (World Bank, 1994b).

Rapid industrialization, however, commands increasingly massive capital investments, which must be provided by domestic savings and foreign investment as well as multilateral development assistance. Indonesia's dependence on foreign borrowing has been overwhelming. Its debt-service ratio (DSR) increased steeply from 14 per cent in 1980 to 32 per cent in 1993, despite the fact that foreign borrowing as a percentage of the government's annual budget dropped from 68 per cent in 1988 to 38 per cent in 1994. In addition, the need for foreign exchange has been further fulfilled through an increase in exports. Shifting from largely import-substitution to export-oriented industrialization has required Indonesia to lower the effective protection rate; in other words, to liberalize its economy (World Bank, 1994b).

The economic crisis of the late 1990s turned everything upside down. The crisis started with a sudden devaluation of the exchange rate. The Indonesian rupiah lost three-quarters of its value before the crisis. Imports became unbearably expensive and foreign exchange-denoted debts – most of which were unhedged – became impossible to pay back. Prices soared to the sky with more than 400 per cent inflation.

Amid popular unrest among the increasingly poor and unemployed people, Suharto, Indonesia's president for 32 years until 1998, was forced to step down. At the end of his presidency, Suharto faced similar crises to Sukarno when he fell from power. The parallel between the two created an atmosphere that, combined with other factors, forced Suharto to step down. Dr Habibie, then his Vice President, took over the job. In the first democratic election, Abdurrahman 'Gus Dur' Wahid became the first democratically elected president. Political reform, until this time, had not paralleled the rapid development of Indonesia's economy.

The first foreign ventures and their problems

Externally driven development is, to some extent, a legacy of colonialism. The colonial countries extracted cheap labour and natural resources from their colonies in exchange for expensive manufactured products. Japan and the US have been the two largest foreign investors in Indonesia. More than 70 per cent of total foreign direct investment, including in the petroleum sector, comes from these two countries. Japan dominates the non-oil sector, whereas most of the oil sector investment comes from the US.

The first large foreign ventures approved in Indonesia since 1966 were Indonesia Asahan Aluminum (Inalum), an aluminium smelter in North Sumatra funded by Japanese investors, and Freeport Indonesia, the largest copper and gold mining venture in Irian Jaya, financed by American investors. Both of these foreign ventures are plagued by severe environmental impacts that affect the local community in the form of untreated toxic waste dumping. Aside from environmental impacts, the projects have had severe social impacts as well. Freeport reportedly used the Indonesian government and the military to violently curb an uprising by the local community of Amungme and Komoro, including the torture and murder of citizens living on property controlled by Freeport. The Amungme, an indigenous tribe of Irian Jaya, sued Freeport for environmental and human rights violations in the US (Kitazawa, 1990; Gitlitz, 1993; ACFOA, 1995). The case was brought under the US Alien Tort Claims Act and is currently under appeal.

These two anecdotal cases illustrate the significant environmental and human rights impacts of the first foreign ventures in Indonesia. There are many other similar cases such as Dukuh Tapak, the site of a recent project in Central Java. The situation is discussed in more detail below and is explored as a case that could be successfully resolved through the use of a mediation mechanism.

Environmental and human rights conflicts in Batam

The central environmental human rights issue in Batam is the distribution of benefits and costs between a myriad of actors: between Singapore and Batam (Indonesia), between Batam and the rest of Riau, between Batam and the rest of Indonesia, between local people and recent settlers, and among the various ethnic groups of recent settlers.

The distribution of benefits between Singapore and Batam is strongly correlated with the proportion of factors of production contributed by the two countries. In the Sijori scheme, Batam contributes cheap labour and land. Compared with the skills, technology, capital and entrepreneurship contributed by Singapore, the financial value of Batam's contribution is relatively low. Consequently, the economic benefits reaped by Batam are low. As experienced by other export processing zones, the main benefits reaped by Batam are local employment and consumption of locally produced goods. With a minimum wage of less than US$1 per day, the consumption that contributes to the local economy is limited to cheap food bought from informal food stalls and housing in illegal settlements. Most of the products sold in Batam, even food products, are imported.

External costs are mostly borne by Batam in the form of environmental and human rights conflicts. Indeed, the permission to pollute is one of Batam's 'comparative advantages'. For some industries and companies, stringent environmental regulation in Singapore makes costs of compliance high and is considered to be a comparative disadvantage. For pollution-intensive industries relocation to Batam from Singapore is attractive. As an interview with a shipyard manager in Batam revealed, even if they had to comply with all the Indonesian environmental regulatory requirements, it would still be less costly to operate in Batam than in Singapore.

Currently, electronics manufacturing is the single largest sector in both Batam and Singapore. The electronics sector, like other industries in Batam, is export oriented. If the intent is to penetrate domestic markets, companies locate not in Batam but in Java. Moreover, electronics companies in Batam are subsidiaries of larger TNCs and are almost entirely foreign-owned. Exports from these companies tend to be intra-industry and intra-corporation exports. The end products of Batam production processes are usually intermediate products or components and final packaging is done elsewhere. Finally, the added value absorbed by Batam is relatively low and is gained largely through local wages.

The Batamindo Industrial Park, the industrial site chosen by most in the electronics industry, is partly owned by Singapore and uses Singapore's Economic Development Board for marketing. Out of a handful of industrial parks existing in Batam, only Batamindo shows signs of success. Most of the other 'industrial parks' are merely barren open spaces.

The benefits of the growth of the electronics sector for the local economy are dubious. Every 1 per cent of economic growth in the electronics sector adds only 0.36 per cent additional employment opportunities.[1] Most of the inputs into the industry are imported rather than made locally. In 1995, the electronics sector spent about US$750,000 on Indonesian-made products, only about one thousandth of the island's GDRP.[2] This sector is relatively capital-intensive and most workers are paid close to minimum wage so their contribution to the local economy is marginal (BIDA, 1997). Nevertheless, the manufacturing sector, led by electronics, generated the largest employment opportunities with 67 per cent of total employment in 1995,[3] followed by the construction sector (16 per cent). In 1995, Indonesian workers constituted nearly 99 per cent of the electronics sector workforce. Most of the positions in the uppermost rungs of the management ladder are held by expatriates. Manufacturing was the largest employer of expatriates, with close to 1000 workers (BIDA, 1996).

Labour is supplied by Batamindo's sister company, Tunas Karya Indoswasta. Most of the workers are recruited from outside Batam, mostly from Java. The overwhelming dominance of workers from outside Batam creates tension within the local population. In addition, outside workers are contracted for two years and are not able to live permanently in Batam.

There are also gender issues in the pattern of employment. Almost all female workers – 93 per cent in 1995 or more than 35,000 women – are employed in the manufacturing sector. Most of these are young women between 18 and 22 years old who work in the electronics companies in the Batamindo Industrial Park (BIDA, 1996). An interview with an unidentified official revealed an interesting reason behind the biased recruitment: the combined effect of workers who are young, non-local, female and temporary is expected to yield a high level of employee obedience.

In addition to social problems, the people of Batam also bear environmental costs, which may be very high. When Dr Habibie took the chairmanship of BIDA and redirected Batam's development, he envisioned Batam as becoming a site for environmentally friendly industries. He drew up a Negative Industries List that identified polluting industries that would not be allowed on the island. The List, however, did not provide clear definitions or standards to determine what constitutes a polluting or non-polluting industry. Surprisingly, he perceived the electronics industry to be a clean industry. The sad fact is that it is not; the electronics industry deals with many toxic and hazardous substances, and Batam is not well equipped for disposal of such substances. Moreover, the electronics industries were located in close proximity to reservoirs into which toxic substances have seeped and now contaminate the drinking water. Batamindo, for example, where most of the electronics industries reside, has no toxic and hazardous waste management system. A visit to a number of these industries revealed that toxic and hazardous wastes are either dumped in ordinary municipal waste facilities or piled in the vicinity. When the rain comes, these carcinogenic substances are washed into the neighbouring reservoirs. As a result, water from the reservoirs is hardly potable. To fulfil the demand for drinking water, most of the middle- and high-income households purchase bottled water. The poor have no choice but to drink the contaminated water.

A direct result of rapid physical development is the expansion of construction. Construction, the second largest sector in Batam, has extensive impacts on soil erosion. In Batam, land can only be leased from the government with 30-year concessions, extendable to 50 and 80 years. To prevent speculation, BIDA stipulates that development of leased lands must begin immediately. To demonstrate efforts to develop their land, many leaseholders simply clear the land and keep it cleared upon receipt of the concession. The ensuing erosion not only causes deterioration of soil fertility, but also sedimentation of coastal water and drinking water reservoirs, where water supply is already a limiting factor for development. Eroded soil makes the already infertile soil of Batam almost impossible to restore. Sedimentation of the coastal water kills many coral reefs and fish habitats. Economically, sedimentation also hinders development of ecotourism as well as ocean transportation infrastructure. For the poor community in Batam – most of whom are fisherfolk and farmers – diminishing amounts of harvestable fish and increasingly infertile soil hamper their livelihoods.

Meanwhile, squatters have colonized some of the protected forests, whose function is rainwater catchment. Batam's skyrocketing economic growth has left the rest of Indonesia, especially neighbouring Riau and Sumatra as a whole, far behind, and thus it has become a magnet for migrant workers. Both the economy and the local population are growing at an average of 17 per cent annually. Interviews with a number of BIDA officials reveal that the actual population of Batam might be twice the officially reported figure of 200,000 people. Affordable housing facilities in Batam are severely limited, and thus most of the migrants colonize the protected forests and other government lands to establish villages. Increasingly squeezed out of the formal sector, these migrants crowd the informal sector, seeking income as street vendors, drivers, prostitutes or criminals.

In sum, while the benefits of export-oriented industrialization in Batam may be collectively beneficial for both Singapore and Batam, it appears that most if not all of the benefits are reaped by Singapore. Almost all the foreign firms in Batam are actually an extension of foreign firms based in Singapore. In essence, Singapore acts as the mediator between Batam and US, Japanese and other foreign companies. Singapore gains high-end entrepreneurial and managerial jobs, as well as investment returns. In Batam, salary workers and poor informal dwellers are victimized by the social and environmental costs they unfairly bear, while the rich can afford to externalize the costs they should bear onto the wider public. The tension between rich and poor is felt so strongly in Batam that the crime rate is one of the highest in Indonesia. Moreover, in Batam, there is a strong popular perception that Singapore is benefiting disproportionately, fuelling tensions between Singaporeans and Indonesians.

How does Batam cope?

Proponents of the Sijori scheme argue that private sector initiatives are mostly or even solely at the root of the economic development success stories of Batam. However, the reality is that the active support of top government officials in Indonesia, Singapore and Malaysia was key. Prior to the high-profile signing of the Riau Agreement in 1990, economic development in Batam was hardly apparent. Even with high-profile support, the Indonesian government needed to ask a favour from the largest Indonesian business group, the Salim Group, to match eager Singaporean investors in the development of the Batamindo Industrial Park, a joint turnkey project in Batam.

Social and political issues may hinder future development in Batam, especially higher value-added industry. In Batam, as in other parts of Indonesia, the rule of law is weak. For foreign investors who require long-term certainty, support from high-level officials may compensate for the uncertain rule of law. As a result, many investments in Batam include either a member of the First Family, a member of Dr Habibie's family, or cronies of their families. In a climate where state institutions are not controlled, the rule of law is weak and societal institution is non-existent, environmental and human rights conflicts tend to occur. When enforcement of environmental regulations is in conflict with the business interests of high-level officials, enforcement tends to relax. Batamindo, for example, is virtually untouchable.

Formally, the House of Representatives should represent the public interest ranging from national, provincial, to regency and municipal levels. Being a special zone with special treatment from the central government, however, unlike other municipalities in Indonesia, Batam has no local legislative institution. Thus, the local population has no formal means of representation whatsoever to provide input to Batam's development and its related impacts. Since there is no legislative institution in Batam, the decision-making process has been solely at the behest of BIDA.

Fortunately, environmental issues have not been ignored, as evidenced by the empowerment of a Subdirectorate for Environmental Monitoring and Management and the creation of an Environmental Management Team within the structure of BIDA. The individuals assigned leadership roles within these institutions are knowledgeable about and committed to environmental management.

Relying on governmental institutions alone, however, especially small ones such as BIDA, is hardly adequate to ensure due care for the environment, as acknowledged by BIDA staff. In 1996, BIDA facilitated the formation of the

Batam Industrial Environmental Improvement Council (Bina Lingkungan Hidup Batam, BILIK). This is a roundtable in Batam for the industrial community to learn about environmental regulation in Batam and in Indonesia as a whole, and to learn how the industrial community can undertake efforts to mitigate existing and potential environmental problems in Batam. BILIK facilitates interaction not only between the business sector and the government, but also between different interests within the business sector itself. Besides companies whose operations might damage the environment, some environmental consultants are also members of BILIK, and the communication between these various interests ensures that an environmental discourse is maintained. Issues ranging from ISO 14000 to EIA to the lack of government responsiveness to environmental problems have been openly discussed in BILIK. Currently, BILIK has established itself as an information clearinghouse and a mediator for environmental conflicts.

Independent of the formation of BILIK, a similar roundtable was established in Jakarta, the National Pollution Prevention Roundtable (NPPR). As the name suggests, NPPR is a roundtable and no formal or bureaucratic structure exists in the organization of the institution. Members of NPPR are treated equally, regardless of their institution of origin, seniority or bureaucratic position. This way, the roundtable functions as an informal gathering of more than 50 institutions. Realizing the similarities, BILIK and the NPPR established an informal exchange. Key members of one organization participated in meetings and activities of the other.

A good example of BILIK's role as mediator of an environmental conflict in Batam is the case of the Bukit Samyong landfills in Batam. A conflict occurred when the accumulated municipal wastes in Bukit Samyong began to emit smoke and noxious fumes. Since no toxic and hazardous waste management facilities exist in Batam, some of the materials being burned were toxic substances. The health hazards of the smoke, reported by a private company in the neighbourhood, severely affected the workers in the neighbouring factories. The Bukit Samyong landfill is located in the middle of an active Batu Ampar industrial zone. The dualism of governance in Batam hindered immediate action, because BIDA and the municipal government argued as to whose responsibility it was to solve the problem. Meanwhile, these delays affected the workers even more. The reporting company then filed a complaint to BIDA regarding the problem.

Eventually, the issue was raised in a BILIK meeting. The official of the company, who was also a member of BILIK, presented data regarding the increased health problems affecting the workers and showed a set of photographs of the smoke from the landfills. He obtained adequate support from the rest of the BILIK members, who could put sufficient pressure on BIDA to take action immediately. BIDA then took precautionary measures to mitigate the problems in the Bukit Samyong landfill and accelerated the plan to build a more permanent waste management facility in Telaga Punggur, a remote area south-east of Batam.

Up to this point, BILIK seemed to have functioned well. However, when the plan was laid out, the issue of illegal settlers – especially scavengers – who lived in and near the landfill had to be addressed. To mitigate the smoke from the landfill, the entire site had to be covered with soil. The most suitable body of soil nearby was occupied by a row of illegal settlers, most of whom made their living picking up reusable matters from the landfill. As in many other parts of Indonesia, scavengers are an important component of the whole waste management system. None of the members of BILIK had any experience working with the affected community and this community had no formal representation in BILIK. Thus, the fate of this community was left in the hands of a few individuals in BILIK. In the end, proposals were developed to properly manage the resettlement, involve the scavengers actively in the waste management system, and to establish a network with similar communities that have been organized in other parts of the country. Nonetheless, there was no institutionalized mechanism to include the community directly in the decision-making process.

Clearly, even well intentioned individuals in BIDA and BILIK will not be able to represent the voices and concerns of the entire island's community. Without a mechanism for wide public participation, existing institutions may not be adequate to properly ensure that social concerns are taken into account.

WHICH MODEL REPRESENTS THE MOST PLAUSIBLE SOLUTION?

Environmental and human rights issues in Indonesian politics

How are environmental impacts of development being addressed in Indonesia in general? What are the politics behind it? This section addresses the politics of the environment and their relationship with mainstream politics in Indonesia.

During the first two decades of the nation's independence, President Sukarno's socialist politics focused more on national identity building and less on economic development. The lack of attention to economic development generated uncontrollable crises: soaring inflation (more than 500 per cent annually) and income disparity that led to widespread unrest. When Suharto took over the presidential office from Sukarno in 1967, economic development became the most prominent issue in Indonesian politics. Suharto's first political manoeuvre was to place heavy emphasis on economic reform. He installed Western-educated economists as his economic ministers, advisers and economic planners – the 'Berkeley Mafia', as some call these elite techno-bureaucrats, since most of them were University of California Berkeley graduates. He succeeded in reducing inflation to less than 10 per cent annually and achieved a steady economic growth rate of around 7 per cent each year.

Amid the crisis, the Indonesian Democratic Party for Struggle (Partai Demokrasi Indonesia Perjuangan, PDIP) led by Megawati Sukarnoputri – daughter of Sukarno – emerged as the strongest opposition party. The largest constituents of Sukarnoputri were the urban poor and lower middle class, the groups hit hardest by the crisis. Sentiments against Suharto were reinforced by the severe oppression of Megawati's party, combined with nostalgia for her charismatic father.

In arguably the most democratic and transparent election ever in Indonesia, PDIP, predictably, won the election albeit not overwhelmingly. While PDIP gained more than 30 per cent of the vote, Golkar, Suharto's party, won more than 20 per cent, making it the second largest party in the parliament. This is instructive because while Golkar suffered from severe distrust and deep-seated hatred among certain sectors of the population, it still gained ample popular support.

In Indonesia, the president is elected by the People's Consultative Assembly, not directly through the popular election. The coalition among the parties other than PDIP built up a majority – called the Middle Axis – that advanced Gus Dur as another presidential candidate to contest Megawati. Gus Dur, regarded as the most accommodating and respected figure in the field, won the support for presidency, while Megawati won the support for vice presidency. Given the urgent economic problems at hand, environmental issues were not high priorities for the new leaders.

Environmental issues have been peripheral in Indonesia and have always been linked to development issues. As a result of the deliberate integration of environmental issues into mainstream development politics, the term 'sustainable development' has been heavily utilized in the environmental discourse in Indonesia.[4] Admittedly, the Indonesian version of sustainable development puts more emphasis on development than on sustainability.

Indonesian politics are heavily personal and informal, and the president is the centre on which they revolve. The rule of law is lacking and legislative institutions are incapable of functioning as the controlling forces of the bureaucracy. In this political situation, direct access to the executive branch, ultimately to the president, is key. Dr Emil Salim, the State Minister for Population and the Environment during the 1980s, was extremely influential in shaping environmental politics in Indonesia and placing them into mainstream politics. Many observers say that if it were not for Emil Salim, environmental interests would not be a consideration in Indonesian mainstream politics at all. In his first post as State Minister for Development Supervision, being a member of the Berkeley Mafia himself, his role was to ensure that the development process in Indonesia was undertaken as properly and in as orderly a fashion as possible. It is clear that Emil Salim's privileged access to the president was a key factor in his success in developing environmental politics in Indonesia.

The first success in Indonesian environmental politics was the formulation of Law No 4 in 1982 on Environmental Management. Government Regulation No 29 in 1986 on Environmental Impact Assessments was the corollary to this law, requiring all new industrial plant developments to undertake EIA (Analisis Mengenai Dampak Lingkungan, AMDAL) prior to initiating the development. Similar requirements also apply to existing plants. The AMDAL documents – public documents accessible to any interested party – are submitted to a committee. According to the regulation, non-governmental organizations (NGOs) are considered non-permanent members of such a committee, whereas affected communities are permanent members.[5] These legal bases for environmental regulation were the products of concerted efforts by Emil Salim and his key staff at the Ministry, NGOs and academic circles.

The inclusion of NGOs in the AMDAL regulation demonstrates that NGOs are prominent in Indonesian environmental politics. The prominence of the NGOs is largely due to the mutually advantageous relationship between them and Emil Salim. As he had only a small office, Salim saw the advantage of having grassroots support from NGOs. Firstly, NGOs could implement some of the policies that the State Ministry's limited staff could not. Secondly, these NGOs could play the role of watchdog to monitor polluters' behaviour.

In 1988, based on these legislative foundations, the Indonesian Forum for the Environment (Wahana Lingkungan Hidup Indonesia, WALHI), the largest federation of environmental groups in Indonesia, sued a pulp and paper company for widespread air and water pollution, the State Minister for Population and the Environment for enabling the pollution to continue, the State Minister for Investment Coordination for allowing the company to exist, and the Governor of North Sumatra for the inability to stop the company from operating in North Sumatra. This case was the first of its kind in Indonesia. Furthermore, WALHI and four other NGOs sued the President of Indonesia for misusing his authority to divert the use of an afforestation fund to finance an ailing aeroplane factory.

The NGOs' strength and influence in environmental politics created widespread anxiety among mainstream political actors, however, and instigated a reaction to limit NGOs' influence and weaken environmental regulations. One of the concerns was the need to attract more foreign investors, as well as to accommodate trade and investment liberalization. When Indonesia decided to join the free trade bandwagon, many policies considered as obstacles to the free market and thus to the development of the business sector were relaxed. Environmental regulations and the prominent role of NGOs have been seen as a hindrance to investment. As a result, in 1993, Dr Salim was asked to step down, and Sarwono Kusumaatmadja, who previously held a relatively minor role in environmental politics, took over the State Ministry for the Environment.[6]

This political shift had multiple impacts, ranging from the broken link between the NGOs and the State Ministry for the Environment to the weakening effectiveness of the Ministry in challenging investment policies. For instance, the deregulation package of 1994, among other things, stipulates more relaxed regulations on investments and exports, including a deregulation of the AMDAL stipulations. Compliance is now sought through a non-regulatory approach, such as encouraging ISO 14000 certification (contingent on compliance with local regulations), ecolabelling for industrial products, and a programme called 'Proper', which classifies industries into different groups based on their environmental performance. However, no regulatory means exist to enforce these voluntary measures.

Environmental deregulation has had a dubious impact. Although not always the case, foreign investors are likely to bring with them production standards from their country of origin, including environmental standards. Furthermore, overseas consumers of their products are likely to be more critical of the environmental standards such as ecolabels and ISO 14000 certification of their production process than domestic consumers. Relying entirely on these voluntary measures uniformly throughout all investments in Indonesia, domestic and international, may only marginally improve environmental standards in Indonesia. The relaxed environmental regulation, however, will affect the majority of domestic investors in Indonesia. After all, while the role of foreign investment is increasing, the majority of investments in Indonesia are still domestic.

Although the AMDAL is strong, it is hardly enforced in practice. In Batam, non-enforcement is particularly severe. The AMDAL commission for the entire island is housed in the Agency for Research and Application of Technology in Jakarta, not in Batam. Thus, all AMDAL tribunal processes are undertaken in Jakarta, thus severely limiting local participation in the review process. Moreover, an interview with an official revealed that only a handful of companies in Batam actually conducted a full AMDAL process; the vast majority conducted none. Nevertheless, AMDAL is still legally in force, including the stipulation for public participation in environmental management. It could thus form an appropriate legal basis for the intervention of an external mediator.

In 1998, when Habibie took over from Suharto, Panangian Siregar took over the Environmental Ministry for less than one year. Gus Dur's administration chose Dr Sonny Keraf, who has a close affiliation with Vice President Megawati Sukarnoputri, as Minister for Environment. Keraf's approach is totally different from that of Sarwono. Keraf is more progressive and assertive, while trying to recreate the institution as 'the People's Ministry'. Before his 100th day of office, he issued a recommendation to close down the Inti Indorayon Utama pulp and paper plant in North Sumatra, the plant that had been problematic since Emil Salim's era and was not properly addressed in Sarwono's era. While this approach is not easily accepted by the private sector, especially the polluting ones, his efforts have arguably been appreciated by the NGOs.

Keraf's ministerial appointment was by no means smooth. He was barely known in the environmental community. A number of environmental activists – notably Emmy Hafild, Executive Director of WALHI – expressed their disapproval of Keraf's appointment to Gus Dur. This move backfired for Emmy Hafild as the press immediately accused her of seeking Keraf's job, though she denied this. Gus Dur insisted on his appointment, and ignored the NGOs' demand. The NGO community then suggested the establishment of a new Coordinating Ministry for Environment and Natural Resources to coordinate the Ministers of Environment, Energy and Mining & Forestry, which was also rejected by Gus Dur. The last move by the NGOs, after the series of rejections, was to propose the establishment of the Sustainable Development Commission.

Although not immediately rejected, the idea to establish the Sustainable Development Commission was frozen for a long time. The idea was seen as 'creating jobs for quasi-government officials'. In addition, a number of ministers voiced their disapproval. Even the Coordinating Minister for Economic Affairs privately disapproved of the idea. New momentum eventually forced its implementation, however. The momentum was that Indonesia entered a bid to host the World Summit on Sustainable Development, also known as the Rio

Plus Ten Summit. While Indonesia lost the bid to South Africa, the momentum was there for the NGOs to push the Commission agenda to the forefront. The Minister for Environment and the Vice President have finally supported the idea.

Existing models

The following functions could lend themselves to a new environmental problem-solving and mediation institution: act as an information clearinghouse, provide documentation and investigation, conduct shaming, facilitate tribunal processes, or provide mediation and conflict resolution functions. These functions could be undertaken by an independent organization, a programme within an existing institution or a network of institutions. Whatever the role is to be, there are several issues that must be taken into consideration. First, integrity is central, thus the institutional setting should remain impartial. Second, the people involved should possess the required expertise. As a number of people have pointed out, sufficient human resources to establish such a function are as yet unavailable. Five to seven years are needed to prepare the necessary human resources (Isna Marifa, 1997, personal communication).

Mas Ahmad Santosa, Director of the Indonesian Center for Environmental Law, foresees the existing effort to establish an Alternative Dispute Resolution that he has been leading as a plausible model (1997, personal communication). Human resources are to be prepared through an Association of Alternative Dispute Resolution Professionals, which he is currently establishing. Most recently, Santosa has been named to establish a trade and environment commission in Indonesia at the national level. Apparently, Santosa's involvement in the establishment of NPPR – he currently sits on its Steering Committee – and in the Association of Alternative Dispute Resolution Professionals gives him the necessary expertise and credibility to assume the responsibility of establishing the trade and environment commission.

There is a case of alternative dispute settlement – an out-of-court settlement – in which Santosa was deeply involved that merits further consideration. The case may illustrate the vision of an ombudsperson function in the future. Semarang Diamond Chemical (SDC), a joint venture between Indonesia and Japan, was built in 1976 in Dukuh Tapak, Central Java. SDC produces calcium citrate, a substance used to produce sodas such as Coca-Cola and Pepsi. In its operation, it dumped its wastes untreated into the nearby Tapak River, whose water is also used by downstream farmers to water their fishponds and their fields during the dry season. The pollution disrupted the productivity of the fields and fishponds (Santosa and Hutapea, 1992).

A tripartite team that included members from the community, industry and government was established. The parties involved in the team suggested mediation, as opposed to litigation, as the medium of choice to resolve the dispute. Although this was the first mediation case of its kind, it was considered a success on several counts. First, it included non-state actors, especially the affected population, as active participants in the negotiation. Second, the case precipitated calls for more transparency in the decision-making process. Third, widespread media coverage of the case – the first alternative dispute resolution attempt in Indonesia – was highly educational for the general public. And fourth, the commission considered claims for compensation and for a community 'right to know'.

A number of factors contributed to the effectiveness of mediation as an alternative dispute mechanism in the Dukuh Tapak case. The conflict, which had been ongoing for 14 years, was approaching a deadlock: nothing would have been achieved without mediation or litigation. Government officials were supportive of the establishment of the tripartite team (Santosa and Hutapea, 1992). Indeed, this mediation case – and to a larger extent, shaming through the boycott initiated by the environmental NGOs on the side – is an interesting model for an ombudsperson function.

Irrespective of the model, the ombudsperson function must be consistent with environmental politics and culture in Indonesia. As other countries, Indonesia is unique and so are its politics. In other words, the ombudsperson function should be country-specific or even sub-nationally specific. While an international entity might be helpful, it would have to be based on national political patterns. A centralized international ombudsperson function may violate the 'national pride' of some individuals who often use (or abuse) notions of national sovereignty. An ombudsperson function should also follow the geographical trend of free trade arrangements. As shown theoretically and empirically, the geographical aspect of trade liberalization has encouraged the emergence of regional and subregional economies such as the Sijori Growth Triangle. Moreover, the ombudsperson function should grow from existing working institutions with capable personnel already in place. Finally, efforts to establish any institution in Indonesia – subnational, national or international – should be initiated by identification of qualified persons behind the institutions. Gradually, institutionalization of the function, rather than individualization, should take place.

WALHI, the largest federation of environmental groups in Indonesia, suggests the creation of a National Commission on Sustainable Development with a prominent figure such as Dr Emil Salim to chair it. Such an institution has been established in the Philippines. The commission is envisioned to house various, sometimes conflicting, environmental and development interests. The commission may be modelled after the existing National Human Rights Commission, a commission established by the president, which reports directly to him (Anung Karyadi, 1997, personal communication). In the Human Rights Commission's first year, much scepticism was expressed, notably the fear that the commission would serve only as window-dressing put in place by the president as a reaction to the embarrassment caused by the international publicity of human rights violations in East Timor and other parts of Indonesia. Thus, while still under his control, the commission created an image of sufficient attention to human rights issues in Indonesia. In its course of development, however, the commission has become gradually more independent. Due to a lack of alternative channels, many victims of human rights violations in Indonesia file their complaints through the commission. The key to the Human Rights Commission's success, arguably, is its membership. In a political environment where individual figures are very important, the strong integrity of its members contributes to public trust in the commission. As a result, there are more disputes submitted to the commission than it can handle. Since the commission is small and centralized, it lacks adequate capacity to cope with a variety of local issues and thus mostly deals with issues that have national impacts or coverage.

Strong scepticism has been expressed regarding the plan to establish a National Commission on Sustainable Development, however. Among other reasons, its presence may undermine the existence and strength of the Human Rights Commission. Furthermore, it may erode the authority of the Minister of the Environment. If Emil Salim were to become the Chair of the new commission, Sarwono Kusumaatmadja, the current minister of Lingkungan Hidup, may not be happy with the intrusion of another authority in his field. His personal interest in detaching politics from the legacy of the almost legendary Emil Salim may be a strong enough force to oppose the establishment of such an institution. Moreover, there is a deep-seated reluctance on Salim's part to take such a position because it may suggest he has a 'post-power syndrome', which he strongly avoids and denies (Mas Ahmad Santosa, 1997, personal communication).

The 'post-power syndrome' problem is no longer relevant. Whereas Sarwono is no longer a Minister, Salim has proved his ability in being effective inside or outside government as time has passed. The establishment of the Sustainable Development Commission seems to have been undertaken at break-neck speed leading up to the World Summit for Sustainable Development.

BILIK and NPPR provide interesting models, in that they are inclusive. These models involve almost all interested stakeholders. They are much more participatory because, as a roundtable, there is no rigid bureaucratic organizational structure. While BILIK and NPPR were established completely independently of one another by different sets of actors and sponsors and in different sets of politics, they work in a strikingly similar way. As Santosa points out, an ombudsperson function in Indonesia may start from a network of smaller but specialized organizations whose function resembles what a future ombudsperson institution might look like (ibid). Organizations similar to BILIK and NPPR might be established in other regions requiring such an organization. Nevertheless, representation of affected communities in the roundtable may be an imperative to make these models evolve to play the ombudsperson function.

In brief, there are a number of models already existing in Indonesia, including the litigation approach that WALHI undertook, the clearinghouse and tribunal functions demonstrated by BILIK and NPPR, and the alternative dispute resolution that Mas Ahmad Santosa's institution initiated. The future ombudsperson function may combine the strengths of these models and minimize their weaknesses. At the international level, since both theoretical and empirical evidence leads to the emergence of regional and subregional economies around border regions, it seems logical to have either bilateral, trilateral or multilateral networks of BILIK-like institutions. A lobbying body could also be established at the level of the Association of the Southeast Asian Nations (ASEAN), to which nearly all of these border economies belong. Thus, in Batam, for example, BILIK would establish close relationships that lead to a network of similar interests in Singapore and in Malaysia, as it has done with NPPR. At the same time, NPPR, being an institution of national scope, could help foster development of similar organizations throughout ASEAN and undertake lobbying efforts in the ASEAN secretariat in Jakarta. This model has been used effectively by NGOs for various global environmental issues such as climate change. Most likely, this model can also work for environmental problems arising from trade liberalization.

CONCLUSION

Economic and trade liberalization have created severe pressure on local environments and human rights. Although the net impacts of trade liberalization have been a matter of sharp debate, sufficient empirical evidence shows severe negative impacts, as demonstrated by the case of Batam Island in Indonesia. Following the decline in oil export value, Indonesia perceived trade liberalization as an imperative to boost non-oil exports to maintain its foreign exchange earnings.

Thus, the Indonesian government responded to trade liberalization by relaxing obstacles to investment. In Indonesia, unfortunately, environmental regulation was perceived as an obstacle to be relaxed to attract more investors. The deregulation of the environmental stipulation created various environmental and human rights impacts.

In the case study of Batam, environmental and human rights consequences of trade liberalization are apparent. While economic progress has been impressive, environmental and human rights conflicts are more apparent. The absence of formal mechanisms to include public participation in formulating development decisions is a possible cause of the conflicts; weak enforcement of environmental regulation has exacerbated the situation.

What institutional setting is the most plausible solution? In Indonesia, establishing one needs thorough preparation, especially in ensuring the availability of necessary human resources. The institutional setting should emerge from existing institutions that already perform some of its functions, and should be tailored according to Indonesian political culture. Noting that the politics in Indonesia are generally informal and personal, identification of key persons behind the establishment of the institution is essential.

NOTES

1   This figure is one of the lowest, second only to hotel and restaurant sectors, which provide 0.27 per cent additional employment for every 1 per cent of economic growth rate. The highest figure is achieved by the utility sectors (electricity, gas and water) with 3.13 per cent employment growth for every 1 per cent of economic growth, followed closely by various service sectors (2.84) and trade sector (2.7).

2   With current employment of around 60,000 workers in the electronics industry, there will be at the most 4,000 more workers demanded every year. With minimum wage set

at US$1 per day, 5 days per week and 50 weeks per year, total income of these additional workers is around US$1 million. If out of this total, three-quarters of it is spent on Indonesian-made products and housing, there will be US$750,000 per year contributing to the local economy.

3   The electronics industry accounts for approximately 80 per cent of the manufacturing employment in the Batam region.

4   Arguably, it is due to the utilization of this term by the proponent of the inclusion of environmental concerns in Indonesian development that Suharto, the Indonesian President, was willing to sign the Earth Charter, Agenda 21, and the conventions on climate change and biodiversity at the Earth Summit in 1992.

5   The notion of non-permanence has created some problems of interpretation, however. Some interpret that a committee should, but is not obliged, to have an NGO on a committee, whereas others argue that the NGO to be involved depends on the issue and the location. Nevertheless, the inclusion of NGOs and affected communities in the regulation opens an avenue for public participation in development projects.

6   In 1993, the State Ministry for Population and the Environment was divided into the State Ministry for Population, headed by Haryono Suyono, and the State Ministry for the Environment, headed by Sarwono Kusumaatmadja.

REFERENCES

ACFOA (1995) *Trouble at Freeport: Eyewitness Accounts of West Papuan Resistance to the Freeport-McMoRan Mine in Irian Jaya, Indonesia, and Indonesian Military Repression: June 1994–February 1995*. Fitzroy, Australian Council for Overseas Aid

Ahmad, M (1993) 'Model Sijori dan Pemerataan: Sebuah Paradigma Pembangunan dengan Mitos-Mitos' [Sijori Model and Equity: A Development Paradigm with Myths], in Sasono, A, Juoro, U and Makka, A M (eds) *Prosiding Konvensi Nasional Pembangunan Regional dan Segitiga Pertumbuhan* [Proceedings of the National Convention on Regional Development and Growth Triangle], *Jakarta, 16–17 February 1993*. Jakarta, Center for Information and Development Studies and BIDA

Alatas, A (1994) 'Basic Principles, Objectives and Modalities of APEC', in Soesastro, H (ed) *Indonesian Perspectives on APEC and Regional Cooperation in Asia Pacific*. Edited version of Alatas, A (1991) *Asia Pacific Economic Cooperation (APEC): Implications for ASEAN*. Outline of remarks presented at the 'Conference on the ASEAN Countries and the World Economy: Challenge of Change', organized by the Asia Society and Center for Strategic and International Studies (CSIS), Bali, 3–5 March 1991. Jakarta, CSIS

ASEAN (1996) *Subwilayah Ekonomi ASEAN dan Kawasan Perdagangan Bebas ASEAN (AFTA)* [Economic Subregions in ASEAN and ASEAN Free Trade Area (AFTA)]. Jakarta, Department of Foreign Affairs, the Secretariat of the Association of the Southeast Asian Nations

BIDA (1995) *The Annual Report on the Economy of Batam Island 1995*. Batam, Batam Industrial Development Authority and the Central Bureau of Statistics of Riau

BIDA (1996) *The Annual Report on the Economy of Batam Island 1996*. Batam, Batam Industrial Development Authority and the Central Bureau of Statistics of Riau

BIDA (1997) 'BARELANG (Batam-Rempang-Galang): Development Data up to December 1996', Batam, Batam Industrial Development Authority

BPS (various years) *Statistik Indonesia* [The Indonesian Statistics]. Jakarta, Biro Pusat Statistik, the Central Bureau of Statistics

Coedés, G (1918) 'Le royaume de Çriwijaya' [The Kingdom of Sriwijaya], in *Bulletin de l'Ecole Francais d'Extreme-Orient* 18. Translated in Manguine, P and Sheppard, M (eds) (1936) *Sriwijaya: History, Religion, and Language of an Early Malay Polity: Collected Studies by George Coedés and Louis-Charles Damais*. Kuala Lumpur, Malaysian Branch of the Rural Asiatic Society

Coedés, G (1936) 'A propos d'une nouvelle theorie sur le site de Sriwijaya' [A new theory about the site of Sriwijaya], in Manguine, P and Sheppard, M (eds) *Sriwijaya: History, Religion, and Language of an Early Malay Polity: Collected Studies by George Coedés and Louis-Charles Damais*. Kuala Lumpur, Malaysian Branch of the Rural Asiatic Society

Davies, B (1992) 'Cooperation to Spark Regional Growth', *Asia Money and Finance Supplement*, November

Fröbel, F, Heinrichs, J and Kreye, O (1978) 'The World Market for Labor and the World Market for Industrial Sites', *Journal of Economic Issues* 12:4, December

GATT (1994) Final Act Embodying the Results of the Uruguay Round of Multilateral Trade Negotiations. Marrakesh, General Agreement on Tariffs and Trade

Gereffi, G (1994) 'The International Economy and Economic Development', in Smelser, N J and Swedberg, R (eds) *The Handbook of Economic Sociology*. Princeton, Princeton University Press

Gitlitz, J (1993) 'The Relationship between Primary Aluminum Production and the Damming of World Rivers', Master's Thesis, Energy and Resources Group. Berkeley, University of California at Berkeley (unpublished)

Grossman, G and Krueger, A (1991) 'Environmental Impacts of a North American Free Trade Agreement', paper prepared for the Conference on US-Mexico Free Trade Agreement, sponsored by SECOFI. Princeton, Princeton University

Henderson, J V and Kuncoro, A (1996) 'Industrial Centralization in Indonesia', *The World Bank Economic Review* 10

Horn, M (1993) 'Indonesia: New Regulation Allows Existing Export Manufacturing Facilities to Become Special Customs Zone', *East Asian Executives Reports* 15:4, 15 April

Jenkins, L, Stumberg, R, Chang, A and Irving, L (1996) 'WTO Policy on Multilateral Environmental Agreements', paper submitted by the American Society for the Prevention of Cruelty to Animals, The Canadian Federation of Humane Societies, The Humane Society of the United States, Humane Society International, International Fund for Animal Welfare to the World Trade Organization Committee on Trade and Environment. Washington, DC: The Harrison Institute of Public Law, Georgetown University Law Center

Kitazawa, Y (1990) 'The Japanese Economy and South-East Asia: The Examples of the Asahan Aluminum and Kawasaki Steel Projects', in Lim, T G and Valencia, M J (eds) *Conflict over Natural Resources in South-East Asia and the Pacific*. Singapore, Oxford and New York, United Nations University Press and Oxford University Press

Krugman, P (1991) *Geography and Trade*. Cambridge, Massachusetts, The MIT Press

Piore, C and Sabel, M. (1984) *The Second Industrial Divide*. New York, Basic Books

Quick, K (1995) 'Batam: Transformation of an Anonymous Island, to an Instrument for Political Change, to a Model for International Development Cooperation', unpublished manuscript prepared for the Department of City and Regional Planning, University of California, Berkeley, CA

Regnier, P (1987) *Singapore: City State in Southeast Asia* (translated from French by C Hurst). Honolulu: University of Hawaii Press

Santosa, M A and Hutapea, A L P (1992) *Mendayagunakan Mekanisme Alternatif Penyelesaian Lingkungan (MAPS)* [Utilizing the Alternative Dispute Resolution (ADR) Mechanism in Indonesia]. Jakarta: Wahana Lingkungan Hidup Indonesia

Sari, A (1996) 'Leaking Carbon – Calculating Carbon Dioxide Emissions Leakage in the Era of Global Trade Liberalization: The Case of Indonesia', Masters' Thesis, Energy and Resources Group. Berkeley, University of California at Berkeley (unpublished)

Saxenian, A (1994) *Regional Advantage: Culture and Competition in Silicon Valley and Route 128*. Cambridge, MA: Harvard University Press

Storper, M and Walker, R (1989) *The Capitalist Imperative: Territory, Technology, and Industrial Growth*. Oxford: Basil Blackwell

UNGA (United Nations General Assembly) (1992) *The Rio Declaration on Environment and Development: Report of the United Nations Conference on Environment and Development*. UN Document No. A/CONF. 151/26, Vol. 1, 12 August, signed at the United Nations Conference on Environment and Development, Rio de Janeiro, Brazil, June 1992. Rio de Janeiro: United Nations

World Bank (1994a) *Market Outlook for Major Energy Products, Metals, and Minerals*. Washington, DC: The World Bank

World Bank (1994b) *Indonesia Environment and Development: Challenges for the Future*. Washington, DC: The World Bank Environment Unit, Country Department III, East Asia and Pacific Region

Chapter 7

Global Norms, Local Compliance and the Human Rights–Environment Nexus: A Case Study of the Nam Theun II Dam in Laos

Philip Hirsch

INTRODUCTION

The proposed Nam Theun II Dam in Laos[1] has been subject to an unprecedented degree of study, scrutiny and standard setting. It is a project with significant environmental and human rights implications that have become hotly contested at various levels. Recent attempts to apply the findings and recommendations of the World Commission on Dams study to Nam Theun II are but the latest example of international and global institutions' attempt to use this project to try out hitherto little-tested procedures for assessment and planning, particularly in a country with poorly developed civil society such as Laos. Ironically, an outcome of this process has been the elaboration of plans and processes that have engaged rather superficially with Lao social and political currents.

This chapter addresses three overriding themes. The first is the difficulty and ultimate irrelevance and irresponsibility of separating social from environmental impacts of a project whose ecological demands alter both the livelihood and cultural base of the people affected. The second is the set of dilemmas raised by the creation and application of global norms to help justify a project whose host country has poorly established politico-institutional and cultural means of dealing with such norms. The third is the importance of understanding competing agendas in the context of wider and longer-term conflicts, whether they are resource based or geopolitical.

The chapter begins with a background to the Mekong River Basin, the history of conflict and peace in the region, and the various development plans that took shape through the 1990s, notably hydropower development. It then in turn considers the environmental and human rights implications of this development agenda, and the need to pay greater attention to the nexus of these two sets of concerns. The Nam Theun II dispute encapsulates the dilemmas and arguments surrounding hydro-development in the Mekong, and the features of the dam together with the 'architecture' of the dispute surrounding it help to illustrate the three key themes of the case study. Various actors have become involved in the dispute, from the isolated swidden farmers of Nakai in Laos' upper Khammouane Province, to players whose more familiar habitat is the corridors of the World Bank in Washington, DC. The protracted process of decision-making and negotiation around Nam Theun II illustrates the wide range of positions. Ultimately, however, it has been a process that engages rather little with Lao stakeholders.

THE MEKONG RIVER BASIN

The Mekong River Basin is a natural unit covering an area of 795,000 square kilometres and spanning parts of six countries in mainland Southeast Asia – China, Burma, Laos, Thailand, Cambodia and Vietnam. The region covered by the basin has a recent history of geopolitical conflict and cooperation, including in the area of natural resource management. The transboundary aspect of the basin is one of the sources of potential environmental and resource conflict, as each country's use of terrestrial and aquatic resources impacts on other countries' ecosystems. Regional rapprochement in the context of post-cold war easing of geopolitical tensions has permitted and encouraged an intensification of a development agenda based on exploiting natural resources, which has in turn posed potential conflicts between riverine nations and between different interest groups that transcend or lie within national borders.

The Mekong River itself is 4,200 kilometres in length. It is the world's 12th longest river and 10th largest if measured by its discharge volume of 475 billion cubic metres. A highly significant feature of the Mekong River is its seasonal flow fluctuation due to the monsoonal nature of most of the basin, so that the low flow (May) is only about one-fifteenth of the high flow (September). The implications of this variability are manifold, ranging from pressures to regulate in order to even out flood and drought regimes, to susceptibility of ecosystems that have adapted to seasonal variation, to interference in the natural seasonal discharge.

While there are many facets to natural resource development in the Mekong River Basin, all of which have environmental and social implications, the issue of large-scale river impoundment has risen to the top of the eco-political agenda in the Mekong Region. Plans for mainstream and tributary dams in the Mekong Basin are long-standing, but it is only since the 1990s that regional geopolitical and developmental conditions have permitted the investment and cooperation that would allow such projects to be built on a large scale. This has occurred at a time when large-scale river impoundment elsewhere in the world is increasingly being questioned on ecological, cultural and even economic grounds. The World

Commission on Dams report was the culmination of such challenges (WCD, 2000).

The core of the Mekong River Basin development programme is a series of dams on the mainstream Mekong River itself, the so-called Mekong Cascade. While these have been scaled down from their originally proposed heights as so-called 'run-of-river' projects to lessen environmental and social dislocation, there is still sufficient concern over their effects to incur significant delays and raise doubts over whether any dams will be built on the lower Mekong mainstream (Hill and Hill, 1994). The exception is the Manwan Dam on the Chinese section of the Mekong (Lancang) and several other dams currently under construction along this section in Yunnan Province (McCormack, 2001). More immediately significant for the Lower Mekong River is the significant number of proposed tributary dams in Lao People's Democratic Republic (Lao PDR), Vietnam and Cambodia, and to a lesser extent in Thailand, most of whose Mekong tributaries have already been impounded.

A brief history of Mekong development, conflict and cooperation

The Mekong Region has a history of geopolitical conflict over the past several decades. Regimes supported by the US in Thailand, Laos, South Vietnam and, after 1970, Cambodia, were in armed conflict with North Vietnam and communist revolutionaries in many of the remoter rural areas within the Mekong Basin up to 1975. After 1975, most of the region was enmeshed in the cold war. Communist regimes in Laos, Vietnam and Cambodia were set against pro-Western Thailand. Sino-Soviet tensions were reflected in Chinese support for the Khmer Rouge against the Vietnamese-supported Heng Samrin regime. In Cambodia, civil war has meant almost continuous armed conflict up to the present, but this has become more intermittent and 'Cambodianized' since the early 1990s. Thus, the Second Indo-China War engulfed the region from the early 1960s until 1975 and precluded large-scale infrastructure development, while after 1975 until the late 1980s the region was at the front line of cold war divisions. During these periods, the Mekong River served as an axis of division rather than unification. Since the late 1980s, the end of the cold war has been manifest in regional terms by Thailand's desire to convert 'battlefields into marketplaces', Vietnam and Laos' entry into ASEAN, and an agenda of economic cooperation and integration within the Greater Mekong Subregion (Hirsch and Cheong, 1996; Stensholt, 1996; Bakker, 1999).

More specific to the Mekong Basin is a history of cooperation stemming from the establishment of the Mekong Committee in 1957, involving the four lower Mekong countries, excluding China and Burma (Jacobs, 1995). This committee involved the then US allies of Laos, Thailand, Cambodia and South Vietnam. Early on, therefore, there was a conflation of the river management role of the committee and its de facto geopolitical make-up of pro-US states. After the change to communist regimes in Laos and Cambodia and the unification of Vietnam under a communist regime after 1975, the committee went into abeyance and was reconstituted as the Interim Mekong Committee in 1978 without Cambodia's participation. From the late 1980s, attempts were made to reconstitute the committee, including an abortive meeting in 1992 whose aim was to re-admit Cambodia. This false start was abandoned due largely to disagreements between Thailand and Vietnam over which set of rules over water sharing and diversion were to be adopted as articles in the new set of statutes, and hence what degree of veto downstream countries would have over upstream developments. Eventually, the Mekong River Commission (MRC) was formed in April 1995 with the signing in Chiengrai of the Agreement on Cooperation for the Sustainable Development of the Mekong River Basin. The MRC includes the four lower riparian states but excludes China and Burma.

New forces for development

One of the results of the decline in geopolitical conflict and a newly constituted framework for cooperative management of the Mekong River Basin has been an accelerated development agenda based on regional integration. The Asian Development Bank (ADB) has an ambitious but controversial regional development agenda based on integration of Greater Mekong Subregion (GMS) countries, using the river and its basin as a linking metaphor. Such integration has political, economic and physical aspects. Politically, the end of the cold war axis of division has allowed Thailand to engage with its neighbours in a new way as the pro- and anti-communist camps have largely dissolved. The withdrawal of Vietnamese troops from Cambodia in 1989 and the partial process of demilitarization of the Cambodian internal conflict in the early 1990s altered relations between Thailand and Vietnam, and this new footing was consolidated in 1995 with Vietnam's accession to ASEAN. Meanwhile, Vietnam and China have developed a non-military basis for resolving their border conflict, and this too has been eased by the developments in Cambodia. Lao PDR and Burma joined ASEAN in July 1997, while Cambodia followed in 1999. The MRC is itself a signifier of political rapprochement within the region. The Mekong Secretariat has moved its offices from Bangkok to Phnom Penh.

Physically, regional integration involves large-scale infrastructure proposals that would entail massive public and private investments to link the region through roads, railways, telecommunications and an integrated electricity grid. The latter is closely and directly associated with development of the region's natural resource base in the form of large dams on the Mekong and its tributaries for hydropower. A significant issue is the nature of project financing, as an increasing emphasis is placed on raising private capital through build-own-operate-transfer (BOOT) arrangements. This aspect of privatization has implications for social and environmental assessment procedures, since the conditions associated with Multilateral Development Bank (MDB) loans to public utilities may be partly or wholly short-circuited. Nam Theun II is an example of a BOOT scheme, but one that has maintained an MDB role through a proposed World Bank International Development Agency (IDA) loan and guarantee mechanism through the Multilateral Investment Guarantee Agency (MIGA).

New axes of conflict and cooperation

Heightened regional cooperation in the political, economic and physical infrastructure spheres has facilitated development of large-scale project proposals, which in turn have engendered new tensions. At one level, conflicts potentially exist along a similar axis to the geopolitical rifts of the cold war era, but with a quite different basis in the form of competition for natural resources – particularly water – between upstream and downstream countries in the Mekong River Basin. While such upstream–downstream issues pre-date the current era of regional rapprochement, they have only become materially significant with the imminence of several large-scale dams and associated diversion schemes. The MRC has established a basis for cooperation between countries in the area of water management, particularly to deal with projects that involve cross-border development (notably for export of hydropower). With this framework for cooperation in place, actual or potential conflicts between countries have become secondary to more immediate differences between actors along different axes.

The controversy over Mekong development is encapsulated in the debate surrounding proposals for large dams. In Thailand, there is a long-standing controversy at local and national levels over large dam construction. Environmentalists and local people affected by dams have come into conflict with the Electricity Generating Authority of Thailand (EGAT) and others with interests in dam construction. Thailand's sourcing of energy from outside the country's borders is, in part, a response to the eco-political conflict within Thailand itself. Such eco-political conflict occurs along axes that have more to do with socio-economic and ideological positions within and transcending national borders than with interests that can be posed as one country versus another. Different resource sectors also have conflicting interests as a result of the differential impact of resource development; for example, energy generation based on hydropower has an impact on fisheries.

ENVIRONMENTAL IMPLICATIONS OF MEKONG DEVELOPMENT

The environmental implications of accelerated development within the Mekong Basin, and the Mekong Region more widely, are enormous (McCully, 1996). The region has already been subject to widespread deforestation, with loss of about half of the forest cover since the early 1960s. More specifically, dams have diverse environmental impacts. Broadly, these can be categorized into impoundment and barrier effects, although these are related.

Impoundment effects are consequences of flooding the large areas of land required for storage reservoirs. Large areas of forest often need to be cleared. The topography of flooded areas is relatively distinctive and rare riverine valley environments tend to be the ones that are inundated. Reservoir aquatic environments are different from riverine environments in a number of ways, due to their still-water characteristics, thermal stratification and reduced oxygen content. Fish species composition in reservoirs is consequently markedly different from the natural distribution. Reservoirs often provide habitats suited to disease vectors. They can also cause waterlogging of surrounding areas, with effects on surrounding vegetation.

The barrier effects of dams and their associated reservoirs are particularly significant for migratory fish species. The Mekong River is the world's third most biodiverse freshwater aquatic system in terms of ichthyofauna (after the Amazon and Zaire rivers), with an estimated 1,200 species of fish (Roberts and Baird, 1995). Relatively little is known of the patterns of migration and spawning or interdependence between species and their resilience to ecosystem disturbance, but most fisheries experts agree that the barrier effects of dams provide a potentially major – and irreversible – disruptive influence to the freshwater ecology of the Mekong and its tributaries.

Other environmental consequences of large dams include the accessibility to previously isolated areas that comes with associated roads and other infrastructure. Another important issue is the large number of workers brought in during the period of construction, who often hunt, clear land for farming and otherwise encroach on previously sparsely populated forest areas.

It should be noted that proponents of the larger schemes set the dam construction agenda in positive as well as negative environmental terms. Non-fossil fuel based sources of energy have been given a fillip in the context of greenhouse warming. Dams are put forward by some Lao officials as a substitute for logging, the intimation being that without the export income from sale of hydropower it will be necessary to engage in even more environmentally harmful resource exploitation in the form of timber felling. Dams are also promoted as means to solve downstream flood problems within the Mekong's macro-ecological framework, although this in itself is controversial given the complex adaptation of the natural and human ecology of the system to the natural flood regime.

Environmental implications of Mekong hydropower development need to be seen in the light of the alternatives to large dams, and also with reference to the question of economic or other developmental trade-offs. While it is well beyond the scope and purpose of this chapter to assess such alternatives and trade-offs, a few points are relevant. Alternatives to 'renewable' hydro-energy are put forward by dam proponents as dirty, unsustainable, fuel-costly and risky options such as coal- and oil-burning fossil fuel plants or even nuclear power, which is on the agenda of EGAT. Opponents or sceptics of large dams tend to question their renewable status, given their limited life due to siltation, and stress decentralized, smaller-scale, alternative options such as micro-hydropower, solar or wind energy, and also enhanced energy conservation measures. Part of their critique is also of the high-growth, high-energy path of development, which means that the debate tends to bypass the question of which mode of large-scale energy generation is preferable. Furthermore, in the case of Lao PDR, such debates are largely irrelevant, since the proposed energy generation is for foreign exchange and not primarily for electrification within the country. Thus, the relevant issue here is whether the foreign exchange generated by hydropower is worth the environmental risks and losses, and also whether the economic benefits are as great as the dam proponents – most of whom have obvious vested interests – put forward. These issues are dealt with further in the case of Nam Theun II below.

HUMAN RIGHTS IMPLICATIONS OF MEKONG DEVELOPMENT

The human rights implications of development in the Mekong Region, and of construction of large dams in particular, need to be seen in terms of the unequal geographical distribution of costs and benefits (Hirsch, 1988). However worthwhile individual and cumulative projects may appear according to aggregate calculations of rates of return, they invariably require a sacrifice by one group of people in the name of wider benefits for other groups, often located some distance apart. Typically, those people whose homes, farmlands, fisheries and forest resources are most directly affected are geographically, socially, economically and ethnically marginal within the national context in which they live. Thus, among the social issues raised by large dams and their displacement effects are the impacts on indigenous peoples, the degree and nature of compensation, participation in decision-making over the project itself and over resettlement schemes or other mitigation measures (*Cultural Survival Quarterly*, 1999).

However, over and above these immediate questions at a project level are more generic questions that beg consideration in the overall context of Mekong development. Resource tenure and property rights issues are crucial to the human outcomes and direction of benefit streams from projects such as large dams. In many parts of the region, notably the more remote areas typically slated for inundation by dams, rights and responsibilities over the resource base are still ill defined. Ambiguity of resource tenure is due in large part to overlapping formal and vernacular arrangements within national frameworks that do not recognise customary tenure. In part, it is also due to the more specific context of change from socialized and subsistence production to the market economy within various frameworks of privatization, notably in the 'transitional' economies of Indo-China (Laos, Cambodia and Vietnam).

An even wider and more vexing issue in the human rights context is the uneven development of civil society within the Mekong Region, both between and within countries. China, Vietnam and Laos are one-party states with relatively limited opportunity for expression outside the formal party structures. In fact, a considerable degree of debate occurs within such structures, but not in a way that is independent of or in any sense a challenge to mainstream decision-making. In Cambodia, the climate of violence and continuing civil conflict precludes many aspects of civil society, while Burma's repressive State Law and Order Restoration Council (SLORC) regime similarly is not conducive to any open form of challenge over mainstream resource development agendas, however controversial they may be (the Yadana gas pipeline is a case in point). Thailand has the most developed civil society, which is expressed in the relatively open media, oppositional NGOs and frequent challenges to business and state projects that threaten local livelihoods and environments. Some of the more controversial developments that are too expensive socially and politically within Thailand have been shifted to neighbouring countries to serve the Thai market, within the wider framework of Mekong regional cooperation (Hirsch, 1995).

THE NAM THEUN II CASE

Many of the key environmental and human rights issues raised in the context of Mekong Basin development are exemplified by the controversy generated by one proposed hydropower project, the Nam Theun II scheme (hereafter referred to as NT2). NT2 was first conceived and investigated in the mid-1980s, but as of April 2001 it is still under a cloud of uncertainty due to environmental, social and economic concerns. This uncertainty has been exacerbated by the financial crisis in Southeast Asia. The scale of the dam itself, and more importantly, the wide range of actors who have become involved in the dispute, provide many lessons for decision-makers at different levels.

NT2 is the most significant of the proposed tributary dams currently under consideration in several key ways:

- *Scale of the project:* NT2 is important in its own right in terms of power to be generated, investment required, area inundated, range of actors involved and size in relation to the economy in which it is located.
- *Potential impact:* NT2 is important due to the sensitivity of the ecosystems affected, and it also has significant socio-cultural implications as a result of the displacement of communities that would be necessitated.
- *Icon of controversy:* NT2 has become the focus of intense debate and controversy over Mekong development at a number of levels.
- *Test case:* NT2 can be seen as a test case for Lao PDR's hydropower-driven, export-led growth strategy, for the World Bank's continued involvement in large dams worldwide after its withdrawal from Narmada and Arun III, and as a model of privatized, large-scale infrastructure development with MDB support through loan guarantee mechanisms.
- *Internationalization of debate:* Many international players have spotlighted NT2 as an example of a development project with environmental implications despite the fact that it is located in Lao PDR, a still relatively closed country with weakly developed institutions of open governance and civil society.

Nam Theun II Dam: Project background

The Nam Theun II project is located on the Nam Theun River in Nakai District, in the central province of Khammouane in Lao PDR. The dam would flood an area of about 450 square kilometres. This area was quite remote until project preparation got under way in the early 1990s. The project area includes the damsite itself, the inundated area, the rivers affected and the catchment to the dam, referred to here as the Nam Theun Watershed.

The Nam Theun Watershed is defined as the catchment area for NT2. The watershed is located entirely within Lao PDR and encompasses an area of 4,013 square kilometres. The watershed is drained by six main tributaries of the Nam Theun River: the Nam Sot, Nam Mone, Nam Theun, Nam Noi, Nam Pheo and Nam One. The watershed abuts the Vietnamese border. It is largely forested and recognized internationally as an area of enormous biodiversity significance, highlighted by the capture of a sao la (Vu Quang ox), a mammal only positively identified as a new species in 1994. Several other rare or endangered species reside within the watershed. The watershed area is inhabited by scattered communities of indigenous ethnic minorities who are alternatively seen as having adapted their shifting cultivation practices to the natural ecology, and as a threat to the ecological integrity of the area.

The watershed has become part of the project area in a number of ways. First, watershed integrity is seen by project proponents as integral to the viability of the dam, since deforestation and subsequent soil erosion would accelerate problems of reservoir siltation. Second, the watershed has been put forward as a compensatory conservation area to make up for the inundation of forest by the reservoir. Third, those living in the watershed area would be affected by a heightened degree of management that would impinge on their livelihoods.

Under the Nam Theun II scheme, most of the watershed area would be incorporated within the Nakai-Nam Theun Biodiversity Conservation Area (NBCA), to cover the reservoir area and its catchment and to be funded from project revenues. The area cannot be so declared until the dam is approved, as this would contravene the World Bank's regulations concerning financing of dams in protected areas. It should also be noted that this area was slated by the World Conservation Union (IUCN) as a high-priority conservation area before the dam was proposed in its current form. Moreover, it was mooted for Global Environment Facility (GEF) support before the World Bank became involved with the proposed guarantee for private financing of the project (see below).

Nakai Plateau is a distinctive upland environment with ecology quite different from the watershed area. Whereas the watershed is dissected upland forest, the plateau in its natural state consists of open grasslands, pine forests unique to this part of Laos and mixed deciduous tropical forest. It was identified by the IUCN in its protected area prioritization exercise in 1991 as containing an exceptional richness of fauna. During the 1980s, the army-owned Mountainous Region Development Corporation (Bolisat Phatthana Khet Phudoi, commonly referred to in project documents and hitherto in this chapter as BPKP) undertook selective logging of the *merkusi* pine forest for export to Japan via Vinh in Vietnam. Until the early 1990s, the Nakai plateau remained largely forested. However, since 1994 the area to be inundated under the project has been clear felled by BPKP in anticipation of the dam going ahead, despite the continuing uncertainty over project funding. Environmental assessment documents reflect this degradation of the Nakai Plateau environment in a way that favours construction of the dam (relative to the recommendations that could be expected if the Nakai Plateau forests remained more intact). Thus, there is already a pre-emptive process in place being driven by the 'project environment' of which the project consortium and feasibility studies are a part.

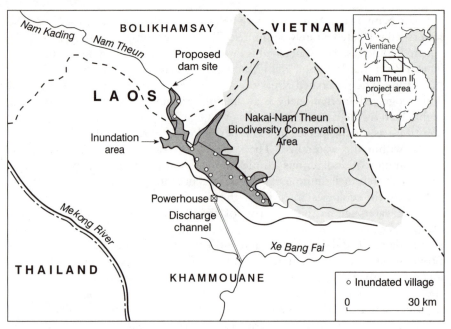

Figure 7.1 *Nam Theun II Project Area*

Project parameters

The Nam Theun II dam is a relatively small physical structure in relation to the size of the hydroelectric project. The main structure is a 50-metre barrage on the Nam Theun River (Figure 7.1). However, the head of water is much greater due to the diversion of water through a tunnel down a 350-metre escarpment into the Nam Kathang valley in Gnommalat District. Full supply level of the reservoir is likely to be 535 metres above sea level and the reservoir will flood 450 square kilometres at the maximum level. The dam would generate more than 1000 MW2 and is said by project developers to have an extremely high factor load of about 80 per cent (typically factor load, or the proportion of theoretically achievable energy output if turbines were running at full load 100 per cent of the time, is less than 50 per cent).

The project will cost about US$1.5 billion at current estimates but this is subject to revision. This is approximately equivalent to the annual gross domestic product of the whole of Laos. Rate of return on investment has been predicted by project developers to be the highest of all projected hydropower projects in Laos at 30 per cent per annum. The most recent economic evaluation studies are less optimistic. While project proponents have suggested a gross annual return to the Lao economy of US$230 million, the economic evaluation report carried out for the World Bank indicated that the net return would be about US$38 million. However, in the absence of a power purchase agreement the returns are still unknowable and are highly sensitive to the unit purchase price agreed between the Nam Theun Electricity Corporation (NTEC) consortium and EGAT, the power purchaser. The economic studies were based on a unit price of 5.7 cents per kilowatt-hour (kWh), but the power purchase agreement (PPA) with EGAT has more recently been negotiated on a 4.3 cents/kWh price (Louis Berger, 1997). Moreover, the regional electricity market is moving towards a spot-price arrangement, so PPAs are unlikely to hold for long.

A significant aspect of Nam Theun II is that almost all the electricity generated would be exported to Thailand. Currently, Laos has an installed capacity of 450 MW, of which more than 80 per cent is already exported. This has been achieved with the Nam Ngum Dam, completed in 1971, and the Nam Theun-Hinboun, Nam Leuk and Huai Ho Dams that have all been completed since 1998. The multiplication of current capacity is thus entirely to serve an export market. Despite an early agreement by EGAT to purchase 3000 MW of power from Laos, there were concerns over this market even before Thailand's recent economic woes, as a result of EGAT's rapid diversification of sourcing to independent power producers. Furthermore, EGAT is no longer bound to take power from NT2 under the terms of the agreement, since project delays will not allow NTEC to deliver power by the contractual dates.

Conceptually, one of the significant points regarding public subsidy to project financing is that NT2 cannot be seen as an infrastructure investment in the sense of facilitating other forms of development through physical provision in the form of extra power or other facilities. Rather, it should more readily be seen as an enclave resource extraction initiative, similar to a mining operation, whose principal raison d'être is to generate foreign exchange in the form of dividends on state-held shares and from resource royalties.

KEY IMPLICATIONS AND ISSUES FOR RESOLUTION

The positive and negative implications of NT2 are numerous and complex. They have generated many thousands of pages of economic, engineering, environmental and social impact studies.[3] For the purposes of this discussion, the key benefits and costs are reduced to the key issues that have entered the public debate. Nam Theun II project proponents promise:

- foreign exchange for Laos, with project revenues in excess of US$270 million per annum;
- an improved standard of living for people on the Nakai Plateau;
- revenues to Lao PDR that allow national development and poverty alleviation; and
- biodiversity protection in the National Biodiversity Conservation Area above the dam.

Critics of Nam Theun II claim that the project will have adverse effects on:

- the environment of Nakai, the catchment and downstream riverine ecology;
- local people's culture and livelihoods; and
- Laos' exposure to foreign debt and risk-prone development strategy.

Large dams have been the subject of controversy for many years, largely due to the social and environmental impacts of such large and localized disruptions to community and ecology. However, the symbolic aspect of dams has also been important. On the one hand, they have been supported by proponents as 'temples to development'; on the other hand, they have been derided by environmentalists and proponents of a grassroots approach to development as part of a development juggernaut riding roughshod over nature and people's lives. Scale is thus inherently important in the controversy over large dams.

Nam Theun II has become involved in such a complex and high-profile controversy largely because of its size, relative to the Lao economy, relative to other dams in Laos and in terms of its impact on vulnerable communities and ecosystems. The controversy has been played out at many levels and locations, from global financial institutions to community meetings, from the corridors of the World Bank to the villages of Nakai Plateau. A particularly striking aspect of the Nam Theun II controversy has been the extent to which it has been played out by non-Lao actors, even within Laos. In part, this is due to the range of interests in the project, and in part it reflects the limited space for open articulation of interests within the Lao socio-political system.

It is important not to view the controversy over NT2 simply in terms of pro- and anti-dam interests. Many issues are raised by NT2 that are not simply questions of whether the dam will be a good thing or not, or whether it is worthwhile in terms of the environment sacrificed for development benefits gained. Rather, there are issues of process, of decision-making structures, of openness, of risk distribution and of power that need to be addressed in order to reflect on the scheme.

AFFECTED ENVIRONMENTS

Inundated area

As indicated, the inundated area is largely located on the Nakai Plateau. Until 1996, the projected area to be inundated was put at 347 square kilometres. Revised topographic maps have since raised this to 450 square kilometres at full supply level. This reduces to 164 square kilometres at minimum operating level. By the time approval is given to commence construction, if this occurs, the area to be flooded will have been largely logged out by BPKP. However, it is important to recognize that most of this logging has occurred *because* of the projected dam, since the move from selective logging to clear felling was done on the understanding that NTEC would be given a green light to go ahead with the project. Other ecological impacts in the inundated area include the conversion of a free-flowing river to a still-water reservoir, with anticipated changes in fish species composition. The gentle topography of the plateau means that an exceptionally large drawdown area would be periodically exposed and flooded on a seasonal basis, and this poses potential hazards to human health as niches favoured by disease vectors are enhanced.

Riverine effects

The Nam Theun II river would be entirely diverted off the Nakai Plateau into a neighbouring river system. The riverine effects of this occur in three main areas. First, a portion of the Nam Theun River downstream of the dam would be effectively dry for a significant portion of the year, and the Nam Kading flow would be concomitantly reduced. This would potentially impact on downstream fisheries, on water available for irrigation and domestic use to downstream communities, and on the Nam Theun-Hinboun hydropower project downstream of Nam Theun II, which was completed in 1998 and which also involves a diversion through an intra-basin transfer. The second riverine impact would be on the receiving river system, the third order Nam Kathang tributary and the second order Xe Bang Fai tributary of the Mekong. The small Nam Kathang would have to be extensively channelized to accommodate the Nam Theun II flows, while the Xe Bang Fai, already susceptible to flash floods, would have to cope with an altered flood regime. Fisheries impacts could also be quite severe. However, baseline fisheries studies only commenced in 2001. Quite significant is the sensitivity of these systems to the management regime of Nam Theun II, so that flood peaks would depend on whether the project would forgo income by holding water back at key flood periods and also on the relative base-load or peak-load function of the dam. Thus, the geographical cost-benefit considerations do not stop with project appraisal prior to construction.

Watershed area

The watershed area would be affected by the Nam Theun II project largely as a result of the increased accessibility that project roads and associated infrastructure bring to the area. Several thousand construction workers will reside at camps during the construction phase. Project proponents foresee a net gain for the environmental integrity of the watershed area if it is funded as the NBCA with project revenues.

AFFECTED COMMUNITIES

Inundated communities

Altogether, about 5,000 people from 28 different ethnic groups in 22 communities would be directly affected by inundation of the Nakai Plateau by Nam Theun II Dam.[4] A key point of contention over the dam has been the issue of whether such communities are to be classed as indigenous people, since the World Bank's Operational Directive on Indigenous Peoples requires certain extra studies and safeguards if they are so classified. While the Lao government and earlier consultancy studies chose to ignore the issue of indigenous status, more recent assessments (notably the socio-cultural study and the panel of experts (POE) review – see below) have unambiguously concluded that virtually all those in the inundation area are indigenous as classed by the Operational Directive.

Resettlement plans initially sought to relocate these communities off the Plateau altogether, but in response to a near universal preference for continued residence at Nakai the current resettlement action plan is trying to accommodate most or all on the southern edge of the reservoir. The two main livelihood options are an agroforestry model whereby the communities would be substantially integrated into an industrial forestry enterprise while maintaining their own small horticultural gardens and woodlots, and a more subsistence oriented model that would allow for wet rice cultivation, gardens and smaller woodlots. The viability of these models is still under study.

Downstream communities

Downstream communities to be affected include those on the Nam Kathang River whose channelization would affect villages in Gnommalat District, those subject to flooding and fisheries impacts by the Xe Bang Fai, and communities on the Nam Theun/Nam Kading whose water supply is reduced because of diversion. Furthermore, there may be minor fluctuations in Mekong River flow during the period of dam filling as the river accounts for 6 per cent of annual Mekong flow. This potentially could affect communities downstream in delta sections of Cambodia and Vietnam.

Watershed area

Communities in the watershed area would be affected indirectly in two main ways. First, they would become the subject of heightened surveillance and restrictions on shifting cultivation and other forest uses that could be expected with implementation of the NBCA scheme. Second, the influx of project construction workers could be expected to have similar social impacts to those documented in many countries where large numbers of relatively well-paid, mostly male, ethnically dominant construction workers are located close to indigenous communities.

THE ARCHITECTURE OF THE NAM THEUN II CONTROVERSY: KEY PLAYERS

Appreciating the 'architecture' of a controversy such as that surrounding the proposed Nam Theun II dam involves more than a simple listing of the actors or stakeholders involved. The controversy is also shaped and structured by key alliances and needs to be seen as a dynamic process with an accumulative addition of new layers, or 'stories', to the controversy, in terms of both the range of actors involved and the complexity of the decision-making process. The key actors (see Figure 7.2) can be summarized as follows:

Project developers

The Project Development Group (PDG) formed the company NTEC, in which the Lao government has a 25 per cent share. This mainly private consortium is

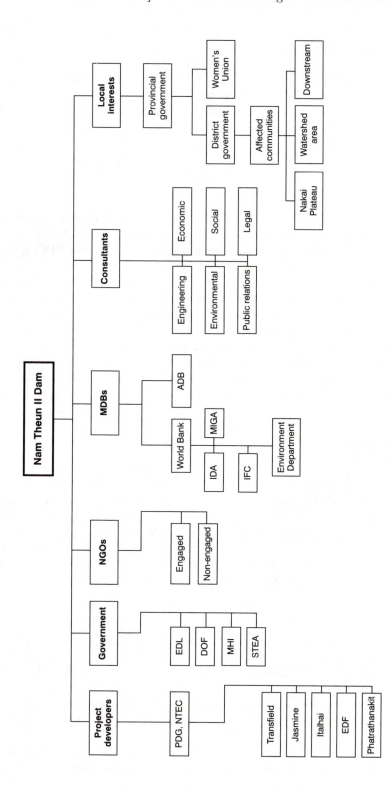

Figure 7.2 *Nam Theun II Key Players*

developing NT2 as a commercial project primarily concerned with generating export revenue. Although the project's financial bottom line is the primary reason for commercial involvement, much of the public discourse of project proponents has been concerned with the benefits NT2 would bring to Lao PDR, its people and environment. It should be noted that the profits to be derived from NT2 are both from ownership-based revenues and from construction contracts, so that some of the partners – notably Transfield (which on-sold its share in the project in 2000) and Ital-Thai – have vested interests in seeing the project go ahead for the up-front construction revenues.

MDBs

In the case of NT2, the World Bank is the key multilateral development bank concerned (the Asian Development Bank is involved in BOOT projects elsewhere in Lao PDR). The International Finance Corporation (IFC) would provide loans for Lao government equity in the project; MIGA is the key to providing guarantees that would convince commercial banks to finance the bulk of NT2; and IDA is providing concessional loans for the macro-economic assessment and the alternatives study, as well as providing the channel through which Lao government infringement of MIGA conditions would be converted into a financial liability to the Bank. A task manager has overall responsibility for coordinating the Bank's multiple involvements with NT2. World Bank involvement also includes the Environment Department, including the Bank's most experienced staff member on dams, Robert Goodland. The Bank comes to NT2 as a complex actor, with internal differences over the project.

Consultants

Consultants are paid by the project developers to carry out the various assessments stipulated by the World Bank. Most of the consultants are commercial consultancy firms from Thailand, Australia and the US, but CARE, IUCN and WCS (see under NGOs below) have served as consultants on the social and environmental studies. It is notable that PDG has retained the services of public relations personnel, including a former Australian television journalist and a Bangkok-based public relations firm (Spindler Associates) who employed a former activist to try to get NGOs on board with the project.

NGOs

Non-governmental organizations have maintained a high profile in the NT2 debate, in part due to the absence of alternative means for expressing critical or alternative voices within Lao PDR's weakly developed civil society. All these NGOs are foreign, although they employ Lao staff. No Lao NGOs are yet allowed to operate. With respect to NT2, there is a fairly clear division between NGOs that have 'engaged' with the project through involvement in the assessment process and resettlement planning, and those that have chosen to remain 'non-engaged' for fear of lending legitimacy to a process in which they feel there is little room for alternative voices. The 'engaged' NGOs include the

Geneva based World Conservation Union (formerly International Union for Conservation of Nature, or IUCN), New York based World Conservation Society (WCS) and the Australia based CARE International. The 'non-engaged' NGOs include the Canadian and Japanese volunteer organizations CUSO and JVC, the Thai-based regional organization TERRA, the US based Consortium and the International Rivers Network, and the Australian branch of the OXFAM network, Community Aid Abroad.

Central government (GoL)

The key central Lao government agencies with roles in the project are:

- Electricite de Laos, the state producer and distributor of electricity;
- the Ministry of Industry and Handicrafts, under whose Electricity Department the project falls directly;
- the Prime Minister's Office which, due to the national significance of NT2 has been closely involved in key decisions;
- the Department of Forestry and, more specifically, the Centre for Protected Area and Watershed Management within whose area of responsibility the National Biodiversity Conservation Area lies;
- the Science, Technology and Environment Agency (STEA), which coordinates decision-making on projects with significant environmental implications, and which has played a key role in the limited participation process;
- the State Planning Commission, which is responsible for national planning and all projects involving foreign aid and investment flows; and
- the military through its Mountainous Regions Development Corporation (BPKP), whose commercial interests in the project area situate it as a key player in the management and implementation of many resettlement and environmental management aspects of the project.

Local organizations

Provincial and district local governments (Khammouane and Bolikhamsay Provinces; Nakai, Gnommalat and Khamkeud Districts) have had relatively little direct role in the assessment process, other than facilitating the studies in a logistical sense. The Khammouane Province Women's Union has been involved in some of the social surveys. Since this is an organization with which many NGOs work on a regular basis, it provides an important link between the sometimes polarized actors in the NT2 controversy.

Local people affected by the project

Local people affected by NT2 include those living in the immediate area of inundation, those living downstream on the Nam Theun River and on the Nam Kathang/Xe Bang Fai into which the dam will divert water, and those living in the NBCA whose livelihoods will be affected by various restrictions on resource use. These people have been visited many times during the assessment process, and in the project's own terms they have been 'consulted'. This must be understood, however, in the light of the very limited opportunities for public debate or challenge within rural Laos, due to both political and cultural constraints. A high level of expectation has been built up through the project preparation process. Moreover, with the logging out of the plateau, a significant part of people's livelihoods has already been destroyed.

The NT2 controversy plays out along a number of axes. NGOs and project developers tend to come into most direct confrontation, with arguments over what model of 'development' is good for Lao PDR, its environment and people. Similarly, several NGOs see the World Bank as essentially in support of the project developers' model of development. GoL and developers share an interest in supporting NT2, although there are critical voices behind the scenes within GoL. The primary negotiation along this axis is the distribution of costs, benefits and risks associated with the project, and to this end there is concern about the inexperience of GoL with complex financing deals such as the BOOT arrangement involved here. There are also tensions and debates within the NGO community, largely along the engaged/non-engaged axis outlined above. While it is possible to see a structural axis of tension between project developers/World Bank on the one hand, and local people on the other, this is not played out through challenge or debate for reasons indicated above.

AN EXTREME CASE OF INTERNATIONALIZATION

A significant feature of the NT2 dispute is the degree to which it has become internationalized. There are several key aspects to this internationalization:

- the function of the dam itself as an exporter of electricity;
- the Mekong Basin context;
- the pivotal role of the World Bank;
- the role of international investors and international finance capital; and
- the role of international NGOs in a country without indigenous NGOs.

The role of influence exerted through NGOs shows some of the complexities of the internationalized debate. On the one hand, international NGOs that have raised concerns about NT2's impact on environment and local people have been branded by some international media, by some within the Lao government, and privately by project proponents, as 'green imperialists'. This is similar to the charges laid by Malaysian Prime Minister Mahathir against international NGOs seen as bent on cheating poorer countries out of the chance to develop. On the other hand, those NGOs concerned more exclusively with biodiversity at the expense of local people's interests have been labelled 'eco-fascists'. This has been most notable in the case of NT2 in a stinging critique by George Monbiot of WCS, and IUCN's support for the project as a means of financing biodiversity conservation in the upper watershed (*The Guardian*, 6 August 1997).

DIMENSIONS OF NEGOTIATION AND CONFLICT: ATTEMPTS AT MEDIATION

The NT2 conflict is the result of an accretion of new issues and new actors over a period of several years. Over time, alliances and divisions have been established, but there is also a contingency to these relationships between different actors. The small-town nature of Vientiane means that those often seen to be on different sides of the debate in the public arena may also socialize and exchange information and views in a less formal setting. The stakes on both sides have always been high and the experience of evaluation, dialogue and debate has raised the project to a very high level in terms of public and vested interest.

The evaluation experience

The Nam Theun II Project has been proposed and evaluated in a number of stages. During the mid-1980s, a pre-feasibility evaluation was carried out through the Mekong Secretariat by the Swiss firm Electrowatt as part of an overall study of the hydroelectric potential of the Nam Theun Basin. In 1990, the Snowy Mountains Engineering Corporation (SMEC), an Australian firm, carried out an EIA for the United Nations Development Programme (UNDP) and the World Bank as part of an overall feasibility study for the project. It was at this point that the project became the subject of wider interest and contestation. Flaws were identified in the Environmental Impact Statement, and the project was put on hold.

Subsequent to the UNDP/World Bank study, which was conducted in the context of a potential World Bank loan to Lao PDR for public project financing, the structure of the project was altered fundamentally by a switch to private financing under a build-own-operate-transfer (BOOT) model. This switch reflects a global trend towards private rather than public financing of major infrastructure projects. However, even advanced capitalist economies have relatively little experience of this model, and it has usually involved controversy over distribution of public and private risk in the financial as well as social and environmental spheres. In the case of a poor transitional economy such as Lao PDR, the main argument and rationale for such a funding model is to reduce the need for massive public debt that would be incurred by a public loan along conventional lines.

Five companies joined Electricite de Laos to form the Project Development Group (PDG):

1 Transfield, an Australian construction giant – initially with SMEC as TRANSMEC, but after SMEC's withdrawal on financial grounds as Transfield, which in 2000 on-sold its share in the project;
2 Electricite de France, a public utility with export contracts in a number of countries;
3 Ital-Thai, a Thai construction firm;
4 Phatrathanakit, a Thai finance company; and
5 Jasmine, a Thai telecommunications company.

The consortium signed a Memorandum of Understanding with the Lao government in March 1993. The consortium was renamed the Nam Theun Electricity Corporation (NTEC) and at the time of writing is still seeking project finance from European and Asian commercial banks. It is understood that such finance would only be forthcoming were the World Bank to use its MIGA to guarantee against sovereign risk. World Bank finance capital is also being sought from the IFC, the arm of the World Bank that lends to private projects that are held to have developmental importance, and from bilateral export credit and loan insurance agencies.

Although the World Bank had supported the earlier SMEC studies, the change in funding model shifted responsibility to new areas of the Bank. Nevertheless, the same Task Manager (Jamil Sopher) was given overall coordination responsibility throughout. In addition to IFC, the MIGA was brought in. The role of MIGA is guarantor of private bank loans against sovereign risk, in cases such as Nam Theun II mainly against breach of contract conditions by the host government rather than against traditional political risk concerns. Also, the IDA is involved, since breach of conditions as determined by MIGA would incur Lao PDR an IDA debt.

Because of its involvement, the World Bank has required a lengthy and costly impact assessment and appraisal process, involving several rounds of environmental, social and economic studies that commenced in mid-1994. Part of the expense of these studies has been borne by the Lao Government, while part has been borne by the project developers, initially as PDG, more recently reconstituted as the NTEC. The World Bank's involvement has been maintained primarily to enable commercial bank loans to be secured through MIGA, but NTEC has also derived public relations value from its required adherence to the Bank's guidelines on environmental and social assessment. It has thereby asserted the moral high ground when compared with purely commercial projects such as Daewoo's Huai Ho Dam in southern Lao PDR. The former Transfield-based director of NTEC has gone so far as to say publicly that if the World Bank were not to become involved then NTEC would also withdraw from the project. Meanwhile the Lao Government has made it known that it is working with the World Bank processes on a trial basis, driven largely by the imperative to gain investment guarantees through MIGA.[5]

The first round of studies under PDG/NTEC was completed in mid-1995 and resulted in an 'Environmental Assessment and Management Plan'. This plan went into significantly more detail than earlier studies, but was subject to criticism from NGOs and Bank staff on a number of points, including:

- vagueness on some key points regarding resettlement;
- failure to identify the affected communities as indigenous people;
- inadequate environmental management plans for the NBCA;
- a too narrowly defined project area, not taking account of downstream impacts;
- lack of attention to alternatives;
- absence of financial risk analysis that takes into account contingencies ranging from rainfall variations to exchange rate fluctuation; and
- retention of a Thai company of consulting engineers to carry out the environmental assessment and resettlement planning; this same company had been used in the earlier SMEC study and has been associated with many controversial dams in Thailand.

As a result of these weaknesses, the World Bank drew up an Aide-Memoire in November 1995 stipulating key further studies to be carried out in the areas of environmental management, socio-cultural analysis, resettlement planning, studies of alternatives and macro-economic analysis. The Lao Government showed some dissatisfaction with this Aide-Memoire, in part because it imposed costs in the form of an IDA loan to finance an economic impact study at the Lao Government's expense. Another sensitive point was the status of affected people as indigenous; it is the Lao Government's position that all Lao citizens are indigenous. Thus, any special treatment on this basis is controversial.

The next round of studies included a socio-cultural survey, a resettlement action plan, an economic impact study, a study of alternatives and a revised environmental assessment and management plan with much more emphasis on the NBCA. The studies were carried out by international consulting firms, with the exception of the socio-cultural survey, which was carried out by the international NGO CARE International. Several 'participatory workshops' were held in Vientiane to solicit comment on the output of these studies. Most of the active participants were representatives of foreign agencies. The Science, Technology and Environment Agency (STEA) hosted and facilitated these workshops.

As part of the World Bank's operating procedure, a Panel of Experts (POE) was established in 1996 to review the studies and assessment process. These experts are supposed to operate independently, but the fact that they are retained by the World Bank raises a question mark over their level of detachment from interested parties. The three experts include a specialist in wildlife and protected area management, a social scientist with experience of resettlement and indigenous people in the region, and an environmental generalist knowledgeable about environment–development trade-offs. The POE reported in February and July 1997 based on brief visits to the NT2 project site and reviews of project documents, together with interviews with some of the interested parties. Their brief reports largely summarized the contents of the relevant studies, and the main departure has been to raise questions over the implementation capacity with respect to key recommendations of the more detailed reports.

Yet another level of appraisal was the setting up in 1997 of an International Advisory Group (IAG) to oversee the process. IAG is made up of prominent individuals including the Director-General of IUCN, the director of Japan's International Development Research Institute, a PNG ex-diplomat, former Indonesian environment minister Emil Salim and the IAG convenor from The Netherlands Commission for Environmental Impact Assessment. Like the POE, IAG made short visits to the project area. Its primary role as defined by initial terms of reference is to monitor compliance of the assessment process with the Bank's Operational Directives 'in letter and spirit', but in discussions with NGOs it claims a wider, and not clearly delimited, mandate. As in the case of POE, the IAG was appointed by the World Bank.

In response to the World Bank and NTEC financed studies, the International Rivers Network has commissioned its own reviews of the documents by several academics. These reviews have contained criticisms both of the studies and of the project itself. Some of the substantive criticisms have been based on the very short period (seven years) of hydrological data used and the high plant factor (a measure of actual versus theoretical energy output were the dam to operate at full capacity year-round) of 81 per cent assumed for the project as compared with typically achieved rates of less than 60 per cent for other rivers in the region.

Throughout the appraisal process, a dilemma for critical voices, notably NGOs, has been to what extent to engage with the mode of dialogue being fostered by NTEC and the World Bank. This applied to the participation workshops and to discussions with POE and IAG. Many of the consultations were held at very short notice and without advance copies of relevant documentation or a clear agenda. Several of the NGOs in Vientiane and outside Laos thus decided to stay away from some of the meetings. Their position was that token consultation is worse than no consultation, in the sense that it legitimizes a flawed process.

Southeast Asia's financial crisis since the floating of the baht in July 1997 has placed new doubts over the project, in at least three main respects. First, since NT2 is primarily an export-related project, the Thai market for electricity determines its relative viability. As early as 30 June 1997, before the baht devaluation, the Bangkok Post's mid-year economic review was casting doubts on the project due to the alternatives available to EGAT through other dams in Lao PDR and through independent power producers within Thailand from whom EGAT is now allowed to source. Second, the companies involved, notably the three Thai companies, have faced severe liquidity problems and Ital-Thai has fallen out of favour with the Thai government owing to a poor environmental and safety record on its urban transit projects in Bangkok. Third, as a bottom line for the appraisal studies was an assured market for NT2 electricity, a key assumption underlying the studies no longer appears valid.

KEY ISSUES OF PROCESS RELEVANT TO HUMAN RIGHTS AND ENVIRONMENT

The NT2 evaluation experience clearly raises many issues over the relative merits and risks of the project itself, and over mitigation, compensation and management measures. However, the experience also raises some key issues of process with regard to project decision-making, who is making decisions on whose behalf, on what assumptions and against what criteria, and with what degree of accountability.

Issues of timing

The process of project planning, assessment, appraisal, implementation, mitigation, management and monitoring is a lengthy, progressive and cumulative one. The point at which any assessment or decision is made will affect that assessment or decision. The POE and IAG have seen the project area from helicopters and have seen that Nakai Plateau is now largely degraded and logged out. It is easy to agree with the conclusion of the assessments that the main area worth 'saving' is in the catchment, and to see that the revenues generated by NT2 can help manage the NBCA. Yet, if the same teams had flown over Nakai a few years earlier, before the anticipatory clear-cutting commenced and before roads into the area were improved, their assessment of the options might have been quite different. Many projects in Lao PDR are currently at a similar stage of planning as NT2 was in 1990. Timing of involvement is thus a crucial issue if other projects are not to be held up as *faits accomplis*, with only the fine details of resettlement and environmental management to be discussed.

Issues of representation

Decision-making is bound up with the issue of representation, since this is part of the planning and assessment process. Participation workshops are open to the public, but also to representatives of organizations that associate themselves with particular perspectives or social actors. Whether it is a government agency representing the 'national interest', an NGO speaking on behalf of the rural poor or the project developer representing the cause of economic development, it is important to delve further into the question to what extent particular actors and decision-makers represent key social or environmental interests. Due process necessitates proper and equitable representation of material and value interests that may genuinely differ, so that rationalistic and centralized exercises in environmental and resettlement planning are themselves part of a disempowering and culturally blind process of project management.

Existing avenues of redress

A final issue concerns existing avenues of redress for parties who feel that due process has not been served. Within the framework of NT2, most of these avenues remain within or close to the structures and procedures set up by the World Bank, for example, the 'public participation' workshops at various stages of assessment. The fact that this process is so close to a party (WB) that is perceived by many actors to have a vested and ideological interest on one side of the debate only serves to undermine the legitimacy of existing process.

This, then, raises the question of what other avenues for redress exist around NT2. Given the limited degree of openness within Lao society and politics, extending also to the Lao media, other avenues tend to go through foreign media and involve the questioning of the whole basis for assessment rather than a dialogue that facilitates good decision-making. Within Lao PDR, particular agencies can be seen to have some degree of autonomy and impartiality. STEA has emerged as one such actor, and support of Lao voices and agencies should be high on the agenda of those wishing to support a more engaged local participation in assessment and decision-making, even where such agencies are not located within 'civil society'. This is particularly relevant in the case of STEA due to its potentially pivotal position but weak standing within the current system. The State Planning Committee is another agency with the potential for supporting more impartial or independent decision-making within the Lao government system.

CONCLUSIONS

Decision-making on projects with inseparable environmental and human rights implications requires enhancement of voices of the most disenfranchised groups and needs representatives who can speak for environments that were not otherwise being spoken for. A challenge for such a process in the case of a country such as Lao PDR is that civil society and representation of marginal interests on the national stage is very weakly developed. To date, this has not mattered immensely for people living in isolated areas, particularly given the fairly egalitarian, participatory and democratic nature of Lao village society. However, as villages get drawn into a wider economic sphere, and more specifically as large resource developments make demands on local resources, so engagement with the wider system becomes inevitable.

What is not inevitable is that this engagement will occur in an equitable or environmentally sustainable way. Relations between centre and periphery may be expected to become more strained and conflictual as development pressures and competition over limited resources increase. In a region with such a recent, long and traumatic history of military conflict, elimination or avoidance of further conflict may seem paramount. However, as the basis for competing interests shifts in part from geopolitical to ecopolitical grounds, it is important to recognize a positive role for conflict, expressed through increasingly open debate, as expression, within limits, of real contradictions. However, this is not a recognition that comes naturally within either the cultural or political systems of Laos.

The challenge for international players in such a context is to engage in these processes in an equitable and legitimate (in both a real and a perceived sense) way. If conflict management becomes the main focus, there is a danger of 'short-circuiting' civil society and preventing local mechanisms from emerging. For all these reasons, the internationalized NT2 experience contains many lessons for those wishing to work towards a key objective: moving the decision-making process back into the national and local arenas while supporting the emergence of means for much wider representation of local interests within that field of action.

NOTES

1   Lao People's Democratic Republic is the official name of the country more commonly known as Laos. When referring to the nation-state, this chapter refers to Lao PDR. Otherwise, the chapter will refer to Laos as a geographical entity.

2   For the purposes of most of the studies carried out for the dam, it was to be a 600 MW baseload project, releasing a fairly steady flow of water to generate relatively constant power. It has been re-designed as a peakload project, hence requiring greater turbine capacity and a more fluctuating water release and power output. This has implications for both the finances and the environmental impact, which cannot be determined from the main studies carried out in project appraisal and EIA.

3   See www4.worldbank.org/sprojects/Project.asp for a list of the more recent project documents provided online by the World Bank. These are the latest in a series of studies carried out since 1989, first by the Snowy Mountains Engineering Corporation,

more recently by the Nam Theun Electricity Corporation and consultants hired by the World Bank to undertake economic, social and environmental assessments of the project.

4   This number is quite small in absolute terms compared with other dams that have received such international prominence. To put this in context, the figure represents a slightly larger proportion of the national population when compared with the numbers to be resettled from the Three Gorges Reservoir in China or those potentially affected by Narmada in India. Nevertheless, in crude terms of 'displaced persons per installed megawatt', NT2 is promoted as efficient and, as a result, much less attention has been given to the social as compared with environmental dislocation.

5   Personal communication from law firm contracted by the Government of Laos, funded by the World Bank, to draw up the NT2 contract with NTEC.

REFERENCES

Bakker, K (1999) 'The Politics of Hydropower: Developing the Mekong', *Political Geography* 18(2):209–32

Cultural Survival Quarterly (1999) Issue devoted to cultural impacts of dams. *Cultural Survival Quarterly* 1

Hill, M T and Hill, S A (1994) *Fisheries Ecology and Hydropower in the Mekong River: An Evaluation of Run-of-the-River Projects*, prepared for Mekong Secretariat, Bangkok, Thailand

Hirsch, P (1988) 'Dammed or Damned? Hydro-power versus People's Power', *Bulletin of Concerned Asian Scholars* 20(1):2–10

Hirsch, P (1995) 'Thailand and the New Geopolitics of Southeast Asia: Resource and Environmental Issues', in J Rigg (ed) *Counting the Costs: Economic Growth and Environmental Change in Thailand*. Singapore, Institute of Southeast Asian Studies, pp235–59

Hirsch, P and Cheong, G (1996) 'Natural Resource Management in the Mekong River Basin: Perspectives for Australian Development Cooperation', Report to AusAID, March

Jacobs, J (1995) 'Mekong Committee History and Lessons for River Basin Development', *Geographical Journal* 161(2):135–48

Louis Berger International, Inc (1997) 'Economic Impact Study Nam Theun 2 Hydroelectric Project: Executive Summary and Overall Economic Assessment', Louis Berger International, Inc, June

McCormack, G (2001) 'Water Margins: Competing Paradigms in China', *Critical Asian Studies* 33(1):pp5–30

McCully, P (1996) *Silenced Rivers: The Ecology and Politics of Large Dams*. London, Zed Books

Roberts, T R and Baird, I G (1995) 'Traditional Fisheries and Fish Ecology on the Mekong River at Khone Waterfalls in Southern Laos', *Natural History Bulletin of the Siam Society* 43(2):219–62

Stensholt, R (ed) (1996) *Developing the Mekong Subregion*. Clayton, Victoria: Monash Asia Institute, pp16–21

WCD (World Commission on Dams) (2000) *Dams and Development: A New Framework for Decision-Making. The Report of the World Commission on Dams*. London: Earthscan Publications

Chapter 8

The Darien Region Between Colombia and Panama: Gap or Seal?

Pascal O Girot

INTRODUCTION

Few places in the world conjure images as powerful as the Darien Gap. This narrow anchorage point between Mesoamerica and the South American continent, straddling Panama and Colombia, is geologically one of the youngest portions of land in the Americas. The Darien is also the southernmost of the five major potential inter-oceanic routes across the Mesoamerican isthmus.

More significant for its privileged geographical location than for its demographic or economic weight, the Darien Gap is a crucial passage point for species from the South and Central Neotropical Regions. As a World Heritage Site and Biosphere Reserve, it constitutes one of the major centres of plant diversity of the Americas, with some of the highest levels of endemism of both flora and fauna. It also houses several transboundary indigenous groups, such as the Kunas, Embera and Woonaan, who have settled the forested lands and coastal shoals of eastern Panama and northern Colombia for centuries.

Today, the Darien Gap is the last missing link in a network spanning over 70,000 kilometres of roads in the Inter-American System in North and South America. With the creation of continental trade blocs, as encapsulated by the North American Free Trade Agreement (NAFTA), the Common Market of the South (Mercado Común del Sur, MERCOSUR)[1] and the Group of Three (Colombia, Venezuela and Mexico), there are compelling macro-economic and geopolitical factors vying for the opening of the Darien Gap. Opening the gap as it were, through building the 129 kilometre-long road link between North and South America, has become a symbol of the forces of integration in the Americas. With the impulses unleashed by free trade policies, many Latin American governments are shifting from protectionist, import-substitution policies towards lower tariffs on trade, as well as multilateral and bilateral free trade agreements. There have been increased hemispheric consultations, such as the Summit of the Americas meetings and the Ibero-American summit meetings, which confirm a unified view of the need to liberalize trade across the Americas. Notwithstanding, at the dawn of the 21st century, the Darien Gap still separates the road networks of North and South America.

The continued existence of the Darien Gap is intimately linked to the vicissitudes of Western hemispheric geopolitics. As a 'natural' barrier between South and Central America, the Gap has served, at least implicitly, to protect the Panama Canal from Colombia's territorial ambitions. More recently, the destiny of the Darien Gap was linked to the Inter American Agricultural System, particularly in terms of countering the spread of livestock and agricultural pests and disease. Since the end of the cold war and the US invasion of Panama in 1989, growing concern over drug trafficking is an issue that has a direct bearing on the continued existence of the Darien Gap.

Whether it is considered a haven for unique remnants of tropical biodiversity, a refuge for surviving indigenous cultures and territories, or as a lost link in a hemispheric network for trade and commerce, the Darien plot is set to unravel in the next decade. The conflict will pit widely differing conceptions of sustainable development, human progress and environmental security against each other. Its outcome is unfathomable unless we compare scenarios and contemplate options for the viable stewardship of one of the most ethnically diverse and biologically rich corners of the world.

This chapter examines the complex web of issues, actors and scenarios involved in the conflict over the opening of the Darien Gap. The central aim is to derive recommendations for future policies and institutional arrangements, including the potential role of a regional or international ombudsperson, in resolving the conflict.

THE DARIEN: GAP OR SEAL?

The physical setting

The Darien Gap is located at the southernmost tip of Mesoamerica as it hinges on the South American continent. It has functioned over the past millennia as a biological corridor and funnel, concentrating species distribution as they interacted and migrated between the North and South American eco-regions.

The continental divide in the Darien is barely 16 kilometres from the Caribbean coast, in the higher tributaries of the Chucunaque River, the largest watershed in Panama (WWF/IUCN, 1997, p226). The long, gently sloping valleys have carved the Darien Mountain formed by the Cordillera de San Blas and higher Serranía del Darien, where the highest peak in the region is located (Cerro Tacarcuna, 1875 m or 5625 ft). The southern portion of the Darien Gap is dissected into a trident-shaped range by the other major rivers in the Darien, including the Tuira, Balsas and Sambú, which drain into the Pacific Ocean through the Gulf of San Miguel. On the Colombian side of the Darien Range, the Atrato River basin, which drains the entire Chocó Department into the Gulf of Urabá on the Caribbean coast, is one of the rivers in South America with the

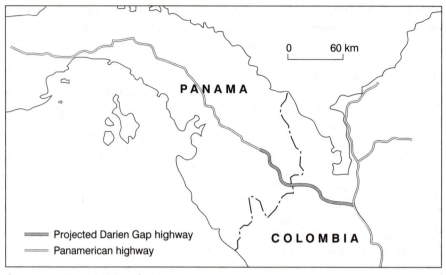

Source: Atlas Mundial, Madrid: Oceano (1992)

Figure 8.1 *Projected Road Through the Darien Gap Region*

largest discharge compared with its drainage area (Parsons, 1967, p2). It meanders into a vast wetlands system as part of the Atrato Delta, which encompasses the Tumaradó swamp. This swamp truly constitutes the greatest natural obstacle to the Inter American Highway, which would have to cross over 22 kilometres of amphibious terrain to reach the border between Colombia and Panama.

The Darien is one of the most biologically diverse and species-rich regions in the Americas. It encompasses ten major vegetation types, including coastal dry forests and mangroves, brackish and freshwater swamps, and various lowland and premontane forests. Its most pristine life zones are in montane rainforests, such as cloud forest, elfin forests and pluvial forests. Darien harbours an extraordinary diversity of species, with over 2440 flora species recorded, high endemism (as high as 23 per cent in the upper mountain ranges) and several endangered species of flora and fauna (WWF/IUCN, 1997, p226). The Gulf of San Miguel houses the largest stand (close to 46 per cent) of mangrove forests in Panama.[2]

On either side of the border, there has been a significant coincidence in the timing of conservation initiatives. The Darien National Park was created in 1980 and covers 579,000 ha; the single most extensive national park in Panama. A Protection Forest since 1972, its establishment coincided with the opening of the road between Bayano and Yaviza on the Panamanian side. The National Park of Los Katíos was created in 1974, covering an extension of 52,000 ha, which was extended to 72,000 ha in 1979 in order to include the riparian forests of the Atrato and Tumaradó swamps. The Darien National Park in Panama was declared as a World Heritage Site in 1981 and as a UNESCO Biosphere Reserve in 1983. Covering an area of 5,790 square kilometres, Darien National Park is the largest park in Panama and one of the largest in Central America

(WWF/IUCN, 1997, p230). However, the definitive legal demarcation of the park's boundaries is still in process, amidst growing pressure over land, resources and territorial rights.

A brief historical background

During most of the 20th century, the Darien has constituted a resource frontier – a source of gold and timber exploited by foreign and national interests. The growing incursions of gold miners, rubber tappers and other adventurers into the Darien brought about increasing pressure on the indigenous populations, particularly the Kuna. With the creation of the Panamanian State in 1903, many of the most isolated indigenous communities were slow to recognize the new national authorities, still pledging allegiance to Colombia. By 1909, the Panamanian government had installed a military outpost in Puerto Obaldía on the Caribbean coast of San Blas. By 1915, the *Circunscripción de San Blas* was created as a territorial administrative unit. The Kuna people had resisted incursions by foreigners for centuries and viewed with similar distrust the competing interests of the Panamanian and Colombian officials. Increasing pressure on natural resources (timber, turtles, tagua nuts) led to numerous conflicts between Kuna communities and outside interests. By 1919, tensions gave way to open conflict between Kuna communities, timber and turtling interests and government officials. This resulted in the 1925 Kuna rebellion in which Kuna leaders rejected forthright any government presence in San Blas, physically expelling all foreigners from their territory (Howe, 1995, p71).

The Kuna (or *Tule*) Revolution, aptly managed by its leaders, benefited from US support, which gave them particular leverage against the Panamanian and Colombian governments. In exchange for legal recognition to their territory and relative administrative autonomy, the Kuna agreed to accept Panamanian sovereignty over this border region. The events of 1925 paved the way for the official demarcation of Kuna territorial claims. In 1938, the *Comarca de San Blas* was created, and by 1945 the Comarca's Organic Charter was passed, guaranteeing territorial autonomy for the Kuna ever since.

The current geographical context

The Darien Gap can be divided into three major cultural landscapes (Herlihy, 1989):

1   The indigenous settlements (Kuna, Emberá, Woonaan) of the upper tributaries of the Tuira, Chucunaque, Sambú and Atrato rivers.
2   The river towns and coastal fishing communities, such as La Palma, Yaviza, Garachiné, Ríosucio, Jaque, Nuquí and Juradó on the Pacific Coast, still dominated by the Darienita or Afrochocoano ethnic group.
3   The Road Axis Cañita and Canglón in Panama, such as Santa Fe, Metetí and Canglón, where the bulk of the Interiorano settlers can be found and along the Carretera al Mar between Turbo and Dabeiba in Colombia, such as the towns of Apartadó, Chigorodó and Guapá, settled since the 1960s by campesino settlers (*chilapos*), cattle ranchers and banana plantation owners.

Figure 8.2 *The Darien Border Region: Colombia–Panama*

These groups are undergoing widely differing demographic transitions and operate in distinct although connected economic networks. The last ethnic group to settle the Panamanian Darien is composed of *mestizo* colonists from central and western Panama, also referred to as *Interioranos*, who began migrating to the Darien in the 1960s, opening agricultural lands around existing river towns, but who migrated more intensively in the 1980s with the opening of the Inter American Highway to Canglón and Yaviza.

The population of Darien Province nearly doubled between 1980 and 1990, from 26,524 to 43,832 inhabitants. If one considers the Districts of the Province of Panama along the Darien Gap Highway, such as Chiman and Chepo, a total population of 76,000 inhabits the Geographic Area of the Darien (*Darién Geográfico*) (República de Panamá, 1997). The annual demographic growth rate of 4.5 per cent for the Darien a whole was twice the average for Panama between 1980 and 1990. It is significant to note that the *corregimientos*[3] experiencing negative population growth are all located in the upper tributaries and areas most distant from the road. On the other hand, those sectors on or closest to the existing road between Chepo and Yaviza experienced the greatest population increases during the 1990s. There is a direct corollary of the opening of the Darien Highway in Panama, that is, major shifts in population distribution, as there is a clear tendency for the most isolated settlements to experience negative demographic growth and out-migration. This remains a powerful argument for those who oppose the opening of the Darien Gap Highway.

The *Interioranos* encapsulate the dominant national culture of Panama and have transformed the identity of the Darien over the past two decades. They are primarily involved in agriculture and are the region's leading rice producers. There is increasing livestock production in the western portion of the Darien, since cattle-raising is strictly prohibited within a 80-kilometre radius of the Colombian border, as a protection measure against the spread of foot and mouth disease (Pasos, 1994).

On the Colombian side of the Darien, settlement history has been more complex and the resource frontier far larger. It shares with the Panamanian Darien a past typical of a resource frontier, marked by extractive cycles of mining and timber ventures. It also shares the cultural features of the Darien, with Kuna and Emberá settlements that span today's border regions. This region has been historically settled by Emberá and Woonaan (also referred to as the Waunana) and black *Darienitas* (also referred to as *Afrochocoanos* in Colombia) located in river towns along the Atrato river and along the Pacific coast. Traditionally involved in subsistence agriculture and fishing, the Chocó Indians and *Afrochocoanos* were progressively incorporated into the Colombian economy through extractive activities such as mining, timber, and especially rubber tapping and *tagua* nut collecting (Girot, 2000). Until the 1950s, trade was essentially waterborne, along most of the Atrato tributaries to trading posts such as Quibdó or Arquía, and linked to the Antioquia heartland by mule trails since the mid-19th century (Parsons, 1967).

The opening up of the *Carretera al Mar*, linking Medellín to Turbo, was completed by the end of the Second World War after 20 years of construction, as a key route for coffee exports. But it was not until the 1950s that road traffic began to spur the settlement of land along the penetration route. Settlements along the road, such as Dabeiba, Chigorodó and Apartadó, progressively grew to become the new economic centre of the Urabá region. As on the Panamanian side, the road transformed the orientation of trade networks in the region, shifting the economic centre of gravity from the waterborne river trade to the automotive traffic along the new road to Medellín. River towns such as Quibdó, Murindó, Arquía and Pavarandó tended to stagnate from the 1950s onwards (Parsons, 1967; Molano and Ramírez, 1996).

The road to Turbo also brought about increased incursions by large consortia interested in developing plantations along the coastal plains of Urabá. The 1960s also saw the growth of banana plantations, particularly by the United Fruit Company, which first exported bananas from Turbo in 1964 at the height of the banana bonanza of the 1950s and 1960s (Parsons, 1967, p76). The bonanza attracted more and more foreign investors as well as Antioqueño capitalists because of its productive soils, climate protected from damaging hurricanes and extremely cheap labour force. Land prices increased more than tenfold during the first half of the 1960s, and by 1965 some 5500 ha were under banana production, producing 3.5 million stems a year (Parsons, 1967, p85).

The banana bonanza had a number of side-effects in the region, the most significant of which was exponential population growth, reaching up to 9.4 per cent annually in 1963, the highest population growth rate in Colombia at the time (Parsons, 1967, p96). Between 1951 and 1964 the population of Urabá increased from 15,700 to over 132,200; by 1985, it had reached 298,047 (Restrepo Forero, 1992, p289). By the early 1970s, the bonanza was over, and much of the excess population was pushed to open up agricultural lands and cattle ranching operations along the tributaries of the Atrato delta and into the Darien. At the end of the 1980s, INCORA (Colombian Institute for Colonization and Agrarian Reform) estimated that there were 6,000 families without land in Urabá, with 3,000 families invading for an average of 1.3 ha per family (Steiner, 1992, p283).

Since the 1960s, low wages and dismal housing conditions in the Urabá banana plantations have fuelled social strife and guerrilla warfare, culminating by the 1980s and 1990s in open armed conflict between insurgent guerrilla forces, the Colombian Army and paramilitary forces. Much of the current pressure on the Darien's natural heritage, notably on Los Katíos National Park, is due to ever-growing numbers of *campesinos* and ranchers displaced by the crisis in the plantation economy of Urabá and by the intensification of armed conflict in much of rural Colombia since the mid-1990s.

At the opening of the 21st century, the Darien Gap stands as a hiatus between two expanding settlement frontiers. The agricultural frontier is active on either side of the Darien, but the acuteness and severity of the processes unfolding on the Colombian side are greater by far than those active on the Panamanian side of the border. This asymmetry is also apparent in terms of the political, economic and military stakes at play on either side of this boundary. The impending humanitarian crisis unfolding in Colombia today unfortunately relegates concerns about the fate of the Darien's natural heritage to a tenuous second place. As we shall document in the following section, the stakes are high and there looms the potential for a compounded cultural, social and environmental disaster.

THE ARCHITECTURE OF THE CONFLICT

Many consider the Darien Gap to be a geographical aberration. The enduring presence of this natural barrier, just 200 kilometres from the busy Panama Canal seems to defy logic. Plans for completing the last remaining (108 kilometre) stretch of the Inter American Highway have been resurfacing regularly since the 1930s. One would be tempted to think that, at the end of the 20th century, the imperatives of commerce and free trade would have easily vanquished 100 kilometres of forest and swamp. The fact that the Gap has endured is an indication of the multiple and often contradictory forces involved, operating at vastly differing scales. From large infrastructural projects decided upon in Washington or Tokyo to local land rights and territorial conflicts involving indigenous groups and conservationists, the future of the Darien Gap does not lie in the hands of any single agent or group of actors, but rather in an array of forces and interests.

The global scale

Hemispheric interests and the Darien

> *If the Berlin Wall fell, why can't the Darien Gap?* Noemí Sanín de
> Rubio, Colombia's Foreign Minister, 1992[4]

Located at the crossroads of the Americas, the Darien Gap is an obligatory passage point for hemispheric politics. Two major geopolitical constructs collide in the Darien: the Inter American System, encapsulated by perennial interests in completing the Inter American Highway, and the intricacies of isthmian geopolitics, illustrated by the recurrent interests in an inter-oceanic route through the Darien. The first seeks to integrate the Americas, North and South, while the second seeks to service world commerce, East and West. Interestingly, both the Inter American Highway project and the Inter-oceanic Canal projects appeal to the same epochal call for globalization.

The Inter American System emerged with the advent of the US as a hegemonic world power in the late 19th century. As a direct corollary to the Monroe Doctrine, the political and economic integration of the Americas was a key geopolitical imperative for the US. This explains in many regards why the decision of whether or not to open the Darien Gap for the completion of the Inter American Highway has been consistently taken, for most of the 20th century, in Washington, DC rather than in Bogotá or Panama City.

During the Fifth International American Conference in Santiago, Chile, in 1923, the Pan American Highway Congress was founded to spur the development of the continent's highway network. The second Pan American Highway Congress, held in 1929 in Rio de Janeiro, Brazil, produced the Convention on the Pan American Highway, literally paving the way for the construction of the 25,744 km highway between Patagonia and Alaska. The Great Depression of the 1930s and the Second World War postponed implementation of the plan until the 1940s. But the war reinforced the conviction that hemispheric integration was a geopolitical imperative for the US.

Between 1943 and 1963, 5,100 kilometres of the Inter American Highway was built between the Rio Grande on the US–Mexico border and Panama at a cost of US$270 million, of which US$170 million was provided by the US Government.[5] It was not until 1955 that a Sub-Committee for the Darien was created at the Pan American Highway Congress and several feasibility studies were commissioned. Four possible routes were highlighted for the Panamanian section of the highway, and nine for the Colombian side.[6] In 1959, the Colombian government incorporated into its highway development plan the Darien Gap Highway (Carretera del Tapón del Darien), projecting to build the 81 kilometres between Guapá, on the Medellín-Turbo road, to Palo de las Letras, on the Colombia–Panama border (República de Colombia, 1991, p12). Several other feasibility studies ensued in 1964 for the 400 kilometre road between Tocumen (near Panama City) and Río León (Colombia), estimated at the time to cost US$150 million (ANCON/Fundación Natura, 1996).

By the early 1970s, the opening of the Darien Gap was an impending reality. The US Congress had earmarked US$100 million for the building of the Darien Gap highway, while Panama was set to contribute US$30 million and Colombia US$20 million (ANCON/Fundación Natura, 1996). By 1972, the Federal Highway Administration had established offices in Bogotá in order to supervise the works in conjunction with Colombia's Ministry of Public Works (MOPT).

In an unprecedented up-staging of international affairs, on 17 October 1975, a US District of Columbia Court ruled in favour of a legal suit presented by the Sierra Club, Friends of the Earth and other environmentalist/human rights advocacy groups, arguing that the construction of the Darien Gap highway would have adverse effects on indigenous tribes as well as the fauna and flora of the region. The court issued an order to the US Department of Transport prohibiting the Federal Highway Administration from pledging funds for the Darien Gap highway until measures were taken to comply with the regulation concerning environmental and social impacts, as stipulated in the 1969 National Environmental Protection Act. Except for sections of the road on the Panamanian side, which were started before 1975, all other US-funded public works on the road were suspended. The US Department of Transport appealed against the court ruling twice, in 1975 and 1977, presenting the additional environmental impact studies that the court required. These studies, conducted by the Batelle Institute in 1975, were followed by other studies unfavourable to the opening of the Darien Gap in 1977 because of sanitary conditions.

In its final ruling, the US District of Columbia Court conditioned the continuation of the works on compliance with US Department of Agriculture (USDA) certification of adequate measures to control the spread of foot and mouth disease, a livestock virus pervasive in South America but still absent in Central and North America. Pursuant to this ruling, agreements were passed between the USDA and the ICA (Colombian Agriculture Institute) to conduct extensive programmes for the control and eradication of foot and mouth disease. These programmes have been ongoing for over 20 years, obtaining by 1991 the long-awaited certification by the USDA. Ignoring the US jurisdiction ruling, the Government of Colombia in 1979 ordered the works to continue, and the 28 kilometre section of the road between Río León and Lomas Aisladas was completed by 1983. Between 1983 and 1992, work on the project was paralysed, as debates concerning the possible impacts of the road continued not only in the US but also in Panama and Colombia.

With the certification by the USDA in 1991, interest in the opening of the Darien Gap has once again been rekindled. As illustrated by Table 8.1, by 1992, of the nearly 400 kilometres of the road planned in 1970, 262.9 kilometres (66 per cent) were built and open to traffic, although only 37 kilometres were asphalted (on the Panamanian side). Another 113.3 kilometres (28.4 per cent) have yet to be completed and 22 kilometres have only partial design and engineering studies. As of 1998, 145 kilometres of road remain to be built, most of which have been designed and engineering studies completed. Intensive collaboration between the USDA and ICA to control the spread of foot and mouth disease has enabled some of the pending restrictions to be lifted from

Table 8.1 *Degree of Completion of the Darien Gap Highway: Tocumen, Panamá–Río León, Colombia, 1970–1992*

Country/condition	1970		1978		1992	
	km	%	km	%	km	%
Panama						
Paved	0	0	0	0	37.0	11.6
Unpaved	0	0	178.8	57	197.3	62.4
Under construction/ improvement	0	0	27.0	8.0	0	0
With complete studies	0	0	111.0	35	81.9	26
With partial studies	0	0	0	0	0	0
Total length in Panama	0	0	316.8	100	316.8	100
Colombia						
Paved	0	0	0	0	0	0
Unpaved	0	0	0	0	28	34.4
Under construction/ improvement	0	0	0	0	0	0
With complete studies	0	0	31.4	38.6	31.4	38.6
With partial studies	0	0	22.0	27	22.0	27
Total length in Colombia	0	0	53.4	65.6	81.4	100
Totals						
Paved	0	0	0	0	37	9.2
Unpaved	0	0	178.8	44.9	225.9	56.8
Under construction/ improvement	0	0	27	6.7	0	0
With complete studies	0	0	142.4	35.7	113.3	28.5
With partial studies	0	0	22	5.5	22	5.5
Total length for both countries	0	0	398.2	92.8	398.2	100

Source: República de Colombia, 1996, cuadro No 2, p5

the US jurisdiction perspective. However, the 1990s have also witnessed a substantial increase in environmental concerns, both nationally in Panama and Colombia, and internationally. Rather than agricultural sanitation, the central contemporary concerns revolve around environmental, security and human rights issues.

The Darien and Isthmian geopolitics

In addition to hemispheric concerns, the Darien is enmeshed in the geopolitics of the Central American Isthmus. The Darien, and in particular the Atrato River, is one of the five major inter-oceanic routes in Central America (see Figure 8.3). The second half of the 19th century saw the isthmus assaulted by the 'scramble for the Canal': rival hegemonic powers vied for the control of resources, territories and colonies. Britain, France and the US as an emerging world power had plans and projects for inter-oceanic canals (Girot, 1994). The events of 1903, when Panama seceded from New Granada with full diplomatic support

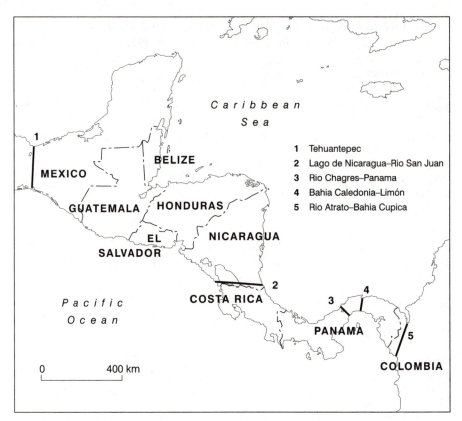

Figure 8.3 *Inter-oceanic Routes Through the Mesoamerican Isthmus*

from the US State Department, precipitated the decision, and the Panama Canal route was the final choice. Previously part of New Granada and then of Greater Colombia, Panama was the Provincia del Istmo. Its secession from Colombia soured relations between the newly neighbouring countries for decades.

The resurgence of alternative canal projects (both wet and dry canals) by rival isthmian nations has been a constant in Central American history, from Tehuantepec, to Nicaragua, to the Atrato (Girot, 1994). Colombian leaders have long sought to have a canal of their own to compete with a Panama Canal they considered as having been annexed by the US in 1903. The historic Canal Zone Treaties signed in 1977 between US President Jimmy Carter and Panama's leader General Omar Torrijos formally marked the end of US control over the Canal, setting a 20-year calendar for the hand-over of installations and institutions. The fact that in December 1999, the Canal Zone passed to total Panamanian sovereignty has rekindled debates about alternative routes, especially in Nicaragua, Honduras and Guatemala.

With the giddy growth of Asian economies in the 1970s and 1980s, the economic potential to use the Darien's unique isthmian position to Colombia's advantage became a major policy issue. The first Plan Pacífico, an Integral Development Plan for the Pacific coast, was approved in 1984 by the Colombian government. It was budgeted for an initial expenditure of almost US$308 million, and was essentially geared towards basic infrastructure and productive projects in forestry, mining, agriculture and fishing. It was also alleged that many of the infrastructure investments were channelled to the mobilization of armed forces in the combat of leftist guerrillas, such as the naval base in Bahía Malaga, 50 kilometres north of Buenaventura (Barnes, 1993, p136).

By 1987, Colombian President Virgilio Barco expanded the Plan Pacífico to an ambitious mega-infrastructure project, involving the creation of an Inter-oceanic Terrestrial Bridge, combining a railway, motorway, canal and oil pipeline, fording the Atrato swamps and across the Baudó range to the Pacific coast, with port complexes and free trade zones on either terminal. A connection with the Inter American Highway was foreseen in the US$4.5 billion programme, enabling Colombia to compete with or even replace the Panama Canal (Barnes, 1993, p136). By 1990, the Plan Pacífico had been fully elaborated into a major development programme for the Chocó Department.

Colombian President César Gaviria settled in 1992 for a more modest Plan Pacífico, arguing that previous programmes were not suited to the environmental and cultural reality of the Chocó. Although a large share of the US$321 million budget was still earmarked for infrastructure development and road building, it placed a clear emphasis on social programmes and environmental impact mitigation (Barnes, 1993). The plan proposed the construction of a new super-port on the Pacific coast, probably at Tribugá Bay near Nuquí, connected to the Central highlands by a highway to Pereira, hub of the Colombian coffee-growing country and Gaviria's main constituency. As Barnes (1993, p139) aptly states: 'What the new Plan leaves out is as important as what it includes'. While downsizing the overall budget requirements for development and infrastructural components, the plan does not formally acknowledge any indigenous or *afrochocoano* territorial rights, a contentious issue since the drafting of the 1991 Constitution. With multilateral financial organizations like the World Bank and the Inter American Development Bank insisting on environmental soundness and social equity, Colombia's government has gone a long way to assuage regional, national and international fears concerning the impact of such large infrastructure projects, although there is also mounting international pressure for the final completion of the Darien Gap highway.

A revealing contrast exists between the terms used in English and in Spanish to describe the Darien; while the English refer to a 'gap', the Spanish use the term *'tapón'* (meaning seal, lid or stopper). Therein lies the query, which provides this chapter with a title, The Darien: Gap or Seal? If one examines recent regional history, the Darien has functioned for the entire 20th century as an effective seal between Panama and Colombia. According to Granados and Solís (2000), the Darien Gap has marked throughout the 20th century the southernmost limit of the backyard of the US.

On the one hand, the 'Gap' refers to the sections of the Inter American highway remaining to be built, not the functional characteristics of this forlorn region of the Americas. On the other hand, many consider that the value of a 'seal' remains to this day, in terms of both containing livestock diseases and stemming the uncontrolled migration of Colombian nationals, with the daunting spillover of the Colombian conflict. The growing concern over increased drug-trafficking, and an acceleration in the pace of *campesino* settlement from either side of the border has resulted in increased rates of deforestation, conflicts over indigenous territories and migrant settlers, and an increased destabilization of the border region as a whole. All of these threats combined are poised to be a major cause of future loss of biodiversity and indigenous land rights. In a sense, the playing field has levelled somewhat since the 1970s, but the stakes have been raised and the number of players has grown considerably.

The post-Rio 1992 climate has favoured the emergence of a number of environmental NGOs and community-based organizations throughout Latin America, including in Colombia and Panama. In a sense, the 20 years of delay in the construction of the Darien Gap highway 'bought time'. Civil society, indigenous groups, special interest groups, environmental and human rights NGOs are present and active, albeit haphazardly, in the Darien; they were not in 1970. During the 19th General Assembly of the IUCN (World Conservation Union), in Buenos Aires in 1994, opposition to the completion of the Darien Gap highway was manifested in Resolution 19.66, noting that it would negatively affect a World Heritage Site, a conservation area of global importance. The Resolution also recommended additional feasibility studies for the improvement of a ferry service on either coast of Colombia or Panama as alternative routes to the Darien Gap highway. Since then, several multi-million dollar conservation projects funded by multilateral organizations such as the Global Environment Facility (GEF) and Inter-American Development Bank (IADB) geared towards flora and fauna inventories and sustainable natural resource use, have centred on both sides of the Gap.

At the national scale

As in most other Latin American countries, Colombia and Panama are undertaking processes of trade liberalization and structural adjustment policies to reduce state intervention in the economy, foster increased privatization and lower trade tariffs. Today, export-led economic growth is considered the key to future development. This is clearly reflected in the three versions of the Plan Pacífico, in which Colombia sees in the Darien the potential of capitalizing on the comparative advantage of its geography. Linking the industrial and agricultural heartland of Colombia to the coast has been an issue for over a century, but at the threshold of the 21st century it has gained particular relevance.

Successive Colombian governments have been clear in their determination to forge ahead with the development of the Pacific coast, giving the theme of the Darien Gap highway a back seat for the time being. Speculative forces fuelled by the prospects of opening up the Atrato and Chocó region by large infrastructure investments have produced a sharp increase in mining and logging concessions in northern Colombia (Barnes, 1993; WWF/PRISMA, 1997). While the issue of the road was central to Colombian national politics in the 1970s, it has been overrun by broader concerns for the development of the Pacific coast. Since the early 1990s a succession of ambitious infrastructure projects for bridging the isthmus of northern Colombia and integrating the Pacific coast into the national economy have been debated in Congress, and presented to potential donors.

Colombia's political history is profoundly marked by regional rivalry and factional strife. As one author puts it, in Colombia, the state is weak, but the bands are strong (Molano and Ramírez, 1996). While initially limited to political activists and armed factions, the *violencia* spread into the countryside in the 1960s and 1970s. With the advent of the Cuban Revolution in 1959, several revolutionary movements emerged, directly opposed to the instalment of capitalist agriculture in the Northern Departments of Córdoba, Antioquia and Chocó. Three main guerrilla groups have operated in Colombia over the past 30 years: the M19, the Fuerzas Armadas Revolucionarias de Colombia (FARC) and the Ejercito Popular de Liberación (EPL). Today, the estimated size of these combined forces is over 18,000 men, of which 15,000 form the FARC, the largest guerrilla group, followed by the EPL with between 3,000 and 5,000 irregular troops (Reyes Posada, 1992). The Darien and neighbouring Departments of Chocó and Córdoba have been the focus of much of the guerrilla warfare, particularly in the Urabá Gulf where major banana and palm plantations and their associated labour forces are concentrated. Many authors point to skewed land tenure, concentration of wealth, dismal labour practices and security conditions as the main causes of the armed struggle (ibid).

By 1991, a new political constitution was voted by a constituent assembly, recognizing for the first time the multicultural nature of Colombian society. Indigenous territorial rights were acknowledged and recognized as inalienable collective property, as was the right to govern their land and resources according to their own laws, customs and political traditions. The Afrochocoano ethnic group was not granted similar rights. While their existence is mentioned in Article 55 of the Constitution, no explicit territorial right was assigned to them (Valencia and Villa, 1992; Barnes, 1993). Over 90 per cent of the nearly 1 million inhabitants of the Chocó Department are Afrochocoano, and they increasingly demand territorial security over traditionally held lands. Indigenous and black organizations have gained considerable visibility, both in the Chocó and the Panamanian Darien and Kuna Yala, over the past two decades, and today constitute key players in the Darien Gap controversy.

The 1980s and 1990s have seen a marked intensification in civil strife and guerrilla warfare. Three major factions contend to control territory, levy taxes and commit indiscriminate murder to dissuade opposition. With increased insecurity and guerrilla warfare at hand, the large plantation owners and cattle ranchers have resorted to forming private armies or paramilitary groups (Reyes, 1992, p63). These, in addition to the Colombian army, conduct counter-insurgency warfare and wreak havoc in communities suspected of collaborating with the guerrillas. By 1997, there were an estimated 400 such paramilitary organizations operating in Colombia as a whole, amounting to over 7,000 irregular troops (*El País*, 1997). The main reasons for the intensification of factional violence in Colombia are linked to the heightened drug war, in part conducted by the US State Department against the drug cartels of Calí and Medellín, the increasing governance crisis of the Colombian State and the continuous factional rivalries between guerrilla groups and paramilitary groups throughout the country. An estimated 35,000 lives have been claimed during the 1990s due to factional violence and drug related crime. Half the kidnappings of the world take place today in Colombia. According to both governmental and non-governmental reports, the bulk of the politically related killing has been recently committed by paramilitary forces, whereas most of the kidnappings have been conducted by guerrilla groups (Shifter et al, 2000).

The intensification of counter-insurgency warfare and heightened citizen insecurity are compounded by the continued involvement of the drug trafficking cartels in the economy of Colombia. Drug lords emerged as crucial economic actors in 1990s Colombia. Their extraordinary wealth provides them with the means to influence land markets, buy favours and even fund and arm many of the irregular troops operating in the country. The Darien is also an important thoroughfare for cocaine trafficking, although most of it seems to be shipped along the Caribbean and Pacific coasts.[7]

In Panama, the intimate relationship between the presence on Panamanian soil of the Canal Zone and the numerous military bases housing the US Joint Chiefs of Staff's Southern Command have weighed heavily on US–Panama relations. The events of 1964, when the Panamanian nationalists stated their open repudiation to continued US presence in Panama, led the way to the Carter-Torrijos Treaties of 1977. Once the handover of the Canal Zone to Panamanian sovereignty was secured, US–Panama relations went through a transition process, particularly after the death of leader Omar Torrijos in 1981 and the take-over by the mid-1980s by strongman Manuel Antonio Noriega. It is paradoxical that the last section of the Inter American Highway to Yaviza was completed in 1988, in the midst of the most serious crisis in US–Panama relations, which culminated with the toppling of the Noriega government by US troops in December 1989.

The 1990s ushered in somewhat less confrontational relations between Panama and the US, geared towards compliance with the calendar fixed for the handover of the Canal in 1999. There appears to have been a resurgence of a national debate concerning the Darien Gap highway. However, its strategic importance is dwarfed at this stage by the momentous stakes at play for Panama in the handover of the Canal Zone.[8] Nonetheless, several key actors are involved in the debate over the highway. As in Colombia, the issue of the road itself is less of a concern than the discussion concerning the style of development these projects take and the possible windfall for resident communities in the Darien.

Finally, there has been a substantial increase since the early 1990s in the number of bi-national sectoral commissions between Colombia and Panama. Established in 1992, the Comisión de Vecindad has functioned as a bi-national forum at the ministerial level between Panama and Colombia. It has fostered several levels of sectoral coordination to address common security, social and environmental issues. In the environmental sector there have been regular meetings between Natural Resource Ministry officials, National Parks Directors and staff involved in the administration of the border park of Los Katíos and Darien National Park. At this stage, these constitute important opportunities for discussing key issues surrounding the Darien.

This bilateral diplomacy and the flurry of commission meetings it has spawned have reinforced the notion that the Darien Gap problem can only be addressed adequately from a truly bi-national perspective. They all point to the creation of a transboundary integration zone, coordinated by institutions built from the forum of the Comisión de Vecindad. This probably constitutes one of the most crucial, albeit tenuous and fragile, initiatives to date concerning the Darien Gap, and above all it involves no other government or international organization apart from Panama and Colombia. This is a far cry from the days when the fate of the Darien was being decided by the US Federal Highway Administration (FHWA) or the USDA in Washington, DC.

At the local scale

Indigenous territories, settlers and refugees

In both the Panamanian and Colombian Darien, indigenous settlements have undergone dramatic demographic and economic change over the past decades, with the exception of the Kuna, who have tenaciously defended their territory and lifestyle from outside encroachment. Today, they represent about a quarter of Darien Province's population (República de Panamá, 1997). As seen earlier, negative growth in the Río Sambú and Río Balsas settlements appears to indicate that the Emberá and Woonaan ethnic groups have seen their most isolated settlements wither (Cansarí et al, 1993). This can be partly explained by the regrouping of Emberá settlements in response to the creation of the Cemaco and Pinogana Comarcas in the early 1980s. Traditionally, a nomadic forest dwelling culture, the Emberá had to sacrifice their transhumance for permanent settlements in order to secure a legally recognized territory in the form of *Comarcas*. There is still a large contingent of the Emberá and Woonaan population that is not located within the two Comarcas. Many of the land conflicts in the Panamanian Darien, particularly with park authorities and conservation groups, involve these landless indigenous people. In Colombia, the growing level of organization of Emberá and Woonaan populations and their official recognition under the 1991 Constitution has secured them territorial claims, particularly along the Pacific coast and in the lower Atrato valley. The range of stakeholders at play in the Darien Gap is extremely diverse and disparate.

Table 8.2 *Yearly Total of Internally Displaced People in Colombia 1985–1999*

Year	Number of internally displaced people
1985–1994	700,000
1995	89,510
1996	181,000
1997	257,000
1998	308,000
1999	288,127
Total	1,823,637

Source: República de Colombia (1999)

In spite of a marked increase in the degree of mobilization of civil rights organizations on either side of the border over the past two decades, the intensification of the civil war in Colombia has produced a sharp increase in the number of internally displaced people fleeing combat zones. According to official data provided by the Ministry of Interior of Colombia the number of displaced people increased dramatically during the latter half of the 1990s (see Table 8.2). Averaging 70,000 a year between 1985 and 1994, the numbers have steadily risen to 257,000 in 1997 and over 300,000 in 1998. It was not until 1997 that the Colombia State recognized the problem and passed Law 387, which defines a displaced person as any person forced to migrate inside the national territory, to abandon his or her place of residence and workplace due to threats to his or her physical integrity, security and individual liberty.

The cumulative number of internally displaced populations in Colombia since 1985 exceeds 1.8 million. The result has been a heightened exodus from war torn regions. Colombia's Ministry of the Interior estimated in 2000 that 400,000 internally displaced people were forced to flee their communities of origin due to armed conflicts, violation of human rights and other acts of extortion, intimidation, etc. This represents 10 per cent of the entire population of Colombia! These migratory flows affect mostly the *municipios* where the armed conflict has been most intense, in particular the Urabá and Chocó regions where both the FARC and the paramilitary forces have been operating. Close to half (44.1 per cent) of the displaced population is composed of families headed by single mothers, 23.2 per cent by youths under 7 years of age and 16.7 per cent by populations belonging to ethnic groups (República de Colombia, 1999).

This massive migratory movement has a direct impact on neighbouring countries such as Panama and Ecuador. Both Panama and Ecuador are particularly vulnerable to the massive inflow of migrants from Colombia. These migrants are often followed by incursions by armed forces, particularly paramilitary groups in pursuit of alleged guerrilla sympathizers. In 1999, some 30 armed incidents took place in the Panamanian Darien, during which eight civilians and two public security officers were killed and villages were pillaged by irregular troops from Colombia. In one of the gravest incidents some 100 irregulars attacked and occupied the town of Boca de Cupe, and a Panamanian police officer was killed and three other civilians injured in the clash. Indigenous organizations both from the Emberá-Woonaan and Kuna ethnic groups voiced their concern and apprehension at the rise in armed violence along the border region. The spillover of the Colombian conflict into Panama is likely to be exacerbated by the onset of the Plan Colombia, a US$1.3 billion military aid package approved by the US Congress in 1999. These developments have heightened the threat of militarization of the Darien Gap, with all the implications of this in terms of human rights, national sovereignty and environment.

CONCLUSIONS, ISSUES AND STAKES

The Darien Gap, both as symbol and reality, was still in place at the dawn of the 21st century. This thin waist of America has for centuries been the object of rivalries, intrigue and myth. From the civilizing zeal of the Spanish Crown to the blueprints of civil engineers of the US Federal Highway Authority, the Darien has somehow escaped the onslaught of development over time. As one of the world's last sanctuaries where a biologically and culturally diverse heritage still live in coexistence, the Darien stands today as a symbol of resilience. What scenarios await this remote corner of the Americas, curiously located at its very centre, in the 21st century?

The stakes are high. As a crossing point between East and West and North and South, the Darien is both a potential route for an inter-oceanic canal and the obligatory waypoint for the last stretch of road linking the Americas. Both of these geopolitical discourses are powerful constructs and essentially reflect the outsider's vision of the Darien. They encapsulate modernity, as did the Panama Canal a century ago. They differ diametrically from the vision forged by those who live, thrive or survive in the Darien today. In contrast to the globalizing vision of modernity, the indigenous vision of the Darien is anchored in diversity and in what makes the Darien unique. These contrasting visions help us to devise several intermeshed scenarios for the future of the Darien, based on a review of the interests and positions of the actors involved.

The environmental dimension: Conserving the natural heritage of Darien

Since the early 1980s, Darien National Park has been recognized as a World Heritage Site. As a tribute to its unique floristic characteristics, with high levels of endemism, this Park has become a symbol of the global struggle for conserving the remaining stands of pristine tropical forests. As in many other regions, the creation of protected areas occurred in response to outside threats, namely the Inter American Highway. Spurred by the continued efforts to resume the construction of the Darien Gap highway, environmental groups and the Natural Resources Institutes of Colombia and Panama worked closely to create 600,000 ha of protected areas by the mid-1980s on either side of the border.

The 20-year hiatus in the construction of the Darien Gap highway enabled international environmental NGOs such as WWF, IUCN and The Nature Conservancy to study and document the region's unique environment. With the IUCN General Assembly's 1994 Declaration, the Darien Gap has become a global conservation priority. The Darien Gap is also a crucial testing ground for the Earth Summit Conventions on Biological Diversity and Climate Change. All the resolutions in international conservation fora, from the IUCN General Assembly of 1994 to the First Latin American Parks Congress, held in May 1997 in Santa Marta, Colombia, have pointed to the importance of these heritage sites not only for conservation biology but also for the moral compromise linked to these Conventions derived from UNCED (United Nations Conference on Environment and Development).

Locally, however, the boom in conservation and sustainable development initiatives has come up against increasing resistance by local indigenous communities. In the Panamanian Darien, ANCON's creation of the Punta Patiño Natural Reserve as a buffer zone for the Darien National Park caused friction with the Congreso General Emberá-Woonaan. By re-settling numerous settlements in the Mogue River Area, in order to preserve the estuarine mangrove ecosystem of Punta Patiño, ANCON has estranged many of the indigenous leaders of the Emberá-Woonaan. Linked to the continued presence of Emberá-Woonaan people outside the comarcas, the resettlement policy is likely to produce future conflicts between settlers, environmental organizations and indigenous groups. Similarly, the creation of the Los Katíos National Park on the Colombian side of the border produced conflicts with local landowners and settlers. However, this local conflict is completely overshadowed by the depth and breadth of the ongoing civil and military conflict unravelling today in Colombia.

The environmental impact of the opening of the Darien Gap highway is no longer based on hypothetical extrapolations. Data collected since the opening of the road to Yaviza on the Panamanian side and to Río León on the Colombian side confirm the devastating effects the new roads have on forest environments. This has also been corroborated by many studies on deforestation in the Neotropical regions of America (Kaimowitz, 1996). Land speculation, deforestation and short-term extractive activities dominate these peripheral economies, and all signs seem to indicate that these trends will continue and increase. Dismal social and economic conditions coupled with the intensification of the armed conflict on the Colombian side of the Darien will undoubtedly lead to significant migration into newly opened lands. By the sheer numbers involved, these migration flows would be unstoppable once a road is built. Governance and control over border migration and traffic would be practically impossible, let alone the livelihood security and protection of local indigenous populations living in this border region.

However, broad national and international support for conservation initiatives such as those set forth by WWF, IUCN, The Nature Conservancy and ANCON in Panama reflect the extraordinary capacity for mobilization that these organizations possess worldwide. The opening of the Darien Gap will most certainly be an occasion for these global organizations to demonstrate their capacity for public advocacy. For instance, it is likely that environmental organizations will closely scrutinize the environmental impact statements drafted with Inter-American Development Bank funding. Further advocacy concerning the Darien is likely to focus on: compliance with both the Convention of Biodiversity and on Climate Change; strengthening the bi-national Commissions on the Environment and on Indian Affairs by increasing their audience and participants; and monitoring the biological diversity of the Darien Gap. There will also be many grassroots activities, including by NGOs, community-based organizations (CBOs) and religious organizations.

The cultural heritage dimension: Promised lands versus ancestral lands

Another major issue at hand relates to the cultural heritage of the indigenous and tribal lands in the Darien. As a UNESCO Man and the Biosphere Reserve, Darien National Park combines a unique natural environment with an extraordinary cultural heritage. Faced with increasing encroachment from settlers and extractive interests, indigenous groups have undertaken momentous mobilization over the past 20 years. Except for the Kuna, whose struggle for territorial autonomy dates back to the 1920s, other indigenous groups such as the Emberá-Woonaan and the Ngöbe-Bugle in western Panama began mobilizing for territorial recognition in the 1970s.

With the creation of the Cemaco and Pinogana Comarcas in Panama in the early 1980s, the Emberá-Woonaan General Congress became the leading forum for political statement of the indigenous peoples of the Panamanian Darien. In Colombia, Organización Regional Emberá Waunana (OREWA) emerged during the same period to defend Emberá-Waunana rights in the Chocó. These organizations have served as a catalyst to rally Afrochocoano and Darienita community-based groups. The future of the '*tierras colectivas*', or the Emberá living on lands outside the Comarcas, is a contentious issue in Panama.

As in many other pristine forest areas of Central America, the Darien has been the stage for a classic confrontation between *ladino* settlers and indigenous groups. With the belligerent history of the Kuna people nearby, the Emberá have mustered many of the negotiating abilities and political savvy of their archrivals. Some of the fiercest battles fought by the Kuna were against *ladino* or *interiorano* settlers over territory. Still today, the Kuna systematically evict and burn the ranches of settlers within their territorial boundaries. These dramatic measures are designed to deter any further colonization movement, thus protecting the Kuna homeland from excessive incursions of market forces into their territory, their lifestyle and traditional knowledge. While territorial claims have gained considerable ground over the past 20 years, indigenous groups are still the social group most vulnerable to market encroachment and resource extraction pressures.

In March 1994, the chief political leaders (*caciques generales*) of the Darien's major ethnic groups (Emberá, Woonaan and Kuna) met in Común, in the Cemaco Comarca, and produced a Resolution of the Indigenous Peoples concerning the opening of the Darien Gap highway. Among the articles contained in this Resolution, there are clear considerations of the lack of indigenous participation in the Comisión de Vecindad, a bi-national, essentially government-run forum concerning border relations between the two countries. As a result of this initiative, the Indigenous Commission on the Inter American Highway was created. Since then, a sub-commission on indigenous affairs and another on environment were instituted as part of the Comisión de Vecindad. These sub-commissions have enabled a greater degree of transboundary coordination between governments. Growing indigenous group claims for greater participation in decisions concerning major infrastructure projects such as the Darien Gap highway could be an opportunity for this commission to broaden its fora to actors from civil society.

Colombia in Panama: Sovereignty in the 21st century

Still a part of Colombia a century ago, the Darien has long been perceived by Colombia as a runaway province. Separated by the Gap, Panama and Colombia share many cultural traits and have a long history in common. However, Panamanians pride themselves on being different from Colombians and enjoy a relatively prosperous life, somehow keeping at bay Colombia's endemic violence and endless political strife. In a sense, the Darien has also been used to seal off Panama from Colombian influence, at least for its first century of existence as a sovereign nation.

Sovereignty is a concept widely assimilated in Panama. Panamanian nationalists perceived the presence of the Panama Canal Zone as a territorial enclave under US jurisdiction, crossing the very heart of the country, as a permanent affront to Panamanian sovereignty. As the Canal Zone ceased to exist in December 1999, attention is shifting back to the borders, and in particular to the Darien. Much of the press and national leaders have denounced the constant violations to Panamanian sovereignty by Colombian paramilitary and guerrilla groups. The economic and political effects of drug trafficking and money laundering are pervasive in Latin America. These forces know no borders and effectively baffle the most elementary notions of sovereignty.

How, then, does a structurally weak state face such formidable forces, which not even the US has been capable of countering? The institutional presence of Panamanian and Colombian government officials in the Darien has been historically tenuous. Shrinking public expenditure budgets with structural adjustment policies have only reinforced the absence of the state apparatus on the frontier. If it cannot effectively control the situation now, it will be less able to do so once the Darien Gap highway is built. US policy-makers who oppose the highway do so because they argue that it will enable the drug cartels to ship their goods overland. The task of controlling the onslaught of traffickers, settlers, poachers, smugglers and illegal immigrants is a daunting one. Throngs of migrants are already entering Panama in spite of the rough terrain and the hardships that crossing the Darien Gap still exact on those who dare.

At this stage, there are few institutional channels through which these issues can be addressed constructively between Colombia and Panama. The creation of the Comisión de Vecindad provides a key forum in which to broadly discuss these issues. Much can be done to strengthen this fragile transboundary institutional linkage. Its fragility is a measure of the relative weakness of each government apparatus. By including a larger number of actors to participate in these fora, it is possible to strengthen the governance capacities in the Darien.

Global imperatives versus local prerogatives

At the dawn of the 21st century, it is worthwhile to ponder the function of sovereignty in an increasingly globalized world. Some utopians sniff the final abolition of borders and boundaries in a true free market world. However, recent global and local events do not seem to corroborate that vision. Boundaries are alive and well and tended to multiply at the end of the 20th century, as we saw in Middle Europe and the former Soviet Union.

Notwithstanding, the trend in neo-liberal-oriented policies favouring the free market over state intervention points to the need to rethink the traditional concept of sovereignty. There has been a notable increase in studies focusing on border regions and transboundary interactions.

More careful study of transboundary linkages, trade, exchange and conflict can provide extremely useful insights into policy options to deal with the Darien Gap. At this stage, the Darien Gap controversy seems to constitute a confrontation between the global imperative of opening to world trade and local prerogatives of who can control the Darien and guarantee its long-term conservation once the road is built. In a study on transboundary cooperation, Malcolm Anderson provides a keen insight on the difficulties of administering territorial sovereignty, which can be applied to the case of the Darien:

> *The policies and practices of the state are constrained by the degree of de facto control that the government exercises over the state frontier. The incapacity of governments ... to control much of the traffic of persons, goods and information across their frontiers is changing the nature of both states and frontiers* (Anderson, 1997).

The opening of the Darien Gap would most certainly change the nature of the Panamanian state and its border with Colombia. There are still those in official circles on either side of the border who view the Gap as an obstacle to hemispheric trade and a fertile ground for subversion.[9]

What is more disturbing is the conviction in official circles that the only way to preserve the Gap's extraordinary biodiversity is by opening the Gap to free trade and global commerce. The other strand of the argument is that if the road is not built it will fester as a breeding ground for guerrillas and drug producers.

Pressures towards economic integration bear directly on the resurgence of projects aimed at opening up the Darien Gap and developing the Pacific region of northern Colombia. Colombia has emerged over the past ten years as a major oil producer, and the new fiscal revenues generated by oil exports make Colombia eligible for large multilateral loans for major infrastructure projects, such as the Plan Pacífico. Colombia has clearly stated that it could finance the Darien Gap highway unilaterally if needed – a clear shift since the 1970s.

The greatest impact of the road will probably be indirect. Through a sharp increase in migration flows, settlers will increasingly encroach into indigenous lands and protected areas and there will be an increased lack of governance in this remote frontier region. As in other highway projects penetrating remote regions, the Darien Gap highway will not necessarily foster local development: it will cater to powerful economic interests in the major industrial centres of Medellín, Cauca Valley, Cartagena and further into Venezuela. If we add to this bleak picture a continued increase in factional violence in Colombia and its likely spillover into Panama, the prospect of opening the Darien Gap highway becomes a matter of national security for Panama, the Canal and US interests still present in Central America.

The future of the Darien and the delinking of issues

Perhaps the greatest threat faced by the Darien is related to the potential spillover of the Colombian conflict, which has already claimed 35,000 lives. The conflict threatens to increase in scale and intensity with the approval of the Plan Colombia by the US Congress and Senate, making Colombia the world's third largest recipient of US Aid after Israel and Egypt. The US$1.3 billion aid package is destined essentially for strengthening the capacity of the Colombian Government's armed forces in their war against drug traffickers and armed guerrillas. Over US$1 billion will go to operations in the southern regions of the Caquetá and Putumayo, for the interception of drug envoys and the physical eradication of coca plantations using questionable means such as massive aerial spraying of herbicides and bio-engineered pathogens. A mere 6 per cent of the total budget is earmarked for the protection of human rights and the response to the humanitarian crisis (Shifter et al, 2000). The total number of displaced people reached 1.8 million in 1999, the third largest in the world after Sudan and Angola (ibid, 2000, p7). The size of this military aid package has elicited fears in neighbouring Venezuela and Brazil. Some analysts refer to this development as the 'Central Americanization' of Colombia, by which the boundaries of the US backyard are shifting further south (Granados and Solis, 2000).

The emphasis placed on a military solution to the Colombian conflict will no doubt exacerbate the impending humanitarian crisis unfolding in the region. It may also have compounded environmental impacts through eradication campaigns and the indiscriminate use of biotechnology. The impact that this will have on the smaller, neighbouring countries such as Panama and Ecuador is unfathomable. In the light of these recent developments, it is unlikely that the construction of the Darien Gap highway will be given a green light, unless it responds to tactical military objectives in an all-out regional war. The potential political cost of protracted military involvement in Colombia is a factor not to be under-estimated; however, it is clear that the main losers will be Colombian people, and particularly those located in sensitive border regions.

At this stage, it is crucial to delink issues such as international security, guerrilla warfare and drug producing from the question of whether or not the road should be built. Not building the road will not necessarily result in greater political stability in Colombia or Panama. Nor does the building of the Darien Gap highway necessarily mean that economic development and prosperity will transform the Darien into an emporium for world trade. Even if the Darien Gap highway is definitely abandoned as a project, it does not in and of itself constitute a sufficient condition for the long-term conservation of its extraordinary natural and cultural heritage.

The Darien Gap entered the 21st century unforded. In spite of its small size and remote location, the forces at play in the opening of the Gap are global in scope. It encapsulates conflicts between modernity and tradition, conservation and development, and between sovereignty, identity and free trade. What is at play in the Darien Gap is obviously more than a pristine forest environment or local indigenous cultures. It will be a testing ground for the future geopolitical make-up of Middle America.

NOTES

1 Free trade agreement between Argentina, Brazil, Paraguay and Uruguay.
2 The tropical wet forest formation extends from the Panamanian Darien into the Colombian Chocó, as both sides of the range share similar species composition. While higher ranges have a floristic composition similar to the cloud forest refugias of highland Chiriquí and Costa Rica, the lower forests have more in common with the Chocó and adjoining swamp forests. In particular, the riparian forest formation, known locally as the Cativo (*Prioria copaifera*), dominates most of the lower Atrato River Delta and associated swamps, as it is a major source of timber for the Colombian market.
3 Municipal administrative unit in the Republic of Panama.
4 Quoted by Jon Barnes (1993, p138).
5 ANCON and Fundación Natura (1996) – This collection of official documents includes a 1996 report from the Transport Ministry of Colombia, National Highway Institute, titled 'Proyecto Conexión Terrestre Colombia-Panamá', these figures appear on p1.
6 Routes included the 540 kilometre route compared with the 81 kilometre between Río Leon and Palo de las Letras (Parsons, 1967, p63).
7 For a compelling account of the cocaine–lobster connection in the Miskito Keys off Nicaragua's Caribbean Coast, see Nietschmann (1995).
8 Stakes include 300,000 jobs, over 3,000 buildings and installations – including airports, communications and radar facilities – in areas of prime real estate, near a major shipping route for world commerce.
9 In a 1993 letter signed by both the Panamanian and Colombian Ministers of Public Transport, sent to the Director of International Programmes of the US Federal Highway Administration, they stated:

> *Our governments have made a strong commitment to preserve and improve the fragile environment and take all necessary measures to guarantee that the road will not be used as access to new land for colonization, but as a 'bridge' to enable all people from the Americas to freely move through our Continent, help preserve our biodiversity and gain valuable knowledge from its study… The Darien Gap highway will improve the image held in the United States and our two countries of road builders so damaged by a history of lack of concern towards environmental issues and prove that development and environment are complementary, rather than antagonistic elements in any society whether developed or not. Furthermore, the connection will stabilize and strengthen democracy in strategic areas of Panama and Colombia that are, in the present state of affairs, fertile land to breed and house guerrillas and drug producers.*

REFERENCES

ANCON (Panamá) and Fundación Natura (Colombia) (1996) *Programa y Documentos del I Foro Internacional sobre Alternativas a la Apertura del Tapón del Darien*, Colón, Panamá, 29–31 March

Anderson, M (1997) 'The Political Science of Frontiers', in Ganster, P et al (eds) *Borders and Border Regions in Europe and North America*. San Diego: San Diego State University Press/Institute of the Californias, p28

Barnes, J (1993) 'Driving Roads through Land Rights: the Colombian Plan Pacífico' *The Ecologist* 23(4):134–140, July/August

Cansarí, R, Castañeda, D and Harp, W (1993) *Estudio Socio-Cultural en tres Regiones del Darien: Río Balsas, Sambú y Garachiné: Un análisis cultural de las comunidades al margen de la Reserva de la Biósfera Darien*. Panamá: INRENARE/UNESCO

Comisión de Vecindad Colombo-Panamameña (1993) *Segunda Reunión de Vecindad Colombo-Panameña: Acta de la SubComisión de Recursos Naturales y Gestión Ambiental*, 9 July, Cartagena, Colombia

Comisión de Vecindad Colombo-Panamameña (1997) *VIII Reunión de Vecindad Colombo-Panameña: Acta de la SubComisión de Recursos Naturales y Gestión Ambiental*, 17 April, Bogotá, Colombia

Congreso General Kuna, Congreso General Emberá-Wounaan (1994) 'Resolución de los Pueblos Indígenas ante la Apertura del Tapón del Darien', Panama (unpublished photocopy included in letter sent to Guillermo Endara Galimany, President of the Republic of Panamá)

El País (1997) Edición América, Año XXII, No 7461, 15 October

Girot, P (2000) *Raíz y Vuelo: El Uso de Recursos Naturales Vivientes en Mesoamérica*. San José: UICN-SUI

Granados, C and Solís, L G (2000) 'Las relaciones Colombia-Centroamérica: Los retos de la fronericidad-Reflexiones Preliminares', paper presented at the regional conference Colombia-Centroamérica: Los Desafíos de la Fronericidad, San José, Costa Rica, 24–25August. Funpadem-Ford Foundation

Herlihy, P (1986) 'Indians and Rain Forest Collide: The Cultural Parks of Darien', *Cultural Survival Quartely* 10(3):46–58

Herlihy, P (1989) 'Opening Panama's Darien Gap', *Journal of Cultural Geography* 9(2):41–59

Herlihy, P (1995) 'La revolución silenciosa de Panamá: las tierras de comarca y los derechos indígenas', *Mesoamerica* 16(29):77–94, June

Howe, J (1995) 'La Lucha por la Tierra en la costa de San Blas (Panamá), 1900–1930', *Mesoamerica* 16(29):57–76, June

Kaimowitz, D (1996) *Livestock and Deforestation – Central America in the 1980s and 1990s: A Policy Perspective*. Jakarta: CIFOR

Molano, A and Ramírez, M C (1996) *El Tapón del Darien: Diario de una Travesía*. Bogotá: El Sello Editorial

Nietschmann, B (1995) 'Conservación, autodeterminación y el Area Protegida Costa Miskita, Nicaragua', *Mesoamérica* 16(29):1–56

Parsons, J J (1967) *Antioquia's Corridor to the Sea: An Historical Geography of the Settlement of Urabá*, Ibero-Americana Vol 49. Berkeley, CA: University of California Press

Pasos, R (ed) (1994) *El Ultimo Despale: La Frontera Agrícola Centroamericana*. San José: Garnier R P

República de Colombia (1991) *Carretera del Tapón del Darien*, Actas del XVI Congreso Panamericano de Carreteras, Montevideo, Uruguay, 6–10 May. Bogotá: MOPT

República de Colombia (1999) Atención a población desplazada por la violencia en Colombia, Red de Solidaridad Social, Informe de Gestión 1998–1999, Bogota, www.red.gov.co/DesplazamientoForzado/index.html

República de Panamá, Ministerio de Planificación y Política Económica, Dirección de Políticas Sociales (1997) 'Situación Social de la Provincia de Darien', Panamá, MIPPE (unpublished manuscript)

Restrepo Forero, G A (1992) 'Un Urabá posible', in *Colonización del Bosque Húmedo Tropical*. Bogotá: Corporación Araracuara, pp287–298

Reyes Posada, A (1992) 'Conflicto y Territorio en Colombia', in *Colonización del Bosque Húmedo Tropical*. Bogotá: Corporación Araracuara, pp55–66

Shifter, M, Graham, B and Scowcroft, B (2000) *Toward Greater Peace and Security in Colombia: Forging a Constructive US Policy. Report of an Independent Task Force Sponsored by the Council on Foreign Relations and the Inter-American Dialogue*, www.cfr.org/public/pubs/Colombia_TaskForce.pdf. Washington, DC: Council on Foreign Relations

Steiner, C (1992) 'Urabá: Un Cruce de Caminos', in *Colonización del Bosque Húmedo Tropical*. Bogotá: Corporación Araracuara, pp275–286

Valencia, E and Villa, W (1992) 'Evolución del poblamiento del Chocó en el siglo XX: el caso del Medio Atrato', in *Colonización del Bosque Húmedo Tropical*. Bogotá: Corporación Araracuara, pp227–248

WWF/IUCN (1997) *Centres of Plant Diversity: A Guide and Strategy for their Conservation*, Volume 3 *The Americas*, S D Davis, V H Heywood, O Herrera-MacBryde, J Villa-Lobos and A C Hamilton (eds). Cambridge: IUCN Publications Unit

WWF/PRISMA (1997) *Fortaleciendo las Perspectivas para el Desarrollo Sostenible en Centroamérica, Panamá: Evaluación de la Sostenibilidad Nacional*, January. Panamá: CEASPA

Chapter 9

Environment, Development and Human Rights in China: A Case Study of Foreign Waste Dumping

Changhua Wu and Simon Wang

INTRODUCTION

In 1949, China faced a massive burden of nutritional deficiency and infectious and parasitic diseases. More than half of the population was expected to die from infectious and other non-degenerative diseases before reaching middle age – a pattern still common throughout the developing world. Since then, dramatic and extensive social improvements have accompanied China's growth. Rising incomes have eased poverty, reduced infant mortality, improved child and maternal health, and lengthened life expectancy. The average life span has risen from 35 in 1949 to 70 in 1998. Infant mortality rate has dropped from 200 per 1,000 people to 31 per 1,000. Infectious diseases, while still a serious problem in some parts of the country, now claim the lives of just around 0.0004 per cent of the population each year (China Ministry of Public Health, 1995).

The achievements in health and life expectancy over the past four decades far exceed what could be expected of China in view of its primary stage of economic development, according to a World Bank evaluation. The decrease in morbidity and mortality rates associated with infectious diseases, in particular, is the most remarkable achievement, and such an achievement can be attributed to an aggressive campaign to improve primary health care and tackle infectious diseases that was enthusiastically carried out by the central government (World Bank, 1997). The campaign aimed to provide the Chinese people with services in family planning, child immunization, improved nutrition and infectious disease control, and access to better education, housing and sanitation.

These improvements have been firmly founded on a broad, publicly financed, disease prevention strategy, coupled with accessible primary health care particularly for mothers and children. This success can be attributed to the capacity of a strong central government to carry out its mandate to bring health to people, by adopting the best of traditional methods and wedding these with modern approaches. At the same time, however, the current transformation of China's health care system to be more market-oriented is causing shock waves in people's lives.

EMERGING ENVIRONMENTAL CRISIS

Accompanying these achievements are some very high costs, both environmental and human. According to the 1996 *State of the Environment Report*, 78 per cent of China's river sections can no longer be used for drinking purposes; 50 per cent of urban groundwater is contaminated; 38.9 per cent of the river sections of the seven major river systems monitored are classified as Grade IV, Grade V or below Grade V surface water standards; and 38.4 per cent of urban river sections are below Grade V standard, which means that the water cannot even be used for irrigation. Pollution in China's seven major river systems is worsening, and polluted areas are becoming larger. In addition, lake and reservoir eutrophication has become serious, and coastal water quality has been declining (National Environmental Protection Agency, 1996a)

Emissions of residential and industrial waste gas have risen with each passing year and pollution from coal burning has worsened. In 1995, China's total waste gas emissions stood at 12.33 trillion cubic metres, an increase of 127 per cent from 1982, and industrial waste gas accounted for 87 per cent of the total. For the long term, there has been a slight decrease of total suspended particulates (TSP) and sulphur dioxide (SO_2) emissions but, in general, all air pollutant emissions have been high and will remain high (ibid). In 1996, the average ambient level of TSP in major cities was 309 ug per cubic metre, more than twice the permissible level recommended by the World Health Organization. Some cities suffer from very serious SO_2 pollution, with an average ambient level nationwide at 79 ug per cubic metre.

Due to the increased number of automobiles in large cities, nitrogen oxides (NO_x) emissions from vehicular exhausts have caught up, and in some metropolitan areas such emissions are the top air pollutant. Areas affected by acid rain expand and suffer from increasingly serious pollution. One recent research report finds that acid rain affects 40 per cent of China's total land area and is especially serious in central China, the country's south-west, the south and the east. In 1996, the annual average pH level of precipitation in 43 cities was below 5.6 (National Environmental Protection Agency, 1996b).

China's industrial solid wastes have been increasing. In 1996, a total of 660 million tons of solid wastes were produced, 20 million tons more than the previous year and an increase of 75 per cent since 1991. Of the total solid wastes produced, 10 million tons were hazardous. In the same year, the total discharge of industrial solid wastes stood at 16.9 million tons, 1.3 per cent of which was hazardous. Due to the lack of treatment capacity, a cumulative total of 6.49 billion tons of solid waste was stockpiled over 51,680 ha of land. In addition, there were nearly 70 million tons of household garbage produced nationwide. Because of the shortage of garbage handling plants, a large amount of garbage has to be stockpiled in suburbs, which has become a major source of pollution (ibid).

Environment and health

Environmental pollution has been identified by the Chinese government as one of the four leading factors that adversely affect people's health and lead to early deaths. The morbidity and mortality rates from respiratory diseases, digestive system illnesses and cancer have been very high and are still rising in China, particularly in areas where problems of air pollution, contaminated drinking water and poor water sanitation are especially serious.

According to the World Resources Report 1994–1995, China's death rate from chronic obstructive pulmonary disease (COPD) is 162.6 for every 100,000 people – five times higher than that in the US. In big cities, an estimated 178,000 Chinese die early every year because of pollutants in excess of standards. In Shenyang, Shanghai and other major cities, the average blood-lead level of children is approximately 80 per cent above what is considered to be dangerous for mental development. Indoor air pollution, primarily from burning coal and biomass for cooking and heating, causes an estimated 111,000 premature deaths each year (World Resources Institute, 1995). Because of air pollution, according to a recent estimate by the World Bank, China loses some 7.4 million person-work-years a year. Meanwhile, with more reaches of urban rivers failing to meet even the lowest standards for irrigation water, access to safe drinking water in the future is threatened for tens of millions of people.

Laws and orders

Recognizing the urgency of these problems, the Chinese government has endorsed a suite of policies to halt contamination of air and water. The success of these policies, which will have a direct bearing on people's health, environmental status and the global environment, depends very much on both the government's continued commitment to these policies and the active participation of the whole society.

Strengthening environmental legislation has been identified as the major responsibility of law enforcement authorities in China. Besides two dozen laws on the protection of environment and natural resources, China rewrote its criminal law in March 1997 and opened doors for punishing environmental destroyers as criminal offenders. The confidence of environmental authorities in law enforcement has been strengthened.

With rising incomes and literacy rates, the Chinese have become increasingly aware of the importance of environmental protection. As shown in recent studies, as communities become wealthier and better educated, they tend to push for stronger environmental regulations and enforcement. Such an awareness could be attributed to the increase in media coverage of pollution events, which brought real pictures of, among other things, the destruction of forests, to people's living rooms. As a result of media coverage, more and more people have realized that they no longer want to breathe dirty air, drink polluted water and eat contaminated foods. It is no wonder that a popular saying in the developed region in eastern China goes like this: house is new, money is enough, but water is foul, and life is short.

Foreign waste dumping: a violation of Chinese human rights

It is difficult for anyone who keeps abreast of China's environment and development to ignore the prolonged media coverage of the controversial issue of foreign waste dumping. It should also be noticed, meanwhile, that a number of more serious popular revolts against environmental degradation, including the series of incidents along the Huaihe River where the people were deprived of safe drinking water, have never been covered by the official media. Under these circumstances, the Chinese government was often forced to react.

Since the latter half of 1996, China's aggressive campaign against foreign waste dumping, as well as the public debate over the issue, has taken on new momentum. For the government, daily coverage by the official media on the illegal imports of environment-damaging industrial and residential wastes, unusual in the number of reports and their investigative nature, laid the groundwork for Beijing to a stage a high-stake, mostly political fight against unfair and immoral practices in international trade.

The battle against foreign junk, as the campaign was officially coined, also provided an extraordinary opportunity for the Chinese government to manifest to its people and the rest of the world that Beijing intends to keep its promise over the protection of fundamental human rights in China. More importantly, it provides an opportunity for China to further clarify to the world that its interpretation of human rights not only differs from the West, but also is highly relevant to Chinese reality.

Through extensive research in both China and the US, we found that in the case of foreign waste dumping, China has effectively and with unprecedented reserve used the weapons of laws and regulations. In China, relationships, or guanxi, are usually the most important currency of business and politics. Although the current battle has not led to increasing xenophobia, Beijing's efforts to explain its human rights record have taken on new, political meanings.

The battle, however, is being waged entirely by the Chinese government and media. China's emerging non-governmental organizations (NGOs) are nowhere to be found. Despite the fact that foreign waste dumping has significant implications for environmental quality and people's daily lives, the general public has not been involved. The lack of genuine public debate and NGO activism suggest that any solution arrived at by the government – on this as well as other domestic or international environmental issues – will be incomplete.

THE EVOLUTION: CHINA DEFINES HUMAN RIGHTS

Evolution of a concept

Achieving sustainable development is a challenge facing all human society. Ever since the Second World War, industrialization has brought rapidly accumulating wealth as well as tremendous and unprecedented problems. How to coordinate economic growth with social and environmental goals has been the subject of endless discussion.

It was the World Bank that first developed the concept of 'equal opportunity of development'. Later, the United Nations Development Programme (UNDP) integrated the human factor into this concept and developed the concept of 'sustainable human development'. In 1987, when the World Council on Environment and Development presented the concept of sustainable development, it focused on the links between the demands of current and future generations. The World Resources Institute added another dimension, 'human health', to this concept and maintained that along with the enhancement of living standards and the conservation of natural resources, the quality of the environment should be protected and improved. Human rights, under this developed circumstance, shall take on new meaning. Environmental rights, first coined in the Tokyo Decision in 1970 by the International Symposium on Public Hazard, represents the further extension of development rights, and the prerequisite for the protection of both rights is international cooperation.

No development, no human rights

Owing to tremendous differences in historical background, social system, cultural tradition and economic development, countries differ in their understanding and practice of human rights.

China has always maintained that the issue of human rights falls by and large within the sovereignty of each country. However, it was not until 1991 that the Chinese government, under consistent Western pressure, offered its first clear, official interpretation of Chinese human rights concepts with the State Council's publication of China's White Paper on Human Rights. The book, however, was rich in China's human rights achievements and relatively weak in theoretical interpretation. In the years afterwards, the government left the work to scholars.

To the Chinese government, basic human rights can be divided into four parts in order of significance: rights to subsistence, rights to development, rights to equality, and rights to freedom, in addition to political rights, religious freedom, economic freedom, and the rights to education and culture. As compared with Western emphasis on freedom of speech as a prominent aspect of human rights, the Chinese government, quoting the Universal Declaration of Human Rights, interprets human rights as, first of all, the guarantee of basic food and clothing. China regards the right to subsistence as the most important of all human rights without which other rights are out of the question. Moreover, without national independence, there would be no guarantee for people's lives. The problem of food and clothing having been solved, the people have been guaranteed the basic right to subsistence (Information Office of the State Council of the People's Republic of China, 1991). To China, in all of human rights, 'the rights to subsistence and the rights to development are the most fundamental human rights, and this is particularly true for developing countries' (*People's Daily*, 1992).

Han Peide, chief author of *Human Rights: Theory and Practice*, a key government-sponsored research project which runs to 1,158 pages and was co-written by more than 50 researchers, argued that Marxist human rights theory, which China sticks to, differs from capitalistic human rights theory. Marxist theory stresses the protection of collective rights as well as individual rights and suggests that rights to subsistence and development are the most important basic human rights. Human rights conditions in a particular country, Han notes, should not be considered separately from that country's history and national condition. To many developing countries, he adds, there would be no other rights for its people to enjoy if there were no national independence or sovereignty or no rights to subsistence or development (Peide, 1995).

Environmental rights and national sovereignty

According to Xie Zhaoguo, author of *On Environmental Rights*, China's interpretation of environmental rights consists of three parts: the right to ecological benefits, which means there should be no discrimination, intervention or exploitation; the rights to economic and financial benefits, which come with the ownership of natural resources; and the rights of a nation or a people to control its environment, which could be interpreted as national sovereignty to environment and independent development of natural resources.

Environmental rights, Xie says, could be in the form of a rights of a country or a people to bring certain natural elements under control. It means, therefore: 'a nation's or a people's sovereignty over its environment, which includes the rights to independent land development, utilization and management; the rights to protect the nation's own environment and its people from pollution and other forms of destruction from the outside; the rights to enjoy the benefits of commonly owned environment, natural resources and heritage in the world; and the rights to participate in international cooperation for environmental protection' (Zhaoguo, 1997).

Chinese scholars also say the reason that they are trying to define the concept of environmental rights, a relatively new concept in China, is the limited nature of natural resources. Environmental rights, these scholars say, is a reflection of the struggle of a country or a region to protect its rights to enjoy the benefits of nature. Setting up a guarantee system, meanwhile, is crucial to the realization of development rights of the developing countries.

The guarantee mechanism should be based on two principles. The first is an equal rights principle, or one country, one vote, which means that every country enjoys equal rights to choose the model of its development free of external interference and pressure. The second is the permanent sovereignty principle, which means that every country has permanent sovereignty over the exploitation and utilization of its natural resources. Foreign development of the host country's natural resources must have the permission of that country (ibid)

FOREIGN WASTE DUMPING

William Ping Chen decision

On 13 January 1997, after a month-long trial covered gavel-to-gavel by the official media and attended by US consulate representatives, Shanghai First Intermediate People's Court sentenced William Ping Chen, chairman of Unity Paper Co. Ltd, a China–US joint venture, to 10 years in prison for dumping foreign waste in China. Chen, 56 and by that time an American citizen, was also slapped with a fine of RMB 500,000 (equivalent to approximately US$70,000) and was ordered to leave the country for good. A highly publicized court drama that placed Beijing in direct diplomatic confrontation against Washington and subjected China's law enforcement to unprecedented credibility tests, finally came to its conclusion.

According to the court document, from July to December 1996, Chen used the name of two fodder trade companies in Zhejiang and Anhui Provinces to import into Shanghai's Wusong harbour 238 tons of American residential and hospital waste. The 16 containers of waste, which originated on the west coast of the US, as local environmental agency and Shanghai Customs officials discovered, were not what the defendant alleged as waste paper or mixed paper, but contained highly hazardous wastes whose imports were banned by Chinese law. Chen, the judge proclaimed, lied about the nature of the imports, attempted to evade customs inspections, caused serious damage to the Chinese environment and put Chinese people's health in danger. Those who commit crimes like this, according to the revised criminal law that went into effect days before the trial, could be punished by more than 10 years in prison.

The case of Chen, the first person to be tried as a criminal and to receive such a sentence since China's law against waste imports came into effect in April 1996, sent a clear signal to the outside world that China had finally become serious about ending foreign waste dumping. In the days before and after Chen's trial, as the drama over foreign waste played out in Chinese courts and throughout the unusually critical official media, the country's law enforcement records were being examined more closely then ever. The government's interpretation of human rights took on new, if not entirely political, meanings.

Waste imports: Sources and numbers

As a major consumer of paper, China has a long history of importing waste paper from the West. Such imports caused few problems, let alone public outcry, for years. In 1993, some 1,300 tons of chemical wastes from South Korea, labelled as fuel oil, were discovered by customs officials in Nanjing, a port city near the mouth of the Yangtze River. Few newspapers covered it. The government, hoping that it was an isolated incident, did little about it. Incidents

Table 9.1 *Chinese Waste Imports 1990–1995*

Year	Total import value (US$10,000)	Import wastes (ton)	Import waste value (US$10,000)	% of total imports
1990	5,334,500	991,542	25,999	0.49
1991	7,379,100	2,114,410	60,610	0.59
1992	8,058,500	5,715,823	134,326	1.67
1993	10,395,900	8,285,361	157,448	1.50
1994	11,561,400	6,668,963	136,067	1.18
1995	13,208,354	6,523,505	172,000	1.31

Source: 1990–1995 China Customs Annual Statistical Report, *Levels of Imported Waste in China*

such as the import of another 6,440 barrels of South Korean chemical wastes from dozens of factories – all labelled on customs forms as engine oil – began to garner attention.

But things got worse. In 1995 and 1996, an average of two waste dumping incidents were reported by the media per week. In April 1996, when some 600 tons of foul-smelling residential waste were discovered in a suburb of Beijing, merely a dozen miles from Tiananmen Square, Chinese bureaucrats were put on full alert.

According to the annual statistics reports of Chinese customs from 1990 to 1995, China imported a total of 25 million tons of wastes, with total import value at US$6.68 billion. In 1995 alone, China imported 6.52 million tons of wastes from abroad, worth US$1.7 billion and equal to 1.31 per cent of China's total imports during the same period. The total amount of imported waste copper and its value shot up by 53.6 per cent and 111.9 per cent, respectively, from 1990 to 1995. The imports of other wastes such as oil residue, used plastics, waste paper and waste ropes and cables all increased dramatically.

Of these wastes, some 50 per cent came from member countries of the Organization of Economic Cooperation and Development (OECD), 16 per cent came from Hong Kong, Taiwan, South Korea, Singapore and Macau, and another 34 per cent came from other regions, mostly Eastern Europe. In 1994, the US was responsible for 21 per cent of China's imported wastes, Japan for 18 per cent, Hong Kong and Russia for 11 per cent each, and Taiwan, Germany, South Korea, Singapore, Spain and the UK, among other countries and regions, for the rest. There have been significant trans-shipments of wastes imported into China from developed countries via Hong Kong and Macau.

It is important to note that some foreign enterprises in China have been directly involved in waste import, processing and disposal. In 1992, there were 195 foreign-funded enterprises in China involved in waste processing with a total investment of US$150 million, an increase of 178 per cent over the previous year. Of these enterprises, Hualong Plastics Chemical Industrial Co. Ltd, of Anhua, Zhejiang Province, was found in May 1994 to have imported 50 containers, or 1,000 tons of waste plastics from the European Union; the company was also found responsible for causing pollution to some 8 ha of farmland with 30,000 tons of residential waste. Chen's (USA) Tongtai International Co. imported approximately 150 truckloads of waste metals, of

Table 9.2 *Sources of Imported Wastes 1993–1994*

Country	1993		1994	
	Quantity (tons) (% of total)	Value (US$) (% of total)	Quantity (tons) (% of total)	Value (US$) (% of total)
OECD	4,630,000 (55.9)	8,570,000 (54.5)	3,360,000 (50.4)	6,560,000 (48.2)
NICs	1,570,000 (19.0)	2,640,000 (16.7)	1,160,000 (17.4)	2,070,000 (15.2)
Hong Kong	890,000 (10.7)	1,180,000 (7.5)	760,000 (11.5)	1,060,000 (7.8)
Singapore	110,000 (1.3)	650,000 (4.1)	100,000 (1.6)	170,000 (1.3)
South Korea	70,000 (0.8)	210,000 (1.4)	110,000 (1.7)	260,000 (1.9)
Taiwan	100,000 (1.2)	430,000 (2.8)	140,000 (2.1)	520,000 (3.8)
Macao	40,000 (0.4)	30,000 (0.2)	30,000 (0.4)	30,000 (0.2)
Russia	690,000 (8.3)	1,250,000 (7.9)	750,000 (11.3)	1,260,000 (9.3)

Source: 1993–1994 China Customs Annual Statistical Reports

which 95 per cent came from the US. Tongtai now owns 10 processing factories across China.

In 1996 alone, a total of 4,100 tons of domestic waste and hazardous wastes were smuggled into China. Most were detected in Guangdong Province whose access to Hong Kong made it a paradise for the trade. In May, Hong Kong's Fuxun Transport Co., trying to deliver 20 tons of what the company clarified was PE film paper to a plastics factory in Dongguan County, was stopped by customs officials who became suspicious at the smell seeping from its containers. It turned out to be the last of 138 shipments of residential waste coming out of the Netherlands. Fuxun was fined RMB 200,000 and ordered to take back the waste, old and new.

In July, five boats filled with used plastics, underwear, diapers and clothes, or 720 tons in total, were caught at the harbour of Shantou and were later ordered to return to Hong Kong, where they originated. In November, another five boats carrying used tyres and rotten plastics were caught running in the Pearl River, and the Chinese buyers, who contacted the brokers only through cellular phones, were nowhere to be found.

Wastes imports: Policy approaches

In pursuing economic development, China's strategy of rapid industrialization has encouraged growth in many industrial sectors that typically generate hazardous and industrial waste, including chemicals, mining, metallurgy, electroplating, steel production, printing and dyeing. National Environmental Protection Agency (NEPA) Administrator Xie Zhenhua's recent testimony to the Standing Committee of the National People's Congress (NPC), during a review of the solid waste law, suggests that the production of industrial and hazardous waste has far exceeded the country's capacity to treat, store and dispose of it safely. Due to limited technology, funding and administrative capacity, the handling and disposal of solid waste in China is still in the initial stage. Most procedures do not meet environmental protection standards. Ineffective waste management practices prevail, resulting in discharges of industrial and hazardous waste, contamination of land, air and water resources, and forgone cost-saving recycling opportunities. Xie estimated that solid waste pollution costs China more than RMB 90 billion (US$10.8 billion) annually (*China Business Review*, 1996).

China's Agenda 21 plan, approved by the State Council in the wake of the 1992 UN conference, estimated that as much as 70 per cent of the industrial waste generated annually in China might be hazardous, and warned that 5.9 billion tonnes of industrial waste occupying 540 million cubic metres have been improperly stored or discarded in recent years. The majority of the waste – which includes hexavalent chromium and polychlorinated biphenyls (PCBs) – is piled on unprotected areas where, according to the Agenda 21 report, it leaches into the water supply, endangering the health of the surrounding population.

Liu Peizhe, director general of the Administrative Center for China's Agenda 21, maintains that 620 million tonnes of industrial solid waste is produced annually, of which about 5 per cent – 30 million tonnes – is hazardous. In a 1994 presentation at a Superfund conference in Washington, DC, Liu estimated that annual production of industrial solid wastes in China has grown by 2.6 per cent since 1980, and that farmland polluted by solid wastes now exceeds 20,000 ha nationwide. In one particularly notorious incident recounted by Liu, a factory in north-east China producing chromium salts piled up 200,000 tonnes of chromium-contaminated waste, resulting in such serious groundwater pollution that 1,800 wells in nine villages had to be abandoned (*China Business Review*, 1996).

China's National Import Inspection Administration reports that during the first half of 1997, 99 per cent of the 3.6 million tons of imported goods met national standards for imported goods (China News Service Bulletin, 1997) According to the official *China Environmental News*, Beijing's means of solving the issue of foreign waste dumping consisted of 'a combination of legislative, administrative, economic and diplomatic means' (*China Environmental News*, 1997). To Beijing, waste dumping is a very emotional issue because it reflects on China's national pride and economic interests. The government formulated its solutions, therefore, by mixing law and order with economics and politics. By strengthening the enforcement of laws and regulations, Beijing tried to punish Chinese and American brokers and to send a message to industry that China is not a dumping ground. With debate on human rights and national sovereignty, the government hopes to bring public outcry under control, and to reconfirm its different interpretations of human rights to its people and the world.

The central government in Beijing appears eager to claim credit for what might have been only a limited success. The government may also have tried to inflate the statistics for political gain. The year 1996 was, in fact, the worst year in terms of foreign waste dumping in China.

Waste imports: Laws and regulations

Foreign waste dumping in China, which was spotted as early as 1994, has begun to garner much attention in China. Having learned the hard lesson that solid and hazardous waste problems are not the exclusive concern of developed countries, Chinese authorities are beginning to address waste management policies, particularly where hazardous wastes are concerned.

Beijing now has a few legislative weapons at hand to fight waste dumping, including the Basel Convention and its new provision on banning toxic waste exports, the Law on Preventing and Controlling Environmental Pollution Caused by Solid Waste. Moreover, the newly revised criminal law for the first time punishes those responsible for waste dumping in China with prison sentences.

Beijing signed the Basel Convention as early as 1989 and in 1991, the Chinese People's Congress, the Parliament, approved it. However, it was not until October 1995, after more than a decade of debate and more than 20 drafts, that the Law on Preventing and Controlling Environmental Pollution Caused by Solid Waste was promulgated on 1 April 1996, together with Temporary Regulations on Environmental Management of Waste Import.

China's legislative efforts are notorious for falling behind the country's social and economic development. However, recent laws against foreign waste dumping have been used effectively by the government as a powerful weapon putting illegal importers and smugglers to the test. In these efforts, the State Environmental Protection Administration (SEPA) and the Customs Inspection Authority have been able to mobilize local regimes to act together.

China's Law on Preventing and Controlling Environmental Pollution Caused by Solid Wastes represents the first milestone in China's fight against foreign waste dumping in China. It bans the dumping, disposing and handling of solid wastes imported from outside the Chinese border. It also bans the import of certain solid wastes for use as raw materials and restricts the import of certain allowable solid wastes that can be used as raw materials.

The effectiveness of this law has since been strengthened by several additional regulations related to the import of solid wastes. These regulations were promulgated, together or separately, by SEPA, the Ministry of Foreign Economic Cooperation and Trade, the National Administration of Industry and Commerce and the National Commodity Inspection Bureau.

However, it was not until 1996 when the revised criminal law came into effect, that foreign waste dumping was constituted a crime punishable by prison sentences. According to the new criminal law, people whose acts result in environmental destruction could be punished under a new crime category called 'crimes damaging environmental resources protection'. The law spells out 12 subcategories of crimes, eight of which, according to legal expert Ying Xiangchao, are new in the light of the development of a market economy (Xiaochao, 1997).

The Law's Item 339, in particular, states that dumping, disposing and handling of solid wastes coming from outside Chinese borders in violation of national regulations should be punished by prison sentences of up to 10 years, plus heavy fines. Those responsible for the acts resulting in serious damage to public property, people's health and environmental protection should serve sentences of more than 10 years.

Basel Convention and the Pinggu incident

China realizes that the final solution to transborder waste dumping must come from international cooperation. China's National Import Inspection Administration, as the semi-official China News Service reported in October, has recently established contract relationships with as many as eight foreign port authorities in order to ensure that goods for shipment to China undergo required inspections before they are put on the ships (China News Service, 1997).

Following a spate of highly publicized incidents involving alleged dumping of foreign waste in China under the guise of scrap imports intended for industrial use, in mid-June 1996, the State Council, China's highest government organ, ordered environmental authorities to stop issuing approvals for imports of all scrap and waste materials. On 26 July 1996, SEPA and four other agencies jointly issued Supplemental Regulations to the Provisional Regulations for Environmental Management of Scrap Imports (Adams, 1997). The document adds 12 new regulations to the import process, in addition to China's first solid waste law that took effect in 1996, which contained regulations governing the import of scrap and waste materials.

The case of William Chen mentioned earlier in this chapter represented the first real efforts by the Chinese government to use the law as a weapon to fight against illegal foreign waste dumping and to punish the persons responsible. Another foreign waste dumping case, in Beijing's suburb of Pinggu County, could shed some light on how the Chinese government has been trying to use international agreements like the Basel Convention, in addition to its own efforts in law enforcement, to protect China's national interests.

In May 1997, it was discovered that Beijing Zhiqiang Caoxian Co. Ltd, a China–Australia joint venture, had dumped 29 containers or 639 tons of what was labelled as waste paper in Beijing's suburb of Pinggu County. Zhiqiang Co., knowing that not all the waste was waste paper, failed to file a report. SEPA and the Beijing Environmental Monitoring Agency conducted field sample inspections of the waste, which originated from Long Beach, California, and was transported via China's port city of Qingdao. They found that less than 10 per cent was waste paper and the remainder was rest room waste mixed with hospital wastes such as needles, drug bottles and rubber gloves. Some of the waste had gone rotten, emitting foul odours and containing live worms. The site was sealed and the waste was later returned.

Speaking to the press, officials of SEPA and eight other government departments including the Foreign Ministry and the Supreme Court, stressed that medical wastes were at the top of the list of 47 types of waste prohibited from export by the Basel Convention and that was why Zhiqiang's import represented a serious violation of the international convention. On 13 May 1997, SEPA filed a complaint to the Secretariat of the Basel Convention, alleging that it constituted a violation of China's national interests.

However, China's attitude towards the Basel Convention has been mixed. When 23 countries first signed the Basel Convention in 1989, it definitely did not ban the international shipment of wastes; instead it merely required that waste exporters must receive consent from the receiving country. Since the US already had laws on the books requiring waste exporters to receive permission from the recipient country, Basel did not establish much that was new. However, China, one of the first to sign the convention, stressed that the revised Basel Convention of 22 September 1995, which contained provisions banning the export of toxic wastes from developed countries to developing countries, could be used as an effective international weapon to fight against hazardous waste dumping in China. China also supported the movement to put out a list of hazardous wastes whose export should be banned, and before the list was finally approved in 1997, worked to drum up support for it.

An opportunity to interpret its human rights

The issue of human rights has always been sensitive in China. While Western countries have been trying to evaluate China's human rights record by their own standards, China has been rather passive in its response, arguing that given the universal principle of human rights in the world, the actual contents and emphasis of human rights can differ from country to country in view of their economic and political development. The Western countries interpret this as China's excuse to ignore such basic human rights as freedom of speech while stressing the need to feed and clothe its 1.3 billion people.

Foreign waste dumping, however, gave the Chinese government an important opportunity to clarify its human rights interpretations in front of its own people and the world at large. The Chinese government seized the opportunity not only to claim the moral high ground, but, most noticeably, also to point out that dumping waste in the developing countries also constitutes human rights violations. In doing so, Beijing points its figure at Washington and other Western countries.

Despite this, China has recognized that the increasing amount of industrial and residential wastes has posed great pressure on the economies of the developed countries. From 1974 to the end of the 1980s, global hazardous wastes increased from 5 million tons to 340 million tons annually, nearly 90 per cent of which was in OECD countries. On the other hand, the cost of waste processing has also shot up, and now the cost for every ton of waste is as high as US$2000. Exporting wastes to other countries seemed to be an easy way out. Exporters, in the name of recycling wastes and increasing the revenue of the developing countries, have been successful in exporting more and more wastes to these countries (Youfu, 1997).

China disagrees with the view of the proponents of exporting wastes from developed countries to developing countries who argue that such trade benefits the latter. Proponents argue that imported wastes are inexpensive, some are entirely free or even enjoy subsidies from the government. Because some of these imports can be used as industrial raw materials, they are conducive to economic development. Moreover, some of these wastes are renewable or recyclable. Chinese scholars argue, however, that waste imports are penny wise and pound foolish for the developing countries. Their potential impacts on the developing countries, in terms of economic costs or ecological destruction, could hardly be overstated.

To the Chinese government, human rights have always been part of international politics. The current international battle over human rights, wrote human rights scholar Xia Guang, is the hot spot in today's world politics. Some Western countries have repeatedly tried to tell developing countries where they have gone wrong in terms of human rights. These Western countries, in their attempt to give monopolistic interpretations to human rights, are in fact trying to control the other, more realistic rights of the developing countries.

The most noticeable phenomenon emerging from the three-year-old drama on foreign waste dumping is China's drive to claim its human rights record and its efforts to re-establish its human rights concept with clear Chinese characteristics.

Beijing's presumed intention could be clearly detected in the official media. An unidentified official from Shandong's Import Inspection Bureau, which discovered problems similar to those in Shanghai, was pointedly quoted by the official Xinhua News Agency in May 1996 as saying that the US likes to use the excuse of human rights to attack other countries, but tries to restrict the export of high-tech products. Why then does it try to overlook the issue of exporting solid wastes? Why has the US not acted to restrict the trans-shipment of its garbage (Xinhua News Agency, 1996)?

A lengthy investigative report in the May 1996 issue of the bimonthly *Green Leaves*, a NEPA publication, concluded that, while China is doing its best to bring pollution under control, a few Western nations, the US in particular, have been trying to export so much toxic waste to China, and treat China as their dumping backyard. Chinese people could not help but be indignant at this criminal act (Haiqiu, 1996, p9).

To the Chinese government, the most salient way to talk about human rights in China is to regard it as an issue of national sovereignty, and even nationalism. In an article published in *China Environment News* on 1 April 1997, Wang Yangzu, deputy administrator of SEPA, called renewed attention to the implementation of China's law on the control of solid wastes. The trans-shipment into China of foreign waste by the developed countries, Wang writes, has not only put China's environment into serious danger, but has also seriously threatened China's national sovereignty and dignity. He says, in our current battle against foreign waste, justice is on our side (Yangzu, 1997).

NGOs: What Has Been Missing?

An emerging civil society

China's economic reforms have created opportunities for Chinese people at various levels but, at the same time, have also exacerbated many of China's increasingly obvious social challenges, including environmental challenges. The Chinese government has begun to recognize the deficiencies of the old centrally planned system. It realizes that its capacity to solve social and environmental problems is limited and that the political structures set up to manage all sorts of social problems are weak. The government's efforts to seek alternatives to address these problems have led gradually to the emergence of social or non-governmental organizations (NGOs).

However, NGOs in China are tied more closely to the government than in many other societies (Knup, 1996). Chinese government officials describe relationships with NGOs as collaborative. Chinese NGO members feel compelled to present themselves as supportive of the postulated social consensus rather than antagonistic to central government policies. The surprising conclusion is that the degree of autonomy of an NGO depends to a great extent on the strength of its ties to influential members of the government (ibid). Government trust has to be bought with a certain degree of restraint in NGO activism. Therefore, Chinese social organizations should be distinguished from Western-style NGOs, and their role and modus operandi can cause confusion if viewed through a predominantly Western lens.

Many social groups seem to have been constituted by and for state employees to carry out activities that do not exactly fit into but complement their ordinary work. They do not necessarily host any ambitions to evolve into independent bodies and may even be transient arrangements, to be dismantled once specific tasks have been performed.

In terms of environmental NGOs, one word to describe them is fledgling. These NGOs are fairly new and are mainly trying to gain an understanding of SEPA policies (Woodrow Wilson Center, 1997). These NGOs could be divided into three kinds: government-organized, or quasi-governmental NGOs, the least autonomous social organizations that are initiated from the top down and established by state agencies or well-known Chinese leaders; individual organized NGOs, which are far more autonomous, more grassroots in nature and whose founders have informal relationships with the government; and voluntary organizations, which are not registered but are the most autonomous organization of all social groups.

Despite their general lack of autonomy, the roles of the emerging NGOs should not be ignored. The clear advantage of government-organized NGOs, like the China Environmental Protection Foundation, the China Society of Environmental Sciences and the National Natural Science Foundation, is their ability to draw together scholars and officials from a wide range of institutions that normally find it difficult to interact in China's highly vertical bureaucratic structure. Viewed in terms of what is currently needed at this stage of China's social development, and seen as growing out of a particular economic, social and political context, these flaws can be seen as assets or, at the very least, as evidence of growing pains. Perhaps the most important achievement of these organizations is that they are changing, in incremental ways, the manner in which average citizens interact with each other and with the state (Knup, 1996).

Foreign NGOs in China

The work of foreign NGOs in China started just a few years ago. With independent funding coming from overseas, foreign NGOs, including environmental NGOs, have been viewed with great interest and some suspicion by the Chinese government.

Chinese social organizations have provided new opportunities for international development cooperation, attracting the kind of support, which would be awkward or improper for government organizations to accept. It has been suggested that when working with China, however, it is important for the Western countries to know exactly what they want out of the relationships but to be prepared to engage on a level that the Chinese feel is important to them. This holds true for NGOs as well. The role of the NGO in China is somewhat unclear. One purpose of NGOs is to initiate and facilitate change, yet this is a new approach for the Chinese culture. It is therefore important for foreign NGOs to proceed cautiously in China, and to work with – not against – the Chinese.

Meanwhile, international assistance can play a crucial role, especially in the first phase of NGO life. Support to organizational development through fruitful international exchanges is of particular importance. Increased communication between overseas donors working or planning to work with Chinese NGOs may help to make the specific characteristics of Chinese NGOs more widely known, so that development projects can build on existing groups rather than introduce artificial structures.

CONCLUSIONS AND RECOMMENDATIONS

Current conditions

Judging from the press reports and official comments in 1997, China has rarely been as open on controversial issues as it has been on the issue of foreign waste dumping. The reasons are clear: foreign waste dumping is an issue about Chinese sovereignty, and it is easier for the government, NGOs and the Chinese from all walks of life to find common ground on an issue that puts China against foreign countries.

Although Chinese law enforcement efforts have always lagged behind reality, on the issue of foreign waste dumping, the National People's Congress, SEPA and the State Council were relatively swift in their actions in cracking down on such unfair trade practices and in punishing the individuals for their crimes.

Since news about foreign waste dumping in China was reported by the country's press, to the end of 1997 when the government claimed victory in its fight against the imports of foreign wastes, no voices of NGOs, either from within China or from outside, had been heard. The Chinese government was not seen as trying to put these voices in check, it was just that no organizations have ever taken a stand on the issue, and that these organizations seemed to have virtually no interest in it. As with other issues, the capacity of the Chinese government to do all is limited, and its efficiency in doing so is low. There are great opportunities for NGOs, either Chinese or international, to play a role. They can do the following:

Engage the government

Foreign waste dumping is an issue that the Chinese government is strongly against. Efforts to endorse the government stand on the issue and facilitate a solution could easily have won the appreciation of the government. However, NGOs missed this important opportunity.

On the basis of working with, not against the government, the NGOs and any international ombudsperson should try their best to identify key issues that could easily win the endorsement of the government, and that are very important to China's environment and development. Such efforts on the part of NGOs should not be regarded as catering to the needs of the Chinese government but should be regarded as a result-oriented strategy.

International cooperation is an untapped area for foreign NGOs

Chinese government is very open with its environmental problems. One reason for such openness is China's dire need for foreign investment and expertise in helping to ease China's environmental woes. Foreign waste dumping is an issue that the Chinese government is not familiar with and needs international cooperation to reach a solution.

For foreign NGOs, facilitating the Chinese government's international cooperation efforts in environment and development is the most important area to work in. A key issue for China's international cooperation is lack of funds. In helping to raise necessary funds, international NGOs can help to exert international influence and pressure to move China to adopt international environmental standards and to sign international environmental treaties, such as that on climate change.

Understand China's environmental decision-making process

A key headache of international organizations and companies working in China is the confusing and often complex power distribution and decision-making processes within the government. Opening the Chinese government to the world is the prerequisite for international cooperation in environment and development. An international ombudsperson could help to increase transparency.

NGOs and an international ombudsperson who work consistently with China could also help the world to better understand and influence the operations, structures and decision-making process of Chinese government. This might not lead to immediate results but long-term benefit to China and the world will prove to be significant.

Pressure is the key task for foreign NGOs

A key conclusion from China's international performance in the past two decades is that pressure from the international community works, especially in relation to improvements in China's environmental protection. China wants to improve its reputation but is moving very slowly. Tacit pressure from the outside is the key.

Pressure on the Chinese government to conform more quickly with international standards in environment and development is now deemed as necessary as ever. This should largely be the job of international NGOs as China's central government restricts domestic NGOs in their funding as well as political outreach efforts.

Working with counterparts in China

The slow development of domestic NGOs in China is rooted primarily in political and economic structures. Chinese NGOs' unfamiliarity and lack of understanding of basic operational principles and process has also contributed to their slow growth and ineffectiveness. A helping hand from abroad means a lot.

For the international NGOs, more time and effort should be spent in cooperating and helping with the development of China's domestic NGOs, in terms of registration, organizational structure, looking for sources of financing and independent planning of activities.

NOTE

1   For a recent report on waste from the electronics industry being exported to China, see Basel Action Network and Silicon Valley Toxics Coalition (2002).

REFERENCES

Adams, C (1997) 'China Slaps Temporary Ban on All Scrap Imports, International Market Insight'. Washington, DC: US China Business Council

Basel Action Network and Silicon Valley Toxics Coalition (2002) *Exporting Harm: The High-Tech Trashing of Asia*, www.svtc.org/cleancc/pubs/technotrash.pdf. Seattle, WA/San Jose, CA: Basel Action Network/Silicon Valley Toxics Coalition

China Business Review (1996) 'China prepares new laws on environmental protection', *China Business Review* August

China Environmental News (1997) *China Environment News* 18 September

China Ministry of Public Health (1995) *China Yearbook of Public Health*. Beijing: China Ministry of Public Health Press

China News Service Bulletin (1997) 'Foreign Garbage Under Control', *China News Service Bulletin* 5 October

Haiqiu, C (1996) 'China is not a dumping ground, but foreign garbage is found in Beijing', *Green Leaves Bimonthly* May, p9

Information Office of the State Council of the People's Republic of China (1991) *Human Rights in China*. November, Beijing: Information Office of the State Council of the People's Republic of China

Knup, E (1996) 'Environmental NGOs in China: An Overview', China Environment Series. Washington, DC: Woodrow Wilson Center

National Environmental Protection Agency (1996a) *The State of the Environment 1996*. Beijing: National Environmental Protection Agency

National Environmental Protection Agency (1996b) *China Environment Yearbook*. Beijing: National Environmental Protection Agency

Peide, H (1995) *Human Rights: Theory and Practice*. Wuhan: Wuhan University Press

People's Daily (1992) *People's Daily* 7 February

Woodrow Wilson Center (1997) 'Discussion with the Chinese Citizen Involvement in Environmental Protection Delegation from the People's Republic of China', Working Group Summaries, China Environment Series. Washington, DC: Woodrow Wilson Center

World Bank (1997) *China's Health Care Reform*. Washington, DC: World Bank

World Resources Institute (1995) *World Resources 1994–1995*. Washington, DC: World Resources Institute

Xiaochao, Y (1997) 'An analysis on the crime of illegally importing solid wastes', *China Environmental News* 28 June

Xinhua News Agency (1997) 'United States has become a major dumper of wastes and garbage in China', Xinhua News Agency News Bulletin, 16 May

Yangzu, W (1997) 'Implementing Solid Waste Law, Strive to Realize the Year 2000 Goal in Environmental Pollution Control', *China Environment News* 1 April

Youfu, X (1997) 'Strategic studies over controlling foreign waste dumping in China', Chinese University of Foreign Economic Relations and Trade, *International Trade Issues Weekly* 26 May

Zhaoguo, X (1997) 'On Environmental Rights', *China Environment News* 10 October

Part IV

Conflicts Over Land Rights

Chapter 10

Environment and Land in Bushbuckridge, South Africa

Robert Thornton

THE BUSHBUCKRIDGE ENVIRONMENT AND POTENTIALS FOR CONFLICT

The Bushbuckridge area of South Africa is a complex and sensitive environment of human settlement, commercial agriculture and nature reserves. The town of Bushbuckridge is a small trading and administrative centre approximately midway on a north–south line between Nelspruit, the capital of Mpumalanga Province, and Tzaneen, a major centre of commerce and agriculture in the lowveld[1] of Northern Province. The area is bounded on the east by Kruger National Park, one of the world's largest game parks, and on the west by the sensitive watershed and forests of the Drakensberg.

The terrain is primarily a sandy plain into the coastal plain of Mozambique. It is naturally bounded on the north by the Olifants River that flows through a spectacular gorge in the escarpment and across the plain into the Kruger Park. The escarpment is a sensitive watershed for much of the lowveld that depends on these mountain streams. The region hosts many wildlife conservation and restoration projects, such as the Kapama cheetah breeding station, and recovery facility for injured animals at Mariepieskop. Some of the most beautiful scenery within the Kruger National Park occurs along this river, which almost bisects the park into northern and southern halves. Waterfalls pour through gorges clad in indigenous vegetation along the walls and floors of the escarpment. Since the political changes of the 1990s, tourism has vastly increased with up to 30 new lodges in the region.

At the top of the escarpment, and around the Blydepoort dam at the bottom, the Blyderivier Nature Reserve is situated. Here the previous National Party government built two government-owned ecotourist camps, The Blyderivier Aventura Resort and the Swadini Aventura Resort. To build them, in the 1950s the new apartheid government had commandeered land from the white farmers to whom it had been deeded in the 19th century by the old Suid Afrikaansche Republiek (known as The Traansvaal). They had removed black African labour-tenants and squatters who had formerly lived there to surrounding areas in Bushbuckridge in the lowveld, and around Graskop at the top of the escarpment. This set the scene for conflict after the African National Congress (ANC)-led government passed legislation that made it possible to reclaim lands that had been removed under apartheid. In this case, claims for restoration of lands had significant implications for all aspects of environmental conservation, with political involvement that went well beyond South Africa's borders. In 1996, claims for land restoration began to centre on the resorts, commercial farmlands and state reserves in the region. The political environment was highly fractured, unstable and uncertain. This chapter examines this complex conflict over environmental resources in Bushbuckridge, placing it in its local historical context, and explores ways in which conflict might best be controlled and moderated.

The political and legal context of conflict

Environmental and ecology issues are overlaid by a complex political terrain. The region is composed today of pieces of two old apartheid 'homelands (also known pejoratively as 'Bantustans'), as well as parts of what was then 'white South Africa' consisting of white-owned commercial farms and state lands, including military reserves and a large airbase near Hoedspruit. Gazankulu, meaning 'Greater Gaza', was created for Tsonga-speaking people. Lebowa, meaning 'Northern' was created for North Sotho-speaking people. Both homelands remained within the South African state instead of taking optional 'independence' as several other homelands elected to do.[2]

The border of the Kruger Park with Mozambique was patrolled by the military to prevent infiltration of anti-apartheid forces until the early 1990s. While Kruger National Park and other forestry and watershed reserves were controlled by the Transvaal Parks Board, homelands were divided into Tribal Trust Lands and ruled by Chiefs (*Makgoshi* [pl] in North Sotho or *amahosi* in Tsonga). They administered through bureaucratized structures called 'Tribal Authorities' that were loosely based on earlier traditional African political systems. The remainder, 'common South Africa' or 'White South Africa', was ruled from Pretoria by the central government as part of the Transvaal Province (after 1910) that largely preserved the old boundaries of the Boer republic.

The entire lowveld region was divided after 1992 by the boundaries between two new provinces, Northern and Mpumalanga, and the old Transvaal ceased to exist. Pre-colonial African polities, however, continued to live in people's imaginations. The land had been contested throughout the 19th century by the Swazi people from the south, the Tsonga-speaking peoples from Mozambique (known in South Africa as 'Shangaans') and the Northern Sotho people of the highveld to the west. African armies from surrounding chiefdoms, raiding parties and bands of hunters swept across the region throughout the 19th century, joined by European hunters, transport riders and prospectors towards the end of the century. Refugees and migrants, prospectors and hunters staked out claims or settled in the region. This led to a complex mix of peoples speaking Swazi (*SiSwati*), Shangaan (*Xitsonga*), Zulu (*isiZulu*), Ndebele (*siNdebele*) and North Sotho dialects (*SePedi, SePulana, SeRoka, SeKgaga,* etc), and other African languages, with Afrikaans and English arriving later. No one speaks only one language, and most mix some or all of these languages in ordinary speech. The African languages are closely related from centuries of trade and conflict – but they are not mutually intelligible.

Boundaries between white-owned farmlands, the apartheid-era 'homelands', chiefdoms, state lands and nature reserves were contested throughout the 20th century. However, this diversity became most salient when land reform initiatives begun in 1992 led to the establishment of local land committees set up around the Tribal Authorities. Ecological regions necessarily spanned most of these boundaries, and jurisdiction is constantly disputed. Pressure on natural resources arises from needs for water, settlement, firewood and occasionally, poaching for game. Wood carvers serving the tourist industry and traditional healers in search of rare medicinal plants place further pressure on resources.

What is known as the 'Transition' in South Africa was a negotiated change of government that led to the National Party (NP) declaring a universal mandate general election. To widespread acclaim, they peacefully handed over the control of government to the ANC after their election victory in seven of the nine new provinces. The NP and its policy of apartheid had been entrenched longer than any democratically elected post-war government in the world.

Apartheid policy had major impacts on environmental issues. In the region considered here, the policy mandated large-scale relocations of populations in order to separate black and white South Africans, and to establish ethnic 'homelands' or 'Bantustans' in which black South Africans were expected to pursue 'separate development'. In the 1950s, black African farmers and farm labourers who had lived along the escarpment and in the lowveld adjacent to it were removed onto 'Tribal Trust' properties away from the escarpment. While it is still unclear what 'traditional authorities' these people originally lived under, relocation distributed people under the authority of Chiefs Moletele, Mogane, Mohlala and Mashile of the Mapulana 'tribe',[3] although there may also have been other people claiming other ethnic identities and political loyalties. They were all removed from bushy mountains and canyons of escarpment, however, and these areas were re-forested, declared nature reserves and protected watersheds. In the lowveld, black people were settled in a strip of land between the protected watershed and the Kruger National Park. A buffer belt of white-owned game farms separated black residents from the boundaries of the vast Kruger Park.

To most outside observers it appeared that the ANC was universally popular all over South Africa and land reform policies seemed to have broad support. Nevertheless, in the middle of 1997, people in Bushbuckridge rose in violent protest against ANC policies and burnt the party's local offices. Although protest was short-lived, it showed that the potential for violent conflict was not far from the surface. Its occurrence on one of the main overland routes to the Kruger National Park threatened tourism, and the protest highlighted unhappiness over land and environment problems in particular.

Three factors are involved. First of all, legislation passed in 1994 made it possible to reclaim land that had been removed by the state on the basis of race under apartheid. Claimants needed to prove ownership or 'beneficial occupation' and removal for reason of race. In Bushbuckridge, a number of chiefs moved quickly to claim land for their tribes. While their claims were initially recognized by government, the new constitution ratified in April 1997 no longer recognized 'traditional leaders' or chiefs as having any special legal or political powers. Moreover, the 'tribe', previously entrenched in apartheid legislation as a cornerstone of 'Separate Development' no longer existed as political entities under the new regime. Consequently, all claims were formally withdrawn in October 1997 by the Commission on Restitution of Land Rights (CRLR). Since many people had not held formal rights to land before removals, and because many were removed for 'race-neutral' reasons such as watershed protection, nature conservation and re-forestation, it was unclear whether any claims would be successful. Among many people, however, there was a clear and strong belief that these areas belonged to them. Expressing his community's disgust with the process, one old Pulana man, a member of a local land committee of the Moletele chiefdom said, 'This government [the ANC government] treats us like Blacks!'[4]

Second, the Northern and Mpumalanga provincial governments, both newly created out of the old Transvaal Province in 1992, came into conflict over which province should administer the Bushbuckridge region. People in the region at first believed that they were to be governed by Mpumalanga Province. Due largely to the administrative structures and geographies of the defunct 'homelands' of Gazankulu and Lebowa, the loyalties of most Bushbuckridge residents seemed to lie with the new province of Mpumalanga rather than Northern Province. When it was finally decided that they would be part of the much poorer Northern Province, activists mounted angry protests against the central government decision. While provincial ANC party members came into line and supported the decision, great resentment continued to exist at the local level, especially among followers of the chiefs. This was reflected as well in the struggle over jurisdiction over the environment, which was the key to control over tourism development.

Third, the struggle over jurisdiction was brought into full relief by the 'Dolphin Deal', a business contract between the Mpumalanga provincial government and The Dolphin Group, an international tourism company based in Dubai. The people's legally mandated rights to land restitution under the new legislation soon came into conflict with the Dubai company's plans, since some of the land they claimed included the prime tourism sites that the Dolphin Group had contracted to develop. The government also attempted to privatize government resorts such as the Aventura resorts, but fell foul of the same legislation. After angry conflict between the provincial and national government, and within the ANC party structures as well, the land restitution commission intervened to temporarily halt the 'Dolphin Deal' and Aventura privatization. Under South African law, land against which restitution claims were lodged could not be sold or transferred until after resolution of these claims. In a search for a solution, the CRLR of Mpumalanga and Northern Provinces began a consultative process. This was coordinated by the Commissioner and the National Land Reform Mediation Panel that had been set up by the Department of Land Affairs (DLA). In the context of what had already become limited violent revolt, the process of consultation led to unexpected outcomes.

The role of human rights in environmental conflict

The primary issues at stake were questions involving the *nature* of rights to land, that is, whether land and restitution rights guaranteed in the Act were based on universal human rights, specific legal enactment, precedent or concepts of usufruct in traditional or common law. The Land Restitution Act of 1994 left these questions to be decided through judicial process in the newly established Land Court. Out of 63,455 land claims countrywide, by 1999 only 264 cases had been successfully resolved (SAIRR, 2000, p149). The legal process still left open the questions of *what* land and *whose* rights. Limits and boundaries of land claims often had to be established anew because of faulty or absent records. Patterns of land use had to be determined since the Act made it possible for claims to be rejected if the Commissioner determined that a greater common good was served by not restoring land. Jurisdiction was often overlapping, since both the provincial and the national governments claimed the right to direct the economic development of the region, especially tourism.

Such conflicts of jurisdiction were instrumental in the 'Dolphin Deal' and Aventura Resorts since both national and provincial governments had declared interests in development initiatives and privatization of government property. Further development of natural reserves, protected watershed and forestry lands had the potential to nullify the rights of people to reclaim land. The implications of this legal fact were not lost on those who had claims to make, of course, but uncertainty existed over how these rights could be asserted. In 2000, new legislation made it possible to negotiate resolution through an administrative process, leaving only the most contentious cases to the Land Court. By 2001, however, with one major exception,[5] little progress had been made anywhere in the lowveld.

The legislation enabled people to make very broad claims based on these rights. Claims could be made on removals conducted over most of the 20th century, from the Land Act of 1913 until the ANC took power in 1994, spanning three major changes of international sovereignty (as colony, dominion and finally republic) and major changes of internal boundaries. With poor record keeping in many rural areas, the legal status, boundaries and even putative ownership were very often in question or unknown. Earlier administrative structures of the old Transvaal and the homelands of Lebowa and Gazankulu had ceased to function with the redrawing of borders and the creation of new provinces with new administration.

Thus, what seemed at first, with the passing of the Land Restitution Act, an elementary exercise of compensation for damages sustained under apartheid, soon became an almost intractable legal and political morass. The government worried about meeting voters' legitimate expectations for delivery on land reform. International conservation and environmental action organizations such as WWF and many local environmental NGOs tried to look after the interest of the natural environment. Attempts at mediation and limitation of threatened conflict motivated all parties, but none of the problems appeared to be easily solved.

If land restitution were to be fully granted to local communities, for instance, the watershed might be damaged by erosion due to grazing and agriculture, as well as poor sanitation and waste disposal practices. Since the escarpment watershed is essential to a vast area, including the Kruger Park and southern Mozambique, this damage would have transnational consequences. The vast floods in the Mozambican plains in 2000 demonstrated this danger.[6]

Many of the removals had been done in order to protect this watershed, and to make the ecological balance of the Kruger Park and other nature reserves more stable. By limiting human occupation – albeit by means of racist legislation and administration – and by clearing a large area of human habitation for game, especially within and adjacent to the Kruger National Park, the ecological resources of the region had been protected. Thus, the attempt to roll back the damages of apartheid might destroy what had been accomplished in nature conservation.

The successful Makuleke land claim on a part of the Kruger National Park (KNP) far to the north highlighted this threat when the Makuleke/KNP Joint Management Board approved limited hunting in the jointly managed part of the KNP in 2000. A large part of the working population of the lowveld also relies on income from these natural resources, from employment in forestry, hotels, resorts and allied businesses, or on employment on plantations and largely white-owned farms. Restoring land to some elements of the population, therefore, stood to disadvantage many workers in these industries. The fact that some were the descendants of claimants did not mean that they wished to lose their jobs in order to secure the rather more tenuous rights to land. The rights of some to lands that had now long since been put to other uses stood to exacerbate conflict in the region since not everyone had access to such rights under the new law. In the background loomed threats of witchcraft accusations and even death as a consequence of jealousy (Niehaus, 2001). Witchcraft accusations in the region led to 389 witch killings between 1985 and 1995 (ibid, p1). Forced relocations and removal of rights to land, together with apartheid policy of 'separate development' of black South Africans in 'homelands' have exacerbated these problems through crowding, social dislocations, and failure of administrative and judicial structures.

Thus, while the existence of the Kruger National Park and the reserves along the escarpment limited the newly mandated rights to restitution, the employment created by the new development extended rights to a better livelihood to many others, and provided many new resources whose usefulness to local communities was only beginning to be explored at the beginning of the new millennium.

The political ecology

The multiple and overlapping conflicts in the region grow out of the delicate balance of political ecology in a highly sensitive part of Africa. The region is home to one of the largest game parks in the world and is an increasingly popular tourist destination. The government of South Africa seeks to encourage foreign investment, but, at the same time, is extremely distrustful of foreign influence, a fear that often amounts to xenophobia.

The natural savannah landscape that today exists in protected reserves harboured tsetse fly and malaria until the early 20th century, and thus resisted both European settlement and dense African settlement. European settlement did not occur until the end of the 19th century, and dense or stable African settlement was largely precluded until the same time by wars and raiding in the area. Today, the physical landscape is a patchwork: there are dense human settlements into which many people were forcibly removed during apartheid, nature reserves, bushveld pasture, game farms and tourist resorts, towns, commercial fruit plantations and some privately owned farms.

One of the chief areas of conflict in the region involves land claims made by people who were forcibly removed during the apartheid years (1948–1994) or even before. One of the most sensitive instances is the area around the Blyde river that flows over the escarpment past layered pink cliffs of ancient sedimentary rocks. The river has been dammed to form a large reservoir around which the Blyde River Nature Reserve is situated. The two associated government-owned Blyde River Aventura camps were aimed at internal tourism and offered cheap holiday accommodation primarily to white civil servants from Pretoria and Johannesburg. Today, they are run as parastatals and are open to anyone as required under current South African legislation.

There were other recreation sites and nature conservation areas built for black civil servants, such as Manyaleti Nature Reserve bordering KNP, especially for those who worked in the old homeland governments. Manyaleti Game Park is now effectively integrated into the Kruger National Park. WWF maintains a training college near it. Other internationally funded initiatives in the area are aimed at arresting poaching and developing community participation and awareness. Adjacent to Kruger Park, other private game parks are owned by international and South African companies. There is likely to be increasing conflict between these concerns and the local communities as increasing efforts to stop poaching and the illicit gathering of medicinal herbs begin to impact more severely on the people in Bushbuckridge. Investment in tourist development may ameliorate conflict if benefits can be equitably distributed. Nevertheless, according to the South African Auditor General 'very few' people have benefited because of the slow pace of land reform, and low capacity of government and NGOs to deliver value to rural people (SAIRR, 2000, p149).

The KNP's 'social ecology' programme was established in 1994 to resolve these conflicts through community fora that attempted to engage local people in conservation issues. It was handicapped by a shortage of resources and personnel. It is characterized by a theoretical weakness since virtually no lowveld people depend on the natural environment, but are rather a 'rural' proletariat who merely live far from cities. Ecological approaches are often irrelevant to social problems, and vice versa. Most programmes have been handicapped by their highly 'technocratic', or 'scientific' interventions when the problems are primarily cultural and political. Indeed, the KNP's 'social ecology' unit was near collapse by 2001.

The Aventura resorts and other lodge sites are among the most sought after resources in the tourism business in the region. Many are within local land claims. It is mandatory under the legislation that adequate 'development plans' for restitution land be submitted before efforts to resolve the claims can begin. Once the claims are resolved, these plans can be made orders of the court. Thus, future development plans have to be integrated with the claims in order to make any progress at all.

THE POLITICS OF LAND CLAIMS AND THE ENVIRONMENT

The claims for restitution of this sensitive land are but one dimension of the current, more general, conflict in the Bushbuckridge area. The 1994 Restitution of Land Act was one of the first pieces of legislation aimed at 'un-doing the harm' of apartheid. While the old apartheid legislation was scrapped, other new legislation affecting development in most sectors of the South African economy were enacted by a new ANC-dominated parliament eager to act for the common good, and for the creation of a New South Africa. Famously, the first Land Act of the Union of South Africa Government, in 1913, allocated 13 per cent of the total land for black ownership and freehold tenure. The drafters of the 1994 legislation held that the 1913 Act on which vast inequalities of land holding was based, had made apartheid possible, and had provided a precedent for further removal of rights to land under apartheid. While this was consistent with the new policy of universal human rights under the new constitution, the long time period since 1913 made the restitution legislation virtually unworkable. This was primarily because of the length of time involved, but also because the nature of land holding, land tenure regimes and the boundaries of the land-units themselves had changed radically over this time period.

Claims were made for land lost over a period of 84 years, a period spanning four generations in some cases. Land was rarely registered formally in the first place in many cases. 'Beneficial occupation' of the land (the legal term for making a living from the land or improving it in some way while being resident on it), rather than formal title, has been held to be the most significant test of rights to the land, but this must be proved in the Land Court. There are archival records relating to tax collection, registration of farm, mine and migrant workers, and records of disputes. These records are inconsistent and their interpretation is often difficult. There are aerial photographs made since the 1950s by the government land survey department, but these are often difficult to correlate with maps and with the registered boundaries of farms in the region. A great deal of meticulous research is involved in recovering information on actual claims, but research skills are extremely limited and the Commission has been severely under-funded from the start.

The restitution legislation stipulates that it must be shown that removals from land were made not simply for practical reasons such as infrastructure development but were also made for racist reasons. This introduces a significant complication in the Bushbuckridge area and, in particular, with respect to the Blyde River claims, since many people were moved during the post-1913 period in order to develop forestry, game parks, watersheds and nature reserves. While these changes in land use were managed by the government officials of the Union (1910–1962) and Republic (post 1963) of South Africa, and were prejudicial primarily to black residents in the region, the reasons for removal were not always strictly 'racist' but were also practical.

The Kruger National Park, for instance, provided a buffer zone and line of control to and from Mozambique. Most of it was established prior to 1913. The KNP also secured what the Boer government saw as its own national heritage in 1898 when it was declared by Paul Kruger, President of the Transvaal Republic, on the eve of the attack by British Imperial forces. In short, motivations were complex – and sometimes racist or nationalistic – but these processes led to the creation of protected watersheds, game reserves and water resources such as the Blyde River Dam. It is not immediately apparent then that the claims made on this land are actionable under the Land Restitution legislation since actionable motives for removal were limited to those that were demonstrably racist.[7] The concession granted by the Mpumalanga Provincial government to the Dubai-based development company made these lands part of a deal that promised significant economic benefits to the entire region but stood directly in the way of settlement of the land claims. The Commission exercised its power to halt all such moves in July 1997, in order to begin a mediation process between all parties concerned, but it did nothing to aid in the solution of the ultimate problems.

The cultural context of land rights

The struggle for land is primarily rooted in the historical identities of the lowveld peoples, rather than in a desire to become subsistence farmers. In other words, it is primarily cultural rather than economic. The region has long been the crossroads of conflict between roughly three broad cultural regions and their associated political regimes. The Tsonga-speakers to the east began to migrate into the area probably in the late 18th century, a movement driven by the establishment and growth of the Portuguese colony of Mozambique, centred on Lourenço Marques (now Maputo), and by the Zulu Empire in the South, centred on Shaka's capitals around Ulundi in what is now KwaZulu-Natal Province of South Africa. The Tsonga crossed what is now the Kruger National Park and began to settle throughout the lowveld. The early Tsonga-speakers in the lowveld were generally held to be part of a broad Tsonga 'nation', especially by the Swiss Romande (Protestant) missionaries who first transcribed the language into a written form and gave it a literature and formal grammar.

The 19th century Gaza state, founded by Shoshanguve, one of Shaka's generals, claimed hegemony over the lowveld region. This was contested by Swazi-speaking peoples to the south, Pedi-speaking peoples to the west and the Venda to the north. Their settlement in what is now South Africa concentrated in the lowveld below the escarpment. There has long been a continuous flow of people back and forth over the South African and Mozambique border. Today it is driven by decades of war in Mozambique during the 1970s and 1980s. Under the policies of Grand Apartheid the Tsonga/Shangaans were allocated a 'homeland' called Gazankulu ('Greater Gaza') that acknowledged – or, some would say, 'created' – a distinct ethnic identity. Under the apartheid legislation, especially the Tribal Trust Acts and the Bantu Traditional Authorities Act, the institution of chiefship and headman-ship was established under South Africa and Lebowa and Gazankulu statutes, given resources, and allocated power under the State President of the Republic of South Africa. The traditional fragmented and mobile polities of the Tsonga-speaking peoples in South Africa became a formally constituted 'tribe' under a 'Chief minister' designated by the apartheid government.

In the early part of the 19th century, the incipient state of Sekhukhuneland (Sotho speaking) to the west and the Swazi state to the south, also had claims on the Bushbuckridge area. By this time, settlement, driving of herds, grazing across the region and hunting were already well established by these distinct African political and cultural groups. From the expansion of the Zulu State from 1818 when the warrior-king, Shaka-Zulu, rose to ascendancy in northern KwaZulu-Natal, the entire region was in social and cultural chaos. People speaking many different languages dispersed in all directions across the Bushbuckridge region where they met and sometimes clashed or sometimes settled peacefully together. The Pulana people and the Tsonga people settled the region in complex arrangements between people and chiefs, creating an ethnically heterogeneous society. In the early 1850s a battle was fought between Swazi raiders and the Pedi (Sotho) speaking people living in the lowveld, who by then called themselves 'Pulana'. According to their oral traditions, the Pulana won the conflict, and the Swazi retreated, leaving many Swazi people behind to settle among the Pulana. Today, the region is one of the most culturally diverse in South Africa.

In addition to the diversity of languages and histories in the region, there are also political differences between the various forms of traditional leadership. Throughout the 19th century, and well into the 20th, Swazi groups followed the Zulu patterns of chiefship under the King. Pedi (North Sotho) chiefships were much less centralized, with independent chiefs (*kgosi*) vying for access to land and followers. Tsonga peoples were even more decentralized and lacked overall authority in the form of a paramount chief or king. In all cases, the chief or 'headman' lacked direct political power and had few administrative functions. He[8] is said to embody the essence and identity of the people he leads, and determines calendrical events –for instance, the first planting, times for initiation of boys and girls, the first harvest – but does not command a hereditary following.

Accordingly, the 'tribe', strictly defined as a set of related kin-groups who follow a hereditary leader from a central lineage, does not exist in southern Africa. Rather, as the oft-quoted Sotho proverb says, 'a chief is a chief by the people': the traditional chief had to attract and maintain a following of clients whom he represented, and to whom he distributed access to land, and, in the past, organized for warfare and for the distribution of its spoils. Under the Union government and continuing under the apartheid government, chiefships were established as local-level government functionaries. Their visible collaboration with apartheid policies compromised their authority severely, but after weathering the political storms of the 1980s and early 1990s that led to the political transition, they had recouped much of their prestige by the turn of the millennium. This was in spite of the fact that the new constitution failed to recognize them at all as legitimate political actors.

Traditional and modern authority in a dual landscape

Traditional chiefs, holding position as a consequence of warfare, conquest or election by a group of followers, were co-opted and incorporated into the administrative structures of government during the 1920s and 1930s. The land was surveyed, divided into farms and sold by government to citizens of the Transvaal, the so-called *Boers* (Afrikaans, lit. 'farmers') and land speculators. This area was among the very last in contemporary South Africa to be surveyed and allocated to white owners.

A 'farm' consisted of a large piece of land that was awarded to a single white male owner irrespective of previous settlements, other patterns of land use, traditional systems of land tenure or political authority. Deeds were granted to these pieces of land under freehold tenure, enabling non-resident land speculators to buy and sell farms. White farmers took ownership of the land and the resident African population was expected to work as poorly paid labourers. While some farms were owned by resident farmers and operated as active farms, others were owned by non-resident businessmen or by interests such as mines, holding companies or brokers. Many non-working farms with non-resident owners and some abandoned farms were purchased by the state to create the homelands. Other farms remained within so-called 'White South Africa', and efforts began in the 1950s to remove black residents from some of these farms.

The farms that constituted the region of the Blyde River Nature Reserve were acquired in this way and incorporated into the nature reserve and park system. As farms changed hands, failed or labour and tenancy arrangements changed, whites generally moved off the land to cities and towns, while black African residents migrated to other farms to seek work, or were forcibly removed. Those forcibly removed during apartheid were resettled, for the most part, on the lowveld 'farms' – that is, surveyed parcels of land originally deeded to white owners and given names such as Dwarsloop, Cottondale and Buffelshoek. These farms soon became dense settlements more like towns than 'rural' areas. All of these were ultimately incorporated into the Homelands of Lebowa and Gazankulu.

New farm boundaries imposed a rigid new pattern of rhomboid-shaped parcels marked by surveyed lines on maps and registered in Pretoria. This pattern overlaid the organic boundaries of chiefships and tribes in dispersed settlements that characterized the region's pre-colonial landscape. Both patterns of land demarcation continued to exist in the minds of the people who lived there, creating in effect two distinctly different landscapes. Traditional boundaries were vaguely associated with historical events such as battles (the battle of Moholoholo Mountain in which the local Mapulana defeated the Swazi invaders in the mid-19th century), or river valleys or hills. Which landscape was actually 'seen' or considered relevant depended on the nature of the dispute and the political authority – whether traditional or state-bureaucracy – involved. With the dual landscapes, two distinctive geographical systems of land tenure and political authority came to exist as overlays of each other. Which system – which geographical or politico-ecological 'overlay' – was salient, depended on the point of view of the observer and the purpose of the observation.

The two systems gradually came to accommodate each other as the followings of different chiefs gradually began to identify different farms as lying within their eminent domain, if not within their political control. This is still true today, with the boundaries of the homelands and the new provinces now adding a further imagined 'layer' to the already complex landscape. The old political domains of chiefs became rather theoretical, but are nonetheless historically real for many residents.

With the introduction of the Land Restitution Act, the alternative geography of chiefly domains suddenly became relevant again. While under apartheid it was 'tribes' or ethnic groups that were removed, under the new South African Constitution of 1996 tribes and ethnic groups had no legal standing. With the new legislation that aimed to reverse apartheid it seemed apparent to the chiefs and their followers that they would be able to reclaim their naturally subsistent rights to the pre-cadastral survey lands of the largely mythical old chiefships. Under the new regime of universal human rights, however, only individuals' rights were accorded recognition. While land and natural resources remained the primary good, the nature of claims to it had changed radically. The change in legal rules was symptomatic of underlying cultural differences. Conflict over ways in which to deal with conflict –that is, the legal, political and constitutional structures themselves – were as important as the conflicts themselves.

CONFLICT MANAGEMENT AT THE POLITICAL MARGINS

The lowveld region in general, and the area of Bushbuckridge in particular, was only incorporated into the South African state near the end of the 19th century, when it came under the control of the government of the old Transvaal Republic, just before it was attacked and eventually defeated by the British Imperial army during the Anglo–Boer War of 1899–1902. The area became a British Colony only from the end of the Anglo–Boer War until the beginning of the Union Government in 1910 when it became a Dominion like Canada or Australia. After this, and especially after the 1913 Land Act, chiefs were effectively incorporated into the larger South African polity. Under the new laws, land belonging to black Africans was to be held 'in trust' by the South African state, and administered by the chiefs. Under apartheid, these lands became 'Tribal Trust' land, with chiefs' near absolute authority directly under the titular State President. As such, they remained out of the normal political structures of the South African state, which was governed by parliament under a Prime Minister. The chiefs then, held their power in a parallel system for black administration which permitted no political activity, while all other South Africans were governed by parliament. Only in the largely symbolic office of the State President did these political systems come together. Politically, the region has always been entirely marginal to the forms of central governmental authority.

A considerable diversity of political forms had only just begun to be consolidated under a common governmental authority – for instance through the establishment of magistrates courts – when the National Party came to power in 1949 and began the reforms that later came to be known as apartheid. Under apartheid, the chiefs were further regulated and used to control labour, political activity of all kinds and to collect taxes. They and their courts were given complete control over distribution of land.

The homeland chiefships, the political structures of chiefs and headmen under them and the 'states' they ruled were all administrative creations of apartheid. The chiefs, however, continued to exercise local political control, including control over land and export of labour, and to carry out all functions of local government until the homelands were dissolved in 1994 immediately after the elections that brought the ANC government to power.

From 1994 until the ratification of the new constitution two years later, political authority was undefined, practically and legally. In practice, however, the chiefs continued to maintain their local authority while the old homeland governments continued in place. Informal organizations of young men, often loosely affiliated to the ANC or the Pan Africanist Congress (PAC) liberation movements, formed 'Civics'. These constituted another layer for informal government.

Under the new constitution the chiefs ceased to exist as political authorities and were given purely ceremonial functions. New Transitional Local Councils (TLCs) were mandated and elected in 1995 but these never materialized. In 2000, The Municipalities Act created large municipalities centred on the old cities, towns and 'townships' (urban African settlements). Elected town councils were given full governmental powers, but chiefs retained the loyalty of most of the citizenry. Indeed, they seem to have gained more loyalty following the municipal demarcations and elections as the ANC-affiliated political structures and politicians were either co-opted into central government, or lost out in the local power struggles.

By 1997, the region had effectively fallen 'out of the state', after less than a century under central-state control under the administrations of the Transvaal Republic, the British Colony, as British Dominion and as Republic of South Africa. Together with other areas where chiefs remained powerful cultural leaders, such as the provinces of KwaZulu-Natal, the Eastern Cape and Northwest, people on the ground began to assert a strong local or regional identity against the central powers located in the commercial and political centres of Johannesburg and Pretoria.

Conflict between levels of government

In June 1997, this assertion manifested itself as open revolt against the ANC government. Roads were blocked and vehicles attacked on the main north–south arterial road, the local ANC office was burnt, schools destroyed in protest and strikes called. While there was some effort to intervene politically, no police or troops were sent to quell the local rebellion. Officials at the national and provincial level ignored the conflict and hoped that it would disappear. It did eventually, but resentments remained high and residents of the Bushbuckridge region felt abused and exploited by both the Mpumalanga and Northern Provincial Governments.

One of the reasons for neglect was the disputed jurisdiction between the two new provinces, Northern and Mpumalanga. The new provincial boundaries followed the boundaries of the homelands created by apartheid and continued to reflect ethnic identities. Although this might seem anomalous in the light of the ANC's antipathy to the homeland governments and the 'traditional authority' of the chiefs, in practice the old homelands had large bureaucracies that could not be dismissed, and it made some sense to transfer homeland bureaucrats to the new provincial administrations. Finally, Nelson Mandela himself declared that the boundaries were final. In support, he cited the international precedent of the Organization of African Unity, whose members agreed that the boundaries of the colonial states must be defended at all costs by their inheritors.

The local people were clearly and overwhelmingly in favour of joining the much wealthier Mpumalanga Province, which had most of the tourism infrastructure and most of the active farms on which people worked, as well as most of the mines. Northern Province was poorer, its capital further away, and is associated in most people's minds with the corrupt administration of the old Lebowa homeland. Worse, most of the people who had been forcibly removed and whose claims were in question were located in Northern Province while the Mpumalanga Parks Board controlled the lands they were claiming. Thus, the land claims were made by people lying across the disputed boundary and between provincial administrations that seemed primarily concerned with defence of their territory.

This diversity has considerable impact on the land-claims issue, and on the nature of the conflict over the preservation of ecological and natural resources. The chiefs were mistaken in their assumption that they would be able to reclaim land under the legislation that seemed to permit precisely this. Confusingly, the new government did grant 'chiefs' a salary, but refused to recognize or pay any of their administrative personnel. Only symbolic, even derisory, functions were allocated to the chiefs such as 'cleaning of graveyards' and 'control of noise pollution'. Several chiefs filed claims over a large number of farms in the nature reserve area and over large areas of adjacent land owned by many other interests. Largely due to the overlap of the two landscapes, traditional and state surveyed, their claims were in conflict with each other. The 'dual landscapes' of the modern state and the African historical imagination were fully in conflict with each other.

Re-assertions of local identity

In the absence of any other functioning government body, the chiefs continued to allocate land and to adjudicate local disputes as they had 'always' done – or at least through most of the 20th century. While people in 1997 refused to pay local taxes to sustain local government under the Transitional Local Councils, they willingly paid the 'chief's levy', collected annually for each household that chose to pay, and fines at chief's courts. This was true even though under the new constitution and legal system none of these fees or institutions existed in South African law and payment could not be enforced nor its use accounted for. This implicit system continued up to the establishment of new local government under 2000/2001 legislation, and seemed to be holding its own against all attempts of central government to modernize. As the young chief Sethlare said to me, 'politics comes and goes, but the chiefs remain'.

Many people seemed to regard the chiefs not as a part of politics, but as a refuge from it. Politics seemed to mean to them a more or less involuntary inclusion in organizations for which they saw no use and from which they received little benefit. But the historical durability of chiefship still gave chiefs no power against constitutional authority of the land claims Commission. Claims made by the chiefs were no longer valid. New claims had to be made by individuals (possibly on behalf of others, so long as the chief was not involved). In the meantime, the Dubai-based group of investors moved closer to effective foreclosure on the land.

The area had effectively ceased to be administered by the institutions of the state; no tax was paid, few services were delivered. In the late 1990s, local government remained almost entirely undeveloped, meeting occasionally at the 'Chicken Licken' fast food shop, for instance, before moving into empty rooms in an abandoned post office in Acornhoek. Jurisdiction at the provincial level remained undecided. Crime rates soared while roads and schools declined rapidly. While chiefs still ran courts that adjudicated domestic disputes, local magistrates were swamped with cases of murder, theft and rape. At the end of 1997, there was almost no mechanism for mediation of any disputes. Only those in which all parties voluntarily submitted themselves for mediation and judgement at public chief's courts received some version of justice.

Conflict between the two provinces continued, while Mpumalanga, in particular, took up a strong independent stand against the ANC central authorities based in Pretoria and Johannesburg. The Premier of Mpumalanga, Matthews Phosa, was removed from power after the central government decided in 1998 to appoint provincial premiers directly from Pretoria, rather than allow them to be elected at the provincial level. In the provinces, however, many people seemed to regard the distant metropolitan centre of the Witwatersrand and Pretoria as a threat to their independence. No longer a magnet for job seekers, and boasting the highest crime rate in South Africa, Johannesburg offered very little of its former allure when it used to attract large numbers of migrants from the lowveld.

Feuding within the ANC and expectations for larger amounts of provincial government autonomy drove a wedge between the provincial and the national governments. Outstanding constitutional questions of degrees of political autonomy, extent of legal jurisdiction and competences of provincial versus national government created a battleground.[9] In April 2001, Thabo Mbeki, President of South Africa, went so far as to accuse the deposed Premier of

Mpumalanga, Matthews Phosa, of being involved in a 'plot' to overthrow the government.

Politics of development

As if to emphasize its political and economic independence from the centre, the government of Mpumalanga entered into a major 'deal' with the Dolphin Group. The 'Dolphin Deal', as it came to be called, was worth R410 million (approximately US$90 million). It was announced by the Mpumalanga government as a *fait accompli* late in 1995. As originally set out, the agreement gave the Dolphin Group exclusive rights to develop the province's very large tourism potential. The announcement was greeted by the press as a major success in attracting foreign investment to the country, but also cast suspicion on the provincial government that had not put the 'deal' out to tender in the normal government channels. In practice, these 'channels' were in any case ambiguous. Premier Matthews Phosa was adamant that the deal was done fairly and that it stood to benefit the province as a whole. His administration quickly fell into line behind him, while the central government challenged him from Pretoria.

Located within Mpumalanga Province are all the principal gateways to the most popular part of the Kruger National Park, and the most expensive private game farms and resorts. Large fruit farms and mines add to the wealth of the province and thus to its development potential. The same economic activities also dramatically increase the danger to ecological and human health. Since the province wanted to develop its ecotourism potential in particular, this was both a threat and an opportunity. Mindful of the international pressure to preserve natural areas and of the need to attract investment, the national and provincial governments were very cautious.

It was clear, however, with so much at stake, that the conflict was political rather than merely administrative, and that it had immense potential impact on the political ecology of the region as a whole. The national Deputy Minister of the central government's Department of Environmental Affairs and Tourism (DEAT), Peter Mokaba, asserted that the provinces must conform with policy and be 'transparent' to the political process. Provincial Premier Phosa, in reply, pointed out that there was no national policy with any bearing on the issue. Political 'transparency' is more honoured in the breach than in the observance in contemporary politics in South Africa, but Mokaba's demand for political transparency – that is, access by the public to the policy mechanisms and administrative procedures – did carry weight since this is a major ANC policy tenet. Premier Phosa again countered by claiming that the 'deal' was simply administrative efficiency: the best way to get the most out of the province's resources.

In April 1997, Deputy Minister Peter Mokaba instructed David Mkhwanazi, who was in charge of environmental affairs at the provincial level, to withdraw the agreement with the Dolphin Group and to begin the process again under the control of central governmental tendering procedures. Mokaba stated that a *political* decision 'must be taken now to avoid obvious embarrassments... The deal was conceived in conditions of secrecy and indeed included clauses that sought to keep its development and implementation secret' (*The Sunday Independent*, 1997, p15).

Mokaba also implied that the provincial government's administration would be 'investigated' if it did not obey orders from Pretoria. In his view, 'political' evidently meant adherence to hierarchy and what amounted to a party line. In a note to the ANC Secretary-General, Mokaba expressed fears that 'foreigners' would be 'given control over the country's natural resources', and that the provincial actions were setting a precedent. Phosa countered this by claiming, evidently correctly, that 'Constitutionally speaking, nature conservation as well as the environment are concurrent legislative competencies of [both] the national and provincial legislatures.'

In other words, jurisdiction in this, as in most other areas we have considered here, was unclear. Phosa hoped that the ambiguity would work to his advantage, but well into 1998, the issue was far from being resolved. Legislative competency (ability to pass laws) does not actually pertain to administrative procedures, party policy or issues of central control versus a degree of provincial or local autonomy in political matters. The concept of 'concurrent' competences between provincial and national governments was the result of compromise between the ANC, which desired strong central government control, the erstwhile National Party[10] and the Inkatha Freedom Party during constitutional negotiations. Much as the US Constitution left ambiguous certain competences and rights between the state governments and the federal government, the South African constitution was similarly flawed, and for similar reasons. All of these issues were effectively engaged in the conflict as it played itself out, and civil war was briefly a plausible threat in the mid-1990s.

Ignoring the ministry's instructions from Mokaba and the implied threat, Premier Phosa and Mkhwanazi re-negotiated the deal with the Dolphin Group. Under the new contract, the Dolphin Group will be given a 25-year lease to develop and administer resorts and game parks in the province. According to Premier Phosa, the secrecy clause – which did indeed exist – was removed and replaced with 'a normal confidentiality clause giving effect to the protection of the commercial trade secrets of Dolphin' (*The Sunday Independent*, 1997, p15). In particular, Phosa acknowledged that the outstanding land claims on the province's nature reserves had not been taken into account, but agreed that this would be done. As long as the struggle remained 'political', that is, largely between leaders of the ANC party, it would not be accessible to the people who were most intimately concerned with the outcome, namely with land claims and seeking protection for the environment.

At the end of June, the Regional Land Claims Commissioner for Mpumalanga and Northern Provinces, Durkje Gilfilan, announced a new initiative to resolve these disputes. This would take the form of a 'consultative process' that would be 'facilitated' by professional mediators from the National Land Reform Mediation Panel. It would seek to involve all of the stakeholders involved in the conflict.

In theory, the Panel was an excellent idea. In practice, it meant that virtually all public initiatives become mired in ongoing 'consultative processes' that are designed to reach consensus, or, failing that, to coerce consensus by public pressure. The Commission hoped to publicize the issues, and thereby make them 'transparent', as well as to seize some of the initiative from the personal struggle that had been waged between the Deputy Minister Peter Mokaba and the Provincial Premier Matthews Phosa. In a press release dated 28 July 1997, the Regional Land Commission announced that the formal, supervised consultation process, known as 'Facilitation' in South Africa government parlance, would:

> *bring land claimants head-to-head with the Aventura ecotourism group and the Mpumalanga Parks Board. The agreement between the Mpumalanga Parks Board and the Dubai-based Dolphin Group, as well as the privatization of the state-managed Aventura resorts, will become a focus of the discussions that will involve state bodies and community groups.*[11]

This was a risky process. In pursuit of its goals, and within its powers as a government appointed commission, the Commission on Restitution of Land Rights (CRLR) had to 'ask the national and provincial governments to give it clarity on the status of the Dolphin Deal, as well as of the land managed by the Mpumalanga Parks Board.'[12] Since Phosa had seemingly won the battle between his province and the national government over the Dolphin Deal, at the cost of considerable political capital within his party, both national and provincial levels of government risked embarrassment. It was evident that there was much that had not been revealed to public scrutiny. The central government proved stronger, however, and in the following year, the Dolphin Deal was invalidated and Phosa was removed from his post.

Attempts at resolution of land and environmental issues

The CRLR for Mpumalanga and Northern Province set up a mediation process to seek resolution through the broadest possible involvement of stakeholders and through research into the history of land settlement, usufruct, rights and deeded ownership. In the mediation process, the CRLR envisioned the inclusion of government departments such as Forestry, Tourism, Environment, Water Affairs, Public Works, Public Enterprises (as owner and administrator of Aventura Resorts) and Security. The latter was included since there was acknowledged potential for violent conflict. In addition, interested NGOs would be brought into the process since many of these were the only effective administrators of resources in the provinces. Any people who had legitimate interest in the land claims process were to be included, such as members of the elected TLCs, the various local 'land committees' that had been set up all over the lowveld when the possibility of land claims was mooted in 1992. Since chiefs did not exist as such under the constitution, they were not to be invited even though they were welcome to attend as private interested parties.

At the first meeting of all stakeholders, things did not go as planned. Originally conceived as primarily an information sharing exercise, the entire meeting was dominated by representatives of the chiefs and the 'tribes' who demanded immediate action on restitution of land. The meeting was opened, as is customary in South Africa, with a prayer. The 'prayer' offered, however, drew heavily if rather loosely on the Babylonian captivity of the biblical Hebrews, and ended with an indirect political challenge: end our oppression by restoring our land to us. Who 'us' was and precisely what land remained an open question. But the openness of the question merely added fuel to the unmet expectations that land would be restored.

It was obvious to the chiefs that they no longer had a direct say in matters. Several spokesmen closely associated with the chiefs under whose names the original claims had been made, however, asserted a unity of purpose based on a claimed ethnic unity as Pulanas. Historically, there was no official recognition of this ethnic label. A new ethnic identity focused on the land restitution issue, and challenging the continued existence of the resort, nature reserves, forestry and watershed land, seemed to be emerging.

The outcome of all of this is still entirely uncertain. Research efforts were hampered by inadequate funding, but were proceeding with all the determination that the small commission could muster. Meetings and mediation forums were continuing and more were planned, but a great deal remained at stake for the future of the environment, tourism, economic development of the region, and the sustainability of its natural and human resources. Great potential for further conflict remained.

CONCLUSIONS

In the current situation, there is significant likelihood of both losses and gains. The potential for continued or escalating conflict is likely to depend on whether the changes take place within a growing economy, or whether the economy fails to perform up to expectations. *Expectation* rather than absolute performance is the key factor.

The complex and overlapping cases discussed here – land claims on the Aventura resorts, violent protest over boundaries and service delivery, the political ecology of nature reserves and protected areas, the negotiation with a transnational development company and the emergence of a militant localism – are all problems of ambiguous jurisdiction and political uncertainty. These conflicts must be decided in the contexts of the South African constitutional framework and global environmental sustainability. Complex local histories of ethnic conflict, disputed landscapes, changing boundaries and cultural diversity set limits on any accommodation or solution to these problems. The region must seek a path of economic development – with or without international involvement – but this will introduce another layer of complexity in problem solving and conflict management. Two scenarios for the future are possible.

Under a zero-sum game scenario, conflict can only increase. This would occur if – as in 2001 – the economy is relatively stable with low growth and high unemployment. African politics is often conducted as if it were a zero-sum game – winner takes all, and what one gains the other must lose. These limits would have to be overcome, and people led to expect that a growing economy free of conflict would benefit all, rather than reward only some, of whom the rest would be jealous.

Under this scenario, however, ongoing mediation and 'facilitation' of dialogue and information dissemination would be critical. Although some elements of government and of the ANC have shown strong dislike of external intervention of any kind, international agencies, NGOs, business people and tourists are already heavily involved in the past and the future of the region. They are likely to come into conflict with local interests. Conflict must be shifted away from destructive government embargoes or points of resistance towards development of international partnerships that can significantly benefit the region at all levels. Under such circumstances, local governments might become more secretive, more resistant to intervention both from the South African 'centre' and from the international agencies. Pressures by international environmental groups to maintain the natural resources for ecotourism groups could be resented and lead to a further decline of the relatively good tourism and investment environment that currently still exists.

Under a scenario of an expanding economy with expectations being met in even a limited way, conflicts could follow a different trajectory. Expanding economic success will inevitably lead to demands for further development. This would threaten the environment in a different way, with the well-known scourges of the more industrialized countries becoming evident. Problems of water provision in the dry lowveld, wastewater management, fertilizer run-off, poaching of game, over-exploitation of resources, and other problems could emerge. Again, a process focusing on identification of developing problem areas and the institution of appropriate control and mediation structures would be essential. Open political conflict and economic resentments would be much less likely, but those economic inequalities that do emerge would create a different set of social problems.

At present, there is a low level of participation in virtually all development and government processes – that is, in politics in general. There is also a low level of provision of government services. People know how to protest violently – as the past has taught them to do – but peaceful mediation of disputes is only known at the local level of the chiefs' courts. Although mediation is being introduced widely as the principle democratic mechanism of South African politics, it often brings limited participation in practice and slows administrative functions as all the stakeholders are consulted. While there are permanent mediation structures set up by the South African government, these are seriously overworked and cannot handle disputes that raise serious constitutional issues, or that involve international parties and transnational issues. There is a clear need here for NGOs that can at least identify these problem areas, define the nature of the problem for the participants and possibly make useful suggestions that would lead to resolution.

NOTES

1   The term 'lowveld' refers to the area below and to the east of the Drakensberg Mountains that divide it from the 'highveld', the broad flat highland area in which Pretoria, South Africa's capital, and Johannesburg, the commercial centre of South Africa, are located. The Drakensburg Mountains are the southernmost continuation of the Rift Valley complex that extends from Ethiopia southwards towards South Africa, where it curves slowly westwards, ending in lower ancient mountains that divide the coastal lowlands from the drier and higher interior. At the southern margin of the lowveld lies Swaziland where some of the oldest metamorphic rocks in the world, the Barberton complex, are found.

2   These were Transkei, Bophutatswana, Venda and Ciskei, the so-called TBVC states. Their 'independence' was only recognized by South Africa who created and maintained 'embassies' and 'consulates' in order to deal with them. These states received virtually all of their funding from the South African government since none was sufficiently efficient, or had sufficient authority, to collect taxes from its own 'citizens'.

3   Research that will establish who lived on the escarpment lands and under which chief's political authority is currently under way, but the history of residence and political jurisdiction, especially over land allocations, is still unclear. Research is being coordinated and conducted by the Commission on Restitution of Land Rights for Mpumalanga and Northern Provinces.

4   Interview 25 March 1997, Buffelshoek, Bushbuckridge North, Northern Province.

5   In the far north-west corner of the Kruger National Park, the Makuleke tribe, a Tsonga-speaking people, were successful in their claim to a piece of the KNP known as the 'Pafuri Triangle'. By agreement, it is managed jointly by the KNP and the Makuleke people as part of the KNP.

6   The flood water in that instance originated from Zimbabwe and Zambia along the Zambezi and Limpopo Rivers to the north, not from the protected South African watersheds.

7   The success of the Makuleke tribe's land claim on the extreme northern corner of the KNP in 1998 helped to establish a precedent in these cases. The Makuleke were the last people to be removed from what is now KNP land, and have remained a relatively coherent tribal group in the extreme north-east of the Northern Province. The case appears much simpler than any other case in the two provinces since only one ethnic group and one chiefdom is involved in a well-supported claim on a single piece of uninhabited land with clearly demarcated borders and well-documented history. It is unlikely to be repeated in any other lowveld case still pending, and is likely to remain significant but unique.

8   Almost universally in southern Africa, the chief or king is male. There is only one instance in which a paramount chief is traditionally female, and that is the so-called 'rain-queen' of the Lovedu, a North Sotho-speaking people of the lowveld, some 200 kilometres north of the Bushbuckridge North area in the hills of the escarpment. There are instances of female chiefs inheriting the chiefship in default of any appropriate male heirs, but this is rare. I shall accordingly refer to the chiefs (traditional authorities) as 'he'.

9   The Western Cape Province challenged the constitutionality of the Local Government: Municipal Structures Act of 1998, while the government of KwaZulu-Natal continued to challenge all legislation which reduced the power of chiefs ('traditional authorities'), especially the Municipalities Act of 2000. Both provinces are ruled by opposition parties, the Democratic Alliance (DA) and Inkatha Freedom Party (IFP), respectively (SAIRR, 2000, p338).

10   At the end of 2000, the old National Party, the party of apartheid, joined with its former opposition, the Democratic Party (DP) to form the Democratic Alliance (DA). They are the majority and ruling party of the Western Cape Province, and official opposition in parliament.

11   Media statement by the Regional Land Claims Commissioner for the Northern Province and Mpumalanga on the start of a consultation process around land claims in the Blyde River Canyon Nature Reserve, Mpumalanga, 28 July 1997. Received by email, from Tony Harding of the Land Restitution Claims Commission (LRCC), awharding@sghq.pwv.gov.za.

12   Media statement, Land Restitution Claims Commission, 28 July 1997.

REFERENCES

Niehaus, I (2001) *Witchcraft, Power and Politics: Exploring the Occult in the South African Lowveld.* London: Pluto Press

SAIRR (2000) *South Africa Survey 1999/2000,* Johannesburg, South African Institute of Race Relations

The Sunday Independent (1997) *The Sunday Independent* 18 May (South Africa)

Chapter 11

Ecological Roots of Conflict in Eastern and Central Africa: Towards a Regional Ombudsman

John Mugabe and Godber W Tumushabe

INTRODUCTION

Eastern and central Africa are plagued by a wide range of inter- and intrastate conflicts. These conflicts are manifested in various ways including deadly violence (loss of human life and displacement of households from their socio-ecological backgrounds) often as a result of military force. The causes of the conflicts are multifaceted. They range from religious differences to stiff competition for access to and control of natural resources such as land, water, forests and fisheries. However, attempts to address many of the conflicts in the region have put excessive emphasis on their political dimensions. Indeed, most of the efforts to resolve conflicts in the region have focused on the political underpinnings without regard to root socio-economic and ecological causes. As a result, they have not been effective in resolving the conflicts.

This chapter argues that most of the conflicts in the region are a result of environmental stress and scarcity. Thus, strategies to resolve them should be considered in a broader conflict resolution framework that takes into account economic, ecological, religious, ideological, social and political sources of environmental stress and scarcity. Such a framework does not tie conflict resolution and/or management to the workings of loose politically driven institutional arrangements. It provides interdisciplinary cognitive structures which are capable of anticipating and managing conflicts. The chapter calls for the formation of a regional ombudsman who could anticipate conflicts and provide holistic resolution and/or management measures.

The chapter is divided into three sections. The first erects a conceptual framework for studying and understanding conflicts in eastern and central Africa based on concepts of environmental scarcity, environmental stress and environmental conflict. The second section discusses the nature and ecological sources of conflicts and their associated human rights abuses in the region. It examines the causation between environmental decline and conflict, that is, how environmental stress and scarcity generate conflicts, and how conflicts themselves are often sources of environmental degradation and subsequent natural resource scarcity. This section also evaluates the adequacy of current national and regional efforts to solve the conflicts.

The last section of the chapter outlines a proposal to establish a regional ombudsman whose strategic role could be to bring environmental considerations to inform conflict management efforts in the region. It suggests a number of characteristics and functions that the ombudsman should possess.

ENVIRONMENTAL–POLITICAL CONFLICTS: A CONCEPTUAL FRAMEWORK

The notion of conflict

Conflicts have been part and parcel of the evolution of human societies for centuries (Bachler, 1994). However, the nature and intensity of conflicts as well as their root causes have changed over time. The changes have generated new terminology around the notion of conflict. We now talk of political conflicts, armed conflicts, environmental conflicts and so on. In fact, the notion of conflict is itself now subject to confusion and misuse. Sometimes conflicts are equated to their causes and at other times to their manifestation. This often generates considerable policy and political implications.

According to Schmid, the defining feature of conflict is 'conflict of interest. Conflict is incompatible interests built into the structure of the system where conflict is located' (Schmid, 1968, p217). Others have defined conflict as violence (see, for example, Galtung, 1969; Bachler, 1994). However, for purposes of our analysis we adopt a definition closer to Schmid's. Conflict, in our view, is disagreement generated by incompatible and/or competing interests and activities. We eschew the view that conflict is violence. Violence, as far as we are concerned, is just one form and often a manifestation of conflict. We can talk of non-violent conflict or violent conflict. Violent conflict is often marked by harmful and destructive actions. The converse applies to non-violent conflict.

Typology of conflicts

Generally, conflict may be either international or local. International conflicts are basically conflicts where the protagonists are sovereign states. Purely international conflicts are not always easy to identify since the original causes are within the jurisdiction of national territory. However, as the conflict assumes new dimensions, new parties including international actors are drawn in either as protagonists themselves or as arbitrators in the conflict; hence the notion of internationalization of conflicts.

The second and most prevalent type of conflict is *local conflict*. For local conflicts, protagonists are not sovereign states but two or more entities (clans, tribes, commercial firms, etc) within a particular state. Most conflicts are caused by differing goals of the parties, structural imbalances and, perhaps most important, resource scarcity and the inevitable struggle by all the parties to have access to these resources. They are the most common, long-standing and complicated kind of conflicts to solve. In addition, they could be internationalized by the involvement (often as arbitrators) of foreign states and/or their entities.

The understanding of the two types of conflicts is essential for evolving the appropriate intervention methodologies that will address their underlying causes. Indeed, a contextual understanding of conflicts is also important in enabling policy-makers to identify their root causes and prescribe long-term measures for their resolution and management (Horowitz, 1985, p564).

Ecological underpinnings

As stated earlier, the lexicon of international studies on conflicts has acquired new phrases that are gaining considerable currency. Phrases such as resource conflicts, economic conflicts, social conflicts, international versus local conflicts, environmental conflicts, armed conflicts and political conflicts are now commonly used in various fora. However, these phrases have not been given internationally acceptable definitions. Indeed, their meaning and policy implications are hotly debated. For the purposes of our analysis, we will confine our discussion to environmental conflicts and how they are related to other forms of conflicts.

In general, the literature on environmental conflicts falls into one of two inclusive categories. The first is that group that focuses on the nexus between environment and national security. It is largely established on the assumption that environmental degradation is one of the major threats to territorial integrity of the nation state, and that conflict is likely to occur in situations of environmental stress and decay (Boutros-Ghali,1992; Brock, 1991). This literature focuses on the creation of regimes that promote the management of the environment in order to maintain national security and peace.

Environmental scarcity is generated by a wide range of interrelated factors. One is ecological vulnerability (sometimes associated with climatic change and drought) and subsequent irreversible environmental degradation. Environmental scarcity is an important motor of change in the economics and politics of control and use of natural resources. Security often strengthens the positions (in many cases political positions) of powerful actors: the redistribution of resources is often in their favour.

Writing on strategies for studying environmental scarcity, indeed causes of conflict, Homer-Dixon states:

> *If environmental scarcity contributes to conflict, it almost always operates with other political, economic and cultural causes. Analysts who are sceptical about environmental scarcity as a cause of conflict often conflate the characteristics of*

> *multi-causality and causal strength by assuming that if many factors are*
> *involved, each must be relatively weak* (Homer-Dixon, 1996, p138).

Much of the interest in the environmental scarcity–conflict nexus has focused on the degradation of ecosystems and the likelihood of interstate conflict over non-renewable natural resources. There is, however, a more complex relationship between environmental change generally and state security. The environment and its natural resources are strategic to state formation and growth. This is especially so in Africa, where economies are less industrialized, economic activities are tied to the availability and use of natural resources, and intra- and interstate competition for resources is pronounced.

CONFLICTS IN EASTERN AND CENTRAL AFRICA

Nature and sources of conflicts

A number of eastern and central African countries have witnessed some of the most violent conflicts and human rights abuses in recent history. Most of the conflicts revolve around competition for access to and control of environmental resources. In a number of cases they have generated armed struggles that tend to overshadow their ecological underpinnings. In Sudan, Burundi, Rwanda and Somalia armed conflicts have been driven by various forms of environmental scarcity and stress. Intertwined with environmental scarcity and stress are poor governance, economic deprivation and human rights abuses that have marked the face of the region.

The inevitable consequences have been violent ethnic clashes, loss of human life, displacement of populations creating transboundary refugee crises, destruction of economic structures and, generally, the destruction of the social fabric of the societies in the region. The transboundary character of the environmental resources and associated ecological problems has transformed some of the conflicts into major international conflicts drawing in a number of sovereign states.

A contextual analysis of the specific interacting factors that generate these conflicts and an evaluation of the prospects for their management and resolution pose one of the greatest challenges to policy-makers and politicians both within Africa and beyond. Crucial to the management and/or resolution of the conflicts are the formulation and implementation of systemic measures that are based on adequate understanding of the nature and dynamic causes of the conflicts, the major players in the conflicts, and the successes and failures of previous attempts to address them. It is also important to appreciate that conflict is essentially an inevitable aspect of human interaction, an unavoidable concomitant of competing choices and inconsistent decisions.

On the whole, the conflicts in the eastern and central African region are so interwoven that any attempt at simplistic categorization may, at best, end up as a futile exercise and, at worst, mislead public policy and practice. However, one common denominator of the conflicts in this region, whether they have assumed international dimensions or not, is that they all have ecological underpinnings. Their resolution must address the specific ecological issues in order to arrive at long-term settlements.

The Southern Sudan conflict

The conflict in Southern Sudan is one of the most prolonged conflicts in the region. From as early as 1983, the Sudanese Peoples Liberation Movement (SPLM) and the Sudanese Peoples Liberation Army (SPLA) have been fighting for greater autonomy for Southern Sudan. Southern Sudan is inhabited by a largely Christian and animist population while the north is Arab and Islamic. The conflict in Sudan has always been described as a religious conflict in which the Islamic regime in Khartoum wishes to rule the whole of Sudan under the Sharia law. The ongoing conflict is therefore seen as a resistance by the people of Southern Sudan against forced Islamization on the one hand, and the right to self-determination of the Southern Sudanese on the other. The conflict has caused a wide range of problems including loss of human life, destruction of economic assets and displacement of households. It is estimated that over the last ten years, more than 50,000 people have died as a direct result of the conflict.

While the Southern Sudan conflict is typically framed around religious issues and differences, its roots lie in competition for access to and control of key natural resources, particularly minerals. Southern Sudan is known to be an area very rich in minerals, especially oil, more adequately supplied with water compared with northern Sudan and very rich in terms of vegetation. It is essentially for reasons associated with control of environmental resources rather than religious factors that the Khartoum regime cannot allow the self-determination of the people of Southern Sudan. If this resource endowment issue is seen alongside the religious reasoning propounded by the Khartoum regime, it is apparent that the latter is actually secondary and less significant.

The Southern Sudan conflict should be looked at in the context of the people of Southern Sudan's right to self-determination. The subject of self-determination as a norm of international law is not yet very clearly understood and is a continuous subject for students of jurisprudence. It is still not agreed whether self-determination should be defined by territoriality, ethno-cultural commonality, subjective collective self-assertion or a combination of all these factors. According to long time Sudan scholar, Abdullahi Ahmed An-na'im the concept has been defined as the right of civil society or segments of it to shape and determine their own destiny within the framework of an established nation state.

Nevertheless, it is important to note that the concept of self-determination and its interaction with the cognate principles of territorial integrity and boundary inviolability since independence, as affirmed in the Organization of African Unity (OAU) Charter and at the Cairo OAU Summit in 1964, has been one of the major sources of contention on the African continent. The claims by various 'peoples' for separate sovereignty outside the decolonization framework and the inevitable stigmatization of these demands as secession has been at the centre of many conflicts on the continent. A fully detailed discussion on the definition of the concept of self-determination is beyond the scope of this study. What is important to note, however, is that the people of Southern Sudan have understood their struggle within the context of an international norm of self-determination.

This conflict is therefore built on the tension between the presumed right to self-determination of the Southern Sudanese and the opposing principle of territorial integrity. Any initiative to resolve the conflict must therefore be able to reconcile the competing demands for self-determination by the Southern Sudanese and for the Sudanese Government to preserve the territorial integrity of the Sudan State. Admittedly, this task is as complex as understanding the norm of self-determination within the context of African neo-colonial states.

The Southern Sudan conflict has been compounded by the involvement of neighbouring states. To the north of Sudan, Egypt depends on the waters of the Nile for its survival. Egypt draws at least 50 per cent of its water from the Nile (see The Nile Waters Agreement, 1959, between Sudan and Egypt for details on water apportionment). Therefore, despite religious and other ideological differences with the military regime in Khartoum, Egypt would not be comfortable with the existence of another sovereign state in the Nile basin. Moreover, there is fear among the Egyptians that self-determination in Southern Sudan may bring about numerous other states, which would be difficult to reconcile with its bid to exercise control or significant influence over the flow of the waters of the Nile.

This conflict is further compounded by the involvement of Uganda. Uganda has long had a political and cultural relationship with the people of Southern Sudan. The people on both sides of the common border are historically linked by language, culture and ethnic origin. Uganda, therefore, has always shown sympathy to the cause of the Southern Sudanese peoples in their struggle for self-determination. Added to this factor is the Ugandan Government's fear of having an Islamic fundamentalist regime on its immediate border. Although this is a very latent reason, there is no doubt that the Ugandan Government would favour an autonomous Southern Sudan as a check on the spread of Islamic fundamentalism from the Islamist regime in Khartoum. It is therefore important to point out that religious ideology plays a highly significant factor in Uganda–Sudan relations and conversely in the entire framework of the Southern Sudan conflict.

As a result of all these factors, a devastating civil war continues unabated and the people of Southern Sudan are subjected to gross human rights abuses, political and religious intolerance, forced relocations and hunger. The religious and ideological dimensions of the conflict inhibit any clear understanding of the ecological underpinnings of this drama and, as such, the plight of the Southern Sudanese. It is now estimated that this brutal war has claimed over 3 million lives of African Southern Sudanese, displaced over 4 million internally and sent over 500,000 as refugees to the neighbouring countries of eastern and central Africa.

Any successful intervention and long-term conflict management in the Southern Sudan conflict must also take into account the South–South dimension of the conflict. This conflict is based on two major factors: first, when Juba was proclaimed the capital city of Southern Sudan, a number of tribes came in and took over land from the indigenous people. These people feel alienated from their traditional lands. Second, there is the occupational conflict between the predominantly agricultural tribes of the Eqatoria Province and the pastoral tribes of the Bahel Gazel and Upper Nile provinces. Therefore, even if the Sudanese Government reached a compromise with the rebel groups in the south, the parties must contend with this problem. Any initiative for dealing with long-term conflict resolution or management in the region must squarely address these realities.

The Rwanda conflict

The Rwanda conflict has persisted for four decades. Rwanda covers a total area of 26,340 square kilometres and has a population estimated at about 8.2 million people. The country is inhabited by two ethnic groups: the Hutu, who are predominantly agriculturalists, and the Tutsi, who are predominantly pastoralists. It is important to note that the two groups are linguistically and culturally closely related compared with many ethnically stratified societies in other countries in the region. However, decades of colonially inspired divisions have cultivated ethnocentric feelings among these two ethnically distinct tribes.

The Rwanda conflict provides perhaps the best direct example of an ecological conflict that has manifested itself in grave political confrontation between the two ethnic groups. The conflict can be explained partly by the scarcity of land resources. The country faces a high population density, estimated at 312 persons per square kilometre. Pastoralist Tutsis demand large tracts of land for their herds of cattle, while the Hutus require arable land for extensive agricultural production. There is, as a result, competition for access to and control of land by the two tribes.

Over the years, the conflict has been manifested in political confrontation – a struggle to retain political power and hence control access to land. The political dimension of this problem is that whichever tribe is in power has control over access to land. Historically, politics in Rwanda have been characterized by exclusion and prejudice.

The Rwanda conflict has been aggravated by the entry of other parties into the political, economic and social pandemonium that has unfolded in what is now commonly referred to as the Great Lakes Region. In the 1980s, the Ugandan Government, which had hitherto been an unwilling host to predominantly Tutsi refugees, expelled most of them from parts of western Uganda and other refugee camps in the country. Those refugees who could not find their way into Rwanda ended up in the National Resistance Army (NRA), then a rebel group fighting the Ugandan Government. When the National Resistance Movement (NRM) took over power in Uganda in 1986, the Rwandese elements in the NRA regrouped and invaded Rwanda in 1992. The fall of the Habyarimana Government in Rwanda, following a successful rebel offensive and the accompanying genocide of nearly a million Tutsi and Hutu moderates, brought the conflict in Rwanda to the centre stage of the United Nations peacekeeping agenda.

The Rwandan genocide is one of the most brutal and vicious premeditated instances of genocide of our epoch. The savageness of the killings and the torture inflicted upon the victims of the genocide were beyond the comprehension of humanity. Along with the genocide, Rwanda suffered almost total destruction of its political and social structures, and a near complete devastation of its economy. The resulting refugee crisis constituted an unmanageable stress for the countries in the region, especially Tanzania and the Democratic Republic of Congo (then Zaire). For example, according to the United Nations High Commissioner for Refugees (UNHCR), as of November 1996 the Kagera Region of Tanzania was estimated to host 617,000 refugees from Rwanda and Burundi, located in 11 main camps.

The Rwanda conflict is compounded by the problems of its immediate neighbours, particularly Burundi and the Democratic Republic of Congo. Burundi's population has the same ethnic composition as Rwanda with a majority Hutu ethnic group and minority Tutsi, and the same occupational differences. In both cases, the Tutsi minority dominates the army and consequently the politics of these countries. Any attempt to resolve the long-term differences between the two ethnic groups in the two countries must be seen within this context. The most difficult problem in the Rwanda–Burundi and Hutu–Tutsi 'jigsaw puzzle' is how to address the resource needs of the two ethnic groups within an agreed political equation acceptable to the protagonists.

The Zaire factor is also now central to resolving the conflicts in both Rwanda and Burundi. Zaire hosts thousands of Banyamulenge, ethnic Tutsis who migrated to Zaire from Rwanda about 200 years ago. Zaire was also a host to over a million refugees who migrated there as a result of the 1994 genocide in Rwanda. During the recent rebellion to oust former President Mobutu from power, the Banyamulenge played a very important and leading role with direct support from the Rwandese Government. The ethnic Tutsis' dominance of the Congo armed forces has generated animosity among the indigenous Congolese, especially in eastern Zaire where it has sparked armed revolts by the Bemba community.

Armed conflicts in Uganda

Ever since the National Resistance Movement Government of President Y K Museveni came to power in 1986, Uganda has enjoyed considerable security in most parts of the country. However, armed insurgency has continued, especially in northern Uganda where the rebel Lords Resistance Army (LRA) has been active. The LRA has been involved in outrageous violations of human rights, especially abduction of children. In their 1997 Report on northern Uganda, London-based Amnesty International estimated that more than 8,000 children have been abducted in northern Uganda since the beginning of the insurgency (Amnesty International, 1997; Human Rights Watch, 1997). As a result of these rebellions, the Ministry of Defense continues to draw the largest percentage of the national budget.

The current government of Uganda has a healthy track record of negotiating an end to conflicts with various armed groups in the country.

However, earlier attempts to reach a negotiated settlement with the LRA were futile. The rebel group has no recognized command structure or political leadership. Whereas these two factors have complicated the resolution of conflict in northern Uganda, the situation has been compounded by the alleged involvement of the Khartoum Government in the conflict. The two countries accuse each other of supporting rebel groups opposed to each other's government. The Ugandan Government particularly accuses the Sudanese Government of maintaining a constant supply of arms, ammunition and other supplies to the rebels of the LRA.

Potential conflict over Lake Victoria waters

Equally important is the possibility of a conflict between Kenya, Uganda and Tanzania over the management and utilization of the resources of Lake Victoria. The lake is shared between the three countries in the proportions of 6 per cent, 45 per cent and 49 per cent, respectively, and is a major source of fishery products to all three countries. With the growth of the fishing industry in the region, there is an increasing incidence of confrontation between fishermen from the three countries. Trade liberalization and the availability of a large market, especially in the European Union, are making fish trade a lucrative business for the three countries.

The growing importance of the fishery industry to the economies of these countries provides a fertile ground for a possible confrontation should there be no established mechanism that can cope and monitor the developments over resource access and use.

Conflicts over pastures in eastern Africa

In addition to the conflicts described, there are latent conflicts associated with access to and control of pastures and pasturelands in countries of eastern Africa. Nomadic groups of Kenya, Uganda, Sudan, Ethiopia and Somalia live in very fragile ecological environments and have had their fair share of drought, diseases and famines. Their very mode of life has been a source of tension among the neighbouring states as a result of cross-border raids. According to scholar Atieno Odhiambo, tribes such as the Turkana, Pokot and Karamajong, the Toposa, Dongiro, and Shangilla, the Gabbra, Omoro and Orma, occupy the margins of the state systems that rule over them. Their very mode of life has been a source of tension among the neighbouring states as a result of cross-border raids.

Continued dwindling of pastures and limited technological abilities to develop new coping strategies are likely to lead to increased inter- and intra-state tensions. Recent border conflicts between Kenya and Ethiopia are evidence of the explosive nature of the continued decimation of nomadic peoples of the region. There are other cross-border conflicts between pastoral communities, including the Kenyan Turkana and the Toposa of Sudan (Lang, 1995). Timberlake gives a detailed account of the Kenyan action against the Karamajong of Uganda (Timberlake, 1992, p170). He reported that, in 1984,

Kenyan helicopters killed several dozen Karamajong pastoralists who crossed into Kenya to raid cattle from the pastoralist tribes just across the border.

In Uganda, the conflict between the state and the Karamajong is a classic example of conflict over mineral resources. Karamoja is known to be one district of Uganda well endowed with mineral resources. It has very rich deposits of gold and other precious minerals. As indicated above, the Karamajong are traditionally pastoralists and thus view the ongoing gold mining activities as a threat to their livelihood. According to the NGO Oxfam International, a South African Company which holds prospecting rights in Karamoja has enclosed wide tracts of land and to a large extent curtailed the traditional movement of persons and animals.

The Karamajong consider it their inherent right to graze their cattle throughout most of northern Uganda and to have access to watering points and other resources in the area. They also consider it their right to share benefits arising out of gold prospecting activities in the area. The Karamoja Development Agency (KDA) formed by local people is an institutional arrangement for coping with this perceived threat. Continued decimation is breeding animosity among Karamajong leaders and pastoralists. The extent to which the resource conflicts are resolved depends largely on how well the Central Government, the KDA, the South African Company and the traditional pastoral communities are able to develop a legal arrangement that will allocate rights of access to and use of the minerals. Such an arrangement should define the nature (quality and quantity) of benefits to be shared among all the stakeholders.

The same problems can also be seen with the Masai pastoralists in the Ngorongoro Conservation Area of Tanzania. The Masai have inhabited the Ngorongoro area since time immemorial. The demarcation of Ngorongoro into a National Park and its transformation into a World Heritage Site has brought a number of parties into a collision course. The Ngorongoro Conservation Area Authority, the World Conservation Union (IUCN) and other international conservation agencies believe that it is their duty to protect wildlife in the Ngorongoro area. The Masai, on the other hand, claim unfettered rights of access to grazing land in the same area according to the Land Rights and Resources Research Institute (LARRRI), a research and advocacy group based in Dar es Salaam. This land use conflict can easily become explosive if not contained. The parties need to be given a platform where they can sort out their differences. Current attempts by LARRRI need to be complemented for such efforts to bear results.

In conclusion, conflicts that have characterized the region for the last two decades arise from problems basic to all peoples: the tugs and pulls of different identities, the differential distribution of resources and access to power and, more often, competing definitions of what is right, fair and just. The resort to violence gives these conflicts a second dimension, that of survival and security. What is required is an institutional arrangement that will facilitate the evolution of political security and stability and equitable economic relations within and throughout the region, as well as guarantee new prospects for development and the fulfilment of basic human needs, including the need for human dignity for all peoples.

THE ESTABLISHMENT OF A REGIONAL OMBUDSMAN

The various conflicts in eastern and central Africa demand institutional and legal arrangements that target their ecological causes as well as their political consequences. Such arrangements must mobilize political support across the region but should be informed by national interests. As we have observed above, most of the conflicts in eastern and central Africa have their sources in increasing interest and competition for environmental resources (for example, land, water, wildlife and minerals) although they manifest themselves into violent political confrontation and gross human rights abuses. Their solution should be searched for and obtained in a broad framework for conflict management and resolution. Institutional and legal arrangements that take into account a holistic approach to resolving regional conflicts should be the main element that distinguishes the present efforts from previous approaches to conflict management in the region. One potential institutional arrangement is that of a regional NGO or governmental ombudsman.

The legitimacy of such an institution and its effectiveness would largely depend on its being politically acceptable to the states within the region. The issue then becomes whether such political acceptability is possible in the present context. This difficulty is best explained by the failure of attempted mediation efforts in the region. For the last five years, the Intergovernmental Authority on Development (IGAD), a club of various countries in the Greater Horn of Africa, has tried mediation between the Khartoum Government and the Sudanese Peoples Liberation Army, the main protagonists in the Southern Sudan conflict. The broader question has also been to resolve the differences between the Khartoum Government and the regime in Kampala. The two cut off diplomatic relations about two years ago. The mediation efforts have been characterized by broken commitments and unfulfilled promises. Personal animosity between personalities in the region has been at the heart of these failures.

International mediation between Uganda and Sudan brokered by the Governments of Malawi, the Islamic Republic of Iran, Libya and more recently South Africa have been to no avail. The main stumbling blocks have been mutual accusations about support for rebel groups. Yet, the cessation of current hostilities between Sudan and Uganda is central to a long-term solution to the conflict in Southern Sudan.

Any institution established to address environmental–human rights conflicts in this region must be concerned about issues of legitimacy. At one level, the question is how the institution will acquire legitimacy to mediate between the parties to the conflict. This involves building the confidence of all protagonists in the institution as the legitimate organ to bring the parties together. At the second level, the institution must be seen as legitimate by states, who are significant players in regional conflicts.

There are three potential institutional routes by which an ombudsman can obtain the requisite legitimacy. The first option is for an ombudsman to be accredited by or affiliated with an existing international or inter-governmental organization such as the IGAD or the OAU. IGAD is a geographic configuration that constitutes what is now commonly known as the Horn of Africa: Sudan, Kenya, Uganda, Ethiopia, Djibouti and Eritrea. However, it does not encompass the entire region that is described as eastern and central Africa. Rwanda, Tanzania, Burundi and the Republic of Congo are not members. For this reason IGAD fails the test: it would not (under its current form) be the best organization to provide affiliation to the proposed ombudsman.

The OAU, on the other hand, includes all African states. Affiliation of the proposed ombudsman to the OAU has the advantage of drawing resources from 'neutral' political parties outside the eastern and central Africa sub-region. In addition, the governance of the institution would be left to states outside the sub-region. On the whole, affiliation with the OAU would enable an ombudsman to gain political legitimacy and respectability among the organization's member states.

Another possibility is for the institution to be accredited by a regional economic grouping such as the Preferential Trade Area (PTA), the Southern African Development Conference (SADC) or the East African Cooperation Secretariat, a loose economic arrangement between Uganda, Kenya and Tanzania that has undertaken efforts to revive the defunct East African Community. The SADC is exclusively an economic club of the countries of southern Africa, while the PTA brings together most of the countries of eastern and southern Africa (with the exception of South Africa). The limited geographic coverage of the East African Cooperation Secretariat excludes it from being a viable option for an ombudsman focused on conflict resolution in the broader region of eastern and central Africa. SADC and the PTA leave out a number of countries like Congo (Brazzaville), the Central African Republic, Cameroon and Gabon, which easily fall within the eastern and central Africa region. Any conflict in these countries would have a very high propensity to spill over to other countries in the region as has been demonstrated by current events in Congo.

Affiliation with the OAU would have both advantages and disadvantages. The main advantage is that the institution would work within the already existing OAU conflict resolution and management framework: the ombudsman could draw on the credibility and acceptability of the OAU among its member states. However, the OAU has had very limited success in its conflict resolution and management responsibilities, which may undermine the credibility of the ombudsman. The OAU has recently been under attack from its critics for failure to prevent or resolve some of the world's most violent conflicts on the continent. Nearly ten years ago, *Africa Confidential* pointed out that if the OAU's new leadership does not make dramatic strides in resolving these conflicts, 'it is hard to see an effective future for the OAU' (*Africa Confidential*, vol 30, 1989, p4). Essentially no such strides have been made in the organization's mediation efforts. The 1994 genocide in Rwanda and the continuing and ever-escalating conflict in Burundi are living testimonies of the complexity of conflict resolution and management both for the OAU and the UN, as well as any new initiatives that may emerge.

In addition, the operations of the institution would be further constrained by the OAU's own operational principles, especially those relating to non-interference in the 'internal affairs' of member states and territorial integrity and inviolability of the boundaries within which independence was attained. It is important to note that some of the most violent and persistent conflicts in the region, like the one in Southern Sudan, are the result of the arbitrary demarcation of borders without due regard to geographical features, human populations or even religious ideologies. Former OAU Secretary-General Edem Kodjo has described the territorial integrity principle as 'a perverse principle with negative effects'. An institution that deals with conflict resolution and management would therefore find itself constrained by such principles.

The second option would be to establish an ombudsman institution as an independent, non-governmental entity. As such, the institution would have its own offices with an established permanent secretariat. As an independent institution, an international ombudsman could draw on examples of already existing institutions. It may, for example, be established following the models of either London based Amnesty International or Washington based Africa Watch. These institutions have built international credibility and legitimacy in traditional human rights circles because of the impact of their work on governments. Although their reports and recommendations are not binding on governments, their reports on human rights abuses have had significant impact especially in international relations of states for which reports have been prepared about violations of human rights. These institutions have built credibility on the basis of their well researched and balanced reporting. The neutrality of their positions on the violations being investigated again reinforces this.

Under this option, an independent international ombudsman would derive legitimacy from quality research and unbiased reporting of the issues at hand. This would enable it to gain general acceptability both by governments in the region and by communities, who would be the main clients. Legitimacy for the institution is essential for its work, particularly if it is going to bring protagonists together to negotiate an end to conflict. The parties coming before it must have confidence that the institution will be capable of providing a remedy for their problems.

The institution would therefore rely on persuasion, since it may be difficult to make the parties to the conflict, especially sovereign states, submit to its jurisdiction. Its legitimacy and respectability would rest on the seriousness of its understanding and analysis of the problems at hand.

The third option is to form an intergovernmental institution negotiated between governments in the region. It may be modelled along the same principles as the European Commission for Human Rights or the African Commission on Human and Peoples Rights. It is important to note that, while the Commission is expected to operate as a human rights ombudsman on the continent, it has not gained the requisite respectability among either member states or the peoples in the region. It is also crippled by its limited scope – the Commission does not allow individuals to bring complaints – and has no powers to compel the member states to submit to its jurisdiction. For these reasons, the Commission has persistently suffered from a crisis of confidence and has constantly witnessed human rights abuses on the continent as an observer rather than a player in the field.

Negotiating the establishment of an intergovernmental ombudsman would be a rather lengthy and protracted process given the political, ideological and even personal differences among the countries and personalities in the eastern and central African region. It would need very skilfully managed negotiations to make sure that the parties reach a consensus on a set of principles and procedures to govern the operations of the institutions. More difficult still is whether the countries of the region can agree on a set of minimum human rights and environmental standards to which all of them would subscribe.

On the basis of the above analysis of the available options, we recommend the establishment of a regional ombudsman as an independent, non-governmental institution. Its primary role would be to bring the ecological dimensions of the conflicts in the region to bear on the entire conflict resolution and management. This is premised on the understanding that the causes of conflict in eastern and central Africa are as diverse as the conflicts themselves. As such, the programme of the institution would need to be inclined towards ongoing initiatives. Most of these initiatives have been under the auspices of the United Nations and regional and sub-regional organizations.

The institution would undertake the following core activities:

1 *Research:* The environment–human rights nexus is rarely understood, let alone appreciated by the protagonists. Empirical research to demonstrate that nexus would therefore help the parties to develop a holistic understanding of their problems. A narrow understanding of the causes of conflict in the region has only served to enhance fears of the participants to the conflict. This broadened approach would encourage innovative solutions that strive to satisfy the hunger of individuals for justice as well as to allay their fears. Research should also help to establish such factors as power relativities, needs of the parties, perceived outcomes, ideological commitments, mutual accordance of legitimacy and the available mechanisms to facilitate the process of conflict resolution.
2 *Facilitation:* A regional ombudsman may also play the role of facilitating ongoing mediation efforts as a means of encouraging the parties to reach a compromise. The institution could provide logistical support, both human and material, to complement the work of local initiatives. Alternatively, the institution could constructively engage state actors to negotiate an end to the conflict.
3 *Monitoring and information dissemination:* A regional ombudsman could also perform the role of monitoring potential conflict situations, disseminating information on the ecological facets of the conflicts, and promoting timely approaches to avoid the escalation of such conflicts.

Finally, it is important to appreciate that conflict management in eastern and central Africa must be seen within a broad spectrum of improving governance at all levels of society. Success will only be achieved if governments in the region are able to practice democratic governance and provide for the basic needs of the majority of the population as well as give a voice to marginalized communities. It is only then that an environment can be created within which intervention by other parties, including a regional ombudsman can be possible and effective.

REFERENCES

Africa Confidential (1989) *Africa Confidential* 30, 1989

Amnesty International (1997) *Breaking the Ten Commandments*. London: Amnesty International

Bachler, G (1994) *Desertification and Conflict: The Marginalization of Poverty and of Environmental Conflicts,* Occasional Paper No 10. Berne: Swiss Peace Foundation

Boutros-Ghali, B (1992) *Agenda for Peace*. New York: United Nations

Brock, L (1991) 'Peace through Parks', *Journal of Peace Research* 28(4):407–423

Galtung, J (1969) 'Violence, Peace and Peace Research', *Journal of Peace Research* 3:167–192

Homer-Dixon, T (1996) 'Strategies for Studying Causation in Complex Ecological–Political Systems', *Journal of Environment and Development* 5(2):132–148

Horowitz, David (1985) *Ethnic Groups in Conflict*. Berkeley, CA: University of California Press

Human Rights Watch (1997) *The Scars of Death*. New York: Human Rights Watch

Lang, C (1995) *Environmental Degradation in Kenya as a Cause of Political Conflict, Social Stress, and Ethnic Tension*. Berne: Swiss Peace Foundation

Schmid, H (1968) 'Peace Research and Politics', *Journal of Peace Research* 5:217–232

Timberlake, L (1992) *Africa in Crisis*, 2nd edn. London: Zed Books

Part V

Conclusion

Chapter 12

Promoting Environmental Human Rights through Innovations in Mediation

Naomi Roht-Arriaza

INTRODUCTION

Like the norms, the institutions at the intersection of international human rights law and international environmental law have grown unevenly. To date, these institutions have proved to be inadequate to the task of hearing and resolving the increasing number of conflicts involving access to and use of resources, as well as the effects of environmental degradation on individuals and communities. Nonetheless, at both the national and the international levels, existing institutions provide lessons in designing effective mediation mechanisms that can promote environmental protection and human rights, as well as economic development.

This chapter has three aims. First, it maps possible modes of mediation in conflicts involving human rights, environmental protection and resource use, and outlines the benefits of a 'soft law', non-adjudicatory approach. Second, it discusses the evolution of the ombudsperson function and evaluates the criteria for success of existing ombudsperson offices in national law. Third, it maps existing international institutions concerned with human rights and environment and evaluates potential insertion points for an ombudsperson-type mediation mechanism.

MEDIATING ENVIRONMENTAL HUMAN RIGHTS DISPUTES

Any institution intervening in an environmental human rights conflict will draw on norms, resources and methods from a number of different traditions: human rights advocacy, environmental advocacy, community development and alternative dispute resolution. Each of these areas brings its own set of methods and ways of operating. Human rights advocates tend to focus on individual rights and have difficulty with group or collective rights. They also focus on civil and political rights and tend to believe in third-party adjudication as the best mechanism for rights protection. Environmental institutions come from a different heritage: they tend not to focus on individual (or group) complaints at all but on scientific knowledge and economic and ecological trade-offs and synergies.

At the national level, a number of states have begun experimenting with 'roundtables', 'stakeholder processes' or 'regulatory negotiations', which attempt to bring together the parties interested in a dispute or set of trade-offs and to structure a discussion aimed at reaching a generally acceptable outcome. These sometimes coexist with citizen suits and other judicial avenues for relief for those affected by harm to the natural environment.

Those working within either the adjudication or mediation tradition undertake some version of four tasks: 1) investigation and fact-finding; 2) advocacy or representation; 3) technical support and capacity building; and 4) dispute intervention. The four are interconnected: for example, the results of an investigation may well push the parties towards seeking a mediated resolution, while advocacy for the party claiming harm may make dispute resolution more difficult.

Investigation or fact-finding includes on-site visits, interviews with participants in a dispute, review of documents and the like, with the intent to compile (and perhaps to publish) a report. Investigation may be particularly important in an environment-related context, where the facts may be disputed, scientific knowledge is incomplete, or one or more parties have difficulty in assembling and understanding complex technical data. It may also aim to establish whether national or international laws have been violated, or to ascertain the needs and desires of participants in a dispute. Investigation may be undertaken with or without a view to later mediation or adjudication; it may simply serve as the basis for publicity or creating political pressure.

Advocacy or representation can include publication of facts in an attempt to 'mobilize shame', lobbying or legal representation before national or international bodies. It may be on behalf of an individual, a local community, an environmental resource, a set of options or development strategies. It may include the preparation of recommendations for the parties. Technical support is sometimes categorized as 'advisory services' when provided to governments in the UN context: it involves providing technical, scientific or legal help directly to one or more parties. In addition to aiding governments, it may involve assisting local groups and institutions in networking and capacity building efforts.

Dispute resolution in the broad sense includes a wide spectrum of activities from 'hard', formal, third party adjudication to informal, 'soft', direct negotiations. 'Hard' dispute resolution involves court adjudication, whether by a regular or specially constituted court, or binding arbitration, where a third party makes a decision that both disputants are bound to respect. The proceedings are adversarial in nature, there are formal procedural rules, once a party has agreed to be bound they cannot unilaterally withdraw without penalty, a neutral third party is empowered to make a decision, and the result is legally binding on the parties.

The foremost existing judicial forum for resolving disputes is the International Court of Justice. The ICJ has an environmental chamber[1] and recently decided a major case involving the environment, which articulated the importance of taking into account the evolving nature of environmental norms.[2] Nonetheless, only states may be parties to a suit before the ICJ: affected communities and individuals have no direct access. In addition, states must consent to the court's jurisdiction. Powerful states, including the US, have repeatedly refused to do so. These limitations hamper the usefulness of the ICJ in environmental human rights conflicts.

Many international environment-related treaties include monitoring and dispute resolution provisions. The Law of the Sea Convention, for example, provides for consultation, conciliation, compulsory arbitration and referral of disputes to the ICJ, and a Law of the Sea Court has recently been created.[3] Like recourse to the ICJ, the arbitration provisions of such treaties are almost never invoked (Chayes and Chayes, 1995). Disputes are generally handled informally because states do not want to cede power to third parties.

Some treaties, like the Montreal Protocol, now incorporate consultative mechanisms as part of their non-compliance procedures.[4] Other environmental treaties provide for compulsory conciliation,[5] but these provisions have not yet been invoked. These mechanisms only apply to a limited number of environmental problems, are restricted to states party to the treaty and do not extend to violations of the rights of individuals or communities.

A wide range of mechanisms for formal arbitration exists at both the governmental and private levels. Most, like those under the International Chamber of Commerce, apply to strictly commercial disputes and have limited relevance. One potentially useful private mechanism is the International Center for the Settlement of Investment Disputes (ICSID). Established by treaty, ICSID provides conciliation and arbitration facilities for legal disputes between a state party and a national of another state party arising out of foreign direct investment. Awards are then treated like decisions of a local court by all state parties (Shihata, 1996). The dispute, however, must be between a government and foreign investor – citizens and communities do not have access. Moreover, both the host and home states must be parties. The treaty could conceivably be modified, however, to allow for easier consideration of environmental harms arising out of transnational corporate activities.

Human rights advocates and lawyers tend to prefer judicialized, 'hard' dispute resolution mechanisms, fearing that more diplomatic approaches will not protect weaker parties. Moreover, judicialized responses develop norms and rules over time, provide some consistency in resolution and, by their nature, require the clarity of a binary outcome – someone wins, someone loses.

Continuing work on more adequate judicial and quasi-judicial mechanisms, however, does not negate the usefulness of more flexible approaches in which outcomes are negotiated by the parties themselves. These approaches, which may include commissions of inquiry, good offices, facilitated stakeholder roundtables, conciliation and mediation,[6] use third parties not to adjudicate, but to obtain or filter information, recommend solutions, ensure all stakeholders are part of the negotiation and/or provide a neutral arena for discussion.

A 'soft' mediation-based approach offers several advantages in the context of environmental human rights disputes. It is better suited for areas of law (like this one) that are inchoate or still under development, or that are easily politicized. It allows for easier incorporation of a multiplicity of parties with interests that do not neatly line up on one side or another of a binary dispute. Moreover, they may be especially salient to environment-related disputes, given that scientific knowledge may be lacking, partial or disputed. 'Soft law' methods have developed greatly over the past few years, aided by the explosion of alternative dispute resolution (ADR) techniques as well as by the spread of community-based participatory methodologies used by development theorists and practitioners. Finally, many cultures lack a strong judicial tradition, view litigation with reluctance and tend to prefer consensus-building approaches to disputes.

Conciliation and mediation approaches to problem solving, however, have their own drawbacks, including a potential tendency to obfuscate irreconcilable conflicts of interest. While many environmental human rights disputes can be settled on the basis of mutual agreement among the parties, with acceptable compensation for losses, some conflicts over control and use of resources are irreconcilable. When there are enormous power disparities among the parties to the negotiation, a presumption that settlement is possible may imply narrowing the range of possible options to the detriment of the weaker party.

Concretely, where a community simply opposes a certain type of resource exploitation on their lands, a negotiation over the mitigating and compensatory measures that will accompany such exploitation has already presupposed a resolution contrary to the desires of the affected community – even if such a settlement is the 'best deal they will get' and even if it is arguably in the interests of larger national or international communities. A negotiations-based approach to conflict must be cautious about such dangers.

WHAT MAKES AN OMBUDSPERSON SUCCESSFUL?

One innovative approach to effective mediation in environmental human rights disputes is to establish an ombudsperson devoted to playing the role of an 'active mediator'. The meaning and role of an ombudsperson has evolved greatly in recent years, both because of the evolution of new norms and the recognition that adjudication approaches may be expensive and distorting of justice. Ombudsperson-type offices are emerging in many parts of the world.

National experiences

The first ombudsperson was created in Sweden in 1809 to consider cases of illegal or unethical acts by governments against citizens. National ombudsperson offices (frequently known as peoples' defenders, advocates, or by other names) now exist in over 100 countries, spanning a variety of systems and cultures. Nearly every country carrying out a reorganization of the state apparatus in the last two decades has included some variant of an ombudsperson office.

In general, the mission of the ombudsperson is to be an independent and non-partisan officer, generally appointed by the legislature, who supervises governmental administration, deals with specific complaints from the public of administrative injustice, and has the power to investigate, criticize and publicize, but not to reverse, administrative action (Rowat, 1985). Besides acting as a mediator to solve specific cases, the ombudsperson may also recommend broad changes in government procedures. The ombudsperson has the power to subpoena witnesses and documents, but often cannot initiate legal action or investigate complaints for which there is a legal remedy. The ombudsperson need not wait for citizen complaints but can initiate his or her own investigations. Once the ombudsperson has issued recommendations, the government must generally respond, explaining why it has rejected the recommendation or how it is being implemented.

As originally conceived, the function of an ombudsperson was limited to supervising the administrative structure of the state and intervening to limit administrative abuses. While most ombudsperson offices continue to focus on administrative abuses, in recent years many (especially in Latin America and Africa) have taken on the promotion and protection of human rights as a central function. Indeed, many reform governments created such offices as a mechanism for reigning in security forces and lawless officials. The emphasis on human rights has given the ombudsperson a broader set of functions, including recommending changes in national laws and administrative decisions, and the overall administration of government entities.

Recent innovations have further extended the potential functions of the office. For example, Norway's 'Ombudsperson for Children' is meant to 'promote the interests of children vis-à-vis public and private authorities and follow up the development of conditions under which children grow up.'[7] This requires the ombudsperson to be alert to the implications for children of legislation, regulations and the actions of authorities and private parties. This expanded and modern model, which is based in part on the idea that children have fewer legal remedies available to them than do adults, has been adopted in Sweden, Costa Rica, New Zealand, Iceland, Austria and partially in several Central American countries (Flekkoy, 1991). The same rationale may apply in the case of the environment.

Along similar lines, the Argentine ombuds office is especially empowered to investigate acts or omissions of public officials that implicate diffuse or collective interests (IIDH, 1996, p23). In Colombia, the ombudsperson may act as mediator between popular organizations and the government when the popular organizations so request; carry out general studies on rights-related matters; and pressure private parties to recognize legislated rights (ibid, p40). A number of offices have recently been set up to deal specifically with environmental issues (either exclusively or as a subset of a larger office) including those in Namibia, Colombia, Philippines, Austria, New Zealand and El Salvador.

Whatever its scope, an effective ombudsperson office requires a clear constitutional or statutory mandate, a clear division of labour with means of referral to other institutions, and adequate funding and staffing. It must provide redress that is quicker and less expensive than that provided elsewhere and easy access for citizens wishing to complain. Most importantly, the ombudsperson must be seen as being both independent of the government and devoid of a partisan political agenda that would allow him or her to be easily discredited.

Where ombudsperson offices have not worked well, they have been merely formalistic palliatives, focusing on peripheral issues because they were unable or unwilling to tackle the hard ones. Accountability to a legislature seems to be less important (especially in the Latin American or African context), mostly because local legislatures have had little credibility themselves. Rather, those ombudspersons who seem to be most effective rely heavily on their individual moral authority, and much of their success depends on the initiative, drive and credibility with the public of the individual occupying the position.

The International Ombudsman Institute (IOI) serves as a promoter, coordinator and training centre for national ombudspersons. Based at the University of Alberta, Canada, it holds congresses and provides support for research into the institution of ombudsperson. It publishes a directory of ombudspersons throughout the world. If an environmental human rights ombudsperson function includes a component of training and coordination with national ombudsperson offices, the IOI would be a natural ally in that endeavour.

International institutions

There is at present no single international 'ombudsperson' per se whose mission is to provide redress for non-compliance with international agreements and norms. However, a number of institutions, both intergovernmental and non-governmental, undertake mediation roles in conflicts over norms and ethics. The criteria for success at the international level are similar to those at the national level: a clear mandate, a source of authority that makes the recommendations likely to be followed by states or other powerful actors, independence and credibility of the investigators and/or decision-makers, relatively easy access for affected parties, and some degree of accountability to either the parent institution and/or the public. And again, the individual(s) involved tend to be pivotal; much of the authority of the institution derives from the personal integrity and reputation of the members of the office, panel or commission.

Intergovernmental organizations generally derive their authority from states, either through a formal treaty that creates the institution and spells out its mandate, or under the auspices of a global or regional institution like the United Nations or the Organization of American States (OAS). Bodies may be permanent, meet regularly for some period of time on an annual basis (for example, the CSD, Human Rights Commission), or be set up on a temporary or ad hoc basis. Intergovernmental organizations in the human rights/environment area lack the power to bind or coerce either governments or private actors: almost all rely on publicity, public pressure and linkages to other 'carrots' or 'sticks' to implement their findings. Very rarely, an organization may directly influence financing, trade or aid decisions. Non-governmental organizations derive their authority from their perceived neutrality, moral authority, or their ability to mobilize key constituencies in major countries to pressure their governments to act.

The objectives of the different institutions range from the very broad – the promotion and protection of human rights, for example – to the specific. Often, the institution's overall objectives will be specified by treaty, by resolution or by a constitutional or 'mandate' document, but the specifics of its intervention will be at the discretion of staff. In other cases, the human rights/environment issue will be a small subset of a larger set of institutional concerns. Funding sources will also vary, from UN or regional organization budgets, to specific funds, to foundations, member state contributions, private individuals or (least often) user fees. A lack of adequate funding in many cases limits the effectiveness of institutions in this area.

Part of the effectiveness of an institution depends on how the interested public gets access to its procedures and to the information generated. Access to the institutions discussed here generally takes place through some version of an initial petition and screening process. The screening may include criteria such as subject matter eligibility, connection to the institution's mandate and exhaustion of other remedies. These admissibility procedures may be more or less formal, and more or less lengthy – they will usually involve some contact with the opposing parties, often in the form of a request for response to a complaint. Once a case has been taken up, institutions differ widely in their treatment. Institutions focused on dispute resolution tend to lean towards greater secrecy, while those whose primary function is making legal determinations will make at least part of the results of their intervention public.

Many institutions require decisions on recommendations and publication to be made by the governing board or equivalent (states parties, board of directors) rather than by staff. Accountability mechanisms in the case of both governmental and non-governmental organizations are undeveloped: there is a significant risk of politically motivated decisions and little beyond public discrediting or the professional reputation or future funding of an organization to ensure accountability. Table 12.1 lists existing international bodies with one or more ombudsperson-type functions.

MEDIATION MODELS AND INSTITUTIONAL HOMES

An international ombudsperson for environmental human rights conflicts could be structured around one of three models and could be placed within one or a multiplicity of international institutions. The right choice of model may differ depending on the institution.

The first model, which could be dubbed the 'great person' approach, relies heavily on the personal prestige and/or connections of a single individual, aided by a small staff. UN High Commissioners and the Carter Center exemplify this

Table 12.1 *International Bodies with Ombudsperson-type Functions*

Organization	Date established
UN bodies	
International Labour Organization	1919
Human Rights Commission	1946
Human Rights Committee	1966
UNEP	1972
Commission on Sustainable Development	1992
High Comm. for Human Rights	1993
Law of the Sea Tribunal	1996
Working Groups and Rapporteurs	varies
Regional systems	
Rhine Commission	1860s
International Joint Commission	1909
Inter-American Commission on Human Rights	1948
European Commission and Court on Human Rights	1950
Inter-American Court on Human Rights	1978
African Commission on Human Rights	1981
Organization for Security and Cooperation in Europe	1992 (CSCE 1975)
North American Commission on Environmental Cooperation	1993
Other intergovernmental	
World Conservation Union (IUCN)	1948
World Bank Inspection Panel	1993
IDB/ADB Inspection Panels	1995

approach, which works to resolve disputes based on the moral authority and political credibility of a particular individual. Compared to a faceless office, an individual can capture public imagination and is personally accountable.

A second model might be termed the 'expert commission'. A small group of 5–15 individuals chosen for their technical expertise or their political connections act as a group to investigate, prepare reports and make recommendations. The World Bank Inspection Panel, the North American Commission on Environmental Cooperation, the International Commission of Jurists and other organizations work on this model. Commissions may be permanent or set up on an ad hoc basis. Commissions may gain political legitimacy from having a broad base; but they may also result in less than unanimous decisions, uneven quality, and more diffuse accountability than an individual.

A third option is a model driven by staff selected on the basis of their expertise or moral authority. A staff-driven model, like that used in national-level work by the ILO, ICRC and most non-governmental groups, would focus more heavily on day-to-day capacity-building, networking and information gathering and dissemination. It might be less effective at mediation and brokering roles, although a staff-driven model could include the option of reverting to the other two models on an ad hoc basis.

An environmental human rights mediation/ombudsperson function could be placed within one or several organizations in the existing United Nations system, within regional systems, within an existing NGO and/or created afresh in a hybrid government–NGO institution. Indeed, the International Ombudsman Centre for Environment and Development (OmCED) was created in 2000 as a joint effort of the Costa Rican-based Earth Council and the World Conservation Union (IUCN).[8] The following section describes possibilities within the UN and regional systems.

United Nations

A number of UN bodies deal with aspects of the interface between human rights and environment. These include the Human Rights Commission, a number of global treaty regimes, the High Commissioner for Human Rights, and the Commission on Sustainable Development. The International Labour Organization also could play a role through its work on indigenous peoples.

Commission on Sustainable Development

The UN CSD was formed to monitor and encourage states' implementation of Agenda 21, the action programme approved at the 1992 Rio Conference. It holds twice-yearly sessions, and has, in recent sessions, considered several of the more contentious areas of international environmental policy, especially forestry. It has little independence from states, however, and no ability to investigate individual or group complaints of non-implementation of Agenda 21, or the related treaties.

Human rights, political and treaty bodies

Six global treaties – on Civil and Political Rights, Economic, Social and Cultural Rights, Discrimination against Women, Children's Rights, Racial Discrimination and the Prevention of Torture – all have expert committees designed to consider states' reports on compliance with the treaty and, in a few cases, to hear complaints from individuals about state non-compliance.[9] The expert committees may receive written complaints and are composed generally of experts (judges, lawyers, law professors) nominated by states and appointed for fixed terms. They rely on information from the parties, do no on-site investigations, and eventually publish their 'views' on whether there has been a treaty violation. While a number of cases involving environment/human rights conflicts have arisen under some of these treaties[10] the treaties themselves touch on environment only tangentially and the complaint process is lengthy.

In addition to these treaty-based mechanisms, the UN Commission on Human Rights has created some 14 thematic rapporteurs or working groups that derive their authority from the Commission rather than a specific treaty. These include rapporteurs or groups on torture, disappearances, internally displaced persons and toxic waste. In the wake of a three-year study by a special rapporteur on the relationship between human rights and environment,[11] there was an attempt to create a permanent rapporteur on the subject, who would have been empowered to receive and investigate complaints and report to the

Human Rights Commission. The proposal was defeated, in part due to opposition from states that preferred environmental issues to be raised in a non-human rights forum.

The Working Group on Indigenous Peoples, also under the general auspices of the Commission, is somewhat *sui generis* in that it serves as a forum for indigenous peoples to meet and formulate joint strategies for work throughout the UN system. Its most important task to date has been the Draft Declaration of the Rights of Indigenous Peoples, now in a process of study pending approval by the General Assembly. The Working Group may convert to a Permanent Forum of Indigenous Peoples which could take on the tasks of investigating complaints by indigenous peoples of violations of their environmental human rights, recommending potential solutions and/or providing technical assistance to indigenous peoples facing resource-related conflicts (see Fergus MacKay, Chapter 1, this volume).

International environmental treaties
Several of the international treaties negotiated at Rio, notably the Convention on Biological Diversity (CBD), touch on the interface between environment and human rights, especially in terms of the effects of resource exploitation activities on biological resources.[12] The Secretariat of the CBD could conceivably take on ombudsperson-type functions if tasked to do so by the Conference of the Parties (or a new subsidiary body of the Convention could be created to do so).

International Labour Organization
The ILO's mission is to protect and promote the rights of workers. It is a tripartite organization, consisting of governments, labour organizations and employers organizations. Thus, while NGOs, indigenous peoples and other groups do not have direct access, they can often make their positions known through labour unions. In addition, the ILO drafted and implements Convention 169, the only binding international instrument at present that includes provisions on the rights of indigenous people to their land, resources and culture.

The ILO combines fact-finding missions, reports and publications with technical support. The International Labour Office has created 14 multidisciplinary teams (MDTs) stationed in various regions, to advise governments, employers' and workers' organizations on their obligations under ILO treaties, to train labour department officials, and to provide good offices (termed 'direct contacts') when labour-related disputes arise (De la Cruz et al, 1996).

The Secretary-General's office
The UN Secretary-General is charged under the Charter with both political and administrative functions. He may appoint such staff as he needs, and is authorized to annually report to the General Assembly and to inform the Security Council of any matter that may threaten international peace and security. Historically, Secretaries-General have often appointed Special Representatives and Personal Representatives to investigate and mediate in

disputes, and the Security Council in 1992 invited the Secretary-General to recommend how greater use might be made of his good offices.[13] While most cases involving the good offices function have involved more than one state, the Secretary-General has occasionally intervened in civil conflicts (for example, Somalia).

It might be feasible to propose a permanent (or ad hoc) Special Representative within the Secretary-General's office who would act as an ombudsperson, investigating cases of environmental and human rights conflict and preparing recommendations for the Secretary-General. Such a function could dovetail with the Social Compact created by Secretary-General Kofi Annan as a way to encourage MNCs to voluntarily embrace environmental and human rights ethics.

The High Commissioner for Human Rights
The closest the UN has come to establishing an ombudsperson for human rights is the Office of the High Commissioner for Human Rights, created by General Assembly resolution in 1993.[14] The Office has a broad mandate which includes playing the leading role on human rights issues, stimulating and coordinating action throughout the UN system, promoting international cooperation for human rights, assisting in the development of new norms, responding to serious violations of human rights, undertaking preventive action, promoting the establishment of national infrastructures, and providing information and technical assistance.[15] The High Commissioner is an Under-Secretary General and had a budget of some US$46 million for 1998–1999.

The creation of the post was the result of efforts going back almost to the founding of the UN. Starting in 1947, states have proposed a UN Attorney-General, a High Commissioner and Regional Commissioners (Clark, 1972). These early drafts were defeated in part because some countries objected to a single individual, rather than a committee more representative of the world's judicial and cultural systems, being responsible for investigating complaints. In 1993, the General Assembly, after much NGO pressure, created the post of High Commissioner.

Within the UN system, the High Commissioner's office may be the most likely and effective 'home' for mediation and ombudsperson functions on environmental human rights. Its ability to do so would be greatly enhanced if it collaborated with UN environmental bodies, such as UNEP and international environmental treaties. In April 2001 the Human Rights Commission declared that freedom from toxic pollution and environmental degradation are fundamental human rights. In a joint effort Klaus Toepfer, head of UNEP, and Mary Robinson, the High Commissioner for Human Rights, agreed to organize an international seminar to explore how environmental and human rights principles can be strengthened (UNEP, 2001). The seminar aimed to influence the second World Summit on Sustainable Development in September 2002 in Johannesburg.

Regional treaty-based mechanisms

Human rights

Human rights commissions have been established by treaty in Europe, the Americas and Africa.[16] The regional human rights treaties in the Americas and Africa refer specifically to environmental rights. The European and Inter-American Commissions on Human Rights investigate patterns of treaty violation and individual complaints, conduct on-site investigations in some cases, hold hearings and publish reports. Both systems also adjudicate certain individual cases through Courts of Human Rights. The decisions of the European Commission and Court are almost always followed, as are those of the Inter-American Court (but not the Commission). The African Commission has been less active, due to both resource and political constraints, and does not have a corresponding court. In addition, these treaties provide for the use of 'good offices' of the treaty Secretariat to settle complaints informally, although the provisions are rarely used.

NAFTA-related

The North American Commission for Environmental Cooperation (CEC) was created through a side agreement to the North American Free Trade Agreement (NAFTA). The CEC carries out some investigative and dispute-resolution functions.[17] A sister organization, the North American Labor Commission (NALC) serves similar goals in the labour rights field. Rather than create new standards or harmonize environmental or labour standards, both organizations aim to ensure that each NAFTA country enforces its own existing laws (NAAEC, 1993). NACEC consists of a Governing Council composed of the three ministers of environment of the NAFTA countries, aided by a Secretariat based in Montreal, and an Advisory Committee with NGO participation.

The Agreement contains three distinct dispute resolution mechanisms. First, state parties may request that the governing council convene an arbitral panel to consider a 'persistent pattern' of non-enforcement of environmental laws. The public cannot initiate, or formally participate in, this process (NAAEC, Pt V). Nor can the Secretariat convene a panel on its own initiative. An arbitral finding against a party may result in trade sanctions, although the process is convoluted enough that the risk is remote.

Second, article 13 provides for investigation by the Secretariat 'on any matter within the scope of the annual program', leading to the production of a report. While the Secretariat has wide discretion to decide whether to proceed, it may not report on issues related to a party's non-enforcement of its environmental laws and regulations, which is the subject of a separate mechanism. The Secretariat submits its report to the Council of Environmental Ministers and, unless the Council objects, makes it public.

Third, under articles 14 and 15, the Secretariat may consider a submission from an NGO or individual resident in any party state asserting that another party is failing to effectively enforce its environmental law.[18] The submission must, among other things, show that it is not aimed at harassing industry and that the matter has been communicated in writing to the relevant authorities of the party. In addition, it must allege harm to the proponent (to date, the Secretariat has defined 'harm' broadly), and show that the petitioner has pursued domestic remedies. After initial enquiries, the Secretariat may bring the complaint before the Council of Environment Ministers with a proposal to develop a 'factual record'. Only if two-thirds of the Council agrees does the proposal go forward – a serious limitation on the panel's independence. To date, the submission process has not been effective in avoiding environmental harm, although it has brought attention to serious environmental problems within the three countries.

International financial institutions

The World Bank Inspection Panel

Perhaps the closest existing analogue to an international ombudsperson function is the World Bank Inspection Panel. The Panel was created in 1993 as a result of widespread complaints about the detrimental social and ecological effects of World Bank-financed projects around the world. It creates a mechanism by which NGOs, local community groups or other groups of individuals (but not a single individual) may seek independent review of a Bank-financed project if they have been adversely affected by the Bank's failure to follow its own internal operational policies and procedures. The applicable 'law' of the panel is therefore the Bank's own internal documents, for example, its operational directives on forced resettlement, environmental assessment or indigenous peoples.

The genesis of the inspection panel came from pressure from donor states, especially the US, for an Inspector General function, together with increasing outside pressure from NGOs to curb the disastrous impacts of Bank projects. One of these projects, the Narmada dam in India, generated so much opposition that the Bank was forced to appoint an independent expert review panel, chaired by Bradford Morse, to 'conduct an assessment of the implementation of the ongoing Sardar Sarovar projects' regarding the displaced/affected population and the environmental impacts, with reference to existing Bank operational directives and guidelines (Shihata, 1994, p11). As a result of the Morse Commission's criticism of the project, the World Bank withdrew its financing (Udall, 1997). The success of this commission helped to set the stage for a permanent institution.

As part of the discussions about establishing an accountability mechanism, the Bank considered the possibility of an ombudsperson for complaints about bank operations. However, Bank staff decided that a panel would be more suitable than a single individual; after extensive discussions, the Inspection Panel was born in 1993 through a Resolution of the Bank's Executive Board.

The Panel is composed of three members nominated by the Bank's President and appointed by the Executive Directors for single, staggered, non-renewable five-year terms. The panel's functions are investigative and advisory to the Bank. Jurisdiction exists over complaints that show a failure 'of a serious character' to follow the Bank's own rules (the applicable 'law'), where the failure 'has had, or threatens to have, a material adverse effect'. The requester must have attempted to bring the matter to the attention of Bank management without resolution. In addition, the Panel can only deal with complaints arising out of the public finance arms of the Bank (the International Bank for Reconstruction and Development (IBRD) and International Development Agency (IDA)) and not its private component (International Finance Corporation (IFC)), and it cannot consider complaints arising out of the actions of a borrower or where a loan has been substantially disbursed.

After a complaint is brought to the attention of the Panel, it generally conducts a preliminary investigation of the admissibility of the complaint, and recommends to the Board whether or not to go forward. However, the Board must authorize the Panel to prepare a report, and must set the terms of reference. If authorized, the Panel investigates and reports back to the Board. Once the report is submitted to the Board, Bank management submits its own report, and the Board decides on a course of action. The Panel may not officially issue recommendations regarding policy or project changes.

Access to the Panel process is limited in a number of ways. Standing to bring a complaint is limited to groups of individuals or organizations in the territory of the borrower, who are, or may be, directly affected (and to Executive Directors of the Bank). There was considerable debate among Bank executives about whether NGOs based in other countries could intervene: while the resolution does not allow complaints based on general public interest, it does allow for representation of local groups by international NGOs, if the local group can show exceptional circumstances and that there is no adequate or appropriate representation in the country where the project is located. Once a claim is submitted, claimants have no further access to Bank management's response or to the proposed terms of reference of an investigation. Thus, claimants are not able to respond to, or even be aware of, arguments that their claim is inadmissible.

The Panel has received 20 complaints to date, carrying out on-site investigations in a number of them. Most claims have involved local NGO activists representing people directly affected by policy violations in the areas of involuntary resettlement, failure to consult with affected people, failure to adequately assess environmental impacts or impacts on indigenous people, and others (Udall, 1997).[19]

Regional development banks (IADB/ADB)
The regional development banks (Asian Development Bank, Inter-American Development Bank) have developed their own variants on the inspection panel procedure. In the ADB, for example, a committee of board members initially reviews a complaint and only if the committee so recommends is an expert panel convened to investigate. Both the ADB and IADB use a roster of experts rather than a named panel to carry out investigations, choosing three roster members for a given complaint based on their expertise, availability and the lack of any conflict of interest. These experts may hire technical consultants to assist them. NGO representatives have found this system less satisfactory, both because of the uncertainties involved and because of the danger that a roster member may tone down his or her criticism in the interest of being nominated to be part of a panel in the future.

GAPS IN EXISTING INTERGOVERNMENTAL INSTITUTIONS

In considering the institutional landscape, several gaps emerge. Human rights complaint mechanisms cannot deal with the economic/scientific/ecosystem aspects of environmental rights issues well, while those techniques that have emerged under an environmental law rubric are usually state-focused, pay little attention to distributional aspects, and do not offer many opportunities for individual or community viewpoints. Even the more recent efforts at ensuring local community participation through environmental impact assessment (EIA) or multi-stakeholder (roundtable) processes cannot deal well with irreconcilable interests, nor do they include mechanisms to make participatory rights effective if national law does not do so. In particular, there are few mechanisms available to make information regarding potential environmental impacts of a given private or public project both accessible and understandable to local communities.

Existing mechanisms are largely state-focused, unable to reach the private entities at the centre of many resource-related disputes. The recent efforts of human rights scholars and activists to operationalize the extension of human rights law to private violations[20] still leaves the state as the responsible party. Efforts to affect corporate behaviour directly, through codes of conduct and the like, are taking place largely outside the formal human rights or environment-related institutions.

At the same time, private institutions are becoming much more central to human rights and environment issues as the state loses regulatory force, the levels of private investment increase relative to public (thus reducing the possible leverage of both aid-granting governments and the public lending sides of MDBs), and the end of the cold war removes strategic incentives to state aid programmes. Under these circumstances, the traditional 'mobilization of shame' that the human rights community has employed against rogue governments is losing some of its force.

AN NGO OMBUDSPERSON?

International intergovernmental organizations may be too bulky and politically constrained to gain the credibility and undertake the subtle tasks required for effective mediation. Could NGOs step into the breach?

The variety and scope of NGOs is, of course, far too great to canvass here, even limiting discussion to those with a primarily global or regional environmental or human rights focus. Many of the more well known of the human rights and environment NGOs, including Amnesty International, Human Rights Watch, Greenpeace and Friends of the Earth, work on a primarily denunciatory model. They see their role as investigating and bringing abuses to public attention, using the 'mobilization of shame' to pressure governments or companies to change their behaviour. While they use many of the same fact-finding techniques as the intergovernmental organizations, they tend to have closer links with local activists, use more on-site investigation, be less reliant on government sources and less willing to keep the results of an investigation confidential. Indeed, the public denunciation focus of many groups tends to lead them to reject any non-public investigation or mediation as at best ineffective and at worst complicit. This reluctance stems in part from a perception that an arms-length relationship to governments is required to effectively pressure for change, that private deals leave them open to criticism from other parts of the NGO community, and that mediation between very unequal partners will rarely produce just outcomes.

Environmental and human rights NGOs have collaborated in the past: for example, the Natural Resource Defense Council and Human Rights Watch carried out a joint project in defence of the civil rights of environmental activists. While the two networks (human rights and environment) are separate, they have a growing number of links. In the developing world especially, the two issue areas tend to overlap, and a single NGO may be able to deal effectively with both sets of issues.

One organization that is well placed to take on mediation functions is the IUCN. Its mission is focused on conservation and biodiversity issues, implemented largely by developing national conservation plans and providing advisory services to governments and agencies. IUCN is a 'mixed' organization, composed of 74 governments, 105 government agencies and more than 700 non-governmental groups. Membership is voluntary, and the organization derives its authority from its scientific and technical expertise, and its ability to funnel funds to national conservation projects.

IUCN works through membership, expert committees and an 820-person Secretariat. A periodic World Conservation Congress sets policy direction and elects a council consisting of a president, treasurer, 24 regional councillors, 6 commission chairs and up to 5 appointed councillors chosen to represent disciplines not otherwise represented on the council.

Another approach is to create a new, stand-alone, institution. Creating and maintaining such an institution, however, is an ambitious undertaking, requiring a sustained and sustainable financial base, a clear mission, and a strong sense of credibility and 'buy in' by a wide range of NGOs, governments and business. OmCED, for example, is proceeding cautiously until it can garner sufficient financial support to build capacities for sustained intervention (OmCED, 2000). Moreover, a stand-alone NGO institution may have more difficulty than an established NGO or government-based mediation effort in convincing governments or other powerful actors to engage its services or respond to its recommendations. The history of efforts in this area illustrates some of the difficulties.

The idea of an international ombudsperson or dispute mediation function for environmental conflicts is not new. The most recent wave of attempts to create a similar function began with the publication of *Our Common Future*, the report of the Group of Experts of the World Commission on Environment and Development (WCED, 1987).[21] The report recommended the creation of special panels or rosters of experts on various aspects of environmental protection and sustainable development. During the preparatory work to the 1992 Rio conference, a proposal submitted by the Pentagonale countries[22] called on UNEP to begin negotiations on the establishment of a commission of inquiry which would assess the facts where concerns had been raised about a given environmental situation. A related proposal would have created a Mixed Claims Commission to deal with transboundary disputes.

A background paper prepared for the Secretariat and Working Group Three proposed a UN Environment and Development Dispute Prevention and Settlement Service (Stein and Cormick, 1991). The idea was to create a voluntary, non-binding and non-adjudicatory dispute settlement procedure. This could deal with disputes involving transboundary effects of activities in one state on other states or on areas beyond national jurisdiction as well as activities in the global commons with effects within a complaining state, and activities within a particular country with international significance. Access was to include NGOs as well as states, but perhaps with some limitation of NGOs to those recognized by a UN body. Proposed criteria included the interest of the parties in seeking assistance in dispute settlement, whether the parties accepted each other's need to participate, whether the issues were specific enough and amenable to some mutually acceptable solution, and the existence of deadlines or other negative consequences of non-resolution – a good beginning list for any dispute resolution function.

The emphasis of the proposal was on dispute settlement rather than investigation, but it did envision the use of an inquiry commission to determine possible approaches to a particular dispute. The proposal involved a treaty-based mechanism which would operate through regional centres, based either in an existing UN agency, the office of the Secretary-General, or as a joint programme of several UN agencies. The service would carry out training programmes and maintain rosters of mediators (by region) and technical experts. A Steering Committee would carry out initial screening as to the appropriateness of intervention. An interesting innovation would be to pair an experienced mediator with a potential mediator from the region; this 'convener team' would then meet with the parties to determine their needs and willingness to proceed. Parties seeking to use the service would be required to agree to a set of written procedures to meet the specific requirements of their situation (Stein and Cormick, 1991, Appendix 3). The authors proposed a demonstration or pilot project as a way of initiating activities.

Despite substantial support from a number of European and some developing countries, the proposal ran into opposition from the then-Bush administration in the US. According to one of the authors, US delegates to UNCED feared undermining existing, more formal dispute resolution mechanisms, and saw no need for additional structures until existing ones had had a chance to prove themselves (Cormick, telephone interview, spring 1997). The proposal was never voted on at UNCED.

The 1995 report of the Commission on Global Governance, an independent group of 28 distinguished individuals, also touched on the need for new mechanisms. They proposed a 'right to petition' UN bodies available to civil society to redress wrongs 'that could imperil people's security if they remain unaddressed' (Commission on Global Governance, 1995, p261). People's security was defined to include both war and conflict, and maintaining the integrity of the planet's life-support systems (ibid, p84). The right to petition would be effectuated through creation of a Council for Petitions, a high-level panel of five to seven persons, independent of governments and selected in their personal capacity, to entertain petitions and make recommendations on them to the Secretary-General, the Security Council and the General Assembly. It would be appointed by the Secretary-General with the approval of the General Assembly and be a council without any powers of enforcement. But the eminence of its members and the quality of its proceedings could foster a measure of respect that gave its conclusions considerable moral authority (ibid, p262).

To date, these recommendations, which required an amendment to the UN Charter, have not been taken up by the General Assembly. Presumably at this point any proposal to house a new institution within the UN would have to be taken up within the context of the Programme of Reform proposed by the Secretary-General as well as within the context of the UN's budget problems.

A group of jurists based largely in Europe and Latin America have continued to seek an appropriate dispute resolution mechanism. In November 1994, 28 lawyers from 22 different countries created an International Court of Environmental Arbitration and Conciliation (ICEAC).[23] Its objective is to facilitate the mediation of environmental disputes with international or transboundary implications. The Court consists of a Secretariat (based in Mexico City, with an office in Spain) and a roster of well-respected international environmental lawyers willing to serve as conciliators and arbitrators.

Access to the Court is open to states, natural or legal persons (ie corporations), who may submit an application for conciliation or arbitration. The Court will then, in the case of conciliation, appoint a commission, and in the case of arbitration, an arbitral tribunal. The applicable law will include treaties and applicable private contracts, general rules and principles of international environmental law, relevant national law (in accordance with general conflicts rules) and any other principles the Court deems relevant. Soft law is thus clearly envisioned, and the use of international human rights law is possible, although not explicitly mentioned.

The Court's statutes also contemplate consultative opinions at the request of any entity. The request for an opinion is to be made confidentially, although the opinion itself is to be public unless the party requesting the opinion objects. Consultative opinions may concern whether a project is compatible with environmental law or may enquire 'whether an action by another person complies with Environmental Law and if not make that information available to the international community'. Cases that may not qualify for conciliation or arbitration may still be the subject of a consultative opinion. In many regards the consultative opinion function shares the features of an ombudsperson.

It is too early to tell what impact this initiative will have. To date, the main problem the Court has encountered is a lack of willingness on the part of states to use its procedures. While NGOs and other non-state actors are willing, the Court requires those seeking an advisory opinion to pay the costs for experts to do on-site investigations; this puts the mechanism beyond the financial capability of many affected communities and NGOs. It illustrates clearly the need for a sustainable funding base if any such initiative is to succeed.

CONCLUSION

This chapter has explored the rationale, models and potential institutional homes for an ombudsperson approach to conflicts involving human rights and the environment. It has especially focused on the role of an ombudsperson in providing a forum for investigation and mediation. Given the issue- and locale-specific aspects of many conflicts, an ombudsperson function could – and probably should – be placed within several institutions at the global and regional levels.

A mediation-based approach could help not only to resolve particular conflicts but also to better define an emerging area of international ethics. In the end, the most valuable contribution of effective innovations in mediation mechanisms is their role in ratcheting up social expectations by providing a space for the powerless to have a voice.

NOTES

1   See Constitution of a Chamber of the Court for Environmental Matters, ICJ Communique No 93/20, 19 July 1993.
2   Case concerning Gacikovo-Nagymaros Project (Hungary/Slovakia), Judgment of 25 September 1997. The case involved a contract between Hungary and Slovakia to build a dam on the Danube River. The dam will allegedly harm the riverine environment as well as local fishing communities. Hungary cancelled the contract, prompting Slovakia to file suit.
3   The International Tribunal for the Law of the Sea was established in Hamburg, Germany, in 1996, with 21 judges from maritime nations. 'UN Swears in Sea Tribunal Judges in Hamburg', *Reuters European Business Report* 18 October 1996.
4   Montreal Protocol, 1991 Amendments (London), Annex III. Under the non-compliance procedure, 'reservations' regarding a party's performance of its treaty obligations come before a 5-member Implementation Committee that attempts to 'secure an amiable resolution'. The Committee reports to the conference of the parties, which may call for further steps. The idea is to create a non-adversarial mechanism to encourage implementation. See generally Handl (1997).
5   See, for example, Convention on Biological Diversity, article 27; Framework Convention on Climate Change, article 14(5).
6   Merrills (1991) distinguishes between mediation and conciliation in the public law context. While conciliation involves presentation to the parties of a set of formal proposals after investigation of a dispute, mediators present their proposals informally and on the basis of information supplied by the parties, rather than their own investigation (Merrills, 1991, p27). Nonetheless, he concedes that the two functions may be blurred.
7   Ombudsperson for Children Act, 6 March 1981, sec 3. See generally Flekkoy (1996).
8   See www.omced.org/background1.htm. IUCN homepage: www.iucn.org. Earth Council homepage: www.ecouncil.ac.cr.
9   International Covenant on Civil and Political Rights, adopted 19 December 1966, entered into force 23 March 1976, 999 UNTS 171; International Covenant on Economic, Social and Cultural Rights, adopted 19 December 1966, entered into force 3 January 1976, 999 UNTS 3; International Convention on the Elimination of All

Forms of Racial Discrimination, entered into force 4 January 1969, 660 UNTS 195; Convention on the Elimination of All Forms of Discrimination Against Women, adopted 18 December 1979, entered into force 3 September 1981, GA Res 34/180, 34 UN GAOR Sup (No 46) at 193, UN Doc A/34/46 (1980); Convention Against Torture and Other Cruel, Inhuman or Degrading Treatment or Punishment, adopted 10 December 1984, entered into force 26 June 1987, GA Res 39/46, 39 UN GAOR Supp (No 51) at 197, UN Doc. A/39/51 (1984); Convention on the Rights of the Child, adopted 28 November 1989, entered into force 2 September 1990, 28 ILM 1448 (1989).

10 See, for example, Ominayak and Lubicon Lake Band vs. Canada, Report of the Human Rights Committee, 45 UN GAOR Supp (No 40), vol 2, App A., UN Doc. A/45/40 (1990).

11 Special Rapporteur Fatma Zohra Ksentini, Report on the Relationship between Human Rights and the Environment, UN Commission on Human Rights, UN Doc. E/CN.4/Sub.2/1994/9 & Corr. 1.

12 See, for example, article 8(j) of the CBD.

13 UN Doc. S/235, 31 January 1992, cited in Franck and Nolte (1993).

14 See GA Res 48/141, 20 December 1993.

15 Office of the UN HCHR: www.unhchr.ch.

16 The European Commission and Court were created by the European Convention on Human Rights and Fundamental Freedoms, 213 UNTS 221, ETS 5, entered into force 3 September 1953. The Inter-American Commission was created by the Charter of the Organization of American States in 1948 and oversees human rights in all OAS states; in addition, it has specific duties under the American Convention of Human Rights, 9 ILM 101 (1970), entered into force 18 July 1978, for those states which have ratified the Convention. The Inter-American Court only has jurisdiction over those states that have specifically accepted its jurisdiction. ACHR, articles 52, 62. The African Commission was created by the African Charter on Human and Peoples' Rights, 21 ILM 58 (1982), entered into force 21 October 1986.

17 North American Agreement on Environmental Cooperation, 14 September 1993, 32 ILM 1480.

18 The definition of 'failure to enforce' is extremely narrow, excluding cases where officials exercised discretion or decided to allocate resources to other environmental matters instead of the case at hand, Article 45, NAEEC. 'Environmental law' is also narrowly defined to exclude natural resource harvesting laws (ibid).

19 See Center for International Environmental Law www.ciel.org/IFI/wbip.html.

20 Most of this work has been in the women's rights area, allowing international human rights law and norms to reach 'private' violence against women, for example. See, for example, UN Declaration on the Elimination of Violence Against Women, UN Doc. A/RES/48/104 (1994). The UN Sub-Commission has commissioned a number of studies that touch on private corporate responsibility for human rights violations. But the legal obligations incurred are still those of the state, to prevent, educate, sanction those responsible and compensate victims.

21 In paragraph 84, the report recommends that states 'may wish to consider the designation of a national council or public representative or "ombudsman" to represent the interests and rights of present and future generations and act as an environmental watchdog, alerting governments and citizens to any emerging threats.'

22 Austria, the Czech and Slovak Federal Republic (at the time), Hungary, Italy and Yugoslavia made up this group; Poland also joined the proposal. A/CONF.151/ PC/L.29, 22 March 1991; A/CONF.151/PC/WGIII/L.1, 27 March 1991.

23 ICEAC homepage: www.envirocom.com/iceac.

REFERENCES

Amnesty International (1992) 'World Conference on Human Rights: Facing Up to the Failures, Proposals for Improving the Protection of Human Rights by the United Nations', *AI Index* IOR 41/16/92, December 1992, p6

Blokker, N and Muller, S (1992) *Towards More Effective Supervision by International Organizations.* Dordrecht: Martinus Nijhoff

Breachy, D (1996) 'U.S.–Mexico NAFTA Pact lots of Talk, Little Action', *Montreal Gazette* 9 February 1996

Bugnion, F (1995) 'The Composition of the ICRC', *International Review of the Red Cross* 307, 1 July, pp427–446

Carnegie Council on Ethics and International Affairs (1997) 'Innovative Human Rights Strategies in East Asia', *Human Rights Dialogue* 9, June

Chayes, Abram and Chayes, Antonia Handler (1995) *The New Sovereignty: Compliance with International Regulatory Agreements.* Cambridge, MA: Harvard University Press

Clark, R S (1972) *A United Nations High Commissioner for Human Rights.* The Hague: Nijhoff

Commission on Global Governance (1995) *Our Global Neighborhood: The Report of the Commission on Global Governance.* New York: Oxford University Press

De la Cruz, H B et al (1996) *The International Labor Organization, The International Standards System and Basic Human Rights.* Boulder, CO: Westview

Flekkoy, M G (1991) *A Voice for Children: Speaking out as their Ombudsman.* London: Jessica Kingsley Publishers

Flekkoy, M G (1996) 'The Children's Ombudsperson as an Implementor of Children's Rights' *Transnational Law & Contemporary Problems* 6:353

Franck, T M and Nolte, G (1993) 'The Good Offices Function of the UN Secretary-General', in Roberts, A and Kingsbury, B (eds) *United Nations, Divided World*, 2nd edn. Clarendon: Oxford University Press, p143

Handl, G (1997) 'Compliance Control Mechanisms and International Environmental Obligations', *Tulane Journal of International and Comparative Law* 5:29

IIDH (Instituto Interamericano de Derechos Humanos) (1996) 'Curso Interamericano sobre Defensores del Pueblo y Derechos Humanos', *Confederias y documentos academicos.* San Jose: IIDH

Kane, J (1993) 'Letter from the Amazon', *The New Yorker* 27 September

Kimmerling, J (1991) *Amazon Crude.* New York, Natural Resources Defense Council

Merrills, J G (1991) *International Dispute Settlement*, 2nd edn. Cambridge: Grotius Publications

NAAEC (North American Agreement on Environmental Cooperation) (1993) *NAFTA Supplemental Agreement: North American Agreement on Environmental Cooperation, North American Agreement on Labor Cooperation, Understanding Between the Parties to the North American Free Trade Agreement Concerning Chapter Eight—Emergency Action.* Washington, DC: US GPO

OmCED (International Ombudsman Centre for Environment and Development) (2000) *Annual Report 2000*, available from omced@ecouncil.ac.cr

Rodley, N (1979) 'Monitoring Human Rights Violations in the 1980s', in Jorge, I, Dominguez, N, Rodley, S, Wood, B and Falk, R (eds) *Enhancing Global Human Rights.* New York, Council on Foreign Relations, pp117–154

Rowat, D C (1985) *The Ombudsman Plan: The Worldwide Spread of an Idea*, 2nd edn. Lanham: University Press of America

Shihata, I (1994) *The World Bank Inspection Panel.* Oxford: Oxford University Press

Shihata, I (1996) 'Implementation, Enforcement, and Compliance with International Environmental Agreements – Practical Suggestions in Light of the World Bank's Experience', 9 Georgetown International. *Environmental Law Review* 37

Stein, R E and Cormick, G W (1991) 'Elements of a United Nations Environment and Development Dispute Prevention and Settlement Service', report presented for the consideration of the Preparatory Committee and Secretariat of the United Nations Conference on Environment and Development, July

Suy, E (1997) 'The Development of Supervisory Mechanisms within the CSCE Framework', in Udall, L (ed) *The World Bank Inspection Panel: A Three Year Review*. Washington, DC: Bank Information Center

Udall, L (ed) (1997) *The World Bank Inspection Panel: A Three Year Review*. Washington, DC: Bank Information Center

UN Centre for Human Rights (1978) Seminar on Local and National Institutions for the Promotion and Protection of Human Rights, 18–29 September 1978, Geneva, UN Doc. ST/HR/Ser A./2

UNEP (United Nations Environment Programme) (2001) *News Release* 49. United Nations Environment Programme

WCED (World Commission on Environment and Development) (1987) *Our Common Future*. New York: Oxford University Press

Wieruszewski, R (1989) 'Application of International Humanitarian Law and Human Rights Law: Individual Complaints', in Kalshoven, F and Sandoz, Y (eds) *Implementation of International Humanitarian Law*. Dordrecht: Martinus Nijhoff, pp441–458

Index